COMPUTER MEDIATED COMMUNICATIONS

COMPUTER MEDIATED COMMUNICATIONS

Bulletin Boards, Computer Conferencing, Electronic Mail, and Information Retrieval

MATTHEW RAPAPORT

John Wiley & Sons, Inc.

New York • Chichester • Brisbane • Toronto • Singapore

In recognition of the importance of preserving what has
been written, it is a policy of John Wiley & Sons, Inc.
to have books of enduring value published in the United
Stated printed on acid-free paper, and we exert our best
efforts to this end.

This publication is designed to provide accurate and authoritative information in regard to the
subject matter covered. It is sold with the understanding that the publisher is not engaged in
rendering legal, accounting, or other professional services. If legal advice or other expert assistance is required, the services of a competent professional person should be sought. FROM A
DECLARATION OF PRINCIPLES JOINTLY ADOPTED BY A COMMITTEE OF THE
AMERICAN BAR ASSOCIATION AND A COMMITTEE OF PUBLISHERS.

Library of Congress Cataloging-in-Publication Data

ISBN 0-471-51642-2
Printed in the United States of America

91 92 10 9 8 7 6 5 4 3 2 1

Searchlight is a trademark of Searchlight Software, Stony Brook, NY.

Squish Plus is a trademark of Sundog Software, New York, NY.

Starlink is a trademark of Galaxy Information Network Inc., Virginia Beach, VA.

SunOS is a trademark of Sun Microsystems Inc., Mountain View, CA.

TBBS/TDBS is a trademark of Esoft, Aurora, CO.

TEAMate is a trademark of MMB Development Inc., Manhattan Beach, CA.

Theos is a trademark of Theos Software Corp., Walnut Creek, CA.

VaxNotes, VMS, and VAX are trademarks of Digital Equipment Corporation, Maynard, MA.

Venix is a trademark of Unisource Software, Boston, MA.

VU/TEXT is a trademark of VU/TEXT Information Services Inc., Philadelphia, PA.

Wilson Line is a trademark of H. W. Wilson Company, New York, NY.

X-Net is a trademark of OST Corporation, Chantilly, VA.

Z80 is a trademark of Zilog Corporation.

PREFACE

I became involved with telecommunications technology in 1981 while an industrial market analyst for a firm in Alameda, California. My boss introduced me to Dialog Information Services, and I became instantly hooked on computer communications as a source of information. By 1983 I was a programmer working on terminal emulation software. As the shop I worked for had no communications test equipment, we purchased subscriptions to various electronic mail and general purpose information services to test out the software. My experience prompted me to pick up my own subscriptions to CompuServe and The Source.

The Source introduced me to real computer conferencing in the form of Participate. A few years later, I had an opportunity to try the Notepad, and I became further intrigued by the variety and potentials of computer mediated communications.

Telecommunications technology has been the sole means of researching this book. About 20 percent of the data was gathered through telephone interviews. Another 40 percent or so, using information retrieval technology, was gathered primarily on Dialog's Knowledge Index. The rest came from dozens of people who patiently answered my questions and commented on the book's development, on-line, using computer conferencing technology.

During the 13 months the book has been in development, I have met (electronically) and talked with people about it on CompuServe, The Source (before it was bought out by CompuServe in July 1989), BIX, GEnie, the University of Michigan's Confer II, and the Well of Sausalito, California, my "home base" since June 1986. The last system has enabled me to exchange electronic mail with many members of the computer communications community, one as far away as Stockholm, Sweden. I have many people to thank for assistance with the research, many more than can be listed here. A few of the persons whose individual contributions were instrumental in forming much of the book deserve mention:

Ren Breck, President of Notepad International, who has shared his insights in the field with me since 1985.

Bob Parnes, President of Advertel Communications, who provided me with a guest account on Confer II at the University of Michigan during the year in which the book was written.

Lisa Carlson of Metasystems Design and Gordon Cook of the Von Neuman Computer Center, who shared with me some of the results of their market research in the conferencing arena.

Peter and Trudy Johnson-Lenz, who coined the term "groupware," and who have experimented with unusual applications of conferencing technology since the early 1980s (To them I owe my appreciation for the value of "software tailorability.")

Jacob Palme of the University of Stockholm, Sweden, who sent me his compilation of features of group communications systems.

Others who deserve mention include the developers of many conferencing systems who sent me copies of their manuals and/or software for exploration. Among these are Charles Roth (Caucus), Karl Denninger (AKCS), Marcus Watts and Mike Meyers (Picospan), Frank LaRosa (SearchLight), Bob Baskerville (TEAMate), and Phil Becker (TBBS).

CONTENTS

1

ORIGINS

ORIGINS   1

1.1   Electronic Mail   1

1.2   EMISARI—The First Conferencing System   3

1.3   Confer—Conferencing Experiments at the
       University of Michigan   6

1.4   The Further Evolution of Conference
       Systems   7

1.5   Philosophical Differences and the Rise of
       Distributed Conferencing   10

1.6   Summary of Computer Mediated
       Communications   11

1.7   The Separate World of Information
       Retrieval Systems   13

1.8   Microcomputers and the Emergence of the
       Small BBS Network   16

1.9　Information Retrieval and Interpersonal
Communications　23

2

SCOPE OF CURRENT CONFERENCING, INFORMATION RETRIEVAL, AND BBS TECHNOLOGY　25

2.1　Promises and Problems　25

2.2　Teleconferencing, Computer Mediated
Cooperative Work, and Computer Mediated
Communications　27

2.3　The Versatility of Many-to-Many
Text–Based Communications　29

2.4　Computer Conferencing in Educational
Institutions　32

2.5　Corporate Application Domains　34

2.6　Factors Contributing to the Success of Public
and Private Conference Applications　42

3

HARDWARE, SOFTWARE, AND TELECOMMUNICATIONS FOUNDATIONS　45

3.1　A Generalized Application　45

3.2　Special Constraints on Information Retrieval
Systems　45

3.3　The CPU　46

3.4   Memory   46

3.5   Mass Storage   47

3.6   The Influence of the Computer Bus   49

3.7   The Communications Hardware   50

3.8   Hardware Constraints on CMC Design   51

3.9   The Influence of the Operating System   51

3.10   The Effect of IBM PC Standardization   54

3.11   The Role of the Modem   54

3.12   The OSI Interconnection Model   57

3.13   The Influence of Data Compression
        Technology   59

3.14   Developments in the Telephone Network   60

3.15   Packet Switching   62

3.16   Other Standards Affecting Interpersonal
        Communications   64

3.17   The Vulnerability of High Bandwidth
        Networks   65

3.18   Future Directions   65

4

SINGLE AND MULTIUSER CONFIGURATIONS

                                                            67

4.1   Variations in Information Retrieval Systems   67

4.2   CMC System Morphology   68

4.3   Data Structures   75

4.4   Architectural Constraints on Software
        Design and Extension   76

4.5   The Influence of the Dial-Up Telephone
       Network   78

4.6   Expanding the System: Multiuser Architectures   79

4.7   Using Single Tasking Systems
       for Multiuser Operations   82

4.8   The Advantages of Multitasking
       Operating Systems   83

4.9   Multitasking and the Requirements
       of the File System   85

4.10   Multiuser Systems and the Telephone
       Environment   86

4.11   Multiuser Systems and Information Retrieval   88

5

DISTRIBUTED CONFERENCING SYSTEMS

                                                       89

5.1   Replicated Text Bases versus Distributed Access   89

5.2   Replicated Conferences on Single-User Hosts   91

5.3   Distribution Techniques   91

5.4   The FIDO Network   93

5.5   Routing Mechanisms   96

5.6   Distribution by Flooding   97

5.7   Some Practical Considerations.   101

5.8   Bridging Networks   103

5.9   The ISO X.400 and X.500 Standards   107

5.10   Other Application-Level Standards   109

5.11   Distributing Information Retrieval Systems   109

6

THE STRUCTURE OF COMMUNICATIONS MODELS 113

6.1	Computer Models of Interpersonal Communications	113
6.2	One-to-Many and Many-to-One Models	114
6.3	Social Origin of Many-to-Many Models	114
6.4	The Role of the User Interface	116
6.5	Communications Structures	116
6.6	Linear Structures and Command Patterns in the EMISARI and EIES Model	117
6.7	Confer and the Appearance of the Comb Model	124
6.8	The Branch Model	137
6.9	The Significance of Navigation and Selection	144
6.10	Philosophical Implications of Conference Structure	146
6.11	Graphics in CMC Systems	147
6.12	Widespread versus Restricted Access and the Role of the Microcomputer	148

7

IMPLEMENTING COMMUNICATIONS MODELS 151

7.1	Communications Data	151

7.2	Physical Text Structures	151
7.3	Program Structures	152
7.4	Picospan and the UNIX File System	153
7.5	Decoupling Internal Structures from the Operating System	156
7.6	File Abstraction in the COM Family	158
7.7	Software Modularization	159
7.8	Source Modularization with Program Libraries	160
7.9	Requesters and Servers	161
7.10	Data Transformation from One Structure to Another	163
7.11	The ISO and X.400 Messaging	163
7.12	Extending Personal Messages to Group Communications	170
7.13	Distributing Information Retrieval	172
7.14	Object-Oriented Programming and Communications Software	174
7.15	Architectures and Tailorability	176

8

COMMUNICATION SERVICES AND SOFTWARE

		179
8.1	Conferencing in The Public Arena	179
8.2	Other CMC Software	197

9

DOMAINS, CHARACTERISTICS, AND IMPLEMENTATION OBJECTIVES

207

9.1	Clarifying Intended Uses	208
9.2	Generic Features of Idealized CMC Software	208
9.3	Human Factors Impacting Required Features	220
9.4	A Place for Electronic Mail	222
9.5	Information Retrieval in Communication Domains	224
9.6	In-House Operation versus Out-Sourcing	225
9.7	In-House Systems	229
9.8	Configuration	230
9.9	The Significance of Tailorability	232

10

ADVANCED FEATURES AND IMPLICATIONS

235

10.1	Graphics Support	236
10.2	Customized Access to External Databases	237
10.3	Improved Information Retrieval for Conference Texts	239
10.4	Automated User Interfaces	248

10.5   Structural Enhancements for Specialized Functions   254

10.6   Customization of the System's Interface   255

10.7   Modifications Requiring File System Enhancements   257

10.8   Effect of File Strategies on Implementing Directory Services   263

10.9   Taking Advantage of Specialized Devices   264

10.10   Developing a System from Scratch   265

10.11   Conclusions   270

11

TRENDS AND SOCIAL ISSUES

   271

11.1   Bandwidth Expansion in Telecommunications   271

11.2   Increasing Desk-Top Computing Power   273

11.3   Recent Growth in the Popularity of Electronic Mail   274

11.4   Niches for Group-Oriented Communications   275

11.5   Bandwidth Plus CPU Power: The Demise of Text-Based Conferencing?   277

11.6   Trends in Public Sector Group Communications   278

11.7   Mass Markets for Group Telecommunications   280

11.8   Mass Market Motivators   282

11.9   The Growth of Ad Hoc Networks and
        Distributed Conferences   284

11.10   The Electronic Tower of Babel   285

11.11   System Specialization   290

11.12   Small Systems as Database Servers   292

11.13   The Promise of a Broadband Integrated
        Services Digital Network   292

12
EPILOGUE

295

APPENDIXES

299

Appendix A   301

Appendix B   321

Appendix C   331

Appendix D   339

INDEX

369

INTRODUCTION

This book is about computer conferencing software, the original "groupware." When Peter and Trudy Johnson-Lenz coined that term in 1978, they defined it as "Intentional *group* processes and procedures, plus the software to support them." It was conferencing technology—computer support for communications among groups of individuals for a variety of purposes—that was foremost in their minds. More recently, the term has been extended (properly, I think) to refer to software that supports the development of information content shared by groups of people or provides support for the flow of work as it moves among working groups. Electronic mail and decision support facilities—such as polls, vote compilations, and information retrieval from management information system (MIS) databases—are usually considered a proper part of contemporary groupware technology. All the primary "groupware products" in the marketplace today include an electronic mail component.

Hardly a week goes by without articles in the trade press about electronic mail (E-mail) and other groupware facilities. Yet that press has almost entirely lost sight of the special features required to support *conversations*, and not just work flow/content management among groups of people. All the best computer conferencing software products contain both E-mail *and* decision support services. They also employ information retrieval technology. Yet they do more; they provide facilities to support the *conversational* aspects of human interaction.

The relative lack of acceptance of these products in the corporate marketplace is due less to technical than to political factors. The availability of this technology threatens the perks, privileges, and traditions of corporate management. The higher up the management scale, the more threatening it seems. Ironically, where the technology is employed, its cost-saving and productivity-enhancing value is directly proportional to the management level that embraces it; the highest levels of management receive the most return for their investment.

At the same time, while corporations have been lackluster in their acceptance of this technology, a significant segment of the public has adopted it. For a few corporations, some large and many small, providing group communications facilities to the public has, in itself, become a profitable business with its own special requirements. This, too, is a part of our story.

Electronic mail is clearly a form of computer mediated communications and is therefore discussed. E-mail is oriented primarily toward individuals, but it can also enhance group productivity. The focus of this book is on those special technologies designed from the beginning to foster the interaction of groups—hence the metaphor of "the conference."

Information retrieval in the professional sense—the searching of scientific, engineering, and business databases for information pertaining to client requests—is not communications with other persons, group or individual. It is treated here because many communications applications also benefit from good information retrieval support. A few of these uses are almost entirely dependent on them. On the other hand, information retrieval specialists can gain much from participation in technical conferences. Finally, many of the user aids applied to contemporary information retrieval systems can, and are, used by modern conferencing systems.

■ ORGANIZATION

Chapter 1 outlines the history of computer conferencing in two forms: centralized and distributed. The history of commercial information retrieval systems is also discussed, as well as the rise of microcomputer bulletin board systems (BBS).

Chapter 2 discusses the public and corporate domains to which computer conference technology has been applied. It also provides some orientation to the wider field of teleconferencing, office technologies, and computer mediated communications. All of these terms are used ambiguously in much of the trade press. Chapter 2 establishes some definitions for our purposes.

Chapter 3 covers the hardware components of a conferencing system: CPU, bus, memory, storage systems, and modems. It also discusses the influence of telephone and other telecommunications networks. There is also an introduction to the International Standards Organization's (ISO) Open Systems Interconnect (OSI) model and the Integrated Systems Digital Network (ISDN).

Chapter 4 begins a discussion of conferencing system features starting with a simple model of a single-user BBS system. It moves from there to a discussion of large-scale centralized conferencing systems.

Chapter 5 discusses distributed conferencing systems. It covers hierarchical, broadcast, and remote-login forms of distribution. The X.400 international distributed electronic mail standard is introduced, along with its related directory standard, X.500.

Chapter 6 is a detailed discussion of the three main communications models, or metaphors: linear, comb, and branch. It also describes the user interfaces of three prominent conferencing systems.

Chapter 7 covers the internal structures of the systems discussed in Chapter 6. It also reviews the internal structure of the CCITT X.400 mail system.

Chapter 8 is a discussion of several popular public communications systems. It also introduces some new models, hybrids of those covered in Chapters 6 and 7. It contains a discussion of some observable trends in public sector conferencing and a brief description of some specific products.

Chapter 9 examines some of the factors to weigh when shopping for a group communications system for corporate or public use. It includes an examination of features present in advanced conference software and considerations regarding the use of third parties to maintain a conference system for corporate use.

Chapter 10 takes up the issue of code customization. This includes an analysis of areas where customization might be warranted, an analysis of different internal architectures, and a discussion of the effects of these architectures on customization efforts. It concludes with some considerations for those who wish to build a system entirely from scratch.

Chapter 11 discusses the technical future of the medium, particularly with respect to the impact of enhanced telecommunications capacity and desktop CPU power.

Chapter 12 is a brief discussion of the corporate political implications of conferencing technology. It begins with a story of opportunity lost in a recent ecological disaster.

Following Chapter 12 are four appendixes and a bibliography. The former contain various product lists, vendor addresses, systems, and other information.

This book is not, strictly speaking, a textbook. Many of its themes are touched upon in chapters throughout the book. It is hoped that, in the end, the reader will come away with a thorough understanding of what a conferencing system is, what it is not, how it is associated with other technologies (particularly the telephone system), and what its possibilities are for social transformation.

The author may be contacted for comments at his electronic addresses:

International UUCP: mjr@well.sf.ca.us

CompuServe Information Service: 70371,255

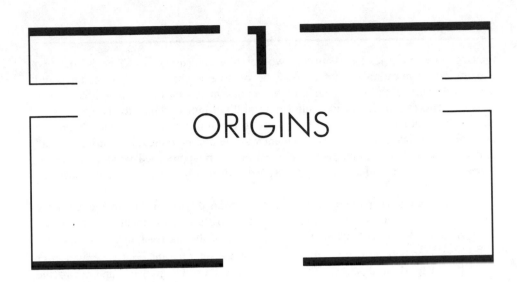

ORIGINS

When computers first appeared in the corporate environment, their primary purpose was the manipulation of numbers. Not surprisingly, the large financial corporations, banks, and insurance companies first adopted the new machines for bookkeeping and payroll purposes in the early to mid 1960s. At the same time, researchers were beginning to explore the computer's potential to manipulate textual data.

Text manipulation of most kinds was impractical before the advent of direct access storage devices (DASD), or disk drives. Before their development in the mid 1960s, the only long-term storage medium was tape. Access to data on tape is sequential only. In the pre-DASD days, sequential file manipulation was a heavily treated subject. On-line interaction with computer data and programs was not common. For these reasons, early efforts in text manipulation were limited to associating text with the results of numeric calculations in output (for example, printing text lines on invoices or paychecks). The advent of random access storage enhanced the potential for text manipulation as well as on-line (interactive) operation. Researchers began to think in terms of using computers to facilitate communication between persons.

The earliest tools for interpersonal communications on large centralized systems were simple message-passing utilities. These allowed an operator at one console to pass a message to someone at another terminal. The recipient, logged in to the computer at the time, could reply by reinvoking the same utility and sending a return message. Only two persons could participate in the exchange. The terminal number of the recipient (the terminal address) had to be entered as a part of each exchange transaction.

■ 1.1 ELECTRONIC MAIL

The next step in the evolution of computer mediated text exchange was the now familiar electronic versions of the mail box. Electronic mail (E-mail) was, and remains, focused on communications between two persons asynchronously. That is, the two persons communicating do not have to be on line at the same time. Each could leave messages to the other and retrieve replies at his or her convenience. Early enhancements to E-mail systems included the ability to forward mail to another person, with or without attachments, and the ability to transmit a message to more than one mailbox. Associated with this enhancement was the ability to create a mailing list and effect a kind of many-to-many communication. This approached what was later to appear in computer conferencing systems, but it differs in three important respects.

1. Each individual participating in such a group discussion has to meticulously maintain a copy of the mailing list. If the lists of participants are not exact matches, some participants will miss pieces of the discussion.

2. New members joining the discussion will see only the material generated *after* they begin participating. There is no means by which they can recoup the discussion to that point. This is true because message collections are stored in a separate file for each participating user.

3. There is no mechanism for organizing separate threads of discussion in a coherent manner. Persons logging in to their terminals might discover they have 30 new messages waiting for them with no way to determine which pertained to what discussions. Users can examine the subject line of each message before reading it, but the organization of the collection is inherently sequential by delivery time. Figure 1.1 illustrates the generic E-mail model.

E-mail has continued to evolve as its usage grows in many corporations. The mailing list problem has been alleviated by the existence of system-maintained group names. The topic organization problem is addressed with keyword selection and filters for subject headings, author names, dates, and so on. Yet E-mail still lacks the more fluid structure of true conferencing systems. Research systems such as MIT's Information Lens and the newer Object Lens have produced very sophisticated and potentially valuable devices for text organization that approach the functionality of computer conferencing, while remaining rooted in an E-mail metaphor: individual mail boxes for each user.

These new technologies are beginning to appear in the marketplace. Current systems have achieved some acceptance in both centralized (mainframe/mini) and distributed local area network (LAN) applications. E-mail does improve corporate communications. Significantly, it does so without imposing on a more politically sensitive form of personal interaction: the corporate meeting.

■ 1.2 EMISARI—THE FIRST CONFERENCING SYSTEM

In 1971 the Nixon administration's wage and price freeze generated a sudden demand for communications and coordination among private sector business, labor groups, and government policy makers. To coordinate the activities of the departments involved, and because of the need to handle reporting and dissemination of information, the Office of Emergency Preparedness (OEP) commissioned Murray Turoff to develop a

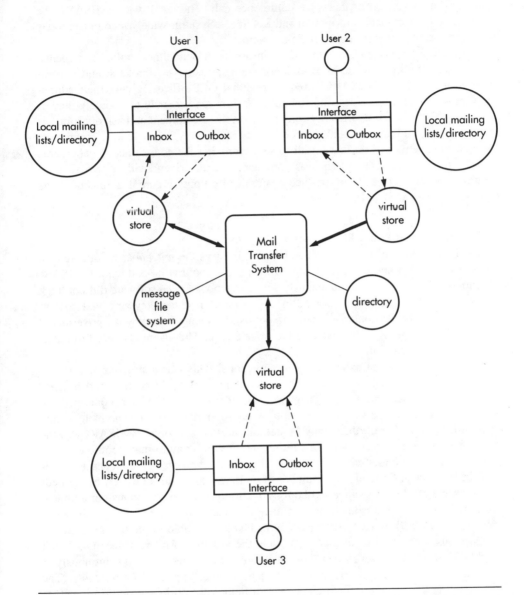

Figure 1.1   The E-mail model. In E-mail each participant has his own inbox and outbasket (sometimes) requiring storage either locally (in a distributed system) or on a central host. Users have access only to messages addressed specifically to them. In some contemporary systems, a user may also be addressed through a "public name" that gets general mail intended for a wide audience.

computer-based version of the voice conference call. The result was EMISARI, the Emergency Management Information and Reference System, widely recognized today as the prototype computer conferencing system.

The price controls created a demand for information, guidelines, policy statements, clarifications, rulings, and so on from labor unions, businesses, brokers, and government administrators. EMISARI linked 10 regional OEP offices, giving their administrators access to time-critical information. Washington was able to update policy as necessary. Those charged with executing it were able to comment and ask questions as the need arose and at their convenience. Policy statements, case rulings, comments, and questions remained on line for all to see, removing the constraints of geographic dispersion and time. The system was completely menu driven, with a provision for creating special commands to produce customized output. Figure 1.2 illustrates the generic conference model.

1.2.1 Features of EMISARI

EMISARI consisted of five key elements. The first was the *notebook*, an open-ended text space to which any number of authorized people could write and read. EMISARI supported any number of simultaneously active notebooks. The software did not track who had read them or what was read by any person. Text was keyword and content searchable. Notebooks contained evolving policy statements issued by the government agencies responsible for administering the price freeze. They were also used to report and comment on the policies.

The *party-line* was an extension of the notebook. This was a structure that stored streams of text grouped by subject. These "conferences" could be searched by keywords, author, date, and so on. They were linked to a directory that contained the names of conference participants. Read-through support tracked the point to which each participant had read, displaying by default only new records. EMISARI was the first system to employ store-and-forward technology in many-to-many conferencing.

Party-line conferences were not further subdivided into topics or branches as developed in subsequent systems. Any number of conferences could, however, be created, and the same mechanism supported both asynchronous and synchronous communications. If two or more persons happened to be connected to a conference at the same time, the text typed by each was made immediately available to the others. Initially, synchronous support was expected to provide the system's primary value. Dr. Turoff quickly discovered, however, that most of the real work was done asynchronously.

The third major component was the *data field,* later expanded into a *table*. The EMISARI system operator could create a data field with a title and description. One person was authorized to write to that field, and many others could examine the results. One of the things typically entered into this field was the number of wage-price freeze violations reported for a given region of the country. Each field represented data from a different region. These fields were grouped together to produce reports. EMISARI would automatically perform regression analysis on the data and project it to the next time period. In this way, OEP managers could track compliance effectiveness from week to week and know if the numbers represented unusual deviations from expected values.

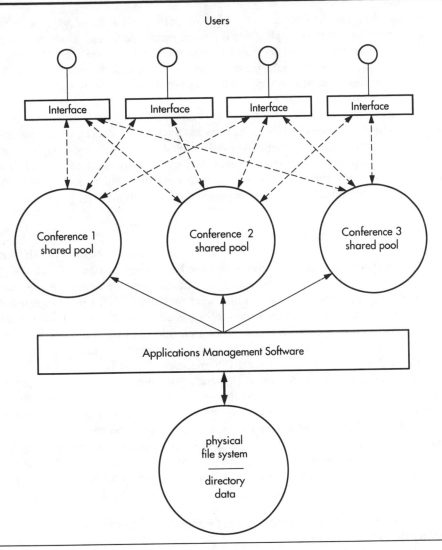

Figure 1.2 Basic conference model. In a true group communications system such as EMISARI, all messages are stored as collections in sharable spaces. Participating users all read the same copy of messages; they have a common access to the public copies. New users joining the conversation "catch up" by reading the stored exchange of earlier conversations. The control lists for private conferences are usually maintained in a central place (logically), and there is no need for private message storage. Individual conferences and all their subconferences are isolated from one another by the applications software, though a few products have the ability to automatically share a subconference between two or more conferences. Without special provision in the interface layer, however, such shared topics will appear more than once to users who are participants of two or more of the conferences involved. This is analogous to the E-mail situation in which a user receives a message two or more times because he or she has more than one mailbox.

EMISARI had its roots in an earlier system built by Dr. Turoff to experiment with *delphic voting techniques*. The Delphi system supported several kinds of voting, including simple accept or reject votes and a seven-point sliding scale vote. These were automatically tabulated with results presented as a single output when all participants had voted. The new system also supported these but delivered the results as another record in a continuing text stream.

Finally, EMISARI supported traditional electronic mail, but with a difference. Mail was not only sent to persons or groups, but was associated with data fields or notebook entries. For example, a person examining a collection of data in fields of a single record would be made aware of comments on that data attached to the field as mail. The ability to manipulate separate parts of records in this way is called *field-addressability*. It is particularly significant for project management applications.

1.2.2 EIES Conferencing System

Later developments in conferencing expanded on many of these elements. After finishing the EMISARI project, Dr. Turoff joined the New Jersey Institute of Technology to do research into the uses, effects, and design of computer conferencing software. In 1975, the EIES conferencing system first went on line at NJIT. EIES is a research system, access to which is sold on a time-share basis to educational and commercial users. Yet its primary purpose is ongoing research into the use of text conferencing and the development of features to support group communication in general.

Although the basic structure of the EIES message stream is identical to that of EMISARI, it added many other support elements. Such things as personal and group-owned notebooks supported jointly authored documents. As with EMISARI, pointers placed in message streams could reference these note files. An expanded directory feature included additional information about participants and became a key feature of many subsequent conferencing systems. EIES also added a special command language used to customize its operation for any given purpose. The data field and table features were made more flexible, but these features were not adopted by other systems.

■ 1.3 CONFER – CONFERENCING EXPERIMENTS AT THE UNIVERSITY OF MICHIGAN

In 1974, Bob Parnes, then a postgraduate student in the University of Michigan's Psychology department, became interested in applying the then-developing time-sharing technology to issues of academic governance. As with corporate meetings, bringing all interested parties together for meetings in a large university can be a daunting task. Many such meetings are convened to vote on issues of university policy involving faculty and administration. More often than not, parties with vested interest in these policies are unable to attend.

In the late 1960s the Computer Science department at the university had created a custom operating system for its new IBM 360 mainframe called Michigan Terminal System (MTS). Dr. Parnes was aware of the work of Murray Turoff on EMISARI, and the later EIES system, but was otherwise unaware of its details. He began to write what became the prototype of Confer, relying heavily on MTS's support for random access to text files. Confer, like EMISARI, was organized around the notion of a conference that contained separate text records. These items were typically proposals to be voted on by policy-setting bodies in the university.

The votes themselves were originally single-line text responses to the item proposals. These, in turn, evolved into multiline text responses. The original single-conference concept evolved into support for multiple conferences, each with its own collection of items and their responses. Further work focused on more sophisticated support for voting and vote tabulation. These features, which included hidden ballots, dynamic value voting, and automatic tabulation, were added to the developing item/response structure.

1.3.1 Synchronous and Asynchronous Communications Structures

Bulletins were an early addition to Confer. These could be entered into a conference stream by any participant in a conference. It was Dr. Parnes' intention to use them for communicating time-sensitive material to be seen immediately by other participants. Bulletins were real-time events. This led to unorthodox use of the bulletin facility for real-time, synchronous chats between persons in a conference at the same time. This usage became a nuisance to other persons in the conference who did not wish to participate in the ad hoc exchange. This, plus the perceived market demand for support of synchronous conversation, led to the creation of a separate facility for synchronous conferencing: the Confer meeting.

Any participant in a Confer conference can initiate a *meeting*. As entries are made, they are immediately displayed to all participants then on line. Dr. Parnes separated the meeting facility from the regular conference to avoid disrupting the latter. Unlike the subsequent development of synchronous "chat" facilities in public systems such as CompuServe, the transcripts of Confer meetings are stored for later review by other conference participants.

Dr. Parnes saw meetings as short-lived devices. Users can post new messages to meetings asynchronously, but Dr. Parnes' intention in storing their transcripts was to allow others to follow the dialogue at a later time, then continue the discussion in the regular conference. That a meeting *had taken place* might be communicated in a conference bulletin. Without such notification, other users might never know of the meeting's existence. It was just this potential discontinuity that prompted the developers of The Notepad (see Section 1.4.3) to combine the synchronous and asynchronous conference forms in one arena.

■ 1.4 THE FURTHER EVOLUTION OF CONFERENCE SYSTEMS

1.4.1 Caucus and Picospan

In 1980 Charles Roth, then at Wayne State University in Detroit, became aware of Confer and communicated with Dr. Parnes about the possibility of porting it to smaller computer environments, specifically to UNIX-based minicomputers. Because Confer was so heavily dependent on facilities built in to the MTS operating system, Charles decided that porting the system would prove impossible, so he began writing his own version of the software. The result was *Caucus*. Written mostly in 1983–84, the product was readied for marketing in 1985. To date Caucus has been the most successful third-party conferencing software, with over 200 installations at the time of this writing. Only VaxNotes, produced by Digital Equipment Corporation and distributed free with VMS-based VAX computers, has more installations.

At about the time that plans for Caucus were being formulated, a grant was made to the University of Michigan to produce a microcomputer (UNIX-based) version of Confer. The result was a product called *Microspan*. This system was in turn rewritten as a commercial product, *Picospan*, by Marcus Watts, who participated in the Microspan project. The basic structure of both Caucus and Picospan is heavily influenced by Confer, though neither product was directly related to Bob Parnes' original system.

1.4.2 Participate

The 1970s were a fertile time for exploration into conferencing models in other places as well. Bob Parnes and Charles Roth were aware only of the existence of EMISARI and the later EIES. Harry Stevens (an active participant on the EIES system at NJIT), George Reinhart, and Peter and Trudy Johnson-Lenz used EIES's Interact script language to develop an environment for the Massachusetts state office of technology called *Legitec*. This system and its successor, Politec, were conceived with the aim of supporting small, very pointed conversational threads. The idea behind these systems was that the response thread would be limited to answering the question at hand or voting on a proposal—with subsequent discussion evolving in other threads.

There were three levels of activity in these two early systems. *Exchanges,* the "conference level," would support any number of subitems called *inquiries*, the "item level." Each inquiry, like an item in Confer, could have any number of responses. Because the system was not designed to foster long-term discussions, text search and filtering facilities were de-emphasized, even though they were already available on EIES.

In 1979 Source Telecomputing Incorporated asked Harry Stevens to build a conferencing system that would operate in conjunction with its venture into public access electronic information exchange, The Source. The result was *Participate version 1,* otherwise known as *Parti,* brought on-line in 1980. It was to satisfy The Source's request that Stevens recast his notion of exchanges, inquiries, and responses into the now familiar tree, or branch, structure of Parti.

In Parti a conference, called a *topic,* starts as a fork in an existing thread of discussion. Subsequent responses to the new topic can also fork off as branches. These branches and their threads of response can be kept indefinitely, or automatically purged after a period of inactivity. The philosophy of Parti was inherited directly from Harry Stevens' earlier work on Legitec and Politec. His goal was not so much to produce a system of infinitely growing response trails, but rather to facilitate short discussions pertinent to a particular topic, searchable in the future by people seeking solutions to problems like those previously discussed.

1.4.3 COM, CoSy, and the Notepad

Jacob Palme of the University of Stockholm in Sweden adopted the Parti model for a system called COM, which was in turn ported to PC-DOS-based microcomputers in the mid 1980s as PortaCOM. At the same time Alastair Mayer, working at the University of Guelph in Ontario, Canada, developed a system called CoSy. CoSy implemented a model that was a hybrid of both Confer and Parti (see Chapter 8 for a discussion of this interesting model).

The Notepad emerged from research done by Jacques Valee in the late 1960s and early 1970s. Roughly concurrent with the development of EMISARI, a grant from the Defense Advanced Research Projects Agency was subcontracted to the National Science Foundation, and from there to the Institute For The Future (IFTF) in Menlo Park, California. Its goal was not so much to develop a computer conferencing system as to do research into conflict resolution. The IFTF developed a model of group interaction in crisis resolution situations. Its model suggested that teams of experts in the crisis subject, provided with immediate reports of persons at the scene of the problem and developing viable alternatives for access to historical information about the situation, were essential to developing viable alterantives for resolution of the crisis.

Dr. Valee was strongly influenced by work previously done at the Stanford University Augmentation Research Center with Douglas Engelbart. An experimental workgroup system called NLS (for oN-Line System) made use of a new breed of bit-mapped terminals developed at the Xerox Palo Alto Research Center (PARC). This system evolved into a product called Augment, designed to foster teamwork in both synchronous and asynchronous environments. The Xerox graphical environment was the foundation of subsequent developments at Apple Computer Corporation over 10 years later. The Augment product has influenced many subsequent products, including bit-mapped document-editing systems and Hypercard. Dr. Engelbart's work has influenced a great deal of the technology applied to groupware products in various environments, though the mainstream computer conferencing systems in use today derive primarily from other roots.

The IFTF developed a computer-based communications system based on an E-mail model called Forum. What the group added to this fundamental model was support for vote tabulation. Yet E-mail itself could not satisfy the communications requirements of the crisis resolution model that IFTF had developed. However, the initial system allowed the group to experiment with other requirements. These included interconnection to telephone systems worldwide, the development of message transmission and format protocols, and the implementation of a user interface that was operable from any terminal equipment. The work on Forum led to the development of PLANET, an acronym for PLAnning NETwork, which added many-to-many communications using the same conference model as the original EIES system.

To support synchronous communications between concurrent participants, PLANET informed users of others joining and writing to the ongoing conference. As new messages were completed, they were automatically displayed to others online, and the entire set of transactions was recorded. Users checking the activity of a topic at a later time could review the discussion as it stood. The system smoothly merged synchronous and asynchronous conferencing into one seamless conversational stream.

PLANET also incorporated voting and tabulation procedures into the conferencing stream in such a way that the process of vote polling and result display would not require disconnection from the thread of discussion. In both Confer and Parti, a message or thread set up to take a vote has a somewhat different structure than a conventional conference stream, and user options are different when responding to a vote. In PLANET, the vote request appears in a stream of text as an ordinary message would. Responses to the voting can be displayed in any number of ways, including character-based graphs, but nevertheless as another message in the flow of conversation. To the developers, this went a long way toward meeting the model for crisis management communications that they had formulated.

In the late 1970s PLANET was reimplemented as a commercial product, Notepad. Notepad borrowed heavily from PLANET and added advanced security features, along with customizable exits permitting commercial users to attach other software directly to the conference. Database search results or newswire reports, for example, could be incorporated directly into the discussion thread.

■ 1.5 PHILOSOPHICAL DIFFERENCES AND THE RISE OF DISTRIBUTED CONFERENCING

The philosophies of EMISARI and PLANET are fundamentally different. Dr. Turoff's goal was, and remains, the development of software that is structurable to meet a wide variety of communications tasks. The PLANET developers, by contrast, sought to produce a system so generalized and simple to operate that it would in itself be applicable to a broad collection of uses. EIES seeks to be moldable as required, whereas Notepad strives for the essentials of group communication no matter what the specifics of an individual application.

During the time that Forum, PLANET, and EIES were evolving, U.S. universities were experimenting with a new kind of computer, the mini, and a new operating system being given to educational institutions by AT&T, UNIX. In 1977 a research group inside AT&T developed an intersystem connection protocol for file transfer and remote command execution called UNIX-to-UNIX-CoPy, or uucp.

The original protocol assumed that each pair of communicating machines was connected directly via telephone links. The uucp software was distributed as a part of subsequent upgrades to the Unix operating system, already a part of many university computer centers. Once established, students around the country began working on software using the protocols to send and receive mail. As the number of nodes quickly grew, a relay feature was added. With this enhancement, it was no longer necessary for a target mailbox's host to be connected to the originating machine. Maps of interconnected machines were published so users of one host could plot a course through intermediate systems to their destination.

As late as 1987 it was necessary for users of one machine to know what specific path(s) existed between their machine and any other to which they wanted to send mail. The uucp E-mail interface permitted a user to create alias names that represented complex routes to other machines, but if some intermediate machine became disconnected from the network, there was no way to know this until the sender's mail was returned as undeliverable.

Enhancements to the system continued. The uucp network capitalized on UNIX's support for scheduled operations and background processes to automate mail forwarding between machines. By 1986 there were 7000 machines worldwide exchanging mail.

In 1980 students at the University of North Carolina and Duke University began to use the uucp protocols to broadcast messages not to individual mail boxes, but to a file directory established on each machine to hold them for public viewing and comment. More interface software was written, permitting users to review, comment on, and post original messages to the text streams. This software was distributed freely to other universities through the file transfer facilities of the existing uucp network.

Conventions were established (see Chapter 5) to prevent duplicate reception of individual messages on machines with regular connections to multiple remote hosts. Broadcast messages were grouped by subject into "newsgroups," which are, for all intents and purposes, separate conferences. Control and creation of newsgroups was performed by ad hoc committees. News about the status of the system and its evolution was distributed to interested parties through the system itself. The interface software continued to evolve, adding sophisticated navigation, search, and response facilities. By 1986 this collection of machines and software, known as Usenet, was a richly featured distributed conferencing system with about 2500 known nodes worldwide. Figure 1.3 illustrates the replicated, distributed, communications model.

What made this system all the more remarkable was its reliability, a product of many redundant connections. No centralized administration existed. The network nodes formed only a loose federation tied together by the interest and energy of its separate system administrators. Yet a given posting to a newsgroup would typically appear on the remotest machines of the net within three days. Many of these continued to use the original uucp transmission protocols for exchanging news, but other exchange protocols, more reliable and faster, are also employed.

The focus of developments in the Usenet over the last few years has less to do with refining the system as a conferencing arena than with handling the rapid growth of the network and its message load. By 1989 there were over 4000 individual nodes and 250 individual conferences being broadcast. There are now four different interfaces in common use. Users in any environment are free to select the interface they prefer, and many support further customization. The spread of UNIX to engineering and research companies has made Usenet an invaluable source of technology exchange between universities and the private sector.

▪ 1.6 SUMMARY OF COMPUTER MEDIATED COMMUNICATIONS

There were several lines of independent computer mediated communications (CMC) development beginning with EMISARI, Confer, Politic and Legitec, and Forum, respectively. CBBS (Computer Bulletin Board System—see Section 1.8.3) begins the line of evolution that led to microcomputer-based communication systems in the late 1970s and early 1980s. The Usenet was another independent line, as was the COM family from the University of Stockholm, Sweden. Solid vertical lines in Figure 1.4 indicate direct technology transfer from one system to another, and the dashed lines indicated a conceptual influence. For example, both CBBS and the Usenet influenced the development of the FIDO network—the former as a microcomputer-based system, and the latter as a distributed system. Politec led directly to Partipate, with COM be-

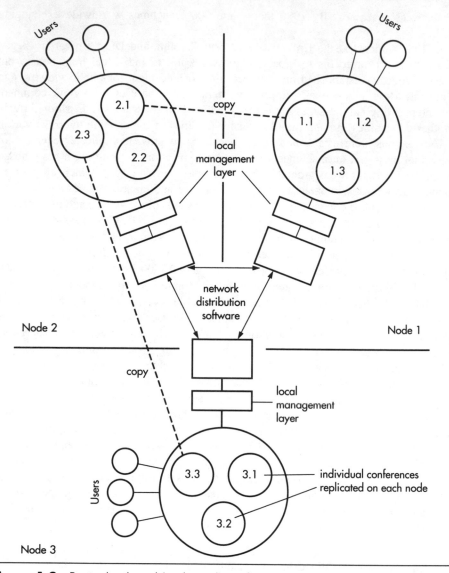

Figure 1.3 Basic distributed (replicated) conference model. In a distributed system the message stores are replicated across machine nodes in the participating network. To the users of these individual nodes, the model appears exactly like that of the basic conference model in Figure 1.2. Messages are not replicated for each user as in the electronic mail model of Figure 1.1. Copies of the message distribution software run on each node of the network and pass messages, commands, and control information to their counterparts on each of the other nodes.

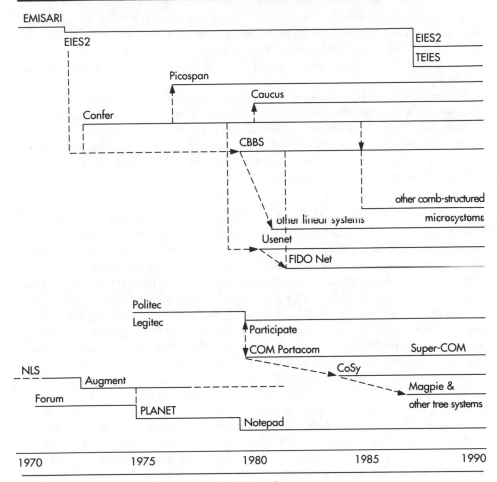

Figure 1.4 Timeline of historical CMC development.

ing a more-or less coincidental development along the same lines. The Forum →
PLANET → Notepad line of development was completely independent of Confer but
nevertheless adopted the basic "comb structure" of the former system.

■ 1.7 THE SEPARATE WORLD OF INFORMATION RETRIEVAL SYSTEMS

By the mid 1970s computer manipulation of text was common enough so that the
majority of documents written by members of the public and private research establishment were maintained in electronic form before printing. This was significant for
those companies whose business was printing collections of abstracts covering many
fields of academic research and business information on public and private companies
in the United States. The availability of this electronically stored text, coupled with
random access storage devices and advances in techniques for quickly finding strings

of text, led to the opening of the first two major information services: Lockheed's Dialog and Dun & Bradstreet's Bibliographic Research Service (BRS) in 1972. The technology of the Dialog-system was derived from a NASA product called Recon, while the Dun & Bradstreet offering had roots in an IBM research system called STAIRS.

Information retrieval systems do not provide interactive communications between persons. Their purpose is to facilitate the recovery of information pertinent to some human query from a large text base. Information retrieval has been an active research subject at least as long as computers have been used to store and manipulate text. This research has focused in two different and unrelated directions: (1) performance and (2) control of the retrieval process.

1.7.1 Factors Affecting the Value of Information Retrieval Systems

Finding strings of text in a large text base, and displaying records containing the string to the user, is a conceptually simple task. The problem becomes interesting when search strings and result sets are combined with Boolean operators (and, or, not) in complex expressions and the text pool becomes very large (hundreds of thousands or millions of records). Even simple searches through sequential collections of records can become abominably slow when the record collection is very large. Publicly accessible text bases such as the Dialog collection are expensive to search, up to hundreds of dollars per connect hour. The value of those systems to the user depends to a great degree on their support for cost-effective discovery and extraction of pertinent data.

The second important research area addresses a breadth-to-depth problem found in all aspects of information retrieval (see Figure 1.5). The problem arises because there isn't always a perfect match between the semantic of a search and the physical text (subject strings) used to carry out that search. If, for example, one wanted to search a large text base for articles on computer conferencing, one might begin with that combination of words as a search term. The term "computer conferencing," though, might appear in any number of records that mention it only in passing. This is the *breadth* part of the problem, also called "recall"—finding too many citations, all of which contain the term or terms of the search but are nevertheless irrelevant to it.

On the other hand, there may be relevant articles in the text base in which the search term never appears. The terms "computer mediated cooperative work," "groupware," or "electronic conferencing" may appear instead. This is the *depth* part of the problem, also known as "precision." The goal is to find *all* articles suited to the real purpose of the query while eliminating citations that are not applicable, even if they contain the search terms. That is, one wants to reduce the recall-to-precision ratio by finding a higher percentage of desirable material while limiting the total material recovered as much as possible. In general, if a query is broadened for the sake of precision (for example, using an "or" conjunction of terms), it will also expand in recall, finding many more irrelevant citations.

In Figure 1.5, the "Information Pool" represents the total amount of information stored in a bibliographic database, with its center representing the information of maximum relevance to a particular search. As contemporary searches get deeper into the

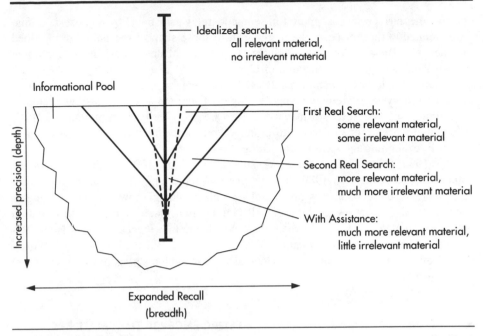

Figure 1.5 The precision/recall problem.

pool, they recover more relevant pieces of information at a cost of also recovering many more less relevant or even irrelevant ones. The dashed triangle represents a search with assistance, possibly using artificial intelligence or other techniques, that achieves a high degree of precision with out too much recall.

Some research systems, such as STAIRS (IBM's STorage And Information Retrieval System), support precision-enhancing features such as term weighting, sentence analysis for co-concurrence of terms, term hierarchies, synonym extraction, and so on. In term weighting, users may specify not only the requirement that a word be found, but the significance of the word compared to other terms used in the search. Co-concurrence has to do with the relationship between two or more search terms appearing in the text and their relationship to one another, proximity, order and frequency of occurrence, and so on. Term hierarchies have to do with association between words whose meanings encompass those of other words; such hierarchies also apply to phrases.

In Dialog, both recall and precision devices rely mostly on the syntactic structure of a text record. Records are subdivided into fields suited to different search demands. If a search term is used in the record *descriptor*, it will have significant bearing on the central theme of the object to which the record refers. The *identifier* contains terms that describe the record in broader terms. Experienced searchers will use these fields to produce sets of records containing search terms with varying degrees of significance. They then recombine these sets in various ways to achieve high-precision searchs. Proximity operators, functions that permit specification of the order and/or word distance between two terms, are an attempt to bridge syntactic and semantic relationships.

On-line thesauri provide support for semantic relevance by allowing users to find terms related to those used in the search. All of these support mechanisms are glued together with Boolean logic, a relatively simple way of describing and recombining various subsets of a large collection of objects.

Systems employing *semantic* analysis, based on term dictionaries, coupled with syntactic rule systems are now being developed. There are a few accessible examples of search assistance software in various forms. One, Verity Corporation's TOPIC, relies on the occurrence of terms to produce "relevance hierarchies" that users may follow in examining recovered information.

The 1985 *Omni Online Database Directory* listed 1100 computer searchable databases worldwide. By 1989 this number had more than doubled. A significant percentage of these databases are found on either Dialog, now owned by Knight-Ridder, or BRS, now owned by Maxwell Online, Inc. Other significant information providers include Orbit, also owned by Maxwell Online; the Dow Jones News Retrieval Service; VU/Text Information Services Inc.; the Wilson Line (H. W. Wilson Co.); NewsNet Inc.; and Mead Data General's Lexis, which serves primarily the legal community.

■ 1.8 MICROCOMPUTERS AND THE EMERGENCE OF THE SMALL BBS NETWORK

Along with continuing developments in computer conferencing and information retrieval, the mid 1970s were a time for computer revolutions in the making. In 1975 Intel introduced the 8080 microprocessor, the first such device powerful enough to make small computers a practical reality. Not long after, the Zilog corporation introduced the Z80, which became the dominant microprocessor for the first generations of microcomputers. In 1977 Digital Research Corporation introduced the CP/M (Control Program/Monitor) operating system, which soon dominated the fledgling microcomputer industry. Given a widely accepted operating system, a microcomputer applications software industry became possible. The pioneers of the microcomputer revolution quickly addressed communications among microcomputers, and among the new machines and older mini and mainframe systems. This ancestry still colors much of the public sector side of computer conferencing more than 10 years later.

The advent of the microcomputer, coupled with the desire to bridge the distance between machines by telephone, created a need for software that allowed:

1. One computer to act as a terminal
2. A second computer to behave as a host
3. Reliable data and command exchange between the two

One problem was that the domestic switched telephone network is inherently unreliable as a data communications medium. Noises that periodically garble voices can destroy data continuity. Large-scale computing centers had machines coupled over long distances, but these systems used private circuits and synchronous modems that performed error-detection and -correction operations between themselves.

1.8.1 Terminal Emulation

A terminal is a human/computer interface device consisting of a keyboard (usually) and a screen, typically a cathode ray tube (CRT). Characters typed at the keyboard are translated into their byte equivalents, eight (sometimes seven) bits in a serial stream set to a pattern of 1s and 0s. Which patterns represent which characters depends on the convention (protocol) being observed by the terminal and the host computer. Both must agree on a standard, or no communication will take place. A device inside the terminal converts digital bytes to electrical signals and places them on one of the wires (again a convention) of a hardware device called a serial port. The port, in turn, is connected either to the telephone network (see Chapter 3 for further discussion) or directly to a host computer. Incoming signals, translated in a reverse process, are interpreted by the terminal hardware as patterns of dots displayed on a screen. Users interpret those patterns as letters, numbers, punctuation, and so on.

In most microcomputers the terminal is not a separate device, but is integrally coupled with the computer so that the micro is host and terminal in one. Characters typed at the keyboard are not sent out a port, but consumed and interpreted by the local machine, which displays them on the screen. In order to connect a microcomputer to a remote host, some software running on the micro must divert keyboard characters to the outgoing lines of a port and capture incoming bytes for display. This process is called terminal emulation because such software makes the microcomputer *appear* to be a terminal from the viewpoint of another computer.

Before the advent of microcomputers, terminal emulation was required in situations where users connected with terminals to one computer were attached, through facilities on their host, to yet another host. The first host, therefore, appears to the second to be a terminal. Remote login, a service provided on some networks, functions in just this way. Other than having to request a connection to a remote host, the operation of this software is completely transparent to the user. On the microcomputer, terminal emulation software is operated by the user to establish a connection to any other host.

Terminal emulation applications were among the first applications widely distributed in the microcomputer world of the late 1970s. There were three reasons for this:

1. Services such as CompuServe and Dialog already existed; there was a ready use for the software.

2. Simple terminal emulation programs are relatively easy to write. Many of the early users of the new technology were technically inclined and had the necessary skills.

3. The use of microcomputers as terminals had two immediate and far-reaching advantages over real terminals: (1) bytes transmitted *from* a host could be captured to local storage devices (disks) for later review, and (2) characters transmitted

to a host could be transmitted directly from disk files instead of being typed during the connection. Because of this, microcomputers could reduce the time users were connected to a remote machine directly or by telephone.

With many remote services, time connected and cost per connection event are directly related. The microcomputer's capacity to reduce connect time gave both the hardware and software technology an immediate boost in the corporate world, and an even larger one in the public sector. Here, use of remote hosts for information retrieval or informal communications with people of similar interests became more affordable. Terminal users had to justify their use of the then-available on-line services directly in terms of cost of doing business. Microcomputer users began to explore some of the available services as a source of *entertainment*.

Many early terminal emulation programs were given away, released into the public domain, or distributed at no cost to the user while the developer retained all rights. "Freeware" is a term often applied to products in this category. Even today, many of the best terminal programs are distributed as *shareware*, a radical marketing concept in which a customer tries a product and sends a specified fee to the author of the software if he or she continues to use it. The prices asked are typically 10 to 20 percent of what a commercial vendor would require. What makes this concept radical is that the author has no realistic way of preventing someone from using the product without ever paying for it. Paying for shareware, however, encourages the developer to support and enhance the product. That many shareware authors do receive a reasonable return in proportion to the popularity of their products is a testament to the enlightened self-interest of the public sector on-line community.

Not long after the development of the first terminal emulation programs, two needs became apparent. The first was born of the desire to make one microcomputer act as an unattended host to another computer or terminal. The second arose from the recognition that program and data exchange could take place between connected systems only if some error-correcting mechanism handled data corruption caused by noise in the telephone network.

1.8.2   File Exchange

File exchange programs operate between computers, rather than from a terminal to a computer. The connection established between a microcomputer and host becomes a channel through which two programs communicate. These programs permit a data exchange that is recorded directly on the storage devices of either machine and not displayed to a user. The two cooperating programs also ensure that the two sides agree on the content of the data.

Error-detecting file transfer protocols have been in use from the earliest days of computing, when the need to transfer files directly between mainframes became pressing. Before this time, the only way to get files from one computer to another was to transfer them on tape. In the early days of microcomputers, programs were similarly transferred on cassette tapes and later on disks. As late as 1978 no standard for error correction had appeared in the microcomputer arena.

In 1978 the CP/M operating system had already begun to dominate the microcomputer industry. In the latter part of 1977 Ward Christensen, who had succeeded in installing the then-new CP/M on an early microcomputer, began to think about a way of exchanging software between other similarly equipped computers. In early 1978 he produced and released to the public domain a program called MODEM, which allowed two microcomputers at opposite ends of a phone line to exchange files. Operators at both ends of the phone line would ready each other for the transmission by voice, place their telephone handsets in their respective modems (see chapter 3 for a discussion of modems), and execute commands on their respective machines—one to send the file, and one to receive.

In 1979 Keith Petersen and Ward Christensen modified MODEM to run in unattended mode. That is, the computer acting as host did not require an operator in attendance to effect file exchange. The operator at the other end of the connection could activate the new MODEM for either receipt or transmission of files. This modification, named X-modem, was released immediately into the public domain, ensuring its domination as an error-detection standard.

1.8.3 The Microcomputer as Host

In 1978 there had been talk among loosely connected computer groups about establishing a nationwide network of systems so news and other information could be exchanged. In short, the computer would provide interpersonal communications services to remotely connected systems. File exchange does not involve interaction with other persons. The new services were to provide a medium for such interaction. Such things as editors and text display software already existed, but they had not been applied to the problem of supporting many user accounts via remote dial-in connections. In the fall of 1978 Ward Christensen wrote CBBS (Computer Bulletin Board System), the first of a long lineage of microcomputer-based group communications software. Like X-modem preceding it, the CBBS software was released into the public domain.

1.8.3.1 Facilities of CBBS

The original CBBS system, first activated in Chicago in 1979, not intended to support file exchange. Its purpose was to reproduce, in computer form, the mundane cork bulletin board covered with thumb-tacked three-by-five cards. Yet this first system was, by today's standards, reasonably sophisticated in several ways.

Users could elect to operate the system through menus or with single-character commands. Commands could in turn be stacked; that is, many commands could be entered on a single line and executed sequentially without further intervention by the user. CBBS divided text records into several fields, including a message number, author, recipient (if desired), subject line, date, and the text of the message itself. The system supported not only simple Boolean arguments in message filtering, but also searches that crossed field boundaries—for example, reading messages posted after some date AND by some author AND containing some string in the subject field. Full text searching was not supported as it is in most true conferencing systems, but many of those systems do not support cross-field selection even today. Christensen's software also tracked each user's read-through point and showed users only those messages they hadn't seen unless told to do otherwise.

CBBS did not further structure the records entered and stored in the system. There were no separate conferences for grouping messages about similar subjects. This lack of structure, coupled with the soon-to-dominate use of these systems as file-exchange engines, continued to characterize most BBSs for many years. This was the primary distinction between BBS and true conferencing systems—a distinction that is today much more blurred. Soon after the development of CBBS, the ability to set up binary exchange pipelines was added to the software. The file exchange capability quickly became the primary reason for calling and running computer BBSs.

1.8.4 BYE and the Hobbyist System Explosion
In late 1979 David Jaffe wrote BYE and released it into the public domain. BYE permitted a remote caller to use the operating system of the host microcomputer as if he or she were using its local keyboard. Programs on the host computer, including X-modem, could be used interactively without the intermediary of a full BBS package running on the host. BYE, of itself, contained *no* message-passing facilities, no interpersonal communications services. It redirected signals from the serial port to those parts of CP/M responsible for keyboard handling. It also intercepted output destined for the console, sending it instead to the serial port.

The appearance of BYE permitted the quick development of BBS applications written in high-level languages (e.g., BASIC, which had appeared by this time for CP/M systems) without having to build elaborate serial port service routines. It was the development of BYE, along with the addition of X-modem to the many BBSs that succeeded CBBS, that established the foundation for the subsequent explosion in small BBS nationwide. In 1980 BBSs in the United States numbered in the low hundreds. Today estimates put the number between 10,000 and 15,000.

1.8.5 The Appearance of Commercial Systems
As with terminal emulators, early BBS software was given away. Shareware distribution continues to account for a substantial number of good programs. Early public domain terminal emulation software differed from commercial versions in many ways. Commercial packages had more sophisticated phone directory managers. They supported proprietary error-detection protocols that, while never adopted as cross-product standards, were typically much faster than X-modem. They began to evolve control languages that were used to automate some aspects of terminal-host interaction. Finally, they typically supported smart terminal emulation, which is the capability of the software to interpret special codes sent from the host meant to manipulate the screen. These codes are used to place data at specific locations of the screen rather than just scrolling everything from the bottom to the top. Early commercial packages were easier to use for people who were not familiar with the process of communicating with a remote computer.

Today both commercial and shareware terminal programs have grown a great deal in sophistication. The best shareware programs have caught up to their commercial brethren in almost every category except for control languages, which have become full-fledged general purpose programming languages in some commercial software. Commercial programs typically support *more* kinds of smart terminal emulation. Similarly, shareware BBSs have grown in sophistication, but commercial host-based programs (conferencing systems) continue to outstrip the relatively simple BBSs in both the number and power of their features. This is primarily due to the considerably more difficult development effort involved. By and large, high-powered host software takes longer to produce, requiring more code than the most sophisticated terminal emulators. It is also more difficult to support many simultaneous users on top of microcomputer hardware and operating systems designed for one user. Large-scale host software typically runs on larger machines. Much of this is changing now, given the advent of very-high-powered microcomputers associated with good multitasking operating systems. It remains true, however, that software running on mainframes is more expensive than the equivalent software in the minicomputer environment. The latter, in turn, is higher priced than counterparts running on micros.

The one place where microcomputer systems, even shareware, continue to outstrip the facilities of larger systems is in the arena of binary file exchange. Although the first microcomputer-based BBS was conceived with text message exchange primarily in mind, file exchange came quickly to dominate the growing ad hoc BBS network. Exchanging *information* via text between users was always possible with these systems, but most of those that followed CBBS did not match its text-handling versatility.

Binary file exchange continues to account for the majority of traffic throughout the nationwide microcomputer BBS network, and X-modem continues to be the single most widely used error-detection protocol (newer, more efficient variants such as Y-modem and Z-modem having become available only since the mid to late 1980s). Most of the better BBS software today supports some functionally adaptable facility for asynchronous conferencing.

This emphasis on file exchange and contemporary developments supporting it is illustrated by the facilities given over to file operations on modern BBSs. The File Cabinet BBS operating out of Bethlehem, Pennsylvania, runs a software package called PC-Board. File operations account for 13 of its 44 main commands. These include such things as marking files for later retrieval, compressing and decompressing file collections (see Chapter 3 for a discussion of compression technology), powerful search functions for files (including the ability to examine libraries of compressed files), and support for optical storage of file libraries. The File Cabinet system has only 10 communications lines, not a large number as some of these systems go. Yet each line supports connect speeds ranging from 300 to 9600 bits per second (bps), and the system's libraries contain some 80,000 binary files.

1.8.6 The Spread of the Mainframe Communications Model

Mainframe- and minicomputer-based conferencing software, by contrast, was conceived for support of communications in natural language between persons. Binary file transfer was not even considered in early systems and has been added to many products because of the demand generated by its popularity on microcomputer BBSs and because the microcomputer has become the preferred means of communicating with even a centralized computer-based conference.

Up through the early 1980s, developments in the electronic conferencing arena focused on a single computing model: the mainframe or minicomputer connected to terminals without CPU resources of their own. Such systems, having been in use for nearly 20 years at that time, were fertile ground for an emerging class of software whose purpose was to enhance communications, problem resolution, and decision-making power of users already tied together by virtue of sharing the resources of the central computer. This being the case, there was no requirement for binary file transfer integration since all files were resident on the same system and therefore inherently sharable.

The developers of conferencing software sought to enhance their products with tools that supported group decision making. Various group voting and opinion-sampling facilities with automatic tabulation and results display appeared in products such as Confer, Parti, Notepad, and EIES. Conference and user directory services, along with some support for cross-field text searching and retrieval, were developed; these foster a group's awareness of itself and its activities. Conferencing systems also allowed for the editing of records after their original entry, making possible jointly authored documents, otherwise treated as store-and-forward conference entries. Early BBSs lacked all these features (though they have now caught up in the arena of textual self-structuring).

The designers of conferencing software from 1971 to the present assumed that their host systems were multiuser in nature. The first BBSs were all single-user environments, and the majority of them continue to be so. Single-user orientation, coupled with the small storage capacity of early microcomputer disks, caused BBS designers to forgo elaborate development of search/retrieval facilities because the message base was typically small, the majority of the disk space being occupied with binary files anyway. Early microcomputers were also slow and could address limited memory. This discouraged elaborate record-structuring schemes because of the system overhead they imposed in both performance and program size.

These limitations were overcome through the 1980s. Multiuser microcomputers were introduced as early as 1981, though for some years their cost was prohibitive for hobbyist users. By 1984 the 64KB memory barrier was a memory itself, following the earlier introduction of the first systems based on more advanced chip technologies: the Intel 8086 and Motorola's 68000. By 1985 it was possible to use a single-user microcomputer as host, and communicate with multiple remote users simultaneously. These systems laid the groundwork for the development of advanced BBS software that began to compete with the more expensive and elaborate conferencing systems running on larger machines.

1.8.7 Microcomputers and Distributed Communications

Shortly after the introduction of the IBM PC in the early 1980s, Tom Jennings, inspired by the success of Usenet, began to develop a set of communications protocols and addressing schemes that would allow the new computers to form a federation of loosely coupled systems to distribute electronic mail and conference texts. The result, in 1983, was the FIDO BBS software and the emergence of the FIDO network. Like other communications software developed for microcomputers in the 1970s and 80s, the FIDO network protocols were placed in the public domain. Their use spread rapidly, and though not as sophisticated in conferencing facilities as more mature software, it has established itself as a de facto standard for distributed conferencing and E-mail exchange between microcomputers in parallel with the UNIX-based Usenet.

Like Usenet, the FIDOnet is a fully distributed conferencing system in which multiple conferences are echoed on individual nodes of the network. FIDO uses the national and international telephone networks and automatic connect and transmission software like its university-developed predecessor. Its message formats, user interfaces, and means of addressing messages are entirely different from those of the Usenet. It has also continued to evolve. In 1989 there were upwards of 4000 machines on the network, a variety of user interfaces, and gateways between the FIDO network, Usenet, and other national and international computer networks.

Today computer conferencing, bulletin boards, and information retrieval systems together form a global web of interconnecting technology. This web is, however, not yet integrated in any significant way. Many of these systems function as stand-alone machines serving hundreds or thousands of users with secondary connections to various international networks. Gateways between centralized conference and E-mail systems, and global networks such as Usenet, MCI mail, AT&T, and Sprintmail are becoming more common. Automatic exchange of conference threads between otherwise centralized systems is growing in popularity, but the different record structures and communication models give these exchanges some rough edges.

■ 1.9 INFORMATION RETRIEVAL AND INTERPERSONAL COMMUNICATIONS

Because of their specialization and the cost of their databases, information retrieval systems remain isolated from interpersonal communications systems. Nevertheless, these systems have grown from a handful in the early 1970s to over 4000 by 1989. General purpose systems such as CompuServe, Delphi, and BIX are experimenting with connections between themselves and the large information retrieval services.

Computer conferencing and information retrieval are merging in two ways, both driven from the conferencing side of the market. First, designers of conferencing software are recognizing the significance of good information retrieval technology in conferencing itself. Computer mediated communications is, to a great extent, an information retrieval challenge. As conferences grow in size and number, the text streams (if they are preserved) are becoming more valuable as sources of information in and of themselves.

To take advantage of this information, software designers must deal with the same problems of precision and recall as designers of information retrieval systems. For readers, navigation through large text bases is essentially a process of finding objects (records, conferences, users, topics, and so on) in which they have an interest.

This is, from the perspective of software design, a problem similar to that faced by persons performing search operations over large business, scientific, or bibliographic databases.

Second, computer conference developers recognize the inherent value of making information already in large text bases (not conferences) available to conference participants. This has caused them to develop gateways, and to find means of making the transition between conference and information retrieval system as seamless as possible. A few designers, taking a different tack, have developed conferencing software around a database management system.

The 1970s proved to be a decade of experimentation and model formulation in conference and information retrieval software. The 1980s have witnessed an explosion in system and user numbers for all sizes and types of software, along with the beginnings of a trend toward interconnection. In the information retrieval arena, the 1980s were years of enormous expansion in the number of databases and in the quantity of information they contain.

Some suggest that the real potential of these systems will not be realized until some settling occurs, so that basic structural models become standardized enough to permit transparent integration of multiple conferencing systems that include large text bases and intelligent retrieval software. Development of both computer conferencing and information retrieval is now driven by the need to make access easier to the public and, ultimately, by the value of computer conferencing and on-line information, as perceived by the business and public sectors.

2

SCOPE OF CURRENT CONFERENCING, INFORMATION RETRIEVAL, AND BBS TECHNOLOGY

■ 2.1 PROMISES AND PROBLEMS

2.1.1 Communications Systems

From the mid 1970s through the early 1980s, the developers of computer conferencing systems consistently predicted that widespread use of the technology was right around the corner. In the opinion of developers, corporate America and the public would soon awaken to the potentials of electronic mail and the many-to-many facilities of conferencing software, and embrace the technology. They believed that the use of computers would move from enhancement of individual activities to the support of work groups through the mediation of computer communications.

In 1988, NETI, a publicly owned company founded by Larry Brilliant to sell and service computer conferencing software, filed for bankruptcy. In 1989 CompuServe Information Service, Inc., the largest general purpose, publicly accessible information provider and conferencing center, reportedly had one-half million users worldwide. In the same year, CompuServe bought out and closed down The Source, 10 years earlier its only rival in the public conference arena. In the mid 1980s other large systems were founded: General Electric Information Exchange, Byte Information Exchange, Delphi, and American People-link.

These continue to exemplify large-scale centralized conferencing in the public arena, though their conferencing facilites lack many of the features available in some of the earlier software developed for this purpose. The first two quickly surpassed The Source in the number of active users. Because usage and subscription figures are confidential, there is no way of accurately gauging the number of people participating in public conferencing, but it is clearly growing.

Beginning in 1984, mid-sized conferencing centers began to make their appearance. These systems are smaller than the four biggest vendors. They are also less expensive for those living within a reasonable calling distance. These mid-sized systems support multiple dial-in phone lines, eliminating most of the busy signals so often associated with earlier single-user BBSs. Most of these systems have enough record organization and navigation facilities to qualify as proper conferencing systems. Their lineage derives from both computer conferencing and early BBSs. All of them contain support for binary file transfer and cataloging. Many have extensive program libraries.

These systems often reside on IBM-PC-like machines running MS-DOS, or UNIX-based microcomputers, or sometimes minis. DOS implementations are not often as broad in overall capabilities as their counterparts on inherently multiuser operating systems. On the other hand, they can be considerably less expensive to implement and maintain, especially if there are but a few phone lines connected to the system.

Single-line BBS systems continue to proliferate and associate in networks. Found on all types of inexpensive microcomputer hardware, they provide an alternative to storing data at a single point. Growth continues in this segment of the communications market, but dollar values are hardly noticeable as the associated hardware/software is obtained inexpensively. This activity is, however, responsible for some overall increase in telephone use.

Although the public's use of computer conferencing has grown steadily in the last five years, private sector usage has continued to grow slowly. In 1982 Gnostic Concepts, a market research firm, pegged nationwide expenditures on computer conferencing at $2.5 million. This same survey projected this market's growth to $90 million by 1990. Real growth since that time, however, has shown these projections to be highly optimistic.

In 1989, there were about 1500 computer conferencing or BBS systems installed in American corporations. Digital Equipment Corporation's (DEC) VaxNotes, with about 1000 installed sites, dominates the corporate market. This software is, however, given away to any DEC customer who uses DEC's popular ALL-IN-ONE office automation software, so there is no way to determine how many corporations actually use VaxNotes.

In the corporation, text-based computer confrencing is perceived as something of a threat to the ritual of the corporate meeting. Where used, it has changed, though by no means eliminated, some of the content and form of face-to-face meetings. Furthermore, operation of the technology requires typing skills, an acceptance of the asynchronous characteristics of the medium, a willingness to participate, and some discipline on the user's part. Participants must actually check a progressing conference transcript from time to time in order to keep up with and take part in developments. For electronic meetings to fulfill their potential, everyone expected to participate must have a terminal or microcomputer on his or her desk, something most high-level corporate executives still strongly resist. All these requirements have retarded the implementation of true conferencing systems.

2.1.2 Information Retrieval Systems

Information retrieval services, begun in the mid 1970s, began to diversify their marketing in the mid 1980s. In 1983 Dialog information services began a less expensive service aimed at the computer-literate public called the Knowledge Index. At about the same time its main competitor, BRS, started a similar lower-priced spinoff of its system called BRS After Dark. Each company has since expanded its services with specialized offerings to the business, scientific, engineering, and medical communities.

Developments in retrieval technology, particularly search assistance software, continue to improve the usefulness of these systems to professional and nonprofessional searchers alike. The 1980s brought expansion in the quantity of available data, and many of the larger systems have publicly stated their intention to focus on retrieval assistance capabilities throughout the 1990s.

Librarians in corporations and universities have been using systems such as Dialog and BRS extensively since the late 1970s. As the number of databases and the data produced per month have increased, research companies, acting as second-order brokers, have multiplied. Research scientists and engineers are frequent users of such facilities, but lawyers spend more money on line than most of the other groups combined. Given the timeliness and historical value of information available in the legal databases, not doing a search in preparation for a significant case is tantamount to neglect.

The value of information now available on these systems has not been lost to business, scientific, and research establishments. Dialog contains over 800 separate databases encompassing almost every field of human endeavor. Included in this collection is a nationwide yellow pages divided into broad industry categories. Dialog catalogs research in fields from astrophysics to zoology, along with all standard business reference sources. For computer users and software analysts, there are extensive collections of computer journals ranging from the highly technical publications of the ACM and IEEE to such popular literature as *Byte Magazine, Dr. Dobbs*, and *Computer Language*.

BRS is similar to Dialog in attempting to maintain a broad range of available databases. Other systems are more specialized. The NewsNet contains over 300 specialized trade and industry newsletters, the kind that typically cost hundreds of dollars a year in subscription fees. VU/Text and DataTimes of Oklahoma City specialize in newspapers—not only the major papers, but local and regional papers as well. The Wilson Line focuses on indexes to journals in many fields. Some of the Orbit databases contain technology information of such sensitivity that federal security clearances are required to search them. This growth trend will continue. Access to these services will become widely available via gateways established through public and private conferencing and electronic mail systems.

▪ 2.2 TELECONFERENCING, COMPUTER MEDIATED COOPERATIVE WORK, AND COMPUTER MEDIATED COMMUNICATIONS

Text-based computer conferencing is a part of a wider domain called teleconferencing. This is in turn associated with other software support tools known collectively as office automation technologies (see Figure 2.1). Teleconferencing includes such things as voice mail, audio many-to-many conferencing, audio plus graphics, and audio plus freeze-frame or full-motion video. Also in the teleconferencing sector are the evolving technologies surrounding multimedia presentation and communications systems.

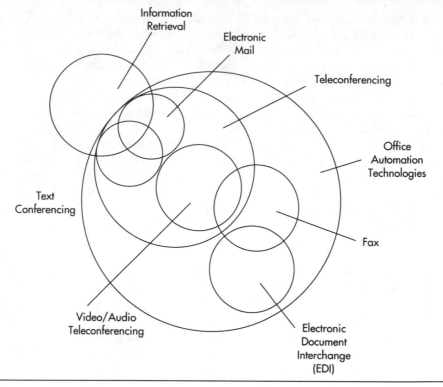

Figure 2.1 The relationship among text-based computer conferencing, electronic mail, information retrieval, and other teleconferencing technologies.

Facsimile (Fax) and electronic document interchange (EDI) are a part of the office automation/technologies arena, although they are not usually considered teleconference technologies. They are communicative, but not conversational. Information retrieval lies outside the office automation technologies, but impinges on it. Technically, information retrieval may be involved in all forms of office automation technology, as well as being a separate area in its own right.

Teleconferencing software and other tools in the office systems group are sometimes called *groupware* because in some sense their purpose is to smooth the exchange and manipulation of information through and among work groups. Some authors divide groupware products into two categories: work flow managers and work content managers. The former focus on human resource management as it relates to data communicated among members of a group. The latter are focused on data organization/presentation and joint document/file manipulation (text, graphics, or both). The larger conferencing systems were conceived with both work flow *and* work content in mind. As things have gone, most of the products involved in interpersonal communication are usually classified with the work flow groupware. Some of the scheduling and project management facilities available in contemporary work flow products cannot be entirely duplicated by any computer conferencing software, without substantial programming and systems support.

Computer conferencing and other forms of text- or graphics-based interpersonal communications systems are also known as computer mediated cooperative work (CMCW) systems. This term may also include much of the teleconferencing domain. Technically, all teleconferencing systems are CMCWs because they employ computers at some level of their operation. The use of computers in video and audio teleconferencing, however, is more or less invisible to the persons participating in such conferences. The purpose of much teleconferencing is to transcend geographic distance and provide a convenient conduit for data or information presentation in an environment that simulates a face-to-face meeting. Except for the ability to later *review* the content of the meeting, time is not eliminated as a factor. Participants must be assembled (however dispersed geographically) at the same moment.

Sometimes the term *computer mediated communications* (CMC) is used to describe the wider view of CMCWs, leaving the latter term to those systems that provide asynchronicity, store, and forward service. Sometimes the reverse usage is seen. The remainder of this book will concern itself with that subset of teleconferencing that is conversational and embraces the computer/terminal/workstation as both a conduit and the primary medium of exchange. Most of these systems are text-based, with some graphical extensions and abilities. Asynchronicity is another characteristic of systems discussed in this book. Some permit conversations between many persons at the same time, but all of them have some means of storing messages and forwarding them to recipients at a later time. The terms "conference," "E-mail," and "BBS" will be used to refer to those specific systems/software. "Communications systems/software" or "interpersonal communications" will be used to name those systems collectively. So as not to confuse "communications software" with "terminal emulation," I will use the latter term only in connection with software supporting microcomputer connections to remote hosts.

▪ 2.3 THE VERSATILITY OF MANY-TO-MANY TEXT-BASED COMMUNICATIONS

All the teleconferencing technologies except computer conferencing and E-mail involve voice. As other technologies are added to voice communications, systems become more expensive to buy and maintain. All voice-based systems except voice-mail are synchronous in nature; the conference participants must be present simultaneously. Voice-mail, though asynchronous, suffers from the same limitations as its E-mail counterpart.

Text-based computer conferencing addresses a potentially wider set of domains than any other teleconferencing or office automation system. Its purpose is the association of ideas and experience of *people*, communicated in written words. The reasons for this association are another matter. Motivations may involve business decisions and millions of dollars, lives hanging on rapid organization of responses to emergencies, the intellectual challenge of a contest, the development of a new technology, or socialization with friends—the development of *virtual* communities.

These applications are not associated with other teleconferencing technologies. They are either dependent on the persons involved being present at the same time, or geared to one-to-one or one-to-many communications. Yet realizing the benefits of this most transforming of teleconferencing technologies requires the greatest commitment to alterations in basic organizational communications structures, channels, conventions, and so on.

The voice-based systems demand less radical changes in communication conventions within and between corporations. Although memos are common, they are typically one-way, broadcast communications between management and employees or point-to-point exchanges. E-mail covers this domain; as a result, E-mail systems are growing in popularity, much more so than conferencing proper. Management decision making and planning has always taken place in face-to-face meetings, that is, synchronously. The implementation of voice or video conferencing facilitates and extends the power of this form of meeting without distorting it beyond recognition.

2.3.1 Relationship between Communications and Other Computer Mediated Services

The broadest view of conference technology's application potential can be seen in the educational and public arenas. The dramatic growth of CompuServe, along with the expansion of midrange systems serving as access points to public communications networks, demonstrates a growing public awareness of the technology. The success of some of these systems is in part attributable to the presence of yet other services about which communication can take place.

At the end of 1989, there were some 250 Special Interest Groups (SIGs) on CompuServe. Each SIG is a conference unto itself with from 10 to 15 major subdivisions. Traffic in these conferences ranges from dozens to hundreds of messages a day. Topics range from the religious and philosophical to the technical nuts-and-bolts of such topics as building homes; buying and selling stocks; programming, operating, and expanding computers; and tasting wine.

Other services are an integral part of the CompuServe Information Service (CIS). There is an extensive on-line ordering and delivery service—an electronic, searchable merchandise catalog. Information retrieval has been a part of CompuServe services from its beginning. These services include searchable news feeds from the Associated Press and United Press International, stock and commodities reports, company information, airline schedules and pricing information, National Weather Service reports, and a gateway service called IQuest. This last is CompuServe's name for its connection to EasyNet, a product of Telebase Systems of Narberth, Pennsylvania. EasyNet is a gateway service, a means of making connections between hosts such as CompuServe and multiple database vendors such as Dialog and BRS (see Chapters 8 and 11).

Finally, there are the games. CompuServe boasts hundreds of games from traditional chess tournaments to mega-wars, a game played by dozens of people asynchronously over a period of many months. With the advent of services like CompuServe, conferencing acquired a new purpose not anticipated or appreciated by the majority of developers and investigators in the field: *entertainment.*

Some of the more complex games on CompuServe have fostered SIGs. These help plan the next game cycle, provide tips and techniques for playing, share strategies, and otherwise communicate with the game's sponsors. Other SIGs serve multiple purposes, with entertainment often counting as one of the more important ones. Face-to-face get-togethers are planned and held all over the country as people who have met only on line wish to socialize in person. Persons who, because of physical circumstances or personality inclination, experience little socialization with their geographic neighbors have fostered a new kind of friendship with others solely through the medium of SIG conferencing and CompuServe's synchronous medium, CB.

2.3.2 The Entertainment Value of the On-line Cocktail Party

CompuServe's simulated citizens band, CB, is a synchronous form of electronic conferencing. Conversations in CB vanish into electronic vapor as conversation scrolls off the screen. They are not stored for later review by others. In CB any number of people can converse with one another as a group as though they were all standing around in a big circle and talking. In fact, The CB experience can be disconcerting at first because one must constantly interpret the stream of text with respect to the conversation being addressed. It is not altogether unlike tuning in and out of background conversations at a party, however, and one soon gets used to it.

Every SIG has a number of CB channels associated with it. On these channels, scheduled and ad hoc meetings are convened to discuss anything and everything having to do with the fundamental focus of the SIG. A participant acts as moderator. A conventional set of signals lets the moderator know you wish to say something or are finished writing. SIG conferences thus remain more focused and orderly compared to the open-ended free-for-all discussions conducted on CIS's open CB channels.

Because conversations on CB channels aren't stored, it is something of a stretch to call them computer conferences. They are, nevertheless, computer mediated text communications, and the entertainment dimension of the medium is nowhere better illustrated than on these channels. On a typical Friday or Saturday night as many as 200 or more persons are engaged in banter about almost anything on the 60 open channels supported by CIS. Private conversations are supported by the same software. It is common for individuals to slip back and forth between public and private conversations, spending several hours a week in this way keeping up with friends across the country or around the world.

2.3.3 The Political Action Potential of CMC Systems

Political action is yet another purpose born of public and educational use of conferencing technology. There are several political forums on CompuServe, disseminating information and opinion about any given issue very rapidly across the nation or the world. The term "electronic democracy" stems from the medium's ability to bring together the actors and those acted upon in a forum where anyone may speak and offer an opinion. This political force has been felt in various parts of the country where issues impacting access to local BBS and conferencing systems were before legislators or regulatory agencies. A few national and state legislators have established small BBS systems of their own to communicate with their constituents, and regional systems whose primary purpose is involvement in local politics and civic affairs have appeared in San Francisco, San Diego, Boston, Chicago, Cleveland, and other cities.

In Santa Monica, California, a BBS is used to connect the city's political administration directly with its constituents. Public debate and lobbying on issues before the city council take place on line. The system is receiving strong support from its community of users.

■ 2.4 COMPUTER CONFERENCING IN EDUCATIONAL INSTITUTIONS

Conferencing in educational institutions is reflected in a number of research and experimental systems, along with the ubiquitous Usenet, which dominates the medium in this arena. There are four or five thousand Usenet nodes nationwide, and several thousand more around the world. The majority belong to educational institutions, many schools having multiple nodes serving different sub-schools or departments. A good number of Usenet nodes belong to corporations, mostly computer or research-related companies.

Usenet conferences range from the very technical through the deep to the silly. Almost every computer architecture, language, operating system, and peripheral type has its own conference, often more than one. User tips, advance product announcements, bug fixes, and evaluations are found there. DBMS systems, spreadsheets, word processors, accounting software, graphics, BBSs, and all manner of utilities are discussed and reviewed. Outside the computer arena researchers and educators use the network to communicate about research and other matters in such fields as astronomy, biology, physics, psychology, sociology, history, the arts, and philosophy. There are conferences with local, regional, national, and international scope. There is a jokes conference, several religion conferences, political forums, current events conferences, and electronic classified ads.

Although Usenet has been invaluable to the flow of information between universities and technology corporations, its high public profile and lack of security features make it less useful for other educational endeavors, one of which is distance learning — an extension of the classroom through the electronic medium. Conference topics can become lecture platforms, and student participation can take the form of responses to the lectures. Essays and written assignments can be transmitted as files or entered as conference items or responses themselves. In the latter case, however, the software must be able to restrict students from seeing others' responses, at least until they have entered their own.

Usenet does not support any of the features required for emulating a formal classroom environment on line. Unless restricted to a small set of machines, all newsgroups are open to public perusal. There is no support for vote-like activities, nor can responses be hidden from other participants until they themselves have responded. A great deal of experimentation in this arena has gone on using centralized systems such as EIES at the New Jersey Institute of Technology (NJIT) and Confer II at the University of Michigan, Arizona State, the University of Illinois, MIT, Wayne State University, and others have experimented with distance learning. Common to all these systems, and to centralized conferencing in general, is the ability to support private conferences. Such systems almost always contain gateways to Usenet as well, so students and other participants may have the best of both worlds.

The University of Michigan's data center has played host to the original Confer system since 1974. Their experimentation with electronic conferencing in education illustrates both its good and its bad points. Successes abound, but there are also some negative themes that appear over and over. Unless participation is mandated by the faculty, it is spotty, at least at the undergraduate level. This, of course, is no different from participation in live classes, and the faculty options are similar: factoring participation into grades, making important announcements on line, and so on. Another problem is an extreme example of the skewed participation curve. In a class of 30 or more people, 5 of them might sometimes generate 30 to 50 messages a day. This endless stream discourages others from participation because so much time is wasted reading through the babble. This curve is well known on public systems as well, but is less extreme because the writers must pay for their time on line.

For example, the curve in Figure 2.2 illustrates a phenomenon commonly observed in many CMC areas both public and corporate. Read/write ratios, the number of messages posted compared to the number read, typically run in the neighborhood of 100:1 in most systems. That is, the average participant will read 100 messages for every one he or she posts. Yet a disproportionately small number of people have much lower ratios, in the 10:1 range. Thus, a relatively small number of people, say 10 percent of the participant population, may account for as much as 80 percent or more of the message traffic. This has occasioned problems, especially when a majority of the user population is not participating just "for the fun of it."

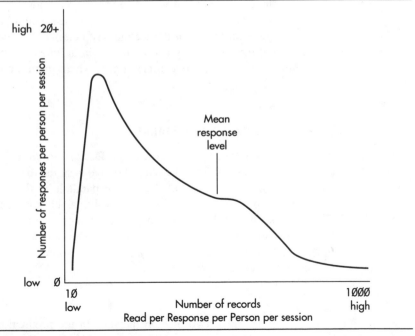

Figure 2.2 The zipped-down contribution curve.

Education has many forms. Awakening Technology of Portland, Oregon, a venture of Peter and Trudy Johnson-Lenz, has been experimenting with the technology to support on-line meetings for self-realization and development. The Johnson-Lenzes were early users and developers of the EIES system at the NJIT. Since 1988, when they formed Awakening Technology, they have been bringing people together in a sort of on-line encounter group. Aside from the counseling value of their work to the individuals involved, they have been active in tuning their environment to address the issues of overall participation, and the contribution curve (Figure 2.2).

They conduct synchronous meetings in which members see their names and the names of other participants displayed in a circle on the screen. Participation is ordered by a token that travels from one name to another. Members may enter comments into the discussion only when they have the token, an electronic version of the American Indian "talking stick." Asynchronous activity is also employed. All members must make a contribution to the discussion before any one of them can enter a subsequent comment. A given conference, or encounter, lasts a set time, typically 10 weeks. On finishing these very specialized sessions, many participants elect to continue as regular members of Awakening Technology's ongoing activities, open only to former encounter group participants.

The Johnson-Lenzes' application of conferencing technology is an example of the flexibility of the medium. Conferencing software is usually employed to increase communications speed and information transfer, but they have used it to produce a methodically paced interaction between persons, emphasizing their demand for equality of participation and thoughtfulness of response. The Johnson-Lenzes' users are atypical in many ways. There is an explicitly declared intention among members of the group to participate regularly. Many of the constraints imposed would be counterproductive in every other domain to which the technology is applied. Nevertheless, they have demonstrated that the technology can be useful in an unusual application. Their approach is closely related to the educational arena, where intention to participate is at least implicit.

■ 2.5 CORPORATE APPLICATION DOMAINS

In the corporate arena, research done by the Metasystems Design Group (MDG) of Arlington, Virginia, and others has identified a number of domains suited to contemporary electronic conferencing technology. Many of these have parallels in the educational and public arenas as well. Some of the domains also involve other software products in the groupware genre, such as schedulers and project trackers. Computer conferencing can act as the cement that binds these various products together, permitting management to schedule resources and assess plans for development, testing, and implementation of complex products or activities.

2.5.1 Coauthorship

Coauthorship is the collaboration of two or more persons in the production of documents. In the corporate world these might be system specifications, user manuals, reports to parent company management, announcements, and so on. In the educational arena this includes jointly authored technical papers, institutional policy statements, and compilations of cooperative research data. A few public systems have even experimented with jointly authored novels.

2.5.2 Decision support

Decision support (DS) is the analysis of data and divergent viewpoints to arrive at group consensus on issues. The groups involved here include technical committees, software development teams, and management groups. Not only conferences themselves, but also the support such systems contain for tabulating votes and probability estimates, are crucial for the effective use of the medium in this domain.

2.5.3 Implementation planning

This is the determination of who will do what, how, and with whom. Research on this use of the technology, conducted by the New Jersey Institute of Technology, has demonstrated that the assignment of leadership roles within a computer conference is crucial to its success in this area. This use of the medium has been demonstrated in the public arena as well, where ad hoc teams of programmers have emerged and produced many useful utility programs.

2.5.4 Project management

Project management is the follow-through to implementation planning. Once plans are formulated, project execution must be monitored. Conferencing technology facilitates communication among and between management and technical teams. Schedules can be posted, time estimates made and evaluated, progress analyzed, problems identified, and resolutions considered. A significant lesson emerging from NJIT research in this area is the need for conference facilitators, whose primary job is overseeing the coordination of multiple conferences or topics that have a bearing on disparate facets of a given project. Field addressability is an important requirement for software employed in this domain.

2.5.5 Interagency Coordination

This domain has been most often associated with nonprofit corporations. Such companies are not necesarily in competition with one another, but they must try to apply the largest possible percentage of their budgets to the direct service of their constituents. Private and government agencies charged with housing the homeless, feeding or providing medical assistance to the poor, preventing the spread of AIDS, and fighting urban drug problems are using this technology to coordinate their activities. This domain may apply to other organizations when their activities require coordination with other companies working on large government contracts or when they are working on projects that involve many kinds of technologies. NASA, for example, uses Notepad for coordinating the design of its new space station and for tracking manned space flights, an activity involving hundreds of individual installations worldwide.

Two networks, Polygon and Pisces, were established by third parties to provide vertical industries with communications and information services. The first is directed at the jewelery, pawnshop, and gun-brokering industries worldwide. Here the communications features of the software are used to set up trades and provide activity information, pricing, and so on. The second is aimed at the global shrimp and fishing industry. Information on storage facilities, prices, and boat availability is provided, as is a medium for communications among subscribers.

2.5.6 Technology Scanning

This is a process for remaining up-to-date on the latest developments and breakthroughs in technology. It is in this particular use that the domains of computer conferencing and information retrieval merge. Information retrieval capabilities are also brought to bear in decision support. In DS, however, retrieved information is brought *to* the conference to support the decision-making process. In contrast, information retrieval is the very essence of the technology scanning process. Here one is not necessarily a participant in the conference(s), but is using the existing records as a database from which to draw information regarding technological problems already solved or in the process of being solved. Access to databases outside the conference is also valuable in this domain. Researchers and engineers in universities and other companies may have published literature available in external databases that contributes substantially to solutions being sought.

This use of conferencing systems is also well illustrated by the global interconnection of universities and technology companies in the Usenet. This network's conferences are used regularly to communicate university research. Research and development in private corporations is less commonly revealed, yet these companies do their part to support the network by forwarding much of its traffic. The evolving technology of the network itself provides valuable insights into developments in many areas of computer science.

Unfortunately, the information retrieval capabilities of most communications products are not wholly up to this task. Conference software search capabilities were not necessarily conceived with information retrieval in mind. Instead they are an adjunct to other system navigation facilities, providing users with another means to find interesting conversations in which to participate. Even this application of search/selection support would benefit from capabilities more like those of the dedicated information retrieval systems, especially as conference volume grows. The primary barriers are the complexity of the software involved and the performance penalty incurred as a result of executing complex searches over large text bases. Information retrieval systems can be optimized for this task, but conferencing systems are more generalized, with many more features to support efficiently.

2.5.7 Technology Transfer

Technology transfer, the transmission of technology from person to person or from one part of a company to another, is a concomitant part of the conferencing process in general, but its most obvious manifestation is found in software support for file transfer facilities. File exchanges are a direct, literal transfer of technology between person and person, company and company, educational institutions, and the private sector.

In large nationally or globally distributed corporations, conferencing is a means by which technological developments in one area are efficiently communicated to other parts of the company. Research and development (R&D) work in one part of a corporation might begin with a technology scan for similar activities in other parts of the company. As technologies evolve, their progress and problems can be communicated in conferences. This provides feedback from other corporate units working in related areas, and avoids the reinvention of technology in distant parts of the corporation.

2.5.8 Product dovlopomont

Product development, building on technology scanning and transfer, brings together the collective experience of individuals in both technical and business-oriented positions company wide. Ideas for new products and services can be communicated to persons whose jobs entail developing product lines. Feasibility studies, investigation of competing products, and unique approaches to product design all benefit from the always available channels of information, feedback, and management control that conferencing technology can provide. In the public arena, products that enhance the use of conferencing technology itself have emerged from the combination of skills and needs expressed through the medium itself.

2.5.9 Dealer and Distributor Support

Dealer and distributor support through computer conferencing allows corporations to maintain high-quality links with their supply and distribution networks. Thomas Malone, of MIT's Sloane Management School, has investigated these relationships. He concludes that "the overall effect of this technology will be to increase the proportion of economic activity coordinated by markets" ("Electronic Markets and Electronic Hierarchies").

The close relationship of few firms in a supplier-purchaser relationship—a hierarchy—is favored when the production costs of a product are relatively high and the product is asset specific, that is, of immediate value to relatively few buyers. Another factor favoring the hierarchy is high product distribution cost. The costs associated with coordination between buyer and seller are relatively lower in hierarchical relationships because the parties involved understand the nature of the complex materials or services being bought and sold. In hierarchies managerial decisions, not market forces, determine design, pricing, quantity, and delivery schedules.

Markets, by contrast, are favored when products are well understood, are easy to describe, and are of value to a broader range of purchasers. These tend to be products whose production costs are low, favoring the entry of more producers who can share in a broader market for the product or service. On the other hand, coordination costs are higher in market-based relationships because sellers must reach many potential buyers. Buyers in turn must spend time and money to identify many potential suppliers and obtain the best price. In these relationships, a broker may act as a middle man between many suppliers and customers to facilitate this coordination. The broker's fee is also factored into the overall cost of doing business for both sides of the buyer/seller relationship.

By reducing the cost of communications *and* facilitating the description of complex products, computer mediated communication pushes hierarchical relationships toward market organization. The rapidly accelerating demand for electronic document interchange (EDI) standards is a predictable consequence of developing market relationships. Brokers are squeezed in the middle because electronic information exchange and information retrieval technology makes it easier for buyers to communicate directly with producers.

Wholesalers are beginning to experiment with this technology by making warehouse inventory, location, delivery lags, and other product information available directly to retail outlets. EDI and other forms of computer communication also make information exchange more efficient for hierarchical business relations. Computer assistance favors both types of relations. Its impact on markets is more dramatic, however, because it raises the value of the production/coordination cost ratio by lowering the cost of coordination. In hierarchical markets, the new technology only serves to increase an already high value in this ratio.

2.5.10 Sales Coordination

On the other side of the vendor relationship equation is sales coordination, another distinct domain successfully addressed by computer conferencing. Here, however, other teleconferencing and related technologies have superseded text conferencing. The most dramatic impact has come from the declining prices of Fax and voice mail. Other developments include the rapid dissemination of price and inventory information to sales forces through portable computers and electronic mail. Conferencing proper comes into play mainly as a means of policy feedback from the sales force to the seller's management. If management is willing and able to respond to such feedback, the result is increasing responsiveness of the seller to changing market demands.

2.5.11 Customer support

Customer support is related to both vendor and sales support, but has evolved a distinct domain. The majority of companies using computer conferencing for this purpose are in the computer hardware or software business. Software developers large and small have a customer base able to take advantage of on-line support services provided through BBS and conferencing systems. Such companies often establish small systems of their own. Typically, these are not fully developed conferencing packages but simpler BBS systems, frequently supporting only one caller at a time.

To reach a wider audience, many of these same corporations will establish conferences on the larger public systems. Most of the better known and larger software developers support their own SIGs on CompuServe, whereas many smaller companies use BIX. The use of conferencing facilities on these systems affords both customer and vendor a rapid form of feedback on product problems and new product developments. On CompuServe, for example, Crosstalk Communications, a division of Digital Communications Associates, Inc. (DCA), maintains libraries of answers to often-asked questions, receives suggestions from its user base, and distributes upgrades to many software modules directly to its customers. This reduces the volume of its shipping department and provides its technical and marketing staff with product ideas and problem information.

2.5.12 Internal Corporate Communications

Corporate policy information, new procedures, the availability of computer resources, and special functions are all effectively communicated via text-based conferences. Because this is primarily one-way communication, electronic mail using distribution lists is also employed successfully in this capacity. Conferencing, however, has the advantage of providing more effective feedback to management regarding announcements and changes. Technical difficulties imposed by new policies can be identified quickly, discussed, and solved efficiently. The morale effects of policy announcements can be assessed, permitting management to respond to real concerns and not the rumor mill.

2.5.13 Team Building

Intracorporate conferences also influence team building, which is particularly important in technical ranks where teams of managers and technical personnel are formed for specific tasks. Conferencing technology helps managers determine which people are most likely to work well together by observing their interaction in conference exchanges.

In this context it is worth noting that such researchers as Turoff, Hiltz, and Johansen found that the success of work-related conferences depends to a significant degree on the existence of general conferences that often have nothing directly to do with the company's business. The existence of conferences that serve no business function, but instead provide users a diversion from business, motivates users to work with the technology and become more adept at its use for business-related purposes.

Conferencing technology has a direct impact on team relationships. It makes widely dispersed technical teams a practical reality. No other teleconferencing medium succeeds so well at keeping geographically dispersed groups in touch with their own work. Even management need not be present in person, but represents itself as conferencing facilitators and coordinators, using the electronic medium to exercise traditional roles.

2.5.14 Professional Devlopement and Organizational Learning

These two domains are mostly side-effects of having and using the technology intended for some other purpose. The former involves general expansion of knowledge in areas related only peripherally to a specific task or job category. Many people with or without the benefit of the technology in their jobs use public systems for this purpose. Organizational learning emerges from management's ability to measure quality of work reflected in the personal energy consumed solving problems or circumventing clumsy procedures and poorly thought-out policies.

2.5.15 Strategic Devlopment

Strategic development was among the uses for which the technology was first developed. Unfortunately, it has probably had the least effect on this domain, because it primarily involves senior corporate management, the very persons who have been most reluctant to participate in the technology. When senior management is geographically dispersed, other teleconferencing technologies such as voice and video conferencing are adopted far more readily than any asynchronous conferencing medium.

2.5.16 International Crisis Resolution and Disaster Management

This is another arena to which conferencing systems were early and successfully applied. The first conferencing system, EMISARI, was conceived with this application in mind. Notepad International Corporation, which bought the PLANET system from Menlo Park's Institute for the Future and turned it into Notepad, organizes much of its business around this function.

Notepad International addresses its niche in the conferencing market by selling connections to its computer, on which the conferences reside. Each conference is customized for its client company, providing any number of extra services from newswire feeds to management support and decision-making tools. The Notepad system is *never* off-line, and its management guarantees accessibility to the system from any telephone network in the world.

The advantages of text-based conferencing in this realm are enormous. Experts from government, industry, and the educational sectors are brought together instantly for discussion about the problem or crisis at hand. The system has been used to coordinate the delivery of emergency supplies to remote areas of the globe, manage the worldwide coordination of short-term crisis relief, and manage other operations requiring intense interaction of people and technology. Examples include manned space flights and amelioration of the effects of earthquakes, oil spills, and nuclear accidents.

At the onset of the Chernobyl nuclear disaster in April 1986, The Notepad coordinated radiation monitoring efforts in Europe, North America, and the Far East. Reactor design experts used the system in conjunction with data from satellite surveys of the stricken area to piece together scenarios that could have precipitated the disaster, and others sought means to ameliorate its effects. The Soviet authorities supplied no hard data until after the acute crisis had passed. When such data became available, the disaster team discovered that the guesses and approximations emerging from the ongoing Notepad discussion (including the use of its delphic voting facilities) had correctly identified the cause, the short-term effects, and the solution to the immediate crisis.

The American nuclear power industry has been using Notepad since the Three Mile Island accident. Nuclear generating plants nationwide are tied together through the Notepad system. About once a month disaster scenarios, generated at different sites, exercise the system. With each drill, plant managers nationwide develop skills in communicating information about the simulated disaster and formulating procedures to deal with it. Local civil authorities are also participants in these drills, using the system to coordinate evacuation plans, medical assistance, and relief efforts.

Crises take many forms. International disasters galvanize large numbers of people and governments into contributing to relief supplies that must be purchased with donated moneys and brought to the site. Organizational politics is minimized because:

- The organization coordinating the relief effort is generally short-lived and has little time to develop a political infrastructure.
- The nature of the crisis, and the public attention cast upon it, demand minimization of organizational politics.

This de-emphasis of the political, coupled with the technical competence and breadth of the crisis team, allow computer conferencing to display its potential.

2.5.17 Public Relations

One aspect of CMC's effect on a corporation's image stems not from any direct use of conferencing, but from the public perception that the company is both willing and able to adopt technology and apply it to the public interest. This association has been made primarily in government agencies and energy companies. Here the existence of an active conferencing system signals that a corporation is ready to manage a crisis should one emerge and that its moneys are being spent to make corporate communications more efficient and therefore less costly.

There is another side to the public relations domain, potentially involving information retrieval technologies in a direct way. Some companies are installing small BBS systems to support public relations. These systems are similar to customer and vendor support systems in size and architecture. Their users are reporters and others in the news media, primarily the trade and industry press, seeking information about the company and its products. Public relations departments fill these systems with electronic versions of product brochures. There may also be E-mail or conference facilities that permit authorized users to ask questions clarifying policy statements or to seek comments on certain issues.

With respect to brochures, product specifications, and other official communications of the corporation, the intended recipients will likely have more than they can print in the near future. Since this information is *intended* by its originators for public release, trade publishers will soon have data resources to sell third parties (probably with royalty arrangements). The most likely customers might be other corporations doing competitor studies, buyers of products looking for new or less expensive sources, market analysts, and so on.

Publishers become on-line information providers, requiring more sophisticated information retrieval support. This is already happening in the form of existing newswire databases. Dialog and other services carry these wires for the producers, who receive their data in turn from corporations. The data bases include publicity and product specification documents and also corporate filings with federal and state governments. The falling cost of mounting data *and* communications services puts the wire publishers in position to augment their databases with conference and electronic mail facilities. The corporate information generates cash flow, and the communications facilities provide user feedback convenient for the marketing and development departments of both the publishers and the corporations that supply the original data.

■ 2.6 FACTORS CONTRIBUTING TO THE SUCCESS OF PUBLIC AND PRIVATE CONFERENCE APPLICATIONS

Successful application of computer conferencing technology depends on a number of different factors, only a few of which are technical. No one conferencing model (see Chapters 6 and 8 for a discussion of the major models) has established itself in all application domains. Some models have been successfully applied to several domains. By virtue of installed base alone, the Confer model (Chapter 6) has proven itself in more arenas than any of the others. Some factors identified with effective use of text conferencing in the private sector include:

1. *Availability.* To succeed, a conferencing system must be readily available to all of those persons who might contribute to and benefit from the process. This includes high-, middle-, and low-level management as well as technical personnel, buying and selling agents, human resources staff, and corporate consultants. Already personal computers, laptops, and workstations number in the millions in American corporations. This number should quadruple by the year 2000. There are a growing number of local area networks (LANs) in corporations, and mainframe systems are being tied to mini- and microcomputers in increasing numbers. To date, only a handful of conferencing software packages will operate across all these boundaries.

2. *Leadership and support.* Every successful application of the technology in the corporate setting is associated with individuals who are given the time to facilitate the proceedings. These people help to keep discussion focused on the problem at hand. When the purpose is decision resolution, participants must understand with whom authority resides. The medium is very democratic, but some individual or group of individuals must have final authority to make decisions based on information transferred. Another important role played by key individuals is that of assisting others in becoming technically proficient with the software itself. The facilitator may or may not function in this role.

   Murray Turoff has observed that the quality of conferencing software depends on its facilities for supporting *expert* users. This consideration is in opposition to most philosophy of software development today. Contemporary wisdom focuses on ease of use and learning, sometimes to the exclusion of flexibility and power. Good conferencing software need not be hard to learn. Once learned, however, the software must support *advanced* use with numerous, convenient shortcuts. If it does not, even the better users will not experience maximum productivity gain.

3. *Purpose.* The most successful systems are established for some clear purpose, usually associated with one or more of the domains cited above. Systems installed for their own sake remain underused and show little payback to the corporation that purchased them. That the use of this technology takes some practice is often cited as a major stumbling block to more rapid acceptance. Given the need to be frugal in resource expenditure, a *purposeful* use of communications technology is essential to successful adaptation. In some application domains,

such as crisis resolution, purpose is imposed by the nature of the problem itself. Here the participants gathered together have little need for facilitators to keep the discussion on track, though they may require the assistance of system experts from time to time. Conversations result in high-quality decisions in a short time. The participants are all authorities in the problem domain, and the urgency of the situation motivates their participation.

4. *Adequacy.* This is a technical consideration to be factored into a purchase decision in association with purpose. The software must be tailorable, adaptable to the purposes for which it was obtained. If joint document authoring is one of the intended purposes, then the software must support ex post facto editing, the ability to alter entry in a text base. Annotation support, the capacity to attach notes to specific documents, is another important feature in this domain. If decision support is involved, then there should be voting and automatic tabulation features. Gateways to databases outside the conferencing arena are also useful in this domain. By contrast, voting is more or less useless in technology scanning, technology transfer, customer/vendor support. Educational systems should support controls on entry and reporting, display of the text base, and so on.

Lisa Carlson of the Metasystems Design Group Inc., has done market research in the teleconferencing area. In one of her reports she concludes that "the most significant factor which distinguishes corporations which are able to make effective and strategic use of communication networks is their focus on networking people together rather then just thinking about connecting machines and data." Companies that implement conferencing systems can tailor them to emulate the existing corporate communications hierarchies, so that employees are communicating only with others at their own level and their immediate managers. Yet the greatest benefits of the technology involve the increased potential for communications across departmental boundaries and management hierarchies. To achieve these potentials, however, corporate management must accept changes in communications channels and adapt to new management roles and styles.

In the public arena, software considerations are somewhat different. Here users often develop a fanatical loyalty to a particular product or conferencing model. Leadership in the business sense is rarely present, though facilitators and helpers are as necessary. Ease of use is even more important in the public arena because the providers are dependent on their subscribers for their income. If systems are too difficult for newcomers to learn quickly, they will not be used. Purpose is diffuse in these systems. People use them for all kinds of reasons, from pure entertainment to political action. The secret to success for many of these systems is the sheer volume of data, services, and people available to each user. Focused purpose is superseded by a "critical mass" of activity that becomes more or less self-sustaining.

Corporate systems need not always have extensive file transfer and cataloging support. By contrast, file exchange is among the most popular reasons for subscribing to a public system. Decision support, while often significant for corporate systems, is rarely useful in the public domain because those participating may have little or no expertise in the issues involved. True experts may be and often are present, but their expertise may be drowned in a sea of uninformed opinion.

The success of public systems has much to do with activity volumes and association with other services. A certain transaction volume in combined services fosters continuing discussion in communications forums. Individual conversations may come and go, but conferences must sustain themselves or they generate no revenue for their providers. This is as true of corporate or educational systems, but use of the system can be to some degree mandated in those systems. In the public arena, participation in communication activities is stimulated by the availability of other services—games, shopping, news, databases, file libraries, and other specialty items—around which interpersonal communications develop. As a rule, however, there is no substitute for a large number of participants.

Computer conferencing has expanded dramatically in scope over the last two decades. Originally conceived as a means of bringing together authorities in a crisis arena, or linking policy makers with those responsible for executing those policies, it has grown to encompass many more kinds of interpersonal exchange, even for entertainment's sake. As electronic conferencing and information retrieval begin to merge, each of the domains applicable to either technology will broaden. U.S. companies are not embracing the technology in a big way; European and Japanese corporations appear more interested. Many of these foreign corporations have already exceeded their American counterparts in productivity; new and more fluid communications technologies will only widen the gap.

3

HARDWARE, SOFTWARE, AND TELECOMMUNICATIONS FOUNDATIONS

■ 3.1 A GENERALIZED APPLICATION

Like word processors, database managers, spreadsheets, terminal emulators, and other general purpose software, computer conferencing systems have been written for every popular microprocessor and operating system combination. Machines as old as the original IBM PC XT or Z80-based computers can reasonably support between four and eight simultaneous users over 1200 bps (bits per second) remote connections. Microcomputers of the late 1980s, costing about as much as the original XT in 1983, can carry as many as 32 simultaneous connections at rates of up to 2400 bps and greater.

■ 3.2 SPECIAL CONSTRAINTS ON INFORMATION RETRIEVAL SYSTEMS

Information retrieval is a specialized discipline that places more demand on disk and memory transfer subsystems. Even BBS and conferencing systems with relatively sophisticated text search and filtering facilities do not have as many searchable fields, output formats, or sheer numbers of records to deal with in an acceptable amount of time. Many conferencing systems retire old messages, topics, or entire conferences after some period of inactivity, thereby keeping their disk space requirements within reasonable bounds. Others scroll off older messages continuously over a period of days, weeks, or months. Even those that maintain their text bases forever have to deal with at most a few hundred megabytes of new material per year. The Usenet is one exception, generating as much as 20 megabytes of new text per day, or about 7.25 gigabytes per year!

45

While some information providers do retire older content, most strive to keep their collections as complete as possible and even extend them backward to include more historical material. The value of many of these databases is proportional to both their historical content and recency of their information. This is especially true of the databases of the legal profession, which become far more valuable as their historical information accumulates. A large information provider might have several terabytes of data on line at any given time. Even smaller systems must plan for data repositories in the multigigabyte range.

These collection sizes put serious information retrieval systems out of the range of most microcomputer configurations. Nevertheless it is becoming technically possible for micros to perform high-volume information retrieval work. Optical disk drives, larger and faster microprocessors, wider databuses, and more installed memory can turn a contemporary microcomputer into a relatively powerful information retrieval engine. Microcomputers can also function effectively as a centralized conference engine, serving as a front-end device for another computer in the role of database server through a high-speed channel.

■ **3.3 THE CPU**

Compared to other hardware components of a system, the effect of the specific CPU architecture is minimal, except in the following instances:

- The raw performance and size of the CPU affects overall system performance. Performance depends not only on clock speed, but also on the CPU's register size and the efficiency of its instructions. Designers strive to get the clock speed high, use large registers, and have the most frequently used instructions execute in the fewest possible cycles. Other hardware components affect performance as well, but the CPU sets the upper limit to any given system's speed.
- The CPU architecture supports the first software layer—the operating system. Although almost any operating system can theoretically be ported to any CPU, some combinations are easier to make efficient. Poorly implemented low-level operating system routines can ruin the performance of even a good CPU. In other words, an efficiently written operating system on a small, slow CPU might run faster than an inefficient operating system on a big fast one.

■ **3.4 MEMORY**

Sequences of instructions (programs) as well as data are stored in memory. Like the CPU, memory's primary impact on an implementation has to do with its speed and the amount present. Some time elapses between a CPU's *request* for data and its *appearance* on the bus (see bus discussion in Section 3.6). The length of this period determines the upper boundary of system performance in data movement.

The amount of memory may have a greater effect on application architecture and performance than does its speed. Even relatively slow memory is usually faster than every other significant subcomponent of the system outside the CPU. Some part of the operating system, executing programs, and data must all reside in memory together. If there is plenty of memory to spare, more code and data can be stored for longer periods. Application design can take advantage of a large memory space, trading it for reduced disk access.

■ 3.5 MASS STORAGE

3.5.1 Magnetic Storage

The average processor instruction takes a few clock cycles. If a CPU has a 10 MHz clock, that might mean that from one to five million instructions per second can be executed. If each of these average instruction executions took one second, the relative time for a memory fetch-write would be several hours, and that for a disk read or write about one month! Disk systems—long-term storage in general—are the slowest overall subsystem of the computer besides the user. As with memory delivery, what counts in disk processing is the time between a request for data delivered to the disk controller circuitry and the appearance of that data on the system bus.

On a single physical disk drive, this time is dependent on a number of factors, including the rotational speed of the disk (latency), the number of tracks on the disk, the speed of the mechanical mechanism positioning the read-write heads (seek time), the position of the read-write head when a new request occurs, and so on. Because the mechanical activity of positioning the heads is the slowest of the various dependencies, disk speed is typically reported in average seek time. If the heads happen to be positioned on the very track required by a data request, seek time will be 0. The requested track might, however, be on the opposite end of the disk (maximum seek time for the disk). Average seek times for magnetic disks manufactured in the late 1980s run from about 15 or 20 milliseconds to about 60 milliseconds, with 30 being quite common. In larger computer installations, the addition of multiple physical drives and drive channels, each with some number of physical drives, adds some time to the average disk I/O. On the other hand, these larger disks are commonly faster internally, and their throughput (see below) is much greater than their microcomputer equivalents.

Another important drive statistic is its data throughput. Given that the physical data has been found, how much of it can be delivered to the computer's bus each second? The transfer rate for floppy disks is around 100 kilobytes per second, while that of a good PC hard disk is as high as one or two megabytes per second. Much of the performance advantage of mini and mainframe computing comes from higher bandwidth in the disk channels. Mini and mainframe disk transfer rates can range from 5 to 50 megabytes per second and more with very specialized hardware.

Software and hardware disk-caching schemes are helpful in both conferencing and information retrieval applications. They are commonly employed on all computer architectures. Caches operate by storing data in memory. When a disk read request is made, the cache mechanism stores sectors physically following the one requested in system or disk controller RAM. In many applications, the next disk request will likely involve one or more of these stored sectors. If so, the cache effects dramatic disk performance increases because disk requests become, essentially, memory requests. In conferencing applications, users spend much time reading conference records sequentially, and caching mechanisms do increase overall system performance related to these operations. In information retrieval, the process of scanning logical records for query matches is greatly facilitated by the presence of records in the disk cache.

On larger systems, researchers have attempted to reduce latency delays and support simultaneous disk activity requests by mounting multiple controllers and read-write heads on a single disk. Such an arrangement might be used to satisfy multiple parts of a single request in parallel. This hardware proved effective in the limited domain of bibliographic retrieval, but was too complicated for use in other kinds of disk-intensive activities (like transaction processing). This has suppressed development of parallel disks and limited their application to only the largest and most demanding bibliographic retrieval systems.

3.5.2 Optical Storage Systems

If magnetic disks are slow, optical drives are slower still, but getting better. The largest optical drives operate with an average seek time of approximately 200 milliseconds and sometimes more. Very large optical disk configurations, called juke boxes, can often store a terabyte or more of data in a space the size of an office desk. They rely on mechanical technology similar to the familiar record juke box to move dozens of optical platters in and out of one, two, or more active drives. With these large collections, seek times on the order of two or three seconds or longer are common.

The advantage of optical storage is not its speed but its enormous data space and relative cost per megabyte. In the microcomputer arena, audio compact disk technology has been transformed into a relatively inexpensive high capacity storage medium. For a few hundred dollars, not counting the drive itself, one can add a CD device to a computer. Each disk costs about $50 and provides up to 250 megabytes of read-only storage. This technology is by no means optimal for computer use, but its volume growth in the audio industry has lowered its cost to a level where small systems can address some serious information retrieval tasks. Since this technology cannot *write* information to the optical disks, the data must come from some other source. A number of vendors, including many of those whose databases also appear through brokerage services like Dialog and BRS, provide their databases in CD-ROM form.

Technology specifically designed for computer use can provide as much as two gigabytes of write-once-read-many (WORM) storage per removable disk on more expensive drives yet still be accessible to microcomputers. Recent developments in hybrid optical-magnetic media have made reusable optical disks practical. The first such commercial products were shipped in 1989, and by mid 1989 one could obtain a magneto-optical drive consisting of removable cartridges, each able to store one gigabyte (1000 megabytes), for about eight thousand dollars. Although it is still expensive, magneto-optical technology is slightly more cost effective than the purely magnetic media of the times—about 125KB per dollar for magnetic media compared to 75KB to 100KB per dollar for magneto-optical media. Note, though, that the cartridges cost only about $400, virtually doubling the byte-per-dollar ratio for every cartridge filled.

Significantly, the access speed of these drives is about 35 milliseconds, with a transfer speed of one to two megabytes per second, properly competitive with magnetic drives.

Storage capacity is critical to all conferencing and information retrieval applications. At least one of the criteria used to distinguish serious commercial conferencing applications software from the hobbyist and casual user variety is its ability to store and track large conference histories. Just what it takes to accomplish this depends on the volume of the message traffic, the number of users, the number of conferences, the availability of compression systems, and other factors. Although all conferencing domains can benefit from extensive histories, some require it, and others get along well without it. Information retrieval, on the other hand, exists almost exclusively to serve those domains that emphasize data volume over all else. In a conference environment, one can always ask a question again, but in bibliographic retrieval, a citation is either present or it is not.

Information retrieval and multiuser computer conferencing applications are both punishingly brutal on disk controllers and drive mechanisms. In medium to large communications systems, the disk drives are probably the most important operational bottleneck and point of failure. In the microcomputer arena, increases in storage capacities and decreases in access time have yet to be matched by large jumps in disk throughput. Even without extensive search and retrieval support, communications applications are as disk intensive as dedicated information retrieval systems. This is one of the reasons why even large conferencing systems do not have more extensive search and retrieval capabilities.

■ 3.6 THE INFLUENCE OF THE COMPUTER BUS

Connecting the CPU, memory, and the external storage system is the computer bus, which is analogous to a highway connecting various cities. Its throughput influences the computer's capacity to run many tasks at acceptable performance levels. Buses carry system control signal information, including the beat of the ubiquitous system clock. They also carry data between devices. The width of its data path sets the main limits on its capacity. Before 1982, microcomputer bus data paths were eight bits wide and could therefore carry one byte of data at a time from one place to any other. By the mid 1980s, 16-bit-wide buses were common, with 24- and 32-bit buses existing in a number of architectures—especially those built around Motorola's 68000 series of processors and their successors. By the late 1980s Intel-based 32-bit buses were making their appearance in the the new IBM PS/2 Microchannel, and EISA (extended industry standard architecture) based machines. In the minicomputer and mainframe world, bus widths of up to 64 bits and more have existed for some time.

Other aspects of the bus design contribute to the performance potential of the hardware. Buses provide the connection paths between external devices and the computer. Special graphics circuitry, additional disk drives, more memory, terminal or communications connections, tape drives, printers, and other equipment must all be able to coexist peacefully on the bus. The what and how of connecting external peripherals to an existing computer system has much to do with the features in its bus.

■ 3.7 THE COMMUNICATIONS HARDWARE

One bus-attached device that is ubiquitous in the micro and minicomputer world is the UART, or universal asynchronous receiver/transmitter. In the conferencing domain, the term "asynchronous" refers to the time-independent nature of interpersonal communications in the medium. In discussion of the electronics of the data communication process, it refers to the synchronization (or lack thereof) in the clocks of connected devices. There are also SRTs (synchronous receiver/transmitters), designed to deliver signals corresponding to one or more synchronous transmission standards.

The UART is involved in all communications-oriented applications involving the serial port. It monitors and effects the control pins of the RS-232 serial interface and is responsible for converting bytes to electrical voltages on the send and receive lines of the serial port. Many devices can be attached to the ports—for example, printers, plotters, mice, writing tablets, and terminals. In the case of bulletin board, conferencing, and information retrieval systems, the device is most commonly a modem (see Section 3.11), the gateway between computer and telephone network. Figure 3.1 demonstrates the relationships among the CPU, bus, memory, and various peripheral devices.

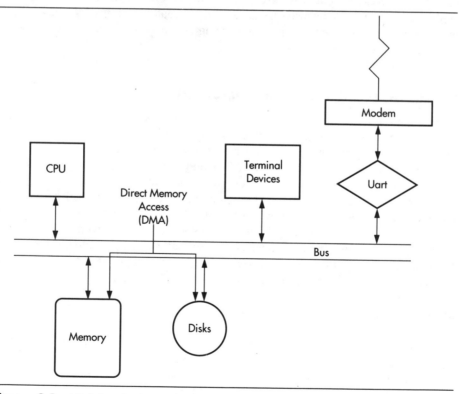

Figure 3.1 High-level relationships among the CPU, computer bus, and other devices.

■ 3.8 HARDWARE CONSTRAINTS ON CMC DESIGN

A system's underlying hardware establishes some design constraints, particularly when it comes to planning for expansion.

A few conferencing and BBS packages are noted for their availability in many environments. From the perspective of the on-line community at large, this is for the best. As hardware platforms become more powerful, performance differences from environment to environment become blurred. Some applications can never have too much power, but conferencing and information retrieval are not among them. This is not to say that size and power requirements do not go hand in hand; but conferencing applications exist to aid communications among human users, and the measure of sufficient power, aside from features of the applications themselves, is satisfactory response time at any designed user load.

There are, nevertheless, advantages to designing and building a system to one environment, including speed and ease of implementation and the ability to provide additions and upgrades to the software's features without concern for the problems associated with generating the same extensions in other environments. Typically, it is not one hardware environment or another that offers these trade-offs, but the operating system—the software layer that acts as the application program's "hardware go-between."

The operating system has the distinction of having become the mechanism through which much software transfer across hardware platforms is achieved. Applications software can, if written in a sufficiently capable language, bypass the operating system and communicate directly with its hardware foundation. In doing so, it wrings the utmost performance from a given hardware configuration. Such an efficient implementation, however, would run *only* on the hardware platform for which it was written. Even minor variations in hardware could require substantial changes to the application code (see Figure 3.2).

To serve in the transport role, a single operating system should be available on a wide variety of hardware; the best example today is UNIX. If arranged properly, the operating system code will be matched efficiently to the idiosyncrasies of each hardware configuration on one side (the "back end"), while providing identical "hooks" into hardware services for applications software on its "front end." If the programmer is willing to trade off a little performance, he or she can move a given application from one hardware platform to another with a minimum of modification (if the operating system does a reasonably efficient job of handling the hardware).

■ 3.9 THE INFLUENCE OF THE OPERATING SYSTEM

Common operating system services include screen and keyboard handling (console communications), disk reading and writing (file handling), and communications with peripheral devices such as printers, plotters, and modems. When high-level languages support facilities for manipulation of serial ports, they typically do so via operating system services.

Although there are many existing operating systems, only a few are widely ported. The Apple Macintosh is a capable hardware platform, but its operating system is pro-

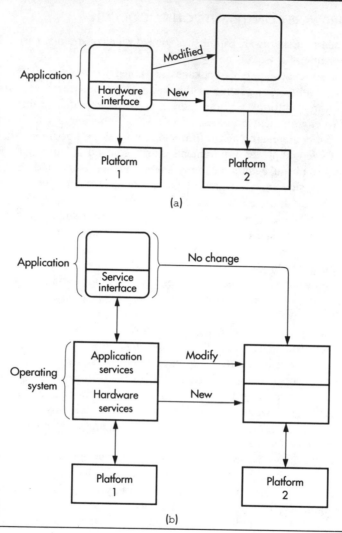

Figure 3.2 Insulation value of the operating system: (a) direct-address application requiring modification; (b) more flexible application. If CMC or other applications are written with modules that address hardware devices or addresses directly, then any change in that hardware or the process of porting the application to different hardware will require modifications to the application code (a). If, instead, the application can make use of services provided by the operating system, then hardware changes or software ports to new environments will not entail application changes, so long as the operating system available in the new environment provides identical application support services (b).

prietary and found nowhere else. A few other operating systems have been integrated with Apple hardware, but these are specialized for purposes such as expert systems development. The Commodore Amiga is also a capable system with an unusually powerful operating system by microcomputer standards, yet it has not achieved any recognition outside Amiga circles.

Microsoft DOS is by many measures a limited operating system, but it has achieved wide recognition and use owing to its availability on machines produced by many manufacturers. With respect to communications, the MS-DOS operating system is fundamentally weak—one might say ridiculously so. Its native communications services are so flawed that virtually all DOS-based communications programs use modules that bypass both DOS and the IBM BIOS (basic input/output system) to communicate directly with the UART.

This would seem a contradiction because these same programs run on machines produced by a great number of different vendors; however, the wide establishment of the AT bus standard makes this case of hardware dependency acceptable to the marketplace. Programmers can therefore depend upon UARTs to behave the same way in different vendors' machines.

The new OS/2 is both more powerful and more demanding of the hardware on which it operates; it provides a suite of efficient routines for manipulating the serial port at the byte level. In the minicomputer arena, DEC's VMS is both capable and widely dispersed, the latter due to DEC's dominance of this market segment. The mainframe world is dominated by IBM and its two primary operating systems, VM and MVS. Only two operating systems—UNIX (and its clones) and Pick—have been ported to a broad range of hardware types from micro to mainframe, running many different kinds of CPUs.

Although a capable system, UNIX has its drawbacks. Its philosophy contradicts that of most modern applications level software. It provides reasonably good communications services and is relatively easy for applications developers to use (not to mention well-known in the development community). Its persistent use in university computing labs since the early 1970s coupled with its flexibility has made it the operating system of choice for many applications where portability to the widest possible range of hardware has been a consideration, even though implementations vary dramatically in efficiency. Table 3.1 presents the compatibility of conferencing and BBS products with different operating systems.

3.9.1 Single Tasking, Multitasking, and Multiuser Operating Systems

For computer-mediated communications the fundamental distinction between operating systems is support for multiuser and multitasking operation. In the mainframe and minicomputer world, multiuser and multitasking operations are a given. The microcomputer arena was not initially geared toward multiuser operation. For many microcomputer applications multiuser means multiple CPUs and a network to connect them. Local area networks, however, are a very expensive way to support computer conferencing.

Multitasking refers to the operating system's ability to support more than one active process at the same time. Multiuser systems are inherently multitasking—each concurrent user must be able to execute at least one task. OS/2 is multitasking, but

Table 3.1 CC and BBS systems OS compatibility

Product	Operating system						
	MS-DOS	UNIX/Xenix	VMS	TOPS	MVS	VM	MTS
Confer			X				X
Participate	X	X	X		X	X	
Caucus	X	X	X		X	X	
Notepad				X			
Picospan		X					
TBBS	X						
AKCS		X					
Magpie	X	X					
FIDO	X						
PC-Board	X						
TEAMATE		X					

it expects a single user to run those tasks; it has no built-in provisions to execute the tasks of different users.

All large-scale and most medium-scale conferencing and retrieval systems are implemented with multiuser operating systems. In these machines, port use by a local terminal or from one a thousand miles away is quite similar. Small business systems can come equipped with six to ten such ports—more than enough for a good start at multiuser conferencing.

MS-DOS is neither multiuser nor multitasking in its native form. Both OS/2 and the Amiga operating system are multitasking but not inherently multiuser. Apple's MultiFinder operating system is not truly multitasking despite Apple's claims to the contrary. This leaves, once again, UNIX and Xenix, the latter a UNIX clone, as the only commonly available operating systems for microcomputers that are both multiuser and multitasking.

■ 3.10 THE EFFECT OF IBM PC STANDARDIZATION

Single user architectures are another story. Because they are less expensive, they are far more common than their multiuser brethren. Single-user systems require assistance in serving multiuser applications; this often entails modification of the hardware and the addition of multiple serial ports. Either the applications software, or a multitasking shell—an applications program that supports the (apparently) simultaneous execution of other programs beneath it—provides these services.

The IBM PC and its descendants have spawned the largest collection of options for turning a single user computer into a multiuser communications hub.

■ 3.11 THE ROLE OF THE MODEM

Modems interpret the digital signals of the UART to the analog telephone system and vice-versa. They are the gateway between the computer and the telephone system or sometimes a dedicated private telephone link. Modems come in two basic varieties: synchronous and asynchronous. Both types function by converting the digital signals sent by the computer's UART or SRT to two or more tones sent across a phone line. In a simple two-tone system, one tone signifies a binary one or set, the other a binary zero or reset. Modems release data coming in to the host CPU and receive data for transmission from the system bus via the UART. This gateway differs from other CPU-to-device interfaces because data can appear in communication buffers at any time—unpredictable from the CPU's viewpoint.

That even relatively small desktop machines can provide extensive communications services is due to the relative slowness of communications devices. Even at 9600 bps, a communication channel is transferring data at only one one-tenth to one-hundredth the average magnetic disk recovery rate—the slowest device on the system! This means that for every character or block of characters communicated between a CPU and a single modem, the CPU has plenty of time to do other things, primarily servicing similar tasks for other connections.

Synchronous modems use synchronized clocks to achieve exceptionally high transmission rates, thereby permitting very efficient use of the phone line. In fact, speed is limited mainly by the accuracy and the speed of the clocks. Data is bundled in packets with header and trailer information, providing a much larger data-to-control ratio than asynchronous modems.

3.11.1 Asynchronous Modems

Though they are efficient, synchronous modems are expensive. Worse, there are competing frame specifications that make communication between modems manufactured by different vendors almost impossible. In the marketplace such modems compete based on their overall throughput and often on their compatibility with IBM-synchronous protocols in widespread use.

Asynchronous modems, by contrast, are relatively inexpensive, and a significant respect for a small set of standards has generated a high degree of intermanufacturer compatibility. Asynchronous modems also monitor frequency switches in the phone line, and they use clocks to determine where one bit ends and another begins. Their tolerance for timing variations is, however, looser, which is acceptable because every ninth or tenth bit transmitted is used to realign the sender and receiver. This generates a 10 percent data-to-control overhead to keep the modems communicating, not to mention any error detection and correction schemes that might be implemented.

Unsynchronized clocks cause the upper limit of detectable tone switches over ordinary lines to peak around 2400 per second. This is the dial-up line's maximum *baud* rate, 2400 frequency shifts per second. Developments in the mid 1980s made it possible to transmit 9600 *bits* per second and more over these same analog telephone lines. The secret lay in making the modem detect more than two frequencies, or sense phase shifts in the tones. Consider that specifying one bit requires two frequencies. Two tones can switch at 2400 baud and transmit 2400 bits in that length of time. Four tones can also switch at 2400 baud, but each tone signifies two bits, for an effective speed of 4800 bits per second. Eight tones will represent all possible states of three bits and achieve a throughput of 7200 bits per second. Sixteen tones achieve 9600 bit-per-second transmissions over the same 2400 baud telephone line, and so on.

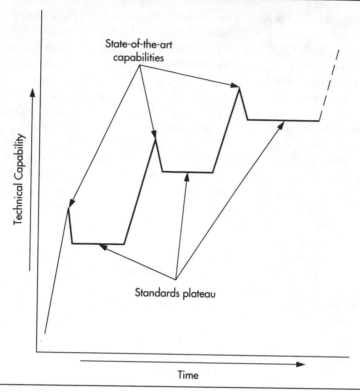

Figure 3.3 Relationship between standards and state-of-the-art technology. As technology develops new capabilities, different and incompatible solutions to similar problems often compete. Even so called state-of-the-art technologies exceed their competitors only in narrowly defined domains. Standards tend to be compromises between existing state-of-the-art technology and the broader economic base of competing, if less efficient, technologies. The establishment of a standard often results in a temporary plateau — a suppression of further technological advance until the parties involved have all produced products compatible with the standard. At this point, new developments will begin to appear, leveraging themselves on the existing standards.

Besides the tone or phase shift mechanism, other effects of ordinary dial-up circuits had to be overcome to achieve these speeds. The dial-up network is not guaranteed to have (and in fact almost never has) matched electrical characteristics from one layer of the network to another. These mismatches cause signals to be echoed, and the echoes can distort the real signal beyond recognition. To operate under such conditions, engineers developed very fast adaptive echo cancelers. It has been primarily the refinement in these circuits that make high-speed dial-up modems workable.

3.11.2 Asynchronous Modem Standards

International standards organizations had only recently agreed to protocols for 2400 bps dial-ups when the new multiphonic and phase technology burst on the scene. Within a few years a new standard, V.32, was established for their interconnection. By some estimates the growing use of this standard, now supported by virtually all modem manufacturers, will enhance the further development of distributed conferencing and information services. Certain problems indigenous to distributed systems are magnified when internodal communications are slow and therefore expensive. As the general purpose telephone network becomes more economical, these problems (see Chapter 5) are to some degree mitigated.

If the flow and transformation of information in the growing networks is to remain predictable, both users and vendors must insist upon control and voluntary respect for limits and approved standards. Communications are especially sensitive because so much money is dependent on so much of it in the present age. As a result, new standards appear and are accepted relatively quickly (Figure 3.3).

Standards compromises are necessary because individual technologies (one vendor's way of doing things) are not always optimal in every possible application—yet all applications want, in the end, to communicate. Other factors include the economic relationship among the vendors and political factors. It is not unusual for the vendor supporting an inferior technology to have more installed units by the time the de jure standard is in place. The advent of 9600 bps asynchronous dial-up modems using ordinary telephone lines represents an eight-fold cost decrease in data communications for persons or corporations using asynchronous technology; therefore, proprietary synchronous standards can now in many cases be profitably replaced with asynchronous systems.

Two standards, V.32 (which covered the physical characteristics of the analog transmission and error correction) and V.42 (covering error checking conventions) have set the stage for an explosion in 9600 bps transmission over ordinary dial-up lines. The error correction procedure, link-access procedure for modems (LAPM), performs the kind of function previously seen in software such as X-modem directly in the modem hardware; it therefore approaches the efficiency of synchronous modems as far as error-correction overhead is concerned. MicroComm Networking Protocol (MNP) is another correction scheme with a significant following.

■ 3.12 THE OSI INTERCONNECTION MODEL

The most far-reaching standard of all is the intersystem connection model propounded by the International Standards Organization (ISO) and the Consultive Committee for International Telegraphy and Telephony (CCITT) in the late 1970s. Although primarily concerned with communications between networks, the ISO model also has implications for some communications between tasks on a single machine. The ISO advanced a concept of interlinked layers. Each performs a specific set of services for the layers above and below it. The ISO and other standards organizations have also suggested interconnect standards—protocols for connecting the services of different layers of the model. Standards like X.25, V.32, and others discussed in subsequent chapters provide services that can be mapped into one of the model's layers.

The ISO built flexibility in two directions. Vertically (between layers), the standard permits the progressive transformation of data meaningful to humans into signals *reliably* exchanged between machines. Horizontally, it allows the interconnection of different networks over bridges that need to perform a relatively restricted set of conversions.

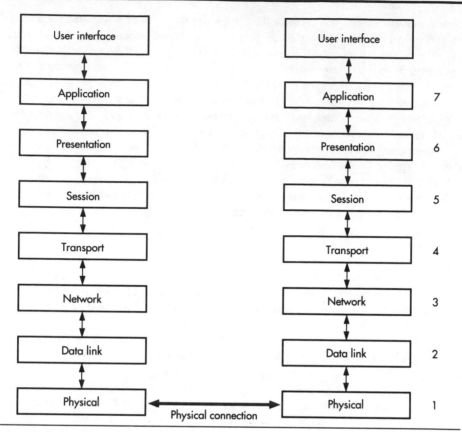

Figure 3.4 The ISO Open Systems Interconnect Model (OSI). *Layer 1*: The *physical* layer provides the physical conduit for electrical or optical transmission of data. This includes twisted-pair, coaxial cable, optical fiber, and radio transmission standards. *Layer 2*: The *data link* layer performs error checking on the electrical signals transmitted through layer 1. *Layer 3*: The *network* layer establishes the basic connection between remote hosts in terms of correct routing of the physical transmission. It also provides reports of established connections from the receiver to the sender. *Layer 4*: The *transport* layer handles data integrity on a point-to-point basis between connected hosts. The *lower four layers* of the model constitute the data transport and integrity mechanisms. *Layer 5*: The *session* layer coordinates interaction between the data coming up from the transmission system and the applications on any given host. *Layer 6*: The *presentation* layer provides code conversion, data formatting, and other translation services specific to the application systems creating or receiving the data. NAPLPS and other graphics standards are examples of presentation layer protocols. *Layer 7*: The *application* layer contains the various functions available to the user in terms of interaction with the network. This has to do with what kinds of applications are available and not their specific user interfaces. The *upper three layers* of the model constitute the host services ultimately available to the end user.

The ISO's model contains seven layers (see Figure 3.4). It is known as the Open Systems Interconnection (OSI) model. All vendor network schemes implement services that reach through all levels of this model from the seventh (application) layer, at least to the third (network) layer. The telephone network, if used as a physical conduit, handles the services required by the first two layers. Each level takes data from the level above it and wraps it in a logical envelope that is meaningful to the same service in another part of the network. As data moves toward the lowest layer, envelope surrounds envelope until converted to electrical (or light) modulation and physically placed on the network. The receiving station strips off envelopes until the data reaches its intended destination: a user, program, and so on.

3.12.1 Vertical and Horizontal Communication Through OSI Layers

The OSI framework is a concept encompassing all that is required to cross the chasm from humanly interpretable data to electromagnetic signals. Some vendor products bridge two or more layers in a single set of programs; others provide services of only partial layers. Theoretically, each product can be connected to any other products performing the functions of the next higher or lower layers. Some products, however, are more conveniently associable than others. The problem of connecting protocols on successive layers of the model is one of constructing interfaces between modules providing different services. Vertical engineering is designed in, and connections can be made as long as the I/O specifications of any vendor's products are available.

The corresponding horizontal connections are a bit more difficult. Every level in one network communicates with a corresponding module in another through the lowest (physical) layer. To work coherently together, products at the corresponding layer in two different networks must *understand* information in their own terms; envelopes themselves must be translated into the form expected by each of the networks for this to occur. In general, the more similarity there is in the networks being bridged, the easier it is to bridge them and to make the bridge both versatile and efficient.

From a practical viewpoint, the top three layers of most products are bound rather closely together, and there is not a great deal of interproduct exchange. The two lowest layers of the model have been more richly developed; many vertical and horizontal bridges exist between products. The middle two layers, transport and network, have also been the focus of some bridging efforts.

■ 3.13 THE INFLUENCE OF DATA COMPRESSION TECHNOLOGY

Compression technology has long been of interest to the data processing community. Concurrent with the development of high-speed asynchronous transmission technology and error correction standards, a wider appreciation for the potentials of hardware and software based data compression emerged. Not only are data communications enhanced by the technology, but dramatic improvements in disk throughput are routinely demonstrated.

Commercial compression systems oriented toward disk data have been around for some time. Squish, for example, from Sun Dog Software of NYC acts to compress or decompress data automatically as it is transferred from disk to memory, but faster and more efficient hardware schemes are becoming available. Though not related to transmission efficiency, these disk-oriented compression systems are of considerable importance to high-volume BBSs because of their beneficial effect on disk capacity.

The growth in data communications volume in the 1980s spurred developments in both hardware- and software-based compression technology particularly in the nationwide BBS network. In the mid 1980s SEA (Systems Enhancement Associates Inc.) released a product called ARC, which became the first widely used compression system for file exchange.

ARC collects files into one ARChive file, and compresses the individual files inside the archive. Early products achieved 10 to 50 percent compression ratios, depending on file type and content. Other such programs followed on the heels of SEA's developments, which were both faster in operation and better in compression, achieving typical ratios of 25 to 75 percent. By 1989 there were four or five competitors in the software compression market, each outdoing the other with every new software release.

While the software "compression wars" continue, both MNP and the LAPM protocols include their own hardware-based compression specifications. These operate directly between the communicating modems, which means that communicating machines need not concern themselves with compressing files *before* transmission and decompressing them *after* reception. MNP supports several levels of compression, each being added as the technology has improved—class 5 MNP compression roughly doubles modem performance. That is, a 2400 bps modem will transmit data streams at effectively 4800 bps. Class 7 compression (not widely supported in 1989) triples performance.

The CCITT V.42bis standard uses another compression technology, British Telecom Lemmpel-Ziv compression (BTLZ). Roughly speaking, MNP class 7, BTLZ, and the best software compression systems are equivalent in compression ratio. It is nevertheless expected that BTLZ in V.42bis will ultimately supplant MNP in the marketplace because it is an international standard; in addition, it makes fewer demands on the modem's CPU than does the MNP protocol. However, MNP has the larger installed base of systems (for the present). Some manufacturers are trying to incorporate both protocols into their products. In fact, the V.42bis standard includes a provision for MNP-compatible operation.

■ **3.14 DEVELOPMENTS IN THE TELEPHONE NETWORK**

The telephone system itself is the last link in the chain of technology supporting computer conferencing and information retrieval systems. Before the AT&T divestiture of 1985, the end-to-end connections between computer and terminal were administered by one company. Now there is a bewildering variety of local and long distance services to account for when building a communications network. Household telephone users have many more service options today than they did only a few years ago, while the possibilities for the corporate network have expanded even further.

The public telephone network is in a state of flux. Present technologies range from state-of-the-art fiber trunks capable of transfer rates of 1 to 500 megabits per second to twisted-pair copper wire that has been in use for 30 years or more. One by one local phone company switching offices are being upgraded to handle more and faster connections.

Pundits disagree about the eventual appearance of the integrated services digital network (ISDN) in the home. Most expect the business environment to have these services—multiple voice and data circuits multiplexed on a single telephone line—by the mid 1990s. This means faster connections and transfer speeds for the information provider or conference host based on higher capacity telephone equipment. User interface designers need not concern themselves with constraints imposed by low-speed dial-up links; since the data network itself will be digital, modems will be obsolete because no modulation of digital data on analog telephone circuits would be required.

3.14.1 The ISDN Phenomenon

In the mid to late 1970s, various standards organizations worked out the basic structures of an integrated services digital network and also sought efficient and flexible ways to use newly appearing channels with capacities of one to five Mbps. Their solution was to divide these channels into subchannels of 64 Kbps. Instead of having 56 Kbps of this set aside for data and 8 Kbps for control information on each subchannel (as is the case with T1 service), the primary ISDN service is a bundle of twenty-three 64 Kbps channels for data (bearer channels) and one 64 Kbps channel for control information (the D channel)—a total of 1.5 Mbps. This is the origin of the 23B+D primary ISDN designation. A subset of this service, 2B+D, consists of two 64 Kbps data channels, and one 16 Kbps control channel. The 2B+D configuration is expected to penetrate noncommercial markets by the mid to late 1990s.

To minimize the required control information, a logical, end-to-end virtual circuit architecture was envisioned, in which packets of information from the same transmission might travel different paths to their destinations. The system would, however, maintain some continuously open channel between the two points during a session. This is called "connectioned service" because it establishes a single logical, if not physical, connection between two points. If broken, data flow ceases until the connection has been re-established.

In the early 1980s, before the ISDN standards researchers had completed their work, an expanded bandwidth potential was demonstrated with a special optical fiber called *monomode*. The more common variety of optical fiber, *multimode*, allows light to bounce a bit off the walls of the fiber pipe as well as to travel straight down the tube. Bouncing light will travel the tube at a different speed than wave forms moving straight along it, and the result is signal attenuation through interference. Monomode fiber, on the other hand, is so thin that it permits only a single wave form to travel straight down the tube, thereby eliminating interference.

If the carrier signal does not interfere with itself, the only limit to its data capacity is its modulation rate. Contemporary laser diode devices have already achieved modulation rates equivalent to 100 Mbps data transfer. Rates of five to ten times that may be possible by the end of the 1990s. The new digital services made possible by this technology are called broadband ISDN, or B-ISDN. A worldwide B-ISDN network would have some astonishing properties (and implications), some of which will be discussed in Chapter 11.

Ironically, the new technology is in some ways less expensive than that required to support narrowband ISDN. The primary delay in implementing such channels in the public phone network is not technical, but economic. Every local telephone office in the world (not to mention every telephone wire) would have to be replaced by monomode optical fiber. Eventually this will occur because the advantages of such a network are too compelling to ignore. When it happens, however, depends on many factors, not the least of which is continuing economic growth and use of existing communications capacity.

■ **3.15 PACKET SWITCHING**

Packet switching technology emerged in the 1970s as a response to the need for transmission of data bursts, which are poorly handled by traditional telephone connections. Circuit-switched telephone channels establish a physical connection between two endpoints that is maintained throughout the call; this connection takes several seconds, while data transmission often occurs in bursts lasting only milliseconds. In a packet system, data is encapsulated in envelopes containing address and other information. These packets are transmitted through physical circuits to intermediary points and routed from switch node to switch node until they reach their final destination. The physical connection network is maintained in a permanently open state by the network administration so that data packets from many sources can travel the network simultaneously. More importantly, separate packets representing parts of one transmission can reach their end points over different physical routes; this permits the network vendors to balance their loading across different routes from second to second. (See Figure 3.5.)

The advent of the packet switch vendors Tymnet, Telenet, and others has had a profound effect on many public conferencing and bulletin board systems: They have made large-scale, publicly accessible information retrieval systems possible and expanded the user base of many medium- to large-scale systems. These vendors cater primarily to businesses with enhanced telephone services normally associated with large volumes of data exchange. Packet vendors may connect client hosts directly to their long distance facilities, or they may use the switching facilities of the local telephone offices; this permits connections between the packet vendors and low-volume users via local telephone calls.

Since the mid 1980s, the most visible service of the packet vendors to individual users has been flat rate connections to multiple hosts in major cities. Persons who regularly use small BBSs in many parts of the country can contract with Telenet (PC Pursuit), or Tymnet (Starlink). If the vendor provides a connect point in their local calling area then many other cities—and *any* host in those cities—can be reached for a flat monthly fee.

These companies also expand the reach of somewhat larger systems by providing them with connection points to other parts of the country. Fees are based on the quantity of data exchanged, active session time, or both; hosts in turn bill their users. Presumably, the packet connect charges are less expensive for the end user than would be a direct long distance call to the host.

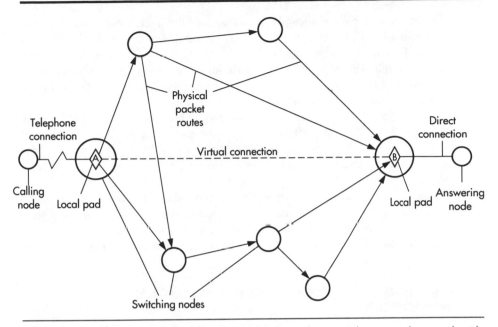

Figure 3.5 Packet switch network. Although packet switching can be used with switched circuits, most of the technology employes virtual circuits. Here a virtual circuit is established between points A and B. From the viewpoint of the application running at both ends, the two points are directly connected. The packets, however (though they comprise a single message), may travel different routes depending on the network load from moment to moment. One of the functions of the packet assembler/disassembler at the receiving end is to collect the packets and put them in proper order for forwarding to the receiving machine. Data and network control packets flow both ways along the virtual pipe, but may or may not travel the same routes.

3.15.1 The X.25 Standard

By 1976 there were several major packet networks in North America, Europe, and Japan. Each used a different protocol to connect itself to terminating equipment, terminals, or other computers. In that year, the United States (represented by Telenet), Canada, and the government-run telephone companies of several European nations pushed the X.25 packet protocol through a plenary session of the CCITT. At the time, no clear consensus on the particular technology represented by X.25 was reached. There were a number of perceived shortcomings and inefficiencies built into the standard from the beginning, yet the need for a standard—*any* standard—had become so desperate by that time that most of the world's telecommunications companies and systems began adopting it immediately.

X.25 brought together service and protocol specifications for physical setup and release of connections between two points. Despite its limitations, technical inefficiencies, and the need for an end-to-end virtual circuit, the influence of X.25 has been profound. One of its effects was to make the need for even higher-level standards immediately apparent. More significantly, it has ensured the interconnection (at least to the OSI network level), of telecommunications networks worldwide. In the 14 years since its establishment, many changes have been applied to X.25, most involving extensions. Though originally valid for connections between synchronous equipment (modems) and packet networks, extensions supporting asynchronous interfaces, ISDN, and LAN connections have been added.

Other developments in standardizing technology (which has a direct effect on the growing network of electronic mail systems) were facilitated by the acceptance of X.25. Evaluation of higher level standards is now practical because of the user base already linked at the middle network layer of the OSI model. The first standard in the seventh layer of the ISO network model—X.400—standardizes the format of interpersonal messages and was accepted in the mid 1980s. To address the need for a universal addressing mechanism among users, hosts, and other network equipment, X.500 has been introduced; and still higher-level standards based on the X.400 set that address conferencing communications directly are in the proposal stages.

■ **3.16 OTHER STANDARDS AFFECTING INTERPERSONAL COMMUNICATIONS**

If conferencing is being addressed directly by standards organizations, can file exchange be ignored? In the United States Intel and DCA Corporation together are sponsoring a protocol, the communicating applications specification (CAS), that permits application level programs of any kind (not just terminal emulators and BBSs) to manage file exchanges. A functionally equivalent international standard is FTAM (File Transfer Access Method). When these standards are accepted, a database user will be able to perform a query and send the results to a spreadsheet on a distant machine without having to deal with intermediate data formatting and communications software.

All communications standards development is being stimulated by the imminent dissolution of many trade barriers in European markets. Economic and trade restrictions of many kinds will disappear throughout Western Europe in 1992. The change is having a far-reaching effect on European businesses' perceptions of their international operations and therefore their data exchange requirements. Dramatic increases in data volumes are projected. After the changeover, European markets will present themselves to U.S. businesses as a larger, more monolithic entity. To compete against this new totality, U.S. and Japanese firms are embracing the standards set by European-based standards bodies. A wide range of specifications for communications is being rapidly formulated and approved; these specifications together form a foundation for international data exchange, addressing everything from physical packet characteristics to the logical structure of documents and messages.

Each standard has leveraged others. The X.25 solution for end-to-end reliable packet delivery has made other higher-level standards possible. At the time of this writing, the IP/TCP (internet protocol/terminal control protocol) dominates the marketable products of the middle network layers. Its competitors are IBM's SNA and the largely untried OSI. Other standards, including X.400 and X.500, are gaining strength at yet higher levels of the general network connectivity model. Each standard provides a larger and more homogeneous virtual subnetwork within which other standards can operate.

Each new development moves the global network toward the goal of universal interoperability between computers and software of different manufacturers. At the same time, the cost of upgrading physical transmission equipment and the ability of the new physical pipeline, monomode fiber, to carry more circuits or data on a single strand is resulting in more and more concentration of these high-bandwidth cables and switches in fewer and fewer locations. This has led to a situation of dangerous vulnerability in the physical telephone network itself.

■ 3.17 THE VULNERABILITY OF HIGH BANDWIDTH NETWORKS

In 1988 a fire in a Chicago telephone switch center destroyed trunk lines servicing the entire midwestern United States. Many logical "alternate paths" happened to run through the same physical switching center. Satellite- and land-based microwave links were of little help because most of their feeds joined transnational trunks in that same center. This phenomenon is not atypical. Engineers designing these modern hubs build redundancy in lines, capacity, and switches within one building; but if that whole building (or the greater portion of it) is destroyed, there is little hope for backup routes that have capacities near that of the primary system.

The primary concern, of course, is for the enormous volumes of financial data and other kinds of intra- and intercompany transactions (purchase orders, inventory updates, and so on) delayed by such disasters; the suspension of a few corporate conferences, or the research department's inability to call Dialog is of little consequence by comparison. Yet this vulnerability of the telephone network is not without implications for those information providers and conferencing centers that survive on a steady stream of usage fees.

As the number of users and data exchange volumes rise, different systems become mutually dependent on one another. One example of this is the growing demand for intersystem file and electronic mail gateways. If a system goes down for just a few days, it can mean a substantial loss of income for the host *and* for other systems connected to it, since their users pay for the privilege of exchanging data with the first system, and so on.

■ 3.18 FUTURE DIRECTIONS

All software advances rest upon hardware and operating system evolution. The modem is a hardware component unique to communications oriented applications, and it influences implementation considerations if not design. Another factor in these applications is the technology of the interconnecting telephone network—all of today's economically significant communications applications are high-volume and schedulable; this permits users of such data to bypass the telephone company in an emergency or as a regular practice. Conferencing, electronic mail, and information retrieval are alone in relying primarily on the public telephone system, with all its strengths and weaknesses.

Computer hardware, including the modem, has expanded dramatically in capacity over the last decade, as has the telephone network, and both remain on a path of explosive development. Operating system technology has also changed, but not to such a degree. Operating system theory and experimental systems have evolved significantly in that period, and the results have found their way into commercial products, mostly in the form of advanced user interfaces. This is not to say that there is nothing new in operating systems. IBM's OS/2 has gained recognition as a serious microcomputer operating system because it offers users a bridge from vintage DOS to a true multitasking environment. New operating systems, however, are more slowly accepted than either new hardware or applications software technology, with good reason.

The operating system is the bridge between the computer's hardware and application software. Reasonably stable operating systems have allowed developers to concentrate on adding functionality to high-level programs, even while hardware platforms have changed under them. The explosion of features in modern applications had to await an expansion in hardware capacity. Such development would, however, have been suppressed if these developers had constantly to port to new operating systems, as operating systems are ported to new hardware.

The biggest changes are probably yet to come. They will involve all the components of the communications system, from terminal to network. In the case of computer mediated communications, no single factor will have as big an influence as what is now happening to the telephone network itself. Throughout the 1980s the capacity of the communications channel between hosts was the primary limiting factor in the performance of distributed communications systems. By the end of the 1990s, these channel capacities may be so high that the bottleneck becomes the protocol translation of data packets from the top of the OSI hierarchy to the bottom and back again. Modern computers able to perform the formatting and translation chores on streams at one to five Mbps will be overwhelmed at 500 Mbps! In all likelihood, the model contributing so much to the developing interconnection of dissimilar systems will have to be partly circumvented to make use of the extraordinary expansion in intersystem capacity for data exchange.

4

SINGLE AND MULTIUSER CONFIGURATIONS

There are several ways to classify conferencing software. This chapter will focus on differences between whole systems, rather than the physical or logical services of specific applications software. Systems include hardware *and* applications software. Here the term includes all aspects of the computer and the communications network in which it is embedded. Some in the field, notably Peter and Trudy Johnson-Lenz, would extend the notion of *system* still further to include that set of persons who comprise the physical system's community of users. The behavior of this group should certainly have an influence on system design.

Application software design is somewhat independent of variations in systems, computers, networks, and so on. A single-user BBS can, as far as the user is concerned, support every service and facility of a multiuser system except simultaneous conversations between two or more remote users. The process of reading, entering, or modifying text may appear the same to the individual user no matter what the underlying implementation. Of course, the facilities and limitations of the target hardware and operating system will influence the implementation of any given feature. Here we will focus on the issues raised by system variations and in Chapters 6 and 7, we will discuss some of the solutions.

■ 4.1 VARIATIONS IN INFORMATION RETRIEVAL SYSTEMS

The biggest variations in information retrieval systems are in the general power and style of their search, selection, and reporting (presentation) facilities. Power, in this case, refers not so much to performance but to the search language's expressiveness. Bibliographic and statistical searching ultimately depend upon matching instances of the database with a query that reflects human intent. Good recall-to-precision ratios are the result of a query's match to patterns in the data that reflect the intent of a user's query.

As with natural languages, as one gains experience with a really powerful, expression-rich search language, one's ability to formulate meaningful (in the database's terms) searches is markedly enhanced. Experimental systems now being developed further aid searchers using artificial intelligence techniques to help find references closely matching the semantic content of the most applicable records uncovered by a preliminary search. Except for performance, all of this is more or less independent of the implementation hardware. There are special design implications if distributed data is involved (see Chapter 5).

■ **4.2   CMC SYSTEM MORPHOLOGY**

4.2.1   Morphologically Independent Functions and Services

Conferencing applications are embedded in the same architectural configurations—networks—as other data transmission or exchange applications. Systems are either centralized or distributed, the latter radically or only partially. Conferencing and BBS software may function in single or multiuser configurations; the latter are always centralized, though they may participate in hybridized networks.

There are also alternatives in the logical and physical configurations of distributed conferences. The logical configuration is the user's model of the system, which can vary independently of the strategy for data and control distribution. Consider the public telephone network; it is typically involved at some point in the link between a user and a communications application and often plays the dominant role in the connection, though it may not play any role. Systems designed to serve LAN, MAN, or other dedicated networks can take advantage of high-speed dedicated communications channels.

Centralized systems are either single or multiuser. "Single" refers to the *system's* support for only one remote connection at a time. On the application level, this distinction is made about a product's potential. Software is single-user if it is targeted at an inherently single-user operating system. A system may appear single-user to the world because it is connected to only one phone line, no matter what its potential internally. Such systems may achieve multiuser effects through distribution.

Inherently single-user software may also behave and look to the outside world as a fully functional multiuser system. The emergence of multitasking shells for the MS-DOS operating system has dramatically expanded the number of BBS packages that are functionally multiuser. A number of products are appearing with specific support for operation under DOS shells which facilitates the development and use of file-handling procedures, synchronous communications between simultaneous users, and so on. This software really becomes multiuser, in the sense that we will use the term.

4.2.2   Single-User Architectures

Every kind of conferencing, bulletin board, or E-mail system must perform certain basic work in the process of accepting new text or displaying it to other users. We can see the issues raised in designing systems for communications applications by beginning with a simple system structure: a single-user computer as host running a single user application with one dial-in telephone line.

Like many other application types, conferencing, E-mail, or information retrieval must coordinate data exchange between users and the computer's other subsystems. In our simple example, we permit one user at a time on the system. We assume there will be more than one person with an account on that system, for that is the nature of our application. We must also decide what role the console operator will play.

Many single-user BBSs are multitasking to the extent that the console operator (usually the system's owner) can operate utility functions of the software or communicate with a user on line or both. Other systems do not provide even this level of multitasking. The operator must close the telephone connection to backup files, add and delete accounts, and perform other maintenance functions. If utilities must run directly in the operating system, then some multitasking shell must be used if the BBS is to remain on-line.

As each user connects and disconnects from the system, it must be able to recycle itself and set up for the next call. This includes the need to detect and respond to sudden disconnections. Sometimes there is a security system that permits only registered users to log in and use the BBS facilities. A special login name (for example, "newuser") may exist to permit nonregistered callers to register and possibly use a subset of the system's features while their registration is being processed. Most BBSs support multilevel security systems, which provide various privileges and levels of authority. In some cases they overlap, and provide some of the function served by "role description" facilities in larger systems. For example, they may permit users read-write authority in some conferences and read-only rights in others.

A minimal BBS typically provides E-mail among users, one or more public message spaces for the bulletin (or conference) part of the system, and some means of navigating through both private E-mail and public message spaces to retrieve items of interest. There are also facilities for uploading and downloading binary files, file directory assistance, and an editor with which to create or change text entries. User directory services may contain lists of user IDs and names. They may also contain address information and collections of keywords describing interests. Some systems do not provide any user directory information. Figure 4.1 places the single-user application in prespective with the rest of its system.

At its core, the system supports some facility to display messages and parts of messages in some order. The fundamental ordering is time sequential, and alternate orderings include reverse time sequential, topic or subject plus time sequential, linked-comment chains, and others based on the values in fields supported by the record format. These may include author, recipient, keywords, words in the text, and so on. More sophisticated ordering support, including system-maintained subject indexes, filters, and customized navigation paths are not typically found on small systems. Many small systems are comment-oriented—that is, users may comment on each message as they see it. Other systems are conference-oriented, in which case user replies are attached to a stream of messages and not to individual records in that stream.

Support for writing records to the text base takes the form of some simple input module that accepts lines of text delimited by carriage returns. Some of these systems

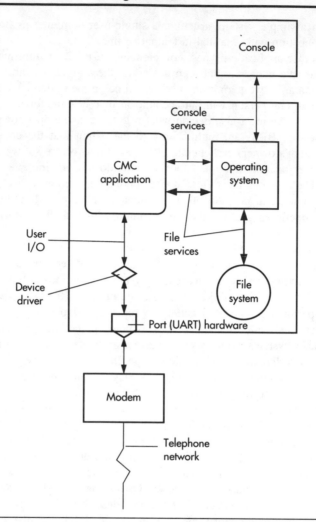

Figure 4.1 High-level representation of a single user CMC system. In this simplified single-user communications systems, the application code communicates directly through its own devise driver with the computer's UART. At the same time, it uses operating system services to perform local console and disk I/O.

generate a prompt signaling of the communication software's readiness to accept the next line. Others have no prompt, and some can be configured either way by the remote user. On some systems, lines entered through the native text input facility are wrapped at preset column boundaries, eliminating the need for a user-generated carriage return at line's end. Once entered, the text can typically be edited by its author before inclusion in the text base.

Editors range from the most primitive of line-oriented devices to sophisticated full-screen editors. Often the user is given a choice. Systems supporting more sophisticated editors usually permit the user to compose a comment and then invoke the communication software's data entry facility, passing to it the newly created text. Ironically, the rise of the microcomputer as a remote terminal device has made the most primitive text entry facilities all the more important. More sophisticated editors and line wrapping devices cannot accept text as quickly as the simpler systems. The microcomputer's ability to upload locally edited texts offsets much of the earlier requirement for good editing facilities on the host.

Some intelligent terminal control is available on most, but not all, small bulletin board systems. For example, users can specify the size (number of lines and columns) of their local screens. This permits clean displays on systems with varying characteristics. Eighty-character lines entered from one system will be displayed as 48-character lines on others, and so on. If the host knows the number of lines supported by a user's terminal equipment, it can support a pager; text scrolling up the screen will pause when the screen fills, and the system prompts the user for some action. Usually the enter key or space bar will display the next screenful of text. Like editors, paging facilities have become somewhat outmoded because text can be captured to local storage devices for later review. More sophisticated screen controls, screen painters, and full-screen editors can actually interfere with text captured for reading off-line.

Other facilities include those required to activate error checking protocols for binary file transfer. Transfer programs are often implemented outside the BBS software itself. When a user requests to receive or send a file, the system executes a separate program that prompts for necessary parameters (file name, type, description, and so on) and initiates the exchange. When complete, the user is returned to the text-oriented facilities of the BBS.

There are many ways to make these features available to users (see Table 4.1). Systems often give users a choice of several levels, or types of menus, or a command mode. Command stacking—the ability to string several commands together—is commonly supported when systems have a command level. Graphics displays may extend the power of menus by allowing users to pick from several items on the same screen page. While no better than most text-oriented menu systems, graphics can enhance navigational facilities by displaying comment titles, subjects, and other messages in a visual structure. This allows users both to select multiple records simultaneously and to see their relation to other parts of the conversational contexts before reading them.

Despite the availability of high-speed dial-up modems and compression systems, communications between BBS and user are still slow compared to the host's connection to its own console. It is for this reason that BBS and conference application interfaces have historically been sparse. Generally speaking, the less time consumed communicating control information (commands *to* the system or prompts for user activity *from* the system), the more time is available for displaying the results and doing other work. The development and acceptance of graphical interfaces and elaborate menu systems is rising in parallel with the penetration of higher-speed modems and built-in compression systems. Menus, for example, compress very efficiently.

4.2.3 Application Interfaces: The User and the Communications Network

Computer mediated communications and information retrieval software are focused in two directions. The first is the user interface and the second is the file system.

Table 4.1 Common features of small BBS/CMC systems

Feature	How supported
login	Unrestricted Restrictions for nonregistered users
Navigations	Menu System Command Mode Graphics interfaces
	Conference/ bulletin/ service indexes
	User specified lists of conferences to visit, etc.
Editors	Line-oriented or full-screen using terminal emulation features
Reading notes	By number, author name, date, since last seen, string in text/subject, etc.
	Scrolling screens, pagers, or full-screen displays using terminal emulation
	features
Writing notes	Line-oriented editors Full-screen editors using terminal emulation features
	ASCII uploads from calling systems, etc.
Electronic mail	Between registered system users Mailing lists, etc.
	Gateways to other systems
File exchange	Command/menu activated upload/ File libraries, or support for binary
	download programs attachments to ASCII notes
User option	Terminals emulated, page length/width
Switches	Graphics on/off, menu vs. command mode, etc.
System auditing/	On-line while system active While not being used, or entirely shut down.
maintenance	
(for sysops)	

Processing work—data transformation—traditionally functions between the interface and file subsystems and is mostly limited to translations between user I/O facilities and files. Some processing occurs in command parsing, search/filtering operations, editing support, and security checking, but user and disk I/O still dominate these applications to a significant extent.

The applications interface must provide some special powers for the system operators (sysops); they must control all activities available to users, in addition to having supervisory control over those users and the system as a whole. Supervisory activities include adding and deleting users, editing or deleting public messages, rearranging the structure of the existing message base, and more. The dichotomy between supervisor and user powers leads to a potential continuum of authority. Between the sysop and ordinary users there may be, for example, assistant sysops with some but not all of the sysop's powers.

The software structure of the user interface—its separation from processing, communications, and file handling logic—is one of the decisions made in the transition from design to implementation (see Figure 4.2). There are many choices. In the early days of BBS software, the interface, processing, and file handling logic were contained in one monolithic program. Early microcomputer languages did not support modularity in program design well. So BBS software was simple enough to make monolithic programs possible. Even today, it is possible to build more sophisticated BBS and conferencing software in this way, because of the relatively simple processing and interface requirements of BBSs combined with the larger memories of contemporary machines.

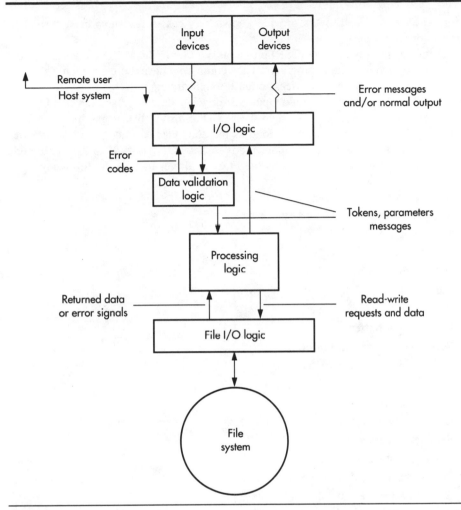

Figure 4.2 Separation of interface and processing logic: one possible strategy for segregating CMC processing logic (security validations, search functions, editing functions) from user and file I/O.

The boundary between the applications software proper and its port-handling systems requires similar consideration. Like the user interface, the code responsible for handling communications can be an integral part of the application module or a separate routine, a *driver*, with which the application communicates.

Device drivers are a modularization contrivance used in all kinds of systems. These are programs loaded into the computer's memory at system or program startup. They connect applications programs and peripheral devices such as disks and communications hardware. As their name implies, they are associated with specific *devices*, one to a driver. These programs service applications by moving data and control codes between hardware devices: for example, UARTs and memory. The CPU and other devices communicate with the driver, sending it commands and getting device status information and data. Drivers provide known services in a standardized format to applications software.

Terminate and stay resident (TSR) programs popular in the MS-DOS world are like drivers in being freestanding programs. They commonly have more abundant services, including liaison with many devices, often through drivers.

In the MS-DOS realm, the Fido Opus SEAdog Standard Interface Layer (FOSSIL) is well-known. FOSSIL is loaded into the MS-DOS driver list or may run as a TSR at startup. It remains in memory as long as the computer is running, and it provides a standard means of connecting applications to and through itself to the computer's serial ports. The services provided by the FOSSIL driver include the following:

Set baud rate

Receive or transmit character with wait

Transmit no wait

Request status

Initialize or deinitialize driver

Raise or lower DTR

Return timer tick parameters

Flush output buffer

Purge output or input buffer

Nondestructive read-ahead

Keyboard read with or without wait

Enable or disable flow control

Extended Control-C or Control-K checking and transmit on or off

Set current cursor location

Read current cursor location

Single character ANSI write to screen

Enable or disable watchdog processing

Write character to screen using BIOS support routines

Insert or delete a function from the timer tick chain

Reboot system

Read block (transfer from FOSSIL to user buffer)

Write block (transfer from user buffer to FOSSIL)

Break begin or end

Return information about the driver

Install or remove an "external application" function

Compare these functions to those provided by the OS/2 device control functions for serial ports:

Set or get baud rate

Set or get line-control characteristics

Transmit immediately

Set or get modem-control output states

Get modem-control input states

Start or stop transmitting

Send or end BREAK signal

Set or get device control block parameters (including 28 control words and flag settings for fine control)

Get communications status

Get transmit data status

Get number of characters in input or output queue

Get UART error or event word

By contrast, MS-DOS provides only the following serial port services through its basic input/output services (BIOS):

Initialize serial port

Output character

Input character

Get serial port status

Although the control features provided by OS/2 better support much greater development of communications services than those of MS-DOS do, the basic services provided by the FOSSIL driver are superior to either native system. In addition, many of the FOSSIL services operate at a higher level than the OS/2 services, considerably simplifying the development of communications code.

Communications libraries produced by third parties are an alternative to writing one's own serial port code or using a permanently resident driver. Collections of routines that manipulate serial port hardware are available for most popular languages and for DBMS system languages such as Ashton Tate's Dbase III and IV, Revelation Technologies' AREV, and other products. For about $100, one can obtain object code (and sometimes source code) for collections of refined, optimized modules for passing information to and from serial ports. Yet another option is to use a language written within a communications system; all of these are associated with existing terminal emulation software.

■ **4.3 DATA STRUCTURES**

The application must support data structures for the storage and exchange of all available message types, along with data describing their relation to users or to other messages. A simple BBS can do quite well with only a few simple data structures; even so, storage of pointer and link information, the use of indexes, mapping of the conference structure into the physical file structure, and the availability and adequacy of operating system services for file manipulation must all be considered.

The number of different storage structures can grow quickly in some designs. BBS public message areas are generally flat; messages are posted on all manner of topics into one virtual space. One of the fundamental enhancements provided by true conferencing systems is some systematic means of grouping messages into discussion threads that not only represent common topics, but may also support the linking of messages to their direct replies. A designer can choose to implement the message space as one large file, or at the other extreme, to create a separate file for every message. Electronic mail can exist in a structure of its own or in the general message space using values in control fields to distinguish it from public messages. File design has a tremendous effect on the implementation of navigation, selection, filtering, and other control facilities.

Most modern BBSs and all true conferencing systems have the ability to track each user's point of last activity in the message base, the read-through point, or last-read marker. There are a number of ways to satisfy this requirement. On one hand, every user can be associated with a unique file or files, one for each conference, containing pointers to the last-read record of conferences or subconferences in which that user participates. Alternately the conference itself and the data structure storing it can be associated with a file holding the required information for all participating users.

As with communications I/O, one has a choice of coding the file handling logic in the applications program or using a separate driver for file operations. Resident file drivers are less common than their communications counterparts; however, file I/O libraries are available for every popular language and effectively serve the same purpose. A more radical approach taken by a few products is to build the communications system on top of a database management system (DBMS).

DBMSs are generalized software systems for the storage, manipulation, and presentation of data as distinct records (or objects) with repetitive structure. Like operating systems, some DBMSs are better suited to communications tasks than others. The ability to manipulate large records, to handle binary and textual data, to support variable length fields of reasonable scope, and to perform well are valuable characteristics for communications applications; in addition, the DBMS should provide for automatic recovery of damaged files and indices, as well as control multiple simultaneous updates to the database (in multiuser configurations) transparently to the communications software itself. An interesting potential in DBMS-based conferencing systems is their capacity to merge the conferencing and information retrieval domains.

■ **4.4 ARCHITECTURAL CONSTRAINTS ON SOFTWARE DESIGN AND EXTENSION**

All communications applications require generic services for reading and writing files. The content of an operating system's file services and its ability to protect files from system crashes determine how well it is suited for these applications. Although it is common (in MS-DOS-based systems) to bypass operating system services to manipulate communications hardware, one never directly manipulates random storage devices (at least not in these applications). Decisions made about employing operating system, file library, or DBMS services for this purpose will influence the ease of implementation and efficiency of higher-level application features.

For example, a user directory maintaining information on user accounts, including names and interests, is a useful enhancement to bulletin board systems. Sysop views of these directory entries may include other statistical information such as conferences visited, notes read or written, files up- or downloaded, and other system activity. Some systems support crosspointers between messages in different conferences or between a private mail message and a conference thread, and so on. Users can navigate across these links, which provides alternate approaches to the message base. The addition of such facilities to existing software is easier with some file designs than with others. For example, a system using one file to contain information about all user activity would smooth the development of a directory feature.

An application's relation to its underlying operating system often has an influence on its extendability. Sometimes the operating system is not rich enough for the task at hand, and application code itself (or external drivers) must make up for the deficiencies; this affects the ease of extending the features of the system.

The target hardware has some influence on our single-user example, but less than it would for other kinds of applications; for example, bulletin board systems can run on the simplest of computers. There is a cutoff point, however, below which the functionality of the system is very much limited by the hardware. Very small systems like Commodore 64s and Atari STs are limited in many ways, such as their ability to handle multiple terminal types and screen formats; these computers have no multiuser expansion potential and they support few languages (compilers), thus limiting their overall value as development environments. Even the more expensive Apple Macintosh and similar machines, though capable platforms in their own right, are of limited value in this domain. In these cases, it is not the hardware itself but its closed configuration and the demand that developers write within the constraints of Apple's user interface that occasions the limits. Economics and market share are the problem for the Commodore Amiga x000 computer line; these machines sport a true multitasking operating system and an open bus, but their small market share has not generated the interest of many third parties for development of communications systems. Despite their limitations, these platforms host a few sophisticated BBS products.

4.4.1 MS-DOS as a Platform for Communications

Despite its limitations in the communications arena, the IBM-PC/XT/AT/386 running MS-DOS has become the platform of choice for small communications applications. The reasons for this are more political and economic than technical.

1. Although the operating system barely supports communications, this fact does not prevent developers from writing code that supports it well. Thanks to the ubiquity of the open ISA/AT bus, code is portable across a wide range of machines from many manufacturers.

2. Hundreds of vendors have products—hardware *and* software—that extend the reach of IBM-PC and clone machines. These include mass storage devices in the gigabyte range, disk management software, multimodem boards, and other

products for BBS maintenance and operation. The sheer number of vendors supplying PC add-ons ensures lower prices than in any other segment of the computer market. In addition, much of this downward price pressure is generated by an enormous quantity of shareware and public domain software.

3. Hundreds of languages are available for these machines. With them come software extensions, drivers, libraries, and utilities. The majority of high-level languages do not provide enough direct support for communications tasks; most, however, including DBMS procedural languages, support linking assembler object code to the high-level language. Furthermore, communications functions are abundantly available. This means that developers with language backgrounds from Cobol to Prolog can produce applications with embedded communications facilities, thus ensuring a great deal of experimentation.

4. Hundreds of finished products exist for these computers. They range from the simplest of BBSs to sophisticated conferencing systems like CoSy, Parti, Caucus, TBBS, PCBoard, Magpie, TEAMate, and more. Many very sophisticated BBS packages are available as shareware for a few hundred dollars or less.

5. IBM clones are relatively inexpensive. An XT-class machine with 20 megabytes of disk running a BBS on a single phone line cost less than $800 in 1989, including software. Such a machine can expand to support up to four telephone lines for a few hundred dollars more. Disk expansion is almost as inexpensive.

Given the dominance of IBM hardware in this area, the weaknesses of MS-DOS have played a minor role in its choice for communications applications. Several UNIX variations run on IBM microcomputer hardware, and these have become the operating systems of choice for multiuser communications. They are, however, more expensive both to obtain and to maintain.

Using a UNIX system is almost as easy today as using DOS or even the Macintosh, although administering such a system still requires significant skill. For these reasons, operating systems other than DOS are almost never used for single user BBSs. MS-DOS dominates this market, and there are still a number of older CP/M-based systems continuing to run on eight-bit computers.

■ 4.5 THE INFLUENCE OF THE DIAL-UP TELEPHONE NETWORK

The final ingredient in our minimal BBS configuration is its relation to the telephone network. Single-line BBSs are almost universally without cost to the caller, other than possible telephone charges. Since their operators make no money but run the boards as a hobby, they rely exclusively on the conventional services of the public telephone network.

A single telephone line can support between one hundred and three hundred people, but in the upper limits of this range, the likelihood of getting a busy signal becomes so great that further growth is stifled. These systems serve mainly local users; most of the callers are willing to tolerate high probabilities of busy signals because, after all, both the BBS service and the call are free. This plethora of isolated small systems serves the purpose of providing a platform for entry-level exploration into the potentials of computer mediated communications.

■ 4.6 EXPANDING THE SYSTEM: MULTIUSER ARCHITECTURES

There are two fundamental ways to expand a single-user system. First, it can become a node in a network of machines, and therefore a part of a larger distributed system. Second, it can function with multiple telephone lines, allowing simultaneous connection by two or more users. Hybrids of the two types are common. Figure 4.3 illustrates several multiuser configuration possibilities.

Considered from a hardware viewpoint, expansion through distribution requires no further investment because little or no change to low-level portions of the communications software is needed. At higher levels of the application, things can get considerably more complex. For this reason, and because the topology of a distributed system is more elaborate than that of centralized multiuser configurations, these levels will be disccussed in the next chapter.

There are four basic strategies (show in Figure 4.3) for multiuser operations. The first and simplest is one in which the application handles all multiuser task switching by itself; for example, TBBS under MS-DOS (see Figure 4.3a). A second strategy uses a multitasking shell to handle task switching (Figure 4.3b). Each executing applications module converses with its own communications hardware, while the shell is used to handle I/O with storage devices through the operating system. Examples include Magpie, RBBS, Wildcat, and others under MS-DOS. The third strategy involves a multitasking operating system using its own device drivers to address communications hardware, file systems, and multiple executions of the CMC application, as demonstrated in Figure 4.3c. An example of this strategy is Picospan under UNIX. The fourth and final strategy, illustrated in Figure 4.3d, is that of a multitasking operating system addressing communications hardware, the file system, and a re-entrant copy of the CMC application. Some examples include Participate under VMS and Confer under MTS.

Multiuser system architectures have been in existence since the mid 1960s. A multiuser topology (the CPU and all services from hardware to the application layer) is a point from which radiates potential simultaneous gateways to remote terminals or to computers emulating terminals. The interconnection is the web of the telephone network or, sometimes, dedicated (always open) lines. There are more kinds of conferencing and information retrieval software running multiuser than in any other architecture because the technology is well understood. Over the years, a very large corpus of techniques for handling user and system contentions of various kinds has been elaborated—computer conferencing, electronic mail, and information retrieval technologies were all born in this environment.

4.6.1 Expanded Services in a Multiuser Environment

With one exception, there are no differences between the services provided by a multiuser system and those of single-user systems on the application level. Multiuser systems commonly provide more features than single-user software does, but there is no reason why this must be so. The exception involves the inherent ability of a multiuser configuration to connect two or more persons simultaneously. There are several variations in this kind of service; the first is illustrated in single-user systems when BBS software allows a caller to converse with the system operator. Communication

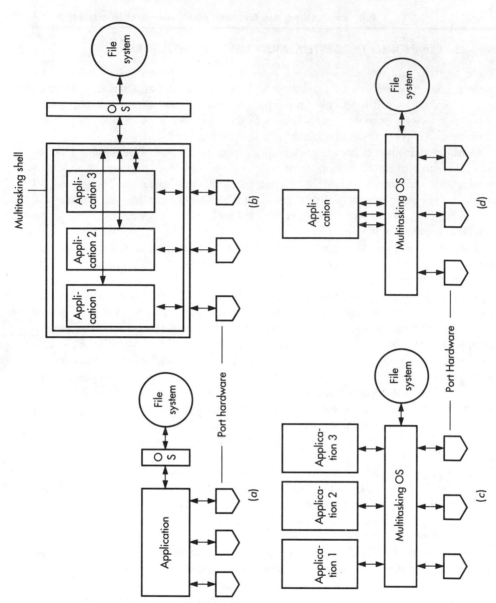

Figure 4.3 Four strategies for multiuser operations.

takes place in real time—each character entered by either user instantly appears on the screen of the other. Although this form of synchronous communication works well enough for two people, it is unwieldy when more than two are connected. As with face to face conversations within a group of people, subdiscussions often occur between members of the group; yet if more than one person's characters were to appear on everyone's screen simultaneously, the result would be uninterpretable. Multiuser systems that support synchronous communications must make compromises to yield intelligible output.

A second approach collects characters into a line, signaled by a carriage return. When a user enters this end-of-line character, the whole line, along with a tag signaling the author's identity, is transmitted to each of the other users. The results are intelligible but not necessarily meaningful, as individual lines from different sources are constantly intermingled. A third and better solution is to group lines into paragraphs signaled by two successive carriage returns. At this point, the conversation becomes coherent, but a new problem arises. As the user's entry is composed, the completed entries of others are being posted. Either the terminal software or the host interface should keep the texts separate. This inevitably involves terminal scripts, customized terminal software, or a login requirement for some minimal set of screen control capabilities. In an interface directed at the widest possible variation in remote screen control support (including none), the interface must either delay the display of other text altogether, or post only a minimal signal that other texts are being composed. Only a few systems supporting synchronous communications also store this conference stream. If stored, the results of the real time discussion can be forwarded to other users asynchronously, providing a mixed mode conference that gives users the best of both worlds.

4.6.2 The Development of Mini- and Microcomputers in a Multiuser Environment

The development of computer conferencing and the appearance of the minicomputer were relatively coincident. Throughout the 1970s the most common platform for mounting such systems was the mini, though EMISARI, EIES, and Confer were implemented on mainframes. The largest public systems, CompuServe, BIX, and GEnie, all run in the minicomputer environment. VaxNotes, the most widely used conferencing application in the corporate sector, is available only on DEC (Digital Equipment Corporation) minicomputer technology.

With the birth of 16- and 32-bit CPUs in the early 1980s, the supermicros— dedicated multiuser microcomputers—began to grow in popularity as a platform for computer mediated communications. Such machines, popularized by Altos and Compupro corporations even before the advent of second and third generation CPUs, support from eight to thirty users and sometimes more. Early models often ran a multiuser variant of the CP/M operating system called MP/M. This operating system was capable of supporting sophisticated BBS and conferencing applications; however, the systems were too expensive to support much experimentation.

Multiuser hardware is distinguished by the presence of multiple serial I/O ports. These computers do not contain separate internal components for communicating with keyboards and monitors as do most single user machines. Rather, their internal architecture is oriented toward stand-alone terminals with their own keyboard and monitor functions. That these terminals may be connected to the system through the telephone network via modems matters not. Such systems require no hardware add-ons to address multiple communications lines and commonly include internal disk subsystems in the 250–750 megabyte range, with expansion ports for adding additional disk capacity externally.

Most modern systems contain multiple CPUs, but not necessarily one per user. There is usually a main CPU, one or more secondary processors handling memory and disk I/O, and one or more CPUs dedicated to accelerating communications (terminal) functions. Multiple primary CPUs are also appearing, thus providing a parallel processing capability. Communications applications are not typically broken into multipule tasks and run on separate CPUs. Instead, tasks started by different users are executed simultaneously. Multiprocessor machines may also provide fault tolerance capability; in the event of processor failure, the remaining central CPUs can continue operations at a reduced performance level. Fault tolerance may extend to other subsystems as well—memory, disk, and buses may be duplicated, resulting in a very low probability of overall system failure.

Multiuser architectures are an obvious first choice for multiuser software development because they remove some low-level considerations from the application layer. Except for monitoring the generation of new records in a shared file, one need only write the software as though it were running on a single-user system; the hardware and operating system takes care of the rest. The primary exception to this simplifying influence is support for synchronous services. Multiuser operating systems like UNIX provide the lower-level interprocess communications services required to hook separate user sessions together. The application software, however, must specifically address these services to support synchronous activities.

The cost of these systems still suppresses their use in the hobbyist communications sector. Fault tolerance comes at a high price; even without it, a small multiuser system of 8 to 12 ports costs $10,000 and more, not including modems and software. Operating systems for these computers are also more expensive than their single-user counterparts, as is applications software. There is little or no public domain or shareware communications software for these architectures, and application prices often vary depending on the number of projected simultaneous connections.

■ 4.7 USING SINGLE TASKING SYSTEMS FOR MULTIUSER OPERATIONS

Of the various single user architectures in existence, only the IBM-style systems have stimulated extensive third-party development of multiuser add-ons for communications purposes; for example, a sixteen-user BBS sporting 256 megabytes of disk storage will run on a PC-AT type machine (either 80286 or 80386) for about $10,000, including software and modems. Essentially one has but to add one or more multiport cards to the expansion slots in the PC.

Each port contains its own UART; some of these cards contain modems built in, as many as eight per card, and prices vary from as little as $1500 for sixteen ports to as much as $5000. The difference reflects the intelligence built into the cards themselves. The least expensive contain little more than the port hardware and UARTs, while more expensive models come with memory used for input and output buffering (the standard

IBM UART has only a one-byte buffer) and their own CPUs. These processors assist in the process of delivering data to, and receiving it from, the PC's main memory. They also support the separation of multiple signals from the UARTs to buffers and the PC bus, a process that would otherwise require special code in the applications or port driver software.

Internal liaison with these communications boards is accomplished with device drivers supplied by the board manufacturer or written by the application developer. Some manufacturers supply drivers and usage documentation, while others supply information needed to write drivers. The features provided by the drivers depend on the sophistication of the port cards themselves. The more expensive cards support byte and block (collections of bytes) level operations, leaving applications software free to deal with higher-level data constructs like strings and records.

■ 4.8 THE ADVANTAGES OF MULTITASKING OPERATING SYSTEMS

The essence of multiuser operation is multitasking—the ability of the operating system to control different applications running at the same time. This is accomplished in a number of ways, but all share a common result: Each separate application receives an allotted slice of CPU time. In a single-processor system, the CPU is running only one process—literally one instruction—at a time. The status of this process is saved while another is run and then recovered again to continue where it left off. This switching process is so rapid that users are unaware of its operation.

This does not mean that it isn't possible to overload such a machine. The result, from the user's perspective, is poor performance, but each user's task still retains its continuity. In multi-CPU architectures, the operating system is responsible for partitioning tasks so that they may run simultaneously in different CPUs. Such coordination is more difficult and costs something in CPU overhead because the operating system must do more work; the overall gains in performance, however, more than make up the difference.

All multiuser operating systems are multitasking, but the reverse is not always true (OS/2 and the Amiga operating system are good examples). MS-DOS must be tricked into multiuser operation; one way of doing this is to run communications applications under a shell that handles the multitasking but is, from the operating system's perspective, a single high-level task. Another approach is to write the BBS or conferencing application itself in such a way as to take care of the task switching that would normally fall to the operating system. Existing products reflect both approaches. DOS, however, does not dominate the multiuser communications arena as it does in the single user world. Here it competes primarily with two other operating systems and a third up-and-coming one.

4.8.1 UNIX in Communications

UNIX is probably the best-known and most widely distributed multiuser operating system in the communications field. There are two basic varieties of UNIX—the AT&T version and Berkeley UNIX. Each has variants (clones) that are also popular. The Santa Cruz Operation's (SCO) Xenix is a clone of the AT&T System V variety, while GNU, from Mt. Xinu (pronounced Zeenu) Corporation is a clone of Berkeley UNIX version 4.3.

The Berkeley version of the UNIX began as a modification of a mid 1970s version of AT&T UNIX and has diverged from the AT&T line ever since. Except for behavior and interface variations in a few utilities, both systems appear very much the same to users. It is their internal structure, the way in which they establish intertask connections for exchanging data and control information, that primarily distinguishes them.

These differences exist well below the level of the application from the user's perspective. UNIX-based communications software runs equally well in either environment. Significantly, though, the variations are but one step removed from the applications layer in the open systems interconnect (OSI) model. This means that the application *software* must be aware of which version of UNIX it is running on. Typically, those parts of the application code relating to communications with the rest of the system are isolated in substitutable modules. Users need not be aware of their existence let alone their operational details, but application developers must be aware of their implications.

The two main versions of UNIX were designed with different lower-level services in mind. For Berkeley UNIX, it was the transmission control protocol at the OSI transport layer, and for AT&T, it was the ISO's own recommendation for transport services. By the late 1980s, both Berkeley Sockets and AT&T Streams had each been connected to the other's transport layer. This flexibility is for the best, but it points out issues that require attention when investigating communications software for this environment. The network-level implications mainly affect distributed configurations. Even in a purely centralized environment however application software must account for the presentation- and session- layer differences between Berkeley and AT&T UNIX. At the applications level, the design and implementation of user facilities, like synchronous conversations or system status and statistics monitoring, are affected by the protocols used in the target system.

4.8.2 VMS from Digital Equipment Corporation

Another operating system contender in conferencing applications is Digital Equipment Corporation's VMS. VMS supports VAXnotes, DEC's own conferencing applications software. Other major conferencing systems have been ported to VMS, including Caucus, Confer, and Participate. VMS has proven itself a capable platform for communications. It has not had the general visibility of UNIX for the following reasons:

- Unlike UNIX, it runs only on DEC equipment. It is not available anywhere else, while UNIX is available on almost every hardware platform in the world capable of supporting it.

- VMS is expensive because DEC hardware, its only environment, is expensive. Even the medium-sized conferencing systems cannot afford DEC VMS machines. Such machines are popular in the corporate arena, and DEC's VaxNotes is a popular applications package in the private sector.

- It is proprietary, its source code is not released by DEC, and it is not for sale. By contrast, it was the availability of UNIX kernel source in the mid 1970s that boosted UNIX to its current level of popularity and universal acceptance in the multiuser arena. UNIX kernel source is no longer so generally available, but it can still be licensed by third parties for application development.

4.8.3 OS/2, the New Kid on the Block

The third contender is a newcomer. Thanks to IBM's advocacy, it should be considered for multiuser communications-oriented development. This contender is, of course, OS/2. Compared to the simplicity of the early UNIX, it is a monster requiring from two to four megabytes of RAM just to run itself. Of course, UNIX never had to worry about maintaining backward compatibility with anything. The RAM requirements are now relatively easy to meet, and OS/2 is endowed with some reasonably powerful support for communications.

OS/2 is, like UNIX and VMS, a true multitasking operating system. It is not inherently multiuser however. All of the special hardware enhancements of the PC environment required under MS-DOS are still necessary under OS/2. Sophisticated serial communications functions under MS-DOS are achieved only through bypassing both the operating system and the BIOS (Basic Input/Output System) and programming the UARTs and interrupt controller chips (interrupt requests) directly. Applications on OS/2 typically run at what is called priority level three in OS/2's hierarchical scheme. Applications at priority three are precluded from accessing the hardware directly. This is necessary to ensure that OS/2 will be able to properly control context switching between tasks. Luckily, the communications facilities provided by OS/2 adequately support multiuser serial port operations.

UNIX, VMS, and OS/2 are not the only multitasking operating systems in common use, though together they probably have 90 percent of this market outside the mainframe universe. Xenix and GNU are not the only UNIX clones in existence either. Other such clones include Microport V, QNX, and Venix; and there are still other multitasking and multiuser operating systems, including Concurrent DOS from Digital Research, OPUS5, Theos, RTX, Interactive, Multilink Advanced, Quick Connect, SunOS, and Pick. Except for the last, the others are primarily found in engineering or educational environments. Pick from Pick Systems of Irvine, California is interesting in that the operating system itself is also a DBMS (Database Management System), and has characteristics that are well-suited to communications software development.

▪ 4.9 MULTITASKING AND THE REQUIREMENTS OF THE FILE SYSTEM

As with single-user systems, the operating system role in multiuser BBS and conferencing software deals not only with communications, but also with handling the file system. File implementations for conferencing take many forms; at one extreme, a single file may contain all conferences on the system, their subsections, notes, replies, and so on. Values contained in fields of the file's records signal their relation to conferences, topics, and other stored material. At the other extreme, every single note, whether one hundred or ten thousand bytes long, is contained in a separate file. The conference or item to which that note belongs is signaled by the contents of fields in the file designed for that purpose. There are actually systems that use this approach, because it has the advantage of greatly simplifying issues having to do with concurrent record updates.

The disadvantage of the latter approach is that the number of files on a system will multiply into the thousands. (Some operating systems can handle this better than others.) While most systems employ filing strategies that fall somewhere between these two extremes, it is worthwhile to note that both extremes simplify crosslinking messages (notes or replies) between conferences or electronic mail—the first because the file manager controls all text associations in a single file, and the second because every note stands alone in its own file and can be associated with any conference, topic, or individual mailbox by adding that conference or topic to the list of its pointers.

Except in the second example, there must be some provision for concurrent operations in the same file. If the applications software is not re-entrant—that is, each user is running his or her own copy of the software—then operating system file locking services may be inadequate because they may not permit more than one program to have the same file open for writing at one time. If used to handle contentions, operating system services must provide at least one locking level below the file itself; for example, at the record. Multitasking MS-DOS shells, like Microsoft Windows and Quarterdeck's Desqview support file locks, but they cannot recognize individual records inside these files. BBS software that uses the file support built into these systems must make some provision for concurrent file updates.

The most common approach is to place entries into a temporary file or holding buffer if a lock is set; when the lock is released, the held record may be added to the file. If the BBS software manages contentions itself or if a DBMS or DBMS-like system is used to manage the files, then locking at the record level is possible. The most common technique at the file or the record level (in the absence of a DBMS) is to maintain a special field called a lock byte, which is set during record or file updates and reset when the update is complete. Before engaging a file for write purposes, the software, the shell, or the operating system must examine this lock byte and act accordingly.

Unlike transaction processing systems, BBS and conferencing software need rarely concern itself with concurrent updates to a single record. If the software permits ex post facto editing, it is usually the message's author or the conference administrator alone who has such privileges. This raises the possibility that both will attempt to edit the record at the same time. Another exception exists if the software supports joint document authoring. In this case, any number of persons may update an individual record. Since such updates could easily overlay one another, it is common to permit only one update at a time; the the first update will be written while further updates are blocked until the record is reread into the other users' edit buffers.

■ **4.10 MULTIUSER SYSTEMS AND THE TELEPHONE ENVIRONMENT**

As with the hardware and operating system, a multiuser system has more options in relation to the telephone network. Strictly speaking, it is not that there are more choices, but that a wider range of options becomes practical. The simplest configuration requires only multiple common telephone lines, and since these lines will be used only for receiving calls, dial-out capability is not necessary. The lines are usually associated in a "hunt group" or on a rotator switch so that the first non-busy phone answers the call. Of course, this simple configuration requires any out-of-area callers to make long distance calls, which will ensure that your user population does not grow too large, especially if you begin to charge subscription fees for your larger, more expensive investment.

If you intend to run a for-profit multiuser BBS, or for some other reason it is necessary to provide for a regional or national user base, some of the system's lines can be serviced by a packet switch provider like Telenet, Tymnet, CompuServe's packet network (CPN), or the packet-switched data networks (PSDNs) supported by each of the Bell Operating Companies. Callers on the other side of the country (or the world) may dial a local number to connect to your system. The packet switch vendor places a PAD (packet assembler/disassembler) at the system site and connects a dedicated line to it. Modems normally connected to some of your system's ports are replaced with serial connections to the PAD, which acts as a multiline modem and handles the conversion between the packets and separate serial streams to and from the system.

Alternatively, the PAD can be mounted on a board directly connected to the system bus. OST Inc. of Chantilly, Virginia, makes such a card which supports up to 256 virtual X.25 connections through a single PC slot. There are few commercial bulletin board systems that contain drivers addressing these cards; they are, however, an attractive option, as they eliminate serial port and modem requirements. Such drivers should appear in due course.

Direct service via X.25 is expensive, usually at least $1500 per month! This price prevents small users from experimenting with packet switching incrementally, which may be possible in the near future under ISDN. Besides monthly service fees, the BBS operator is billed per minute for these connection services, possibly with an added charge for the data transferred in any given session (typically a few cents per thousand characters). Presumably, these charges are passed on to users either as a part of their subscription fees, or as a separate charge. Most cities in the United States with populations over 100,000 are served by packet switch providers, bringing some 90 percent of the U.S. population within local calling distance of such services.

Sometimes, it is the packet vendor itself that moves to promote connections to ordinary telephone-based conference and BBS systems, thereby generating more income from existing capacity; PC Pursuit from Sprint Communications and Tymnet's Starlink are examples. The packet vendor invites callers to use the packet system to call a remote city, and once routed to the vendor's distant PAD, the packet provider makes the last local phone call completing the connection to a distant host. Users are billed a flat monthly rate or an hourly charge for their connection to the packet service. Either way, the call is supposed to be less expensive than a direct long distance phone call. Other options include connections to packet radio-telephone equipment and even the shortwave radio transmission bands. In the latter case, the BBS operator must also be a licensed ham radio operator, as must all callers using this radio technique.

As long-distance companies lower their transcontinental rates, operations like PC Pursuit will be put under economic pressure. The current balance of long-distance direct costs compared to PC Pursuit's flat charges already favors direct long-distance usage in many cases. PC Pursuit is less expensive only if users spend a great deal of time connected to remote systems or if they call a large number of them each month.

■ **4.11 MULTIUSER SYSTEMS AND INFORMATION RETRIEVAL**

Multiuser dedicated information retrieval applications are simpler in principle than are computer mediated communication systems. User and disk I/O dominates their processing requirements even more than in communications applications. The primary processing requirement in information retrieval is comparison operations over the database, which is accomplished by the application software or an underlying DBMS. Records are written at regular, schedulable intervals. What complicates this software is its performance requirement—many databases contain gigabytes of data, and good search and retrieval software provides users with many ways to search, combine, and report results, which can involve millions of comparison and selection operations.

In the PC world, it is primarily the low disk-to-system throughput that makes small systems unsuitable for this task. PCs can exchange hundreds of kilobytes of data per second with their disks. Minicomputers and mainframes can transfer millions in the same time. Until recently, CPU speed—the number of executable operations per second—was another limiting factor; however, as the 1990s begin, microcomputer CPUs operating in the 10 million instructions per second (MIPS) range are appearing on desk tops. This instruction speed brings the performance required in complex searches well within the range of the PC; if only they could get data from their disks as fast as they can process it!

5

DISTRIBUTED
CONFERENCING SYSTEMS

■ 5.1 REPLICATED TEXT BASES VERSUS DISTRIBUTED ACCESS

Adding multiuser capabilities to a single-user BBS is not the only expansion route. Another more radical approach is to distribute the conference itself onto multiple single-user machines. There are two fundamental forms of conference distribution. In the first type, represented by such networks as Usenet and the FIDO network, every individual conference is fully replicated across all participating machines in the distributed network. Connecting to any machine on the network provides access to any conference in which that node participates.

In the second type of conference distribution (illustrated in Figure 5.1), each machine on the network plays host to one or more conferences. If a user is reading or writing to a conference whose host node is his or her local machine, then the system is effectively a single- or multiuser configuration; however, if the conference resides on another host, then participation requires establishing a real-time connection between the local machine and the host node for that conference because no conferences are replicated on other nodes. When users read or write to conferences located on remote nodes, the local interface software connects them directly with those nodes and permits reading and writing directly to the remote shared storage pool. This method is exemplified by VaxNotes running in the DECnet environment. Because it requires the initiation of real-time connections between hosts, it is a practical configuration only in the private sector, where all the hosts involved are controlled by a unified entity. Connections can take a number of forms, from high-speed LAN (Ethernet, for example) links to the dial-up telephone system.

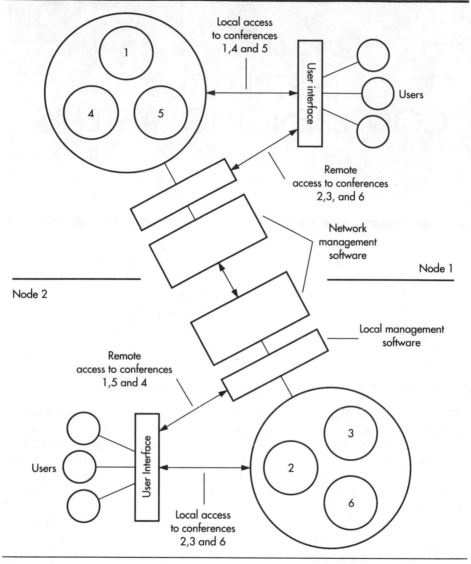

Figure 5.1 Distribution via distributed access.

The VaxNotes configuration is really a form of interconnected multiuser conferencing. In an unmixed replicated configuration, each participant is also the manager of a network node; this precludes the use of dumb terminals on such networks. Of course, a BBS can function as both a node in the distributed network *and* a host for remote users with terminals or computers emulating terminals; leaving this latter possibility aside for a moment, conference participants in a distributed system both read from and write to conference streams stored on their own local computers.

▪ 5.2 REPLICATED CONFERENCES ON SINGLE-USER HOSTS

The person we have called the console operator or sysop in the last chapter is now the conference user, as well as the manager of his or her own local network node. New additions (records) to the conference stream are initially added only to the local node. At periodic times throughout the day—commonly once, in the early morning hours when phone rates are lowest—the conference software activates a telephone connection and dials another network node, or conversely, may receive calls from remote nodes; upon connection, new records added to a conference on the node of reference are sent to the receiving node for further distribution. New records are received from the remote point, possibly sent there by other nodes. A component of the communications software dissects the incoming message stream and assigns each message to a mailbox or a conference.

Application level services are similar to those provided by single-user or multiuser systems. If the user interface is sufficiently differentiated from the rest of the conference software, there exists a potential for competitive development of exotic features, particularly in the areas of searching and filtering. Most of the products operating at this level provide enhanced electronic mail facilities or alternate user interfaces (or both) to the system.

There are some practical realities to face in a distributed environment. As a result, some features available on many centralized systems are not incorporated into distributed systems. Unavoidable constraints are imposed by the intermittent, though regularly scheduled, connection between nodes. Also of concern are the issues of cost, privacy, politics, efficiency, and reliability, which make distributed techniques less suitable than centralized architectures for some uses. However, there are domains to which distributed systems are better adapted than their centralized counterparts.

▪ 5.3 DISTRIBUTION TECHNIQUES

The periodic reflection of new material from node to node throughout the network is sometimes called "echo conferencing." There are three strategies in use for exchanging new material among nodes.

- *Direct connection.* Each node in the network calls or is called by every other node when new records appear. This technique is impractical for all but the smallest networks, though the FIDO network uses just such a strategy for the exchange of electronic mail (point-to-point exchanges).
- *Broadcast flooding.* Each node calls or is called by other machines in proximity to it, sending and receiving new records (see Figure 5.2a). Some machines will make long distance connections, while others are purely local. Receiving machines, in turn, connect with others, and these to yet others. This technique is analogous to ripples spreading from a handful of pebbles tossed into a pond. The outcome is a simulated data broadcast that spreads throughout the network. Mechanisms exist to limit the number of duplicate messages transmitted or to eliminate them when received; this is necessary because many hosts will have neighbors in common.

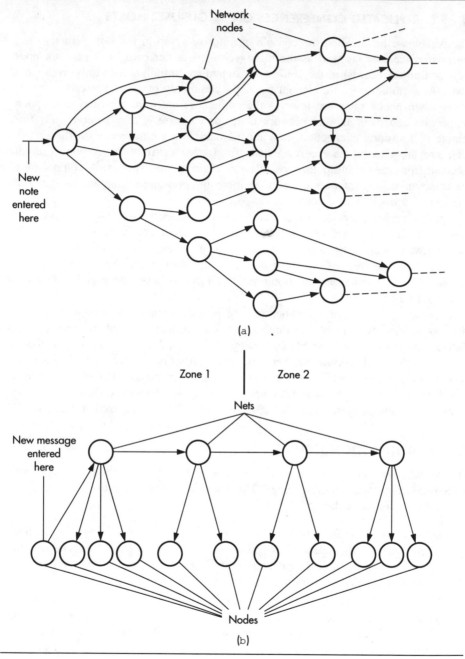

Figure 5.2 Broadcast versus hierarchical distribution.

- *Domain hierarchies*. In this scheme, a local node exchanges conference data with a designated subregional machine. The subregions forward it to regional nodes, which communicate with national nodes, which perform international distribution tasks. On the receiving side, each appointed focal node communicates with the centers below it, which contact the individual nodes in their regions, subregions, and so on (see Figure 5.2*b*). This is the echo method adopted by the FIDO network for conferences. Duplication of messages is theoretically prevented, but may occur in real situations because some node-level machines may send new conference material directly to other nearby node level systems.

The point-to-point technique is suitable for very small collections of machines because each must contact or be contacted by the others. Its virtue is its simplicity. It is viable for electronic mail exchange, provided the network administrators maintain a complete system list—a map of the entire network—on every node. The FIDO network does exactly that. Larger networks use the technique to provide real-time remote-login capability. Usually associated with networks of larger (hence multiuser) computers, remote-login essentially permits a terminal on one node to become a terminal on another and manipulate the remote host as if it were local.

■ 5.4 THE FIDO NETWORK

FIDO is a popular BBS package that runs on MS-DOS-based microcomputers. The FIDOnet software operates at the transport level of the OSI seven-layer hierarchy and has been ported to many platforms, including Macintosh, Commodore, and Amiga computers. The FIDO software is strictly single-user, but the network protocols permit any machines supporting them to exchange messages directly, point-to-point. The FIDO software costs $175, but the message exchange protocols are public-domain.

In 1986 FIDO's E-mail facilities were extended into "public mailboxes." Mail could then be sent to many machines at the same time, and many persons could read these public messages. At that time, there were two machines exchanging public mail, soon to be called "echo conferences." By the end of 1988 there were several thousand machines echoing conferences among themselves. The original point-to-point exchange of material quickly became inadequate, so FIDO system operators agreed in 1987 to establish a hierarchical addressing scheme that permitted an orderly transfer of data from one geographic location to another. Although private mail is still primarily sent point-to-point, the hierarchical domain scheme facilitated the exchange of conference data and was rapidly adopted as a means of identifying machines for mail exchange (see Figure 5.3).

Each node on FIDO net stores a list, literally the telephone number, of every other FIDO machine in the world participating in the network. This list contains the name of the node administrator as a synonym of its address. To send mail to a user of a machine who is not the operator, one must know the address—the machine number—of that user. It is up to the local software to map user names to individual mail boxes below the machine's node number.

The FIDO node number is a combination of three levels of hierarchy. The first, or zone, is the international designation; for example, 1 is the United States, 2 Europe, and 3 the Pacific basin. Zones are divided into two different overlapping classification

```
user   1:125/101
         ↑                                    FIDO Address
     Zone ↑
       Net ↑
         Node
```

`user@fnode#.nnet#.zl.fidonet.org`	Form for sending mail from the Internet to the FIDO net. Note that zone #1, North America, is currently the only zone that supports this service.
`uucp gateway`	Form for sending FIDO mail to the uucp network. The main gateway machine is 1:125/406. The first line of the message text contains the address of the uucp user in one of the two formats below.
`host!host!host!...!user`	Old style path-routing uucp address.
`user@host`	New style uucp address for machines supporting uucp domains.
`user%host.uucp@gateway`	For sending mail from the Internet to the uucp network from a machine that does not support automatic internetwork routing. gateway is an Internet machine that gateways mail between networks.
`user@host.BITNET`	For sending mail from uucp to the BITNET where the local mail software supports the pseudodomain .BITNET, or routes through a gateway that supports it.

Figure 5.3 Some examples of address formats within and between networks. Many more examples and explanations can be found in the Users' Directory of Computer Networks by Tracy Lynn LaQuey, published by the University of Texas System Office of Telecommunication Services, 1989. Appendix B of this book contains a generic list of protocols for mail exchange between disparate networks.

schemes—nets and regions. Nets occupy a geographic area on the order of a few counties, and regions are larger state-level groupings. A node is an individual machine attached to a net or a region. Association with a net or region depends on geographic location and the density of other FIDO nodes in the area, among other factors. Each node has a number and is associated with either a net or a region, but not both.

In a 100% distributed network, each user *is* a node operator. The cost of transcontinental, or even transglobal mailing, is borne entirely by those who use the network and is proportional to their use. Though simple, this topology is being fostered by declining long-distance rates on the dial-up telephone network, and even more so by the availability and declining price of high-speed dial-up modems. As the cost-per-kilobit ratio continues to decline, it becomes practical to use a simple but direct configuration for an increasing proportion of the total amount of data exchanged between nodes. If a node has other users—that is, it is a single or multiline BBS in its own right—then the node operator must have some local arrangement with his or her users regarding the cost of exchanging mail. It is possible for individual nodes to make arrangements with their net or regional contacts for mail forwarding, which opens up some potentially cost saving techniques. If the node operating as a net nucleus or regional focus carries a large enough volume of data, it may be cost-justified to permit or originate connections through a packet service.

High-speed modems with sophisticated compression and error checking are another alternative. They are less expensive all the time, but still beyond the reach of most small node operators. If the financial arrangements are satisfactory to all parties, a focal machine at a given level in the hierarchy may act as a high-speed data conduit to other systems at its own level; this, of course, entails yet other arrangements with those hosts for further distribution to the next lower level in the hierarchy. Most of the FIDO regional and net level nodes now employ HST modems operating at 14.4 Kbps, which exchange as much as 10 megabytes of echoed conference data each day.

Echo conference distribution involves just such negotiations. Each node operator makes arrangements with the local net or regional node for echoing conferences to and from that local node. Typically, the terminal node will do the calling in a prearranged time window; mail and conference entries coming to and leaving from that node are exchanged, and the cost is borne by the node operator exactly in proportion to his or her traffic volume—including the volume of conferences being echoed! The node operator also subscribes, on a monthly or yearly basis, to the transport services of the machine at the next level up in the hierarchy. This defrays the operator's cost of maintaining the node and its calls to other net- or regional-level machines; operators at this level have calling-window and cost-distribution arrangements with one another.

The FIDO network itself is dynamic. The node lists maintained by each machine have only to do with point-to-point mail. Conference echoes are always routed through the domain scheme, though the hierarchy itself is fluid. Any operator at the lowest level of the hierarchy can elect to move up a level by supporting other nodes below him- or herself. Since private mail is still, for the most part, routed point-to-point, the relative size of an echo center has only to do with the number of conferences echoed and the attachments required to receive them. For example, a node in Provo, Utah, may connect with another in Salt Lake City for some portions of its echo mail, and another in Denver or New York to receive conferences echoed across the Atlantic.

■ 5.5 ROUTING MECHANISMS

FIDO relies on *domain naming* for its addressing. That is, each node has a unique name associated with a specific node one level up in the hierarchy, its domain. By contrast, uucp mail uses a technique called *source routing*. In this mail network, all machines are technically peers; there is no hierarchy. Any machine can establish a direct connection with any other machine on the network, but mail can be (and usually is) also routed from machine to machine along a path assigned ahead of time by the user on the source machine. Each machine maintains a map—phone numbers and connection information used by the link-establishing software—of the machines it contacts on a regular basis.

The connection maps of each machine must intersect with those of other nodes, and it is the mail originator who ultimately must build a path from map to map (most machines maintain copies of most maps) ending at the remote machine. A uucp address is a string of machine names ending with a user who receives the mail on the last machine. Each individual node has a name that is unique only to the extent that all nodes with which it communicates have no other *immediate* or *second* generation neighbors bearing the same name.

uucp and Usenet maps are not used by the mail exchange software in any automatic way, as are the corresponding FIDO maps; the connections established in FIDO are imposed by the map, whether direct or via the net and regional centers. In uucp, because of an enormous redundancy in the web of interconnecting nodes, there may be any number of alternate routes between two systems. Recent extensions to mail protocols include a convention for establishing network-wide unique names; this permits the development of automatic routing systems based on the source-path-routing technique.

Mail software has been enhanced to build routes automatically from a combination of machine and user names that appear in the maps contained on each host. These developments, coupled with almost total compliance with the network-wide naming standard, result in a virtual domain-naming system from the user's viewpoint. Mail is still associated with a route specified from end to end, beginning with the source system. Construction of the path is, however, transparent to the user, who need only name a user on a machine.

There are some difficulties with this approach. The primary problem is the lack of provision made for rerouting around temporarily disabled machines if they happen to appear in the path list. Although there are well-established and reliable centers that regularly carry long distance traffic, there is no guarantee that any given machine, especially in nontrunk nodes, will always be available. The result is returned mail, bouncing back to the originating user from the last system reached in the path. Of course, this problem can occur on the FIDO network as well, but if it does, it is only the operators at the affected hierarchy level who must coordinate calling schedules and distribution paths. By contrast, *every* node operator throughout the uucp network must become aware of a problem with a given node and make appropriate adjustments to the maps.

On the other hand, there are some advantages to source routing. It is inexpensive and facilitates network extensions on an ad hoc basis. New nodes can be added

anywhere on the network without coordination with existing nodes; so long as at least one machine already on the net will agree to exchange mail with the newcomer, it is, in effect, added. The next time the existing node's map is updated and distributed throughout the network, the new node's name will appear on it. In fact, it is not even necessary that a node, or group of nodes appear on any map so long as the sender is able to specify a proper end-to-end path beginning with the last mapped node. Of course, such a nonmapped node cannot participate in the netwide naming system or be reached using automated path building software.

■ 5.6 DISTRIBUTION BY FLOODING

The Usenet broadcast uses the source-path technique just as FIDO uses its hierarchy. Rather than bearing the burden of maintaining an up-to-date dictionary or map of the entire system, each node must only be aware of a few neighbors. For the transmission to take place, at least one of those neighbors must connect to another that is not a part of the common set of neighbors; this next "outside" machine must have at least one neighbor that satisfies the same condition, and so on.

At its simplest, the entire network becomes a star or a string of machines like beads on a thread. A directed graph of such a network—a digraph, with circles representing individual nodes, and lines representing connections (telephone links) between nodes—must be at least weakly connected; there must be at least one traceable path from each machine to every other node. If, for example, a critical machine link is inoperative, the net would behave as two separate networks, each unaware of the other's existence. News is not routed end-to-end as is mail. Instead, each node simply uses the existing mail exchange software to echo news (conference texts) to all its immediate neighbors. So long as the network is fully connected, the news will eventually reach every machine on the network (see Figure 5.4).

Figure 5.4 illustrates a complete flooding network. Network A is strongly connected to B through node F. Network B is weakly connected to A through node G and strongly connected through H. If node H failed, messages would travel from network B to network A, but not the other way around. The reverse holds for node G. If node F fails, the two networks would be completely isolated.

A partitioning of the Usenet is unlikely as the network now exists because of its redundancy and well-established ad hoc hierarchy of trunkline nodes to which smaller sites are connected. Many lines on the network graph are connected to machines with neighbors qualifying as gateways to the rest of the network. Usenet is also older and much larger than FIDO. Large universities, technology corporations, and the regional Bell Operating Companies maintain reliable high-volume nodes, so these sites, used for mail *and* net news distribution, maintain state-of-the-art connection technologies. Some of the trunk centers are connected with others by fiber-optic cable. Data exchanges occur every hour or even more frequently.

Consider also what happens to terminal nodes of the FIDO network if their net or regional nodes are disabled. Those operators must spend time making financial and call-scheduling arrangements with other net-level nodes, or they might have to change their machine names (numbers) because the original number may be used by another

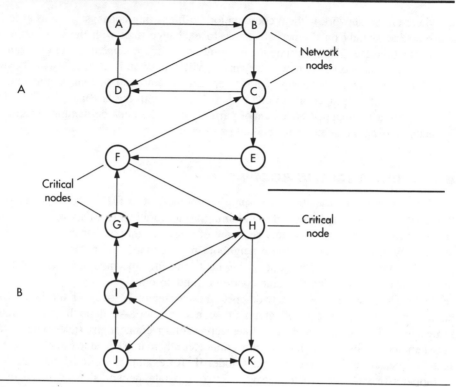

Figure 5.4 Connected graph of a broadcast type network. In this illustration, two networks, A and B, are connected through three nodes: (G), (H), and (F). Node (F), in network A, is the most critical point of failure because it is responsible for both transmission to and receipt of messages from network B. Nodes (G) and (H) in network B are partial failure points. If (G) fails, network B can recieve but not send messages to A. If (H) fails, B's messages can be sent to A, but none can be received.

node in the new net. In Usenet, the disappearance of even a large trunk node only means that the reflected news will reach that center's neighbors via other machines (unless that disabled node was the only neighbor).

5.6.1 A Few Difficulties with Duplicated Message Bases
One of the technical problems arising from conference distribution is message duplication. By establishing distribution conventions among the human operators of the network, the FIDO network minimizes (but does not eliminate) this problem. On the sending side, each node checks a list of nodes already having the message before forwarding conference material. This list is appended to the end of each message by each machine through which it passes (it is stripped in the user interface, and therefore invisible to human readers). If the receiving machine is already on the list, the sender removes the message from the list of those queued for transmission, and if not, the sender appends its own ID to the list and transmits it. This eliminates most but not all duplicates. The rest are handled on the receiving side through examination of the

message author, date, subject, and reply-to fields of a record; any that exactly match existing records are discarded. The FIDO software is also capable of generating a guaranteed unique message ID for every text created on the network, so the receiving software need only compare a text's ID to those already present in its message base.

The hierarchy-less configuration of Usenet makes duplicate detection on the sending node more difficult; this network therefore relies on detection at the receiving end. Before 1987, its method was identical to the first FIDO technique—examining the header fields of a text and comparing all their values to messages already present. Since that time, participating sites cooperate in generating a network-wide unique ID for every message. Contemporary Usenet software maintains a dictionary of all recently seen IDs and compares new ones to this list. The list recycling period is long enough to ensure that no number is discarded before any message with that ID could possibly reach a given machine. In the current network, this is typically a matter of a few days.

5.6.2 Advantages of Replicated Distribution

So far as computer conferencing and electronic mail are concerned, distributed systems have three technical advantages over a centralized configuration. One is the independence of the conference from the status—the availability—of any one machine at any given time; if a centralized conference host goes down, its conferences are temporarily suspended. In a distributed system, especially one using the broadcast technique, no single machine can halt the whole conference. The second advantage has to do with efficient use of telecommunications links between machines on the net. In centralized configurations, capacity is wasted while lines remain open and underutilized. Systems wait for users to make decisions or type text. Transfers in distributed systems can take advanage of the full capacity of available communication channels, and lines remain open only as long as required for exchange of new material.

The third advantage is the overall data volume that must be transported among network users to read from and write to a conference. Under typical read/write ratios (the amount of material read divided by that written by each user), the amount of data moved around a distributed, replicated conference is less than that communicated to users of a centralized system.

Consider a simplified centralized system with a 10MB text base and 100 users. If each user reads 100KB a day and writes 1 KB (a 100/1 ratio typical of crisis resolution applications), then the total data transported through the user population each day is (100KB + 1KB) × 100 users, or 10.1MB. If the read/write ratio is 10,000/1 (more typical of public use), this model will ship 10.01MB per day. In a similar-sized, purely distributed (and replicated) network with 100 systems, in which each starts with the full 10MB base and a read/write ratio of 100/1, each machine will have to receive, at a minimum, 1KB from every other machine (99 x 1). This set of transfers is repeated 100 times (once for each machine) for a total transfer of 9.9MB. If the read/write ratio is 10,000/1, the total data shipped in the distributed configuration is only 99 (machines) x .01KB x 100 users or 99KB/day. Of course multiple (redundant) links between nodes (with message duplication) will cause data volume to be larger than suggested in this minimal model. Yet even this effect is mitigated by high inter-system channel capacities and the capacity to batch messages for efficient transmission if dial-up connectionc to remote hosts are required.

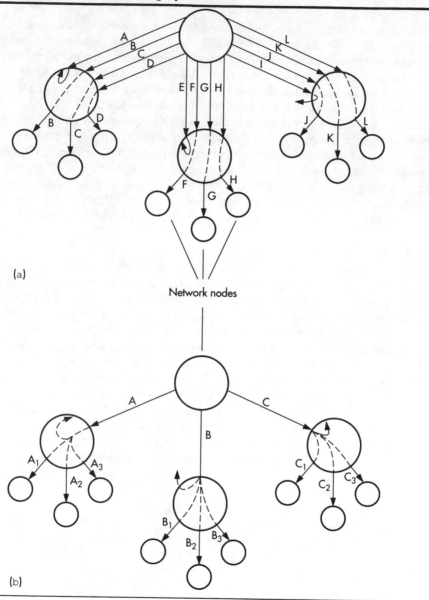

(a)

Network nodes

(b)

Figure 5.5 Routing multiple instructions with and without remote execution.

5.6.3 Remote Login and Remote Program Execution

Services provided in some network and internetwork environments like remote program execution—the ability to direct a remote node or a set of such nodes to execute some program on each machine—are very useful. Suppose, for example, that one wished to provide for the automatic execution of a DBMS routine on a set of nodes in a network. This routine might assimilate transmitted data and combine it with local data to produce the results. Rather than try to coordinate the execution of these routines on all machines, which would require a search and decision regarding the presence or absence of transmitted data, the starting machine need only transmit instructions for the routine's execution along with the data.

In Fig. 5.5a, separate messages must be transmitted from the node starting the transaction to each of the addressed remote nodes. Several individual messages will pass through the same intermediary node, destined for nodes yet another hop away. However, only one message is required from the head node to the secondary level in Fig. 5.5b. This message contains not only the request for data from the secondary nodes, but also instructions to replicate the request and send it along to the tertiary level; this replication process is an example of remote execution.

Remote login is another powerful service provided on a few large-scale networks. It is essentially the interactive side of remote execution. As early networks of microcomputers primarily served to provide sharing of expensive peripherals, large-scale dispersed networks can provide for sharing of expensive computer resources located at but a few sites. Besides on-line connections to supercomputers, remote-login facilities permit utilization of interactive software and databases available only on certain nodes. This permits the entire network to specialize in certain areas, with each node providing services not present in the others.

The value of these last two features of distributed systems emerges from the fact of distribution. Neither makes sense in a centralized configuration, because any authorized user of a centralized host can execute any software available on the host. These features are not so much advantages of distribution as they are extras—facilities required to provide the same internal functionality as any central multiuser system. Having these features does make a distributed network as a whole potentially more powerful than any single centralized machine. Conference applications per se, however, have no requirements that warrant the potential inherent in large-scale network specialization, with the possible exception of specialized database access.

▪ 5.7 SOME PRACTICAL CONSIDERATIONS

5.7.1 Message Bases out of Phase

Distributed systems like single-user BBSs do not typically support real-time synchronous communications; in this case, it is the result of a double asynchrony. Centralized conferencing is asynchronous when users are not logged in at the same time, but if multiple simultaneous logins are supported, then synchronous conferencing is at least theoretically possible. Distributed systems support asynchronous conferencing (in the conventional sense) and multiple simultaneous connections on *different* machines that are not typically in dedicated continuous contact with one another.

The conventional layer of asynchrony operates as users read and write to conferences at random times. Therefore at any one time, the copies of conferences on various machines are not identical. Because they are inconsistent, they are therefore asynchronous in another sense as well. On a central system, a conference is always consistent—identical to itself, but when multiple copies are involved, the copies never quite match unless there has been no activity (no new records added to the conference) since the last entries were distributed to the entire network.

In theory, dedicated high-speed connections can nearly eliminate the consistency problem. Such connections, which emerged in the late 1980s, now obtain between most of the largest trunk nodes in Usenet. The ebb and flow of activity among machines on or next to trunk sites has become so fast as to make synchronous exchange possible, but the cost of doing so restricts implementation to a small group of big machines. The majority of the network must still wait a few hours at least for conference updates, and although this is quite satisfactory for much conferencing activity, it puts distributed systems at a severe disadvantage in some conference domains.

Overhead in data exchange volumes and double asynchrony are two technical disadvantages of a distributed configuration, and there are other problems of a political and administrative nature. For example, not every machine on the network carries every conference. There are now over 400 newsgroups on Usenet, and new groups come and go daily. If selectivity were applied only at terminal ends of the network, this wouldn't be a problem, but some conferences are eliminated at nonterminal nodes (nodes that forward news to others) for political or economic reasons (or both). The subject matter of a particular conference may have political implications; economics may be a matter of system size—the inability of a given node to contain all the events and information that transpire on the net.

5.7.2 Class Stratification in User Populations

Other problems with distributed configurations are inherent and have no convenient solution. In a large network, some machines may be only minutes apart; that is, new conference entries on one machine may appear on others in minutes or hours. On the other hand, machines in remote parts of the network may not receive the new information for one or two days, thereby producing classes of participants. Upper-class nodes have far more influence on the course of a conference than users of lower-class nodes do, simply because they have faster access to new material.

The volume of news engenders another problem because of the varying storage capacity of network nodes. Not only will machines carry and pass different subsets of all the conferences, but texts are retained for different periods. Some machines will keep messages around for months, others for weeks, and smaller machines can afford to keep them only for days. If users are not participating frequently enough, they may miss entries entirely. Even when they do not miss messages, backward references may be traceable for some period on some machines and impossible to follow on others. This problem has spawned a common practice of excerpting sentences or paragraphs from prior messages in the body of a new entry; this custom solves the citation problem (if context is respected) but it increases the volume of data transported throughout the network because the texts of many messages contain lines copied from earlier postings as reference anchors!

5.7.3 Directory Services in Replicated Systems

Another problem in this vein has to do with the lack of distributed directory services. For example, Usenet has no inherent directory system; while individual nodes may (and often do) maintain files that users can search to find people with common interests or discover electronic addresses, there are no such facilities serving the network as a whole. Usenet *is not* unique in this regard; it is an endemic problem with echo conferences of all kinds. Many small networks are sharing conference streams (see Chapter 8); all of these use the replication technique. In reading through a conference on one node of such a network, there is rarely any indication of where particular messages originate (the Internet is an exception). A user may attempt to get directory information on a given author, for example, only to discover that the person in question is not local to the user's node.

The significance of good directory services was never lost to the developers of the larger centralized communications systems. Being able to find biographical information about conference participants or to determine who has read what in a particular topic are among the important services provided by more elaborate conferencing packages. The availability of this information enhances the sense of community in a group communications environment. It may also provide essential information to users who wish to query others on a private basis.

There is nothing to prevent the distribution of directory (participant) information. Problems to be solved are analogous to those facing distributed systems in general. These include volume and maintenance (update) issues; to date, however, developers of distributed systems have not thought it important enough even to try to deal with the problems, leaving some of them to future resolution in network-wide, universal directory services.

5.7.4 Historical Contingencies

The FIDO exchange protocols were developed as an extension of application-level software. They were imposed from the top, and any machine capable of supporting their functionality will operate as a node in the FIDO network. Usenet was evolved on top of an existing physical protocol for formatting and encapsulating messages for routing from machine to machine. An accepted set of standards for making connections— mutual recognition between machines—also existed, and the software required to establish these connections was universally available on UNIX-based hosts.

The FIDO network is composed primarily of single user machines in which the system operator *is* the user. The hierarchical FIDO network is a working compromise among many factors, including transmission efficiency and ease of use. By contrast, Usenet is composed mostly of interconnected multiline computers, centralized multiuser systems in their own right. Personnel with the skills required to maintain these systems and their network are always available. Because it grew in an ad hoc way, its interconnections are complex; it pays a price for redundancy but gains an extraordinary resiliency as a result.

▪ 5.8 BRIDGING NETWORKS

There are other networks besides FIDO and Usenet in widespread use. Some of these, like DEC's EasyNet, IBM's Vnet, and the Xerox Internet are associated primarily with those corporations and their customers. Others, like the Arpanet, CSNET, the BITNET, and ACSNET are primarily educational, with some corporate participation. (CSNET is uncommon in deliberately functioning as a net of networks—a meta-network.) The military has its own network—the MILNET—as well. Each of these has counterparts in other countries.

Each of these networks arose from a perceived need or desire to link together computer users with common interests. Some of these nets have nodes belonging primarily to one hardware type, one operating system, a common middle- to upper-level communications protocol, or a shared general purpose like research. The best-known example of linkage at the middle layers of the ISO model is Internet, whose many hosts all employ the terminal control protocol at the transport layer on top of the Internet protocol at the network level. The traffic in each of these is composed of mail, files, and sometimes conferences—analogous to Usenet. A few, the uucp network included, sometimes support remote program execution.

There are also networks of very different kinds, optimized for speed, remote program execution or data acquisition at the expense of size; local area nets (LANs), corporate wide area networks (WANs), and metropolitan area networks (MANs) fall into this category. Though typically controlled by a single entity—in other words, centrally administered—these networks are still collections of semiautonomous users with their own computing resources. They could support conferencing of either a distributed *or* a centralized nature (via remote login), taking the best from both worlds. All must provide various levels of service between user applications on multiple hosts and the lowest levels of the electrical or optical system physically connecting them. However they are supported in each vendor's products, their functional operation can be mapped into one or more of the layers of the ISO seven-layer connection model.

5.8.1 Three Bridge Strategies

Bridging dissimilar networks has become an important technological, economic, and political issue. Resources are wasted as users on various networks must solve similar problems without the benefit of interconnection. To bridge networks, dissimilar protocols must be translated because services operating at equivalent layers of the OSI model cannot understand the conventions of their counterparts in disparate networks. There are three logical translator configurations.

- Performing translation entirely on one network, demonstrated by Fig. 5.6a; as far as Network B is concerned, it is communicating with another network exactly like itself.
- Providing translation services through cooperation of both networks (Fig. 5.6b); both networks are aware of the other's differences.
- Performing translations for nets connected through a special device (a dedicated piece of hardware, or possibly another network—see Fig. 5.6c). In this case, both networks view each other as being exactly like themselves.

The third approach is potentially the most efficient and versatile. The bridge device examines network traffic; if addressed to the other network, translation takes place and data is routed across the bridge. The hardware and software dedicated to translation and

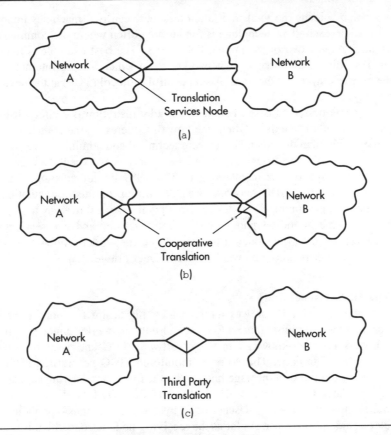

Figure 5.6 Three internetwork translation strategies.

bridging services can be optimized for that task, achieving high throughput for fully translated and rewrapped data blocks. Bridging devices can serve as hubs for more than two networks at a time; this method is used most often in connections between high-speed LANs (or LANs and WANs). It is the most expensive in capital outlay. The presence of special hardware demands maintenance and administration practical only in applications where all networks are under some umbrella jurisdiction—campuses and large corporations come to mind.

The second approach involves software on both networks but no special hardware. A standard network node is appointed to bridging tasks. Software running on bridge nodes of both networks communicates with itself across the bridge, acknowledges the exchange of data bound for the local net, and performs translations. This process is less efficient than the first approach because the software on both ends runs (usually) on generalized hardware supporting a user population with other computer services. Yet it may, to some degree, be optimized.

For one thing, the software on each end has primarily to concern itself with translations to and from its own local protocols. On the bridge side, it may exchange data in an intermediate form, only partly translated into the protocols of the other side;

thus cooperation spreads the total translation task between two machines imposing a minimum load on each. This technique is found most often where the communicating networks share one or two of the middle OSI layers. The best example is Internet, a collection of medium- and large-scale networks, all of which use the Internet protocol (IP) at the network layer and the transmission control protocol (TCP) at the next higher (transport) layer.

The first technique serves best where network administration is entirely distributed and no umbrella authority exists. Often, the thrust of interest in the connection comes more from one side than the other. Even where technical and administrative conditions would permit a cooperative bridge, a single-sided one is less expensive because only one network must spend time maintaining it. The 1989 implementation of a bridge between Usenet and the FIDO network is an illustration of this configuration; both employ proprietary communication services from level seven all the way through level three. Each uses the public telephone network for level one and two services. Both have been linked to the OSI model at the level three (network) layer with interfaces to X.25, but this link is not employed by the FIDOnet bridge.

5.8.2 The FIDO-Usenet Bridge

The bridge built by Tim Pozar was motivated by his desire to connect the FIDO network to the older and more famous Usenet and uucp networks. Since the protocols of each network are well-known, Tim wrote software (in C and assembler) that ran exclusively on a FIDO node. This software monitored FIDO net traffic for the string "uucp" placed at the top of a message body. When it finds such a string, it takes these messages, translates them into the files and formats required by the uucp protocol, and forwards them to a uucp or Usenet node by the usual means—periodic dial-up polling by one side or the other. As far as the receiving node is concerned, it is dealing with another uucp-based machine. This node contains the FIDO machine on its node map, and considers it a uucp node that happens to be named FIDO! Mail and net news destined for FIDO and beyond are routed to the bridge as uucp data. On the FIDO side, this time as receiver, the bridge software translates the uucp containers into FIDO containers and passes them into the FIDO network.

The FIDO-Usenet bridge illustrates the complexity of the bridging task. The software has about 100,000 lines of source code and serves to route only text data. The uucp network supports both binary data transfer and remote program execution; the former is supported in FIDO, but neither service is supported across the bridge.

Because of the complexity of the translation task, electronic mail is always the first and often the only kind of traffic that can pass between networks; even conferences, which are, after all, streams of text, are not typically visible across a translating gateway. The FIDO bridge is an exception. Other services supported on homogeneous networks, including binary file exchange, presentation level graphics, remote login, remote program execution, and domain addressing (network-wide naming) are almost never supported across network boundaries. One exception to this rule exists among much of the collection of academic and research networks called the Internet. Not only E-mail, but remote login and execution, Usenet conferences, and even a synchronous communications facility called Internet Relay Chat (IRC) are widely available. These services are made possible by exceptionally high-bandwidth dedicated connections between the participating networks in the Internet. The presence of these services demonstrates the potential inherent in high-bandwidth connections.

5.8.3 E-mail Service Standards

Because electronic mail is popular and because all of these large-scale networks support mail, it is not surprising to find that E-mail is the first and often only application supported in internetwork traffic. Conferencing, mail, and most other applications users are familiar with function at the highest, or applications layer, of the OSI model. User and vendor demands have driven the ISO and other standards organizations to focus on agreements for this upper layer, now that the lower three layers are relatively well-developed. This still leaves layers four through six trapped in a mire of competing protocols (including the ISO suggestions). The parties involved recognize that if protocol agreements can standardize the highest layer of the system, then lower-layer conversions will not impose translation requirements in the most important segment of the model—applications software for end-users.

The ISO has therefore developed and ratified the X.400 text-message format standard. Its importance is signaled by the appearance of products and the pledge of most network vendors to support it before it was ever formally adopted by the ISO. Like other ISO and CCITT standards, X.400 is a standard for *internetwork* exchange of text records. The standard does not purport to address protocols inside networks managed as one domain (say a corporation, university, or government). Mail exchange is the most common application, but documents or files consisting of text or binary information are also supported. Although many network software vendors have pledged to support it inside their networks, it is not required that they do so in order to be X.400 compliant. Rather, they must support gateways (translators) to and from X.400 format in any connection *between* their product and other networks.

■ 5.9 THE ISO X.400 AND X.500 STANDARDS

X.400 is a set of standards. Each one deals with a different subset of the information associated with text messages, and the set comprises a complete message handling system (MHS). It includes user agents (UAs), software devices that communicate directly with the end user; message transfer agents (MTAs), independent programs serving a computer installation moving messages between UAs through intervening MTAs; and the protocols used to communicate between them. These standards are described in the CCITT *Red Book* of 1984, and updated in the *Blue Book* of 1988, ratified in 1989. Because it is so important and because there is a high-level model of text-based communication implied in it, we will take up the X.400 set in some detail in Chapter 7.

The X.400 specification, however, says nothing about one of the toughest internetwork problems—that of finding addresses. To this end, the ISO proposed the X.500 suite, which takes advantage of message ID specifications and incorporates them into a global internetwork directory system. The X.400 standard accounts for the generation and recognition of an internetwork-wide global address, but not a way to produce that address as the result of a user query. That is, it provides no directory service analogous to the telephone white and yellow pages. The X.500 specification addresses that need.

As with the X.400 proposal (Sec 5.10), there are competing directory systems. Internet users have access to a distributed domain name service (DNS), which functions to generate addresses (paths) for names, as X.500 is supposed to do. X.500, however, provides for much more; it functions as a general database of information about users *and* systems. Its data structure is hierarchical in nature and provides information about objects of many kinds. Besides users, these include shared resources like programs, CPUs, output devices, or any other discreet object nameable in a large network. Like X.400, X.500 addresses the inherent autonomy of distributed systems by being broken up into subcomponents, directory user agents (DUAs), directory service agents (DSAs), and the protocols required for their interconnection, both to each other and to the directory data structure itself.

Even X.500, when fully implemented, will not provide some fundamental services associated with centralized conferencing software since its inception. Given a network-wide X.500 directory, it will be possible to find biographical information about conference participants whether local or remote and to assemble a list of participants in a given conference and to crossreference this list with common interests, geographical locations, and so on. It will not, however, be possible to determine who has read a given message or what messages a given user has read in a conference. This information is immediately available in centralized configurations, and also in non-replicated distributed configurations like that of VaxNotes. To provide such a service in a replicated system, however, would entail network-wide transport of information regarding read messages on each participating node. Even ignoring the time-lag problem, such data would add enormously to the overall volume passed across the net, and could quite possibly require more resources than the distribution of the messages themselves.

5.9.1 Barriers to X.400 and X.500 Implementation

The main barrier to rapid implementation of X.400 and X.500 is economic in several senses. First, vendors have much invested in proprietary E-mail, conference, and directory systems. Most pay lip service to the value of global connectivity, but they are not at all sure that adopting the ISO standards will be good for everyone. Second, the development and testing of standards at the highest level of the OSI model is complex and expensive. At the time of this writing, there is no definitive way to demonstrate across-the-board compliance with the X.400 specification, let alone X.500. It is not easy to organize the required resources on both sides of a network gateway so that crossovers are properly implemented and tested. Third, there is the issue of how one network charges for another's traffic.

So long as few gateways exist or costing and charge back arrangements are established ahead of time, all is well. Yet if everyone supported the OSI application level standards, the resulting automatic connectivity would be offset by an increase in the complexity of tracking the traffic for purposes of distributing the costs. An agreement analogous to international postal treaties permitting free flow of mail across national boundaries is required.

∎ 5.10 OTHER APPLICATION-LEVEL STANDARDS

The ISO X.400 and X.500 recommendations are not the only protocol suites vying for the attention of application vendors. IBM and DEC would like very much to see their own systems become more widely adopted. In the mid 1980's the Usenet and uucp networks settled on a reasonably flexible physical standard for text messages defined in document RFC822. This standard addresses the same format issues as X.400 but not its whole message exchange model. Besides E-mail, the Usenet news conferences are gatewayed between networks more often than any other single service; because of this, and the historical significance of the uucp and Usenet networks, RFC822 and a newsgroup structural standard, RFC1036, have gained significant acceptance in the internetwork community.

∎ 5.11 DISTRIBUTING INFORMATION RETRIEVAL SYSTEMS

Turning once again to information retrieval, we can begin to see why such systems are rarely associated with distributed configurations. In one respect, information retrieval shares some common problems with the field of distributed computing in general. One of the goals of heterogeneous distributed computing systems is to make use of idle machine capacity; tasks that are not restricted (by nature or by administrative reasons) to running on specific nodes could use the resources of idle nodes. Problems include finding a node with the necessary resources, routing the data and instructions to that node, and getting the results returned to the proper place. These entail complex intersystem and interapplication communications, CPU-intensive no matter what the communication standard adopted. If the network is connected by dial-up telephone lines or dedicated but relatively slow long-distance links, the time wasted in establishing connections and routing will likely wipe out any gains made by distributing the computations.

This is not to say that information other than personal and group communications is not exchanged within and between existing networks. The Internet contains many repositories of text and binary data: programs, compilers, maps and other graphical data, documents, indexes, and so on. These may be retrieved by any user on the Internet, or machine gatewayed to the Internet through some translation point. Significantly, however, users must know what they want and where to get it. The network has no automatic means of finding the data in response to a user query.

One possible distributed information retrieval configuration would replicate all or most of the data over all the nodes of the network. This has the advantage of making most retrieval operations local. The update cycle of information retrieval data supports such a distributed scheme because new material can be added incrementally at regular scheduled intervals. Such a configuration also helps to ensure access to data for members of the network, even if one or more nodes are temporarily out of service. So long as the network supports either remote login or remote execution (in this case of a query statement), the data can be obtained from some other node. Good information retrieval databases are, however, very large. There are few machines on any network that can afford to provide the space required.

Distributed nonreplicated databases, however, are especially sensitive to the network's overall traffic load. A user query could involve one or more machines, none of which are known to the user. Like a distributed name server, the distributed data server would have to route the request to all possible information servers in the network (imagine the overall computation and communication overhead encumbered by hundreds of these requests introduced each minute throughout the network).

Storing enough classification information for the local data servers to know *which* network machines had relevant data would increase performance markedly at the cost of extra overhead to maintain the local dictionaries. Much of this cost could be mitigated by the introduction of a few specialized dictionary servers to the networks. A querying node would address the nearest dictionary server machine, determine where the data is likely to be, and then issue the appropriate retrieval instructions from only these machines.

In any case, the overall network resources consumed by a query are still expensive. Some results might be available in seconds if the data was on the local node, but it might take minutes, hours, or even days to return data from remote nodes, depending upon the connection configuration and the exchange technology used—dial-up telephone, dedicated high-bandwidth cable, and so on.

The nonreplicated form of distribution has one very attractive feature—although few machines can maintain a very large database, the network as a whole can maintain a database far larger than any single machine. Even databases in the terabyte range become feasible if distributed across dozens or hundreds of machines, provided there is an efficient way to recover the data. Unfortunately (for now), except where the network is relatively small and the machines are connected by dedicated high-speed links and controlled by one entity, there isn't any way to accomplish this task without dedicating most of the network to it.

Response delays of several hours or even a few days may be acceptable for many kinds of interpersonal communications. This is almost never the case in information retrieval applications, where professionals are accustomed to response times in the seconds, and anything more than minutes is rarely acceptable. The DecNet architecture would support this kind of information retrieval operation, but it has not been used extensively for large-scale information retrieval tasks. Whatever the distributed architecture, the ability to make information retrieval work in such an environment depends on the bandwidth and moment-by-moment availability of internodal connections and the existence of a distributed data dictionary.

The dictionary is a repository of meta-data—data about the distributed database. Data dictionaries describe the structure of the data, its fields and their characteristics, and the location of the data. Like the database itself, the dictionary can be either distributed or centralized. If the database is entirely replicated, then the dictionary might as well be also. The same mechanisms used to update the data can be employed to update the dictionary when necessary; however, if different data are localized in different parts of the network, it may still be practical and cost effective to replicate the dictionary. The dictionary is smaller than the database and therefore easier to replicate and maintain across the network. Replicating the dictionary also means that each node on the network can determine *where* to go for other data prior to making a network connection.

If it is impractical to replicate the dictionary (say for political or security reasons), then one or a few machines may become network dictionary servers. One network-wide dictionary server is impractical in large networks because of the traffic it would service and because it is a single point of failure for the information retrieval system. Dictionary servers, whether one or many, also require more coordination among system operations and administrative staffs. Most network nodes will, at the least, maintain their own dictionary of local data. A query begins by searching the local dictionary and moves on to the server dictionary only if the data being sought is not on the local node.

In the next chapter, we will look more closely at user interface models and conference metaphors that have evolved in the various configurations we have considered here.

6

THE STRUCTURE OF COMMUNICATIONS MODELS

In this chapter, we will discuss communications models on two levels. The first concerns mapping conversations between persons—the communications model itself. The second level deals with the implementation of that model in the function of the user interface.

■ 6.1 COMPUTER MODELS OF INTERPERSONAL COMMUNICATIONS

6.1.1 Models as Communications Pipelines

When computers mediate communications between persons directly, they assume the role of pipelines and stores. They support each user's ability to filter an unmanageably large communications torrent, thereby producing an acceptable quantity and quality of response. What constitutes an acceptable quantity is purely in the eye of the beholder; this is true for quality as well, but metrics associated with precision and recall can be applied. The effect is that of a window onto a river of dynamically evolving discussion streams generated by other human beings. There are opportunities for professional association, entertainment, and political activity embedded in the circulating and ever-changing conversational repository. Fluid operation of each environment requires some practice, and conference software operation and presentation differ from system to system.

In human conversation, the meaning of a statement depends in part on its context, which is set by related statements of other persons, the conversational environment, and other factors. Context in the computer conference stems from an association of messages in some structure. There may be several structures or a hierarchy of structures involved. To appreciate the potentials of a conference application, the user must comprehend something of those structures and their relation to the tools used to manipulate them. Facility with this medium does not come automatically, but instead requires effort and practice on the user's part.

The versatility with which the computer allows the user to manipulate and enhance this contact depends on many factors, including historical influences on the software developer; available technology at the time of development (hardware and software); presuppositions respecting connection technology, standards, and design motivations (both technical and personal); the selection of physical structures for the data; and interface implementations. In this chapter we will explore particularly the effect of the last two factors.

■ **6.2 ONE-TO-MANY AND MANY-TO-ONE MODELS**

By the mid 1970s, electronic mail had proven itself an adaptable substitute for many purposes otherwise handled by voice-based telephone conversations. It does not convey information contained in intonations and inflections or other vocal cues, but its store-and-forward features are more than adequate compensation in many domains. The value of asynchronous capability was a fundamental assumption of electronic conference designers. This led them to examine other venues of human communication in which more than two persons were involved. The more people required to address a project or make a decision, the more difficult it is to coordinate their available time.

Some communication requirements involve many people on only one end of the conversation. Office memos broadcast from upper management to the employees of a corporation and memos or status reports from many employees to one executive are examples. Electronic mail can address these domains rather easily, except for a possible problem with message classification on the part of a recipient. If a user logs on to a mail system, he or she may discover 20 or 30 unread messages, which might concern a number of subjects. Users can usually look over the message subject fields, and thereby control the order of what they see, but this is a purely manual process. However, structured conferences support subject association automatically. Communications software developers focused on arenas in which many persons perform roles of both recipient and originator of information exchange. These range from informal association to professional gatherings to the formality of a courtroom, with many variations in between.

■ **6.3 SOCIAL ORIGIN OF MANY-TO-MANY MODELS**

Confer began with a model of persons who happened to be university faculty members examining arguments on administrative, financial, and academic proposals and registering their votes. It was but a step from there to debating the same proposals in the electronic forum along with the voting. Parti's founder, Harry Stevens, did his early research into electronic polling devices used for voting and learning feedback in live gatherings, classrooms, lectures, and other formal meetings. Jacques Valle and other developers of PLANET and Notepad began with a vision of the communications that might go on among experts in a given domain discussing some critical occurrence in the field. Their goal was to help move information quickly from experts present at the physical site of some event to others scattered around the globe and back again.

6.3.1 Personal Roles in Many-to-Many Communications

One of the overall structuring mechanisms adopted by every system is the concept of *roles* played by individual participants in the system's activity. Roles have two aspects; one is a participant's social function in relation to a conference or organization, and the other is his or her privilege or power to control the conferences' physical contents. In the latter aspect, roles vary from that of a superadministrator who can exercise all possible control over conference material provided by the software or system, to that of a user who can only read conference proceedings. Most systems support only a few role distinctions. There may be two types of administrators and two or three levels of user privilege. A user's control over his or her own text once it is released to the conference also varies from system to system. Customization of privileges on a conference-by-conference basis is supported on the better systems.

Informal role distinctions have much to do with creativity and spontaneity in the conversation itself. Administrative roles and user powers are formally enabled with software switches. Social role differentiation within a conference is not often formalized in special powers supported by the software. Most of the research conducted in the use of conference software has identified a need for persons whose activity helps stimulate the participation of others. This requirement is one of the distinguishing characteristics of electronic conferences, as compared to E-mail and information retrieval applications, and it is also a factor that hinders the acceptance and widespread use of text conferencing. Sometimes system administrators are also supposed to function in the "social facilitator" role, but the two jobs require different skills, tact and patience being common to both.

Application administrators should have a gift for attention to detail. They are responsible for the security, performance, and availability of the conversational arena; lower-level administrators assigned to one or a few conferences may have overall responsibility for their contents and conduct. In some application domains, there is also a need for individuals who encourage others from the user's perspective. As a system becomes a more important component of organization-wide communications, the role of the user-stimulator becomes that of user-expert-assistant. Those who contribute a great deal to the early adoption of a new communications system can become knowledgeable assistants and guides to new users.

6.3.2 Public and Private Conferences

Lack of adequate role support in contemporary communications products is reflected in crude support for private conferences in most systems. Most systems support some provision for limiting conference participation; conference content can be filtered and restricted in many ways, one of the most common being to close the conference to all but a named set of individuals. Maintaining the list of individuals eligible to participate in one or more private conferences is sometimes like mailing-list administration in electronic mail systems; the task is usually relegated to the individual conference administrators.

Few systems have the ability to link conference eligibility to corporate job functions—named classes—in which employees work. *Manager*, *director*, *engineer*, *office administration*, *systems*, *technical support*, and *customer support*, are examples of such classes. Many corporate communications requirements are related to the interests and activities of one or a few classes, while others cut across class boundaries and are project- or mission-related. Conferences should be related to these groups by name, and indirectly through these names to eligible participants—the individual users. Not only conference privacy but all administrative role distinctions should be supportable in this way.

■ 6.4 THE ROLE OF THE USER INTERFACE

The conceptual model meets the implementation model in the user interface. The interface is a collection of stylistic techniques for delivering data to and receiving input from a user. Its output reflects the structural levels superimposed on the organization of records that comprise the substance of communications. It is also the set of powers that the software gives the user to manipulate this data, along with its style of presentation.

At its most basic functional level, the user interface accepts commands and displays results. Some research into communications and information retrieval interfaces suggests a need for the interface to initiate action with the user. Rather than having to execute a series of operations to find new data, databases and conversational repositories might *interrupt* the user from time to time and *inform* him or her of new information. It should be convenient for the user to ignore the interruption. Modern E-mail systems provide some of this, but are unable to distinguish between important messages and junk mail. Research systems exploring sophisticated filtering systems, like MIT's "object lens," approach this capability.

Terminal emulation programs with capable script languages, or special communications programs written for the purpose, can at least automate the collection and some filtering of new information. Once available on the local workstation, review is largely up to the user. Current filtering and selection technology is relatively crude, but it is possible to incorporate author name, subject and word identifiers to support some of the qualitative judgments of users.

■ 6.5 COMMUNICATIONS STRUCTURES

Between the physical storage and the presentation of text there is a virtual structure—a logical framework in which the conversation object (the individual text record) is placed. To become an expert at manipulating the text already in the system and to participate fully in its generation, a user needs to understand the particulars of this logical structure as it pertains to his or her environment. The tools provided by the application software affect the data reflected through these structures. The power to manipulate the environment depends first on system constraints and presentation capabilities, and second on the ability of the tools or tool-building elements to operate flexibly on data shaped by conceptual structures.

In the 1970s and early 1980s, three primary structure models evolved. The first—the linear model—appeared in EMISARI and carried over into EIES at the New Jersey Institute of Technology. The second—the comb or book model—appeared in Confer at the University of Michigan. The Confer model has influenced more systems throughout the 1980s than all the others combined. The branch model, elaborated in COM from Jacob Palme of the University of Stockholm in Sweden and in Harry Stevens' Parti, was formulated in the late 1970s.

Each of these models is "formal" in the sense that individual contributions are attached to whole conversations as a single thread and not directly associated with any *specific* comment besides the one that began the chain. In the 1980s developers began experimenting with a fundamentally different model—one in which each comment might have other comments explicitly linked to it. This informal comment-in-context or comment-oriented model plays an important role in the current development of text-based communications systems (see Section 6.10 and Chapters 8 and 9). First we consider the three formal models in the context of their user interfaces.

■ 6.6 LINEAR STRUCTURES AND COMMAND PATTERNS IN THE EMISARI AND EIES MODELS

EMISARI was the first system to approach computer mediated management of human communications in a holistic way. It offered an uncluttered model for text organization (see Figure 6.1), a set of physical data structures containing relatively rich information *about* data instances (records), and a tool set permitting a wide range of mechanisms for threading through or filtering data. EIES communication structures include an open text space; individual mail boxes; records with defined formats (traditional flat-file database organization); binary attachments; personal and group notebooks; delphic voting, tabulation, and display; and tables. This last feature, the ability to express data in two dimensional tables and manipulate them for display (for example displaying only summary rows, or projecting values in the manner of a spreadsheet), is unknown in other conference software other than direct descendants of EIES, which adopted the EMISARI organization model and enriched the data structures. EIES extended the EMISARI tool set and added new facilities to customize the controls by combining commands—along with parameters, iteration, conditional execution, and so on—into scripts.

6.6.1 Virtual Structures In EIES

The EIES conceptual model is a time-sequential string of records hung from a first record. The first, or header record, is the starting point of a *conference*. The significance of conference differentiation in the text collection is two-fold: First, it sets the overall subject and establishes the basic communication structure; second, all the tools operate at the conference level. For example, a search for a particular combination of characters can apply to some subset of a conference's records or operate across *all* conferences on the system.

Structural variation is illustrated by the ordinary conference structure and the notebook. In conferences, participant entries are organized by time sequence, while in notebooks, the entries may be rearranged into any order by the users.

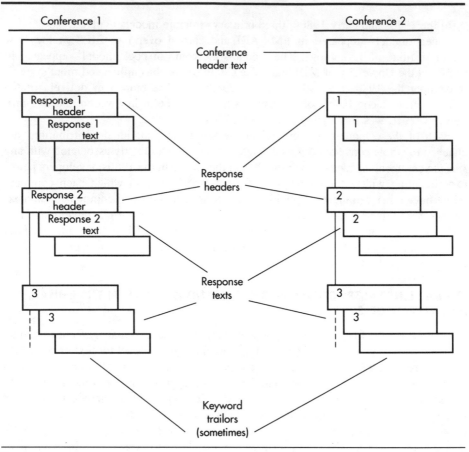

Figure 6.1 The linear communications model. Each conference is distinguished by a number and title. There may also be a text describing the purpose or content of the conference in general terms that may be displayed with a conference directory facility, if available. Responses to the conference merely follow a linear time sequence, and they may be grouped by keywords or other mechanisms if supported by the software. Keyword lists may be stored in either the reponse header records or in a trailer to the message text. EIES is the only major CMC system that uses this model; many early microcomputer-based BBSs also used it, but it has largely disappeared in favor of other structures.

Although the model is simple, EIES tools transform it into a variety of structured spaces. Users construct substructures by changing the set of filters used to organize the individual notes. The power of EIES' navigation facilities has partly to do with its extensive field addressability—the capacity to retrieve any note by its ID or keywords or otherwise manipulate data in specific record fields.

The same filters can apply to searches in the whole communications space. For example a string search on a keyword might result in the following display:

```
MATCHES FOUND FOR ITEMS:
C10 CC25, C10 CC56, C123 CC44, C234 CC89, C234 CC117, C234 CC118,
C420 CC19

7 MATCHES FOUND.
GET/DISPLAY (Y/N/T/#)?n

DO NESTED SEARCH(Y/N)?y

SEARCH CHOICE?
     .

     .

     .
```

In this example, the system returned seven records spread across four conferences. These can be re-searched, displayed, or thrown away. EIES supports searches on author name, date ranges, keywords, full text, record numbers, and any other values in fields defined for a specific conference. Only one field type can be searched at a time, however, so the nested search ability is important. The initial search might cover a keyword, while a subsequent search restricts the output by dates, text strings, or other factors.

6.6.2 EIES Electronic Mail

EIES has a powerful E-mail system. It supports one-to-one and one-to-many connections, along with mailing lists and reading aids. For example, readers can gather together all mail from one person and read it in reverse time sequence. Binary attachments to mail are also supported; presumably, the receiver has the software required to interpret them. Mail records can also reference conference records by including the conference record's unique ID. While reading mail, a user can jump to referenced records and examine them, later returning to the mail facility. This feature is not automatic, however, and is achieved by manipulation of EIES commands in scripts, coupled with the ability to execute such scripts from anywhere in the EIES environment.

6.6.3 Other Structures in EIES

Surveys are a special structure designed to get and process answers to questions. Results can be automatically tabulated and displayed in a number of forms; they can be admixed with conference texts, notebooks, or electronic mail via the editor or automatically assimilated as a table record. Conversely, comments in conferences can contain embedded pointers that allow users to follow a reference trail using EIES navigation commands.

Real-time synchronous conferences are supported by changing a single characteristic of the software's behavior. In a real-time conference, new records are displayed immediately to others viewing the conference at their time of entry (when the author commits a completed text to the conference). In asynchronous conferences, concurrent participants are informed about newly posted records but must deliberately issue a command to retrieve them; all messages are stored for later asynchronous retrieval and comment by other users.

The EIES text editor is an old-style line editor, sufficiently powerful to perform any normal editing and block transfer tasks executed on a line-by-line or line-range basis. Text from any part of EIES can be cut and pasted into editor buffers, modified, and then placed in any other part of the system. This permits fluid exchange and enhancement of documents throughout all EIES record types. The editor illustrates twin design goals. First, it gives users enough power to manipulate text in any way they may have to; second, it ensures that the system, including the editor, is accessible with as wide a range of terminal equipment as possible.

6.6.4 The EIES User Interface

The EIES user interface is command- and not menu-driven. Menu interfaces have emerged only since the early 1980s when higher speed modems (1200 bps) became common. When known, commands are more efficient because they do not require the transmission of menu screens. Commands on EIES are composed of one or more characters associated (possibly) with conference, message, and line numbers (lines within a record). For example, the verbs in the left column of Figure 6.2 are associated with the objects on the right to produce commands.

Commands are constructed by combining a verb with an object along with referents to messages in any of EIES' structures. For example, GC85,N would connect to conference # 85 and extract new comments. GN22NP5L1-15T gets notebook #

	Verbs			Objects
A	Add		A	Associations
C	Compose/Send		D	Directory
CA	Copy & Add		C	Conference
CY	Copy		G	Group
D	Display		K	Keys
E	Explain		M	Message
EX	Exchange		MG	Member/Group
F	Find/Search		N	Notebook
G	Get		NC	New Comment
L	Let		NM	New Message
O	Organize		NP	Notebook Page
P	Print		RM	Reminder
R	Review		SA	Storage Area
S	Set/Send		SP	Scratchpad
SN	Set Negative		SS	System Status
			T	Time & Date

Figure 6.2 Command verbs and objects in EIES.

22 page 5, lines 1 through 15 text part only, ignoring any binary attachments. Commands can also be stacked. For example, the command above could be followed by a ';' and then another command, and so on. This further increases the efficiency of the system's operation. For example, all of the interaction in Figure 6.3 could be eliminated with gc123,y,n;+scm 4/20/89;+gcc,y—that's "get conference 123, show me the status of conference participants, don't show me the new messages, set conference marker to 4/20/89, and show me everything entered since then."

```
INITIAL CHOICE?+gc 123
Public Conference:  FUTURE OF TELECOMMUNICATIONS (123)
You are the only member active.
MEMBER STATUS (Y/N/A/O)?y
UP TO 1818 [member name] [(nickname,NNN)] [(member role, e.g.
   ORGANIZER)]
UP TO 1815 [member name] [(nickname,NNN)]
UP TO 1812 [your name] [(nickname,NNN)]
UP TO 1800 [member name] [(nickname,NNN)]
367 items.   CC 1850 Written on  5/24/89  10:55 AM

38 new text items.
ACCEPT ABOVE ITEMS (Y/N/#)?n

CONFERENCE 685 CHOICE?+scm 4/20/89
Marker now reset.
CONFERENCE 685 CHOICE?+gcc
ITEMS (#/#-#/LAST #)?[return entered]
6 new text items.
ACCEPT ABOVE ITEMS (Y/N/#)?y

C123 CC1845  [remark author's name] (nickname,NNN)   4/21/89
   2:00 PM
KEYS:[key words if any given by originator]

Body of text...
   .

   .

   .
end of text...

C123 CC1846  [remark author's name] (nickname,NNNN) 5/20/89
   10:46 AM
KEYS:[key words]
```

```
Body of text...E class [Technological Forecasting], I had the

  .

  .

  .

end of text...

  .

  .

  .

[to end of message 1850]

CONFERENCE 123 CHOICE?+cc
Entering Scratchpad for CNNN Composition:
1? begin comment text here...
2? continue comment text...
3? .
N? .
N? end of comment text
N? +
Associated Comment(#/CR=None)?
Keys (word/phrase/CR=None)?
OK to Send? y
Added as C123CC1851
```

Figure 6.3 EIES conference status display and control example.

Each comment is identified by author, date and time, the author's nickname and ID number, the comment's ID number expressed as CNNN CCNNN, and the number of lines in the comment.

After reading through these comments, the user elects to enter one. The command +cc for "compose comment" takes the user into a scratchpad area—the editor's buffer—which may or may not contain text from previous work; one can either use this text or clear it. One can also force it cleared with +cnc—"compose new comment." A + on a line by itself signals the end of entry. At that point, the system allows the user to associate the message with another, add some keywords, and add the message to the conference. Further editing is also an option. One very interesting command, +gwcc, permits a user to group a series of conferences and collect all their new notes without having to move from conference to conference. This, in effect, creates a user-tailorable conference, at least as far as concerns reading notes. Messages can be composed and sent to any conference from anywhere in the EIES system. For example, a user viewing a new note in a conference on information transfer can assimilate it in his or her personal scratchpad and send it, with or without other text appended, to another conference.

EIES developers were never blind to the obscurity of this kind of control interface. Given their desire to exchange a minimum of control information, they allowed users to pick their way through conference and other message streams by letting them deal with one number or command-part at a time. At EIES' first prompt INITIAL CHOICE? a user can enter a ? and see a list of possible first-step commands. Further explanation of any of them is available. Once reminded of the numeric value of a

```
SEARCH CHOICE                        FOR BRIEF EXPLANATION, TYPE:

SEARCH BY
  NUMBERS/NAMES        (1)                ?1 and ??1
  STATUS/TYPE          (2)              NOT AVAILABLE
  COMBINATIONS         (3)              NOT AVAILABLE
  FROM-TO-DATES        (4)                ?4 and ??4
  WORDS/PHRASES        (5)                ?5 and ??5
  ASSOCIATIONS         (6)                ?6 and ??6
DISPLAY STRUCTURE OF
  KEYS                 (7)              NOT AVAILABLE
  ASSOCIATIONS         (9)                ?9 and ??9
  SEQUENCES            (10)             NOT AVAILABLE
SEARCH CHOICE?9                        NOT YET IMPLEMENTED


SEARCH CHOICE?5
WORDS/PHRASES (/TEXT/TEXT/)?/your string here/another/etc./
KEYS ONLY (Y/N)?y
ITEM RANGES (#-#,#-#/LAST #/CR=LAST 100)?last 135
(*LAST*:135 items scanned)
Matches found for items:
C982 CC31

1 Matches found.
GET/DISPLAY (Y/N/T/#)?y
  .
  .
  .
```

Figure 6.4 EIES search functions. This entire search could be executed from anywhere with the command +GCNNN,n;+F,5;/text to search/,y where "NNN" is a conference number. If this first command were absent, the system would search the conference currently referenced by the user, or the whole system if the user were not inside a conference. The options marked "NOT AVAILABLE" were not available to me in my role as visiting user.

command, the user may enter it and switch to the control module for that subsystem. An initial choice of 2, for example, results in the following prompt: CONFERENCE (NAME/#)? A ? at this prompt will yield a list of conference names and numbers the user can read, among other material. This is a classic incremental menu system that encourages rapid development of skills in combining commands. An example of interaction with an incremental menu appears in Figure 6.4. In this case, the user entered a ? in response to the EIES prompt SEARCH CHOICE?

The EIES model relies completely on a user's ability to slice up a monolithic collection of notes with powerful utilities. The linear model has fallen into disfavor; in some ways this is unfortunate, because it is the most easily manipulated by smart interface software; every response in the system is only one level away from the top of the organization chain. This provides developers with a simple anchor point from which to create numerous "virtual organizations" from which users can select to suit their purposes. "Intelligent interfaces" that can rearrange the ordering of responses in various ways are more difficult to build when new entries must be mapped to more complex logical organizations.

Most subsequent developers factored human communication into a hierarchy of two or more levels and gave nonadministrative participants the power to generate original entries and new topics at a level *below* the conference. Confer was probably the original expression of the popular two-level system known as the "comb" or "book" model.

■ 6.7 CONFER AND THE APPEARANCE OF THE COMB MODEL

Like those of EIES, Confer conferences are created by persons having special administrative authority. Conference subjects, however, are too broad to contain a coherent time-sequential thread of commentary coming from large numbers of users. As in a crowded party or a professional conference, groups of persons will break up into separate discussions. The conference subject encompasses subdiscussions as a whole, but they are otherwise specialized conversations. One of the measures of a good face-to-face convention is the degree to which ad hoc discussions are supported and related to the overall theme of the conference.

On Confer, subgroups are called items. Attached to conferences, they form the spine of the comb (see Figure 6.5). Items delimit discussion subthemes inside the conference. Each item is followed by one or more comments in an otherwise EIES-like sequential stream, the teeth of the comb. From the item level, a Confer conference looks pretty much like an EIES conference. The difference is that users with ordinary privileges can *create* new items. This permits users, like the people at a party, to form their own discussions or subgroups as the need or desire for them arises.

This could, of course be arranged in EIES by associating subthreads with certain keywords, but it would not be an automatic process. In Confer and other comb-structured systems, the interface software by default will usually move from item to item within a conference, displaying new entries to each user. Distinctions between item *types* also occurs underneath a conference, which support all types of items concurrently. Types include several vote and survey variations (one variation per item),

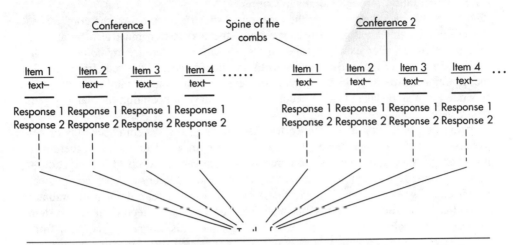

Figure 6.5 The comb communications model. Each conference consists of any number of *items* or *topics*. Each of these is associated with an opening text that describes the purpose of the topic or asks a question. Topics may be created by users in most circumstances; these topics form the spine of the comb. Below the topic level, responses fall in linear time sequence exactly like that of the linear conference model seen in Figure 6.1. These are the teeth of the comb. This model is very common because it achieves a good balance between a user's ability to start discussions on new topics and is simple to visualize at the same time. Like the linear model, each response also has a header portion which contains information such as author's name and date and time stamps. Header or trailer records may contain keywords if supported by the software.

an essay type (participants are restricted to making one entry in the item), and the common conference type. A special type, the bulletin, crosses item boundaries and informs an entire conference. It is like an individual response automatically posted to *all* items, except that it also appears immediately (in real time) to anyone who happens to be working in the conference when the bulletin is created.

It was the abuse of the bulletin facility, among other things, that led Bob Parnes to create a synchronous conference type. Confer real-time conferences are stand-alone objects, unrelated to other conferences. They are called *meetings* and can be created by any user. Inside a meeting, new entries are automatically displayed to all users then in the meeting. As users join and leave a meeting, their coming and going is signaled to others then on-line. As in conferences, the text of the meeting is stored for later asynchronous review. The meeting facility was designed to support short synchronous discussions when these were necessary or desirable and was separated from the asynchronous part of the software so as not to clutter items and threads with large amounts of text. Meetings can be extended asynchronously, but a meeting participant may also extract parts of the meeting and post them as records in an appropriate conference.

6.7.1 Navigation through Combs in Confer

Given the changes occasioned by the creation of substructures below the conference, the utilities provided to control user review of the text stream must also be attuned to the difference. For example, one enters a Confer conference by *joining* it. In EIES, one may *get* records associated with any conference, if desired, from outside the conference structure. In Confer, the conference is a context within which many separate discussions take place. It becomes the boundary of operation for many system commands.

If the user is joining a conference for the first time, the system checks his or her permissions for that conference. Public conferences are open to all users; there are, however, private conferences and conferences open to various levels of participation—multiple roles. To manage this, Confer maintains a user directory for each conference. When entering a conference for the first time, each user is asked for a biographical sketch of a few lines. This becomes part of the user's record in the system directory, searchable by other conference participants. This biography may vary from conference to conference so that user interests are related directly to the conference subject.

Unlike EIES searches, those of Confer will not cross conference boundaries. The search will return a list of item *and* response numbers that contain the strings sought. This list can be assembled as a single group of texts (a set) which can be the subject of further analysis or many display variations. Confer is one of a few systems that support some Boolean (and/or) operators in its search facility. It does not support parenthetical groupings of Boolean terms, but the set gathering abilities of the search command can achieve some of their effect with successive subqueries. Search commands can be modified to operate within an item or across a range of items, including the entire conference, but not other conferences.

Confer informs the user of the appearance of new responses in items already seen and of the existence of entirely new items. The command r new displays the new responses, and i new displays the new items and their responses. The same command with a modifier, i new browse would display the full text of the record entered to create the item (the item header) and then only the first two lines of subsequent responses. The command i new nor would display new item texts and skip the responses. When each new item is displayed, the user is given the option of RESPONDing—adding a comment to the item; FORGETing (see Section 6.7.2); or PASSing—moving on to read the next item.

6.7.2 Filtering and Display

The connection model envisioned by Bob Parnes was not exactly the same as that of Murray Turoff. Dr. Parnes envisioned more of an institutional system with a higher percentage of connections made by dedicated higher-speed lines, and terminals with some minimal display formatting capability. As a result, Confer is command-driven, like EIES, but its commands are English words and modifiers. Confer has editing facilities much like EIES and supports an extraordinary number of display formatting and content summarizing options. For example, the user entry item ? will elicit the response shown in Figure 6.6.

Note how many of the command modifiers in Figure 6.6 pertain to the format of the text display, how much is displayed, and in what order. Others have to do with enabling flexible response origination by the user. Users can, to some degree, customize their use of the system by establishing defaults for frequently used combinations of the above modifiers. Lists of default settings are maintained by the user in a personal "parameters" collection. If no modifiers are used (as in the example below), and there is no parameter list, the system uses defaults compatible with the most primitive user I/O devices.

```
DO NEXT?   i ?


The ITEM command lets you view the items in the conference.
Use the ENTER command to enter items.

The display of an item normally consists of the descriptor, the
text, the related items, all the responses to the item, and a
prompt for your response.  There are many modifiers that you can
use to modify the action of the item command.  The ITEM com-
mand given unmodified will display just the first "new" item
in the conference.

Two modifiers, *FILE* and *PRINT* are common to every command.
Enter "?" at DO NEXT? to find out how to use them.

The following are the possible modifiers of the ITEM command:


        all              [item number list]  pause
        browse           lifo                 previous
        change           load                 respond
        date             new                  reverse
        >date            next                 scan
        etc              nod                  text
        exact            nof                  this
        filesave         nop                  unseen
        first            nor                  *
        focal            nos                  "..."
        follow           not                  *dummy*
        forgotten        nov                  <index category>
        headers          pass                 {myindex category}


It is often appropriate to specify more than one modifier.  If
you do, use spaces to separate each one.
```

The ALL modifier displays all the items in the conference except forgotten, retired, updated or deleted ones.

The BROWSE modifier will cause Confer to print out just the first two lines of each response rather than the full response.

The CHANGE modifier will let you change your responses to the item or items you've specified. It is equivalent to saying CHANGE at the RESPOND, FORGET, OR PASS prompt.

The DATE modifier will cause Confer to print out the date each response was made. The date will appear just prior to the response.

The >[date] modifier restricts the output for the items designated to only the responses given since the date specified. The date must be given without embedded blanks (e.g., >10/29/82 or >Oct29 or >Tuesday).

The ETC modifier causes the items to be displayed in a logical sequence determined by each one's Next=field. The first item displayed will be the one named with an item number modifier, and thereafter items will be displayed in order until an item does not have a Next=field.

The EXACT modifier tells Confer to leave the left margins of your responses exactly as you entered them. That is, you don't want Confer to do automatic formatting of your response entries.

The FILESAVE modifier will cause each of the items named to be placed in a separate temporary file called "-item.nnn" where nnn is the number of the item in that file. In addition, Confer will build a temporary file called "-filesave" that will have the appropriate commands to save the "-item.nnn" files to a *FS tape.

The FIRST modifier restricts the display to the first item that satisfies the rest of the command specifications. It is usually used in conjunction with the FOCAL, NEW, UNSEEN, or * modifiers. The FOCAL modifier causes the items in the "Focal items" index category to be displayed.

The FOLLOW modifier causes the items in your personal "Follow these items" category to be displayed.

The FORGOTTEN modifier causes the items you have forgotten to
be displayed.

The HEADERS modifier causes Confer to print out a one line
header rather than the three line descriptor.

The [item number list] causes the item or items whose numbers
are given to be displayed. Elements in the list must be separated by commas; a range of items is designated by a dash. There
must be no spaces imbedded in the list. For example,
10,12,15-20.

the LOAD modifier causes the item (or items) named to be transferred to your Confer buffer file rather than to be printed at
your terminal.

The LIFO modifier causes the responses on the item (or items)
named to be printed out in reverse chronological order (Last
In, First Out).

The NEW modifier causes all the new items in the conference to
be displayed. Whenever you join the conference you are told
which items are new.

The NEXT modifier causes the item defined in the "Next="
field of the most recently displayed item to be displayed.
If no "Next=" field was defined for that item, then the
numerically next item will be displayed.

The NOD (nodescriptor) modifier causes the item to be displayed
without their three line descriptors.

The NOF (noforget) modifier expands the display to include all
retired, updated, and deleted items, along with their retired
and deleted responses, as well as any items you may have
forgotten.

The NOP (nopause) modifier instructs Confer not to pause to
ask you if you want to VIEW REMAINING TEXT at those spots
where the item author has specified a pause with "==".

The NOR (noresponse) modifier displays the items named without
their responses.

The NOS (noseparator) modifier is used to suppress the printing
of the dashed line separator between responses.

The NOT (notext) modifier displays the items named without their texts.

The NOV (noverify) modifier will suppress printing of the item numbers when you ask to have the output directed to *FILE* or *PRINT*.

The NRI (no related items) modifier displays the items named without the reference to their related items.

The PASS modifier causes the item display not to pause after each item to get your response. It assumes you want to PASS on the response to every item named.

The PAUSE modifier causes Confer to pause after it prints out the descriptor for each item. At the pause prompt, the viewer is able to indicate if the rest of the item should be shown or if it should be forgotten.

The PREVIOUS modifier gives the first valid item prior to the one most recently displayed.

The RESPOND modifier tells Confer you want to respond directly to the item or items named. You'll see the item descriptor, then immediately be prompted for your response.

The REVERSE modifier cause the items you've named to come out in reverse order (highest=numbered item first).

The SCAN modifier causes Confer to print out the three line descriptors of the new items. SCAN can only be used for new items.

The TEXT modifier restricts the output to just the textual portion of the item. TEXT is equivalent to NOD NRI NOR.

The THIS modifier causes the item most recently specified in a command to be displayed.

The UNSEEN modifier displays the items that you have not yet seen, but are not "new".

The * modifier displays the currently defined * (star) items.

The "..." modifier (where ... is a character string) restricts
the output to just those items that have the character string
designated between the quotes in their headers.

The *DUMMY* modifier is the fastest way to remove items from the
"new items" list. Say: I NEW *DUMMY*

Enclose the name of an index category between angle brackets to
have Confer restrict the output to just the items in that
category. E.g., ‹confer›

Enclose the name of a myindex category between curly brackets to
have Confer restrict the output to just the items in that
category. E.g., {computers}

Figure 6.6 Control options of the ITEM command (from Confer's on-line help database).

Confer, like EIES, limits the size of regular conference messages. Initially this was a consequence of an operating system constraint, but it proved a useful source of information in its own right. If individual responses to an item can take any length, a user has no a priori way of determining how much text is present in new material. By restricting the size of individual responses to about 1.5KB (about 4K in EIES), a user can estimate the maximum number of lines he or she will see when reading through new comments, because the software reports the number of new responses to each item. If a user's response exceeds this size limit, the software automatically breaks it up into two or more records, giving each its own number. Figure 6.7 is a sample Confer session in a conference with new *responses* to one item and several new items.

DO NEXT? join "network:control"

CONFERence for NETWORK:control
organizers: [organizer's name], [NNN/NNN-NNNN]
            [organizer's name], [NNN/NNN-NNNN]

New responses on items:
 123

New items: 200-205
DO NEXT? r new

Item 123 09:32 Jun27/89   85 lines   98 responses

```
[item originator's name]
[item title]

   2 new responses.
Aug06/89 23:36
123:97) [response authors name]: body of text...
 body of text...

   .

   .

   .

 last line of body...
- - - - -
Aug07/89 09:27
123:98) [response authors name]: body of text...
 body of text...

   .

   .

   .

 last line of text...

RESPOND, FORGET, OR PASS: ['ENTER' is same as PASS]

DO NEXT?  i new

Item 200  09:16 Jul25/89    15 lines    4 responses
[item originator's name]
[item title]

Text of item...
Text of item...

   .

   .

   .

last line of item header text...

   3 responses
Jul25/89 10:59
200:1) [response author's name]: body of text...
 body of text...

   .

   .

   .
```

```
 last line of text...
 - - - - -
 Jul25/89 11:28
 200:2) [response author's name]: body of text...
   body of text...

   .

   .

   .

   last line of text...
 - - - - -
 Jul25/89 13:30
 200:3) [response author's name]: body of text...
   body of text...

   .

   .

   .

   last line of text...
 - - - - -
   RESPOND, FORGET, OR PASS:    res

   GIVE YOUR RESPONSE
 > Text of response...
 >.
 >.
 >.
 > last line of response...
 >
   EDIT, VIEW, CANCEL, MORE, OR DONE:    done
   This is response 200:4
```

Figure 6.7 Example of Confer conference flow (user's input is underlined).

The power to *forget* an item first appears in the comb architecture. In the simpler EIES structure, one can always decline to read the contents of any conference simply by not GETting it. Once inside a conference, any comment may relate to any other or to none; there is no inherent organization below the level of the conference. In Confer, the existence of a sublayer suggests the relative specificity of discussions under *items*. The model has a convenient organization for supporting this simple filtering mechanism. Users with no interest in a particular item's theme can simply FORGET the item, and the system will stop displaying new responses to it. Subsequent searches over that conference will also ignore matches in forgotten items. It is, of course, possible to include those comments in a search with use of the search modifier NOFORGET.

```
RESPOND, FORGET, OR PASS:   ?
```

The possible answers to this prompt are:

respond	forget	pass		
stop	again	text	new	date
change	edit			
enter	transmit	note	bulletin	
query	participants			
mine	lifo	"..."	[integer]	
anonymous	pseudonymous			
myindex	index	follow		
browse	nobrowse			
summary	mysummary			

Figure 6.8   Options available at the confer RESPOND prompt.

The suggestions made by Confer at the RESPOND prompt are the most commonly used. Just as those in EIES, many (but not all) Confer commands will operate from many levels in the system. These commands, illustrated in Figure 6.8, will all work at the RESPOND/FORGET/PASS? prompt.

Each of these may be further expanded by entering the command word followed by a ?. For example, ? transmit, will extract a tutorial on intraconference personal messages (see Section 6.7.5). FOLLOW marks the item as one belonging to a personal collection of items that the user wishes to follow on a regular basis. The only difference between setting up a follow list and the default behavior of the system, (in other words, showing you what you have not *forgotten*) is that the follow list allows a user to read through new responses to items of special interest and still visit other new responses later. It is, in effect, the opposite of FORGET, a kind of PRIORITY-GET. It does *not* permit users to collect items across conference boundaries.

6.7.3   Creating New Items and Responses.

New items are generated by any user with the ENTER command. The system prompts for the number of the item that most inspired the one being created. If one is given, it appears as PRIME=NNN in the item's opening header and can be used to link related items together. Confer then prompts for the TEXT of the item-opening record. This text can be of any length—a book if necessary—and it is not broken up as are comment texts that may follow. Confer recognizes a special character-position combination in this text and uses it to make reading entries easier. If the item originator enters two equal signs (= =) in the first column of some line, text display to other users will stop at that point, and the reader is asked whether he or she wishes to read the rest of the opening text. This = = marker can be used as many times as desired in the opening-item record. Persons who create new items are encouraged to use this facility liberally as a matter of politeness to readers who may not want to read a long opening text once having seen the first few paragraphs.

6.7.4 Association Mechanisms

Indexing is another service supported by Confer. Indexes to conferences can be put together manually by conference administrators with the assistance of software tools available to them. An index is a topical reference to subjects based on words or phrases found in the text of comments. The index crossreferences these subjects with the items and specific comments that pertain to them. Users may then gather all of these items and comments together and read them without specific reference to their item or comment numbers. User indexes are similar, except they are generated by each user on a per-item basis. In this sense they are akin to the "follow" command.

FOLLOW sets up a virtual index to topics in which a user is keenly interested, MYINDEX allows a user to classify items of interest in named registers and read new comments on these items one group at a time. The conference index capability adds another dimension to the conference system by allowing users to cut across item boundaries and read comments regarding a given subject no matter what items they may appear in. Of course, discussion continuity is lost because the individual comments read in this way are not part of a single conversation; however, if the purpose of the session is to find information already present in the text base, there may be no need to maintain this continuity.

Confer's search facilities permit examination of keywords, titles, or the whole text of items. It includes support for the Boolean operators "and" and "or." Search results are collected into sets like the results of index operations; these sets can serve as targets of subsequent search or other commands such as read or browse. This set generation capability, similar to that produced by EIES searches, represents the best available fusion of communications and information retrieval technology at the present time. Although both EIES and Confer support subsequent searches over user generated sets, neither allows crossing one set with another to find records common to both; the Boolean "not" operator is also not available. This is a critical operator in information retrieval operations, because it permits the subtraction of information already reviewed from new sets, as well as filtering term associations. Unfortunately few conferencing packages support this operator.

Both Confer and EIES support a user directory. To some people in the computer conferencing field, lack of a good user directory and complimentary user-status information all but disqualifies a system from serious consideration as a conference system. Both the EIES and Confer directories allow users to find others with similar interests or skills. They identify users by name and system ID—both searchable fields. It is also possible to search the directory by geographic location–for example, one may want to find all users in Denver, Colorado—or by keywords that represent interests or skills.

Both EIES and Confer maintain usage logs for each user on a per-conference basis. Upon entry to each conference, EIES asks each user if he or she wishes to see these statistics, showing the last note read by each member. On Confer, the QUERY command is used for much the same purpose. For example, QUERY 1,5,7,9 RESPONSES will show not only how much each conference member has read in each of the specified items, but also how many comments each has written along with the sum of their line counts!

6.7.5 Alternate Communications Structures in Confer

Confer items are tailorable in yet other ways. When a user begins a new item, he or she is asked to pick from a list of possible structures and restriction sets. For example, experiments in on-line classrooms use a particular item switch that prevents students from seeing the comments of others on a given question until they have entered their own. Another variation collects essays from participants. These essays have no length restrictions, and they are not broken up into separate comments as occurs in the standard item format; but only *one* essay or comment may be entered per participant.

Confer has a somewhat novel variation on electronic mail. Users have multiple mail boxes—one for each conference they have joined. Transmitting mail to a fellow participant, or to many of them at once, is convenient, with many options from which to choose, as are the read and disposition features. Users are informed of new private mail as they enter each conference. The mail and conference facilities share a single interface in both style and content, though there are a few keyword differences between them.

The message is more like a private note passed across the table of a face-to-face meeting—except that the other participants cannot see it being passed. Mail can be transmitted (in fact, `transmit` is the keyword) from almost any prompt in the system. Confer looks at the conference directory to determine if the recipient is a member of the current conference; to transmit notes to someone not in this directory, a user must `join` one of the conferences to which that user belongs. This is not E-mail, strictly speaking, but another tool designed to expand the use of the conference arena. It provides a place for remarks having special significance for two or a few persons (arranging a luncheon appointment, passing confidential information, and so on).

The message system has one feature not otherwise available in the conference arena—messages can carry binary attachments. These include compressed files, executable programs, bit-mapped screens, spreadsheet or database files, and other features. The message disposition prompt permits message manipulation through the Confer editor (if text) or any host resident tools available to the user. Confer supports user exits—escapes—to the underlying operating system and its facilities. It contains direct support for text or binary feeds (from the conference or the message system) into system files for further handling.

6.7.6 Communications Beyond the Borders of the System

One of the facilities present on most large systems—Confer's platforms are no exception—is system-wide electronic mail. On MTS at the University of Michigan, Confer treats all its text as native MTS files. Confer output files, generated by users from inside Confer, are perfectly compatible with the MTS E-mail software. As a result, Confer messages or conference streams (called "confers" by users) can be piped outside the Confer. Texts can be moved from one conference to another via the Confer editor and external files. Strictly speaking, writing software to perform these transfers automatically, would be outside the scope of the conferencing application. It would also further solidify the original Confer's dependence on the MTS operating system! Confer's recent porting to DEC's VMS helps make the point. The compatibility between Confer *files*, and VMS *tools* was one of the more difficult problems encountered in the VMS port.

6.7.7 The Influence of the Confer Model

The basic comb architecture has influenced more conference system development than any other fundamental model. Some of the systems appearing in the late 1970s and the early 1980s were direct descendants of Confer in that their developers had experience with Confer and deliberately adopted its structural paradigm. Microspan, another University of Michigan project, is an example that was designed to demonstrate conference capability like that of Confer in smaller mini- and micro-computer installations. Picospan by Marcus Watts is a commercial version of Microspan, developed under a National Science Foundation grant. Neither of these systems set out to find a "better paradigm" for interpersonal communication. Their goals were to take an existing high-level concept and implement it on other system architectures. By the time of the Microspan project, UNIX had become the de facto standard operating system for university minicomputer installations, and was soon to appear on new microcomputer architectures. This timing, along with its tailorability, multiuser, and multitasking support, made it the operating system of choice for most subsequent development. Many of these variations have appeared in systems hosting conferences for public, nonprofit, corporate, and other commercial purposes. We will cover some of these in Chapters 7 and 8.

Although the comb model helped alleviate a problem associated with the earlier linear model of EIES, it did not cure it completely. Human conversations, if they are not formally controlled, drift from subject to subject. For instance, a user posting may make three points, while the next posting addresses only one of these three, and in response to that, yet other comments that divert the overall subject still further. The ability to start new *items* in comb systems is supposed to eliminate this problem. The shift in topics — topic drift — is often subtle, and users are often unwilling to direct attention to a new *item* because it is easier to continue the discussion under the original one.

■ 6.8 THE BRANCH MODEL

In response to the tendancy of topics to drift in subject, several developers conceived and implemented another communication paradigm known as a "tree" or "branch" structure. Harry Stevens' and George Reinhart's Participate, or Parti for short, is the best known example of this architecture. Independent development of the same concept by Jacob Palme of the University of Stockholm resulted in Com, and later PortaCom.

Participate was conceived with the intention of facilitating large numbers of short discussions on specific topics. A relatively high-quality search-and-retrieve system permits users to scan many short "conferences" and collect results for analysis. Fig-

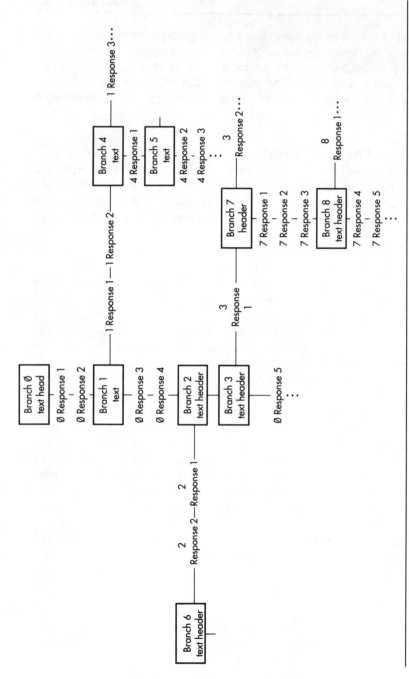

Figure 6.9 The Participate branching model. All conferences begin at and trace their origin back to branch 0. A new branch may start at any point, and has the status of a conference in itself. The branch-starting texts appear as a message in the sequence of responses to the parent branch. Further responses to the parent continue in a time-sequential fashion, while the new branch begins with response 1 to its header text. Branches may be interspersed among many comments in a parent or may occur one right after the other. Any user may start a new branch unless specifically prohibited from doing so by restrictions specific to the conference or user. This model is used by Participate and the COM family of CMC packages.

ure 6.9 illustrates the Participate superstructure. The entire arrangement begins with a root conference containing responses much like those of EIES or Confer. Each Parti comment displays the name of the comment's author, the date and time of its posting, its sequence number in the conference, and the number of characters in the comment. Conference title, author, origination date, and subject are displayed each time a reader encounters new material in a given conference as illustrated in Figure 6.10.

6.8.1 Structure of Participate

Parti branches are rooted in notes inserted into a conference stream for that purpose. They are not connected to any specific response in a thread, but to the thread itself. Suppose a Parti conference had 25 notes in it; note 10 of that conference could be a root for another branch. Presumably, this branch was put where it was because it is re-

---

```
"CONFERENCE TITLE" by [CONF. ORIGINATOR] May   27, 1989 at 22:11
about CONFERENCE SUBJECT......
(25 notes)


12 (of 25) [COMMENT AUTHOR] May   30, 1989 at 15:38 (1240
characters)


body of comment...

    .

    .

    .

end of comment 12 body

13 (of 25) [COMMENT AUTHOR] June 3, 1989 at 10:32 (2420
characters)


body of comment...

    .

    .

    .

end of comment 13 body

    .

    .

    .
```

Figure 6.10 Participate conference flow.

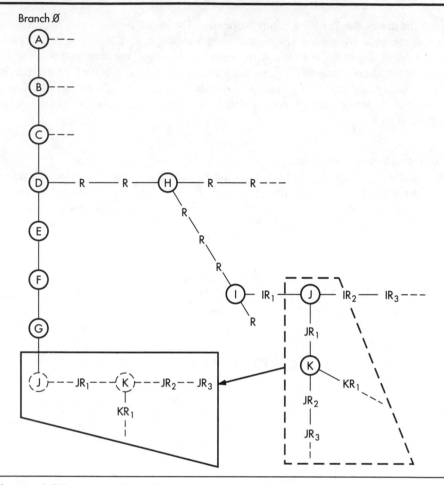

Figure 6.11 Moving branches in participate. A branch started in an inappropriate place, along with all sub-branches of that branch, may be disconnected from its parent and attached to the end of branch 0. In this illustration, branch 0 consists of nothing but branches starting conferences.

lated to the parent conference, and specifically because one of the other notes between 1 and 9 inspired someone to start a diverting thread. Note 10 might or might not have something to say about the first nine notes of the thread, but its real significance is to introduce the new subject. Its header (conference title, subject, author, and so forth) references the *new* branch, not the old one. Note 11 of the original thread would logically be the next note on the old theme after number 9. Of course, branches can come off the original topic at any point.

Once begun, a new thread becomes an "original thread"—a parent—that can spawn other branches. This splitting and splitting again can go on indefinitely, though the software contains switches that permit system administrators (not individual conference administrators) to limit the allowed branch depth (see Figure 6.12). Users originating branches have the power to disconnect sub-branches from their branches if they feel that the tributary is not sufficiently related to the subject of the parent. When this happens, the split-off thread and any further subthreads grafted to it move automatically to the end of a default list of branches (illustrated in Figure 6.11). This list usually consists of nothing but branches; every note on it is a branch root.

Access switches available on a per-user/per-conference basis in Participate vr.4.x.

```
ACTION ==> (Inbox) profile "[conference name"] access

["conference"] by CONF. AUTHOR, Apr. 23, 1989 at 12:30 about
[CONFERENCE SUBJECT]
(nn notes) (Questions: nn)

You have the following access permissions:

Can read the opener of this item: Y
Can read a note sent to this item: Y
Can send a non-branching note to this item: Y
Can create a branch topic off of this item: Y
Can send a poll in which addressees cannot view the results: Y
Can send a poll in which addressees can view the results: Y
Can join this item to receive other people's notes: Y
Can leave once joined: Y
Can vote (if a poll): Y
Can delete another user's note sent to this topic: N
Can delete the entire item: N
Can modify addressees, retention, subject, or opener: N
Can use MODIFY ACCESS on this item: N
Can profile addressees or branches: Y
Can profile members or acknowledgements: Y
Can use PROFILE ACCESS on this item: Y
Can use MODIFY ORGANIZER to become the organizer of this item: N
Can profile the votes (if a poll): Y
Can use PROFILE ACCESS <username> on this item: N
```

Figure 6.12 Participate control switches.

6.8.2 Presentation of the Model: The INBOX Reference Point

An irony of the Parti system is that the distinction between conferences and sublayers is completely blurred because of the potentially unlimited possibility for diversion. *Every branch or thread is a conference unto itself.* Each conference has a name, and users participate in them by "joining" them as they do in most other systems. As users log onto the system, an *inbox* notifies them of new material in conferences they have joined. It is like a menu of conferences and other notes attached to conferences followed by each user. The inbox also discloses the presence of personal E-mail divided into regular and priority categories. An example of a user's inbox is shown below.

```
SEGMENT   NAME (# OF NOTES)


   1   Urgent Notes (0)
   2   Personal Notes (2)
   3   [conference1 name] (5)
   4   [conference2 name] (12)
   5   [conference3 name] (4)
   6   [conference4 name] (6)
   7   [conference5 name] (3)


ACTION on 32 Inbox Notes ==> (Read)
```

In the above example, the conference names could be branches occurring anywhere in the Parti system. There is nothing to signal the user that "conference4" was originally a branch of "conference2," and that "conference5" is related to "conference4," and so forth. Since every branch has equal status, users need not participate in the original topics from which these branches have sprung. The numbers following the conference names show the number of notes posted *since* this user last visited the system.

Some of these notes might, of course, be roots of subsequent branches, but there is no way to tell until they are read. If one of the notes is a root of another branch, the system asks the user if he or she wishes to join that branch after displaying its root note. To participate in a subsequent branch, a user must explicitly join it. Once joined, new notes appearing in the branch will become visible in the user's inbox.

6.8.3 Navigation and Selection

Users can elect to read one conference at a time, pausing or not pausing between each note (including new roots). They can order the system to display all the notes from the conferences without pausing even between conferences. They can read specific notes or browse notes, displaying only their subjects' authors and a user-specified number of lines of the text body. The software has a broad range of features supporting user navigation through the labyrinth of branches. Searches can be performed over branches for text in subject headers or comment bodies and can be limited to a specified branch depth, or performed over all existing branches in the system. Searches may also include date and time delimiters and author specifications; for example, "find since 12/12/89 from rapaport." Parti's search facility supports neither Booleans nor nested searches.

6.8.4 Alternate Communications Structures and Control Mechanisms

Participate, like both Confer and EIES, supports delphic voting and automatic vote compilation. Branches can either be regular topics or vote requesters. If the latter, the system prompts for the kind of vote involved. Examples include yes/no, numeric ranges, or picking a value or item from a list. Parti has an extensive searchable user directory, but no per-conference user-status reporting. It shares with EIES the ability to post a note to persons or conferences from any point in the system. That is, a user can read a branch and write a note to an individual or a comment to another branch, or both at the same time. This flat command structure is the source of much of the software's flexibility. The Parti text editor can transport text from one conference to another. The user help facilities are similar to those of Confer. A question mark followed by a command will elicit a description of the command's purpose and use.

Participate spares its users the complexity of EIES' global commands by supporting fewer overall operations. For example, it is not possible to send a note from a thread to another user or topic in a single command. It is possible, by naming different entities on a .SEND line, to distribute original notes to multiple conferences or users at the same time. Command stacking is supported as in EIES, using a semicolon between separate commands.

Participate originated later than either EIES or Confer. The microcomputer was already making some impact on the data communications industry. Parti's developers envisioned somewhat higher speed connections and wished to position themselves to take advantage of coupled software running on remote microcomputers. Consider that the transmission of inbox information requires time; at least one screenful of text must be placed on a user's terminal each time it is displayed. EIES saves this time, yielding a faster but more difficult interface. Given the evolution of technology at the time of Participate's development, its designers believed that the advantages of the inbox mechanism outweighed the need to consume the transmission time to make it available.

6.8.5 Three-Dimensional Models and Two-Dimensional Views

The Parti model lends itself to many small conversations addressing very limited subjects. This is exactly what its creator intended. Harry Stevens' idea was to allow people to shift discussions from one subject to another as they were inspired to do so. A root node in the middle of another thread need not be a direct comment to the note preceding it, or for that matter any note in the thread. The model does alleviate but does not eliminate the problem of topic drift, and it brings about another, possibly more severe, problem.

Suppose a user is following a thread to which a branch is attached. If the user does not elect to follow the branch and join that discussion, subsequent branches that may be of interest will never be seen; they will never appear in his or her inbox. A search might uncover the branch, but such a search must be conducted deliberately by the user on a periodic basis with a command like PROFILE "item" [BRANCHES] [DEPTH#] [STARTING_NOTE#]. This command will display the titles of branch headers of all branches to a specified or arbitrary depth starting from a given point. If substantial time has passed since the creation of the first sub-branch of the original thread, there may be many subsequent branches; this search may take a great amount time. The PROFILE command modifier that limits the depth of branch-reporting alleviates this problem but returns us to the original problem of losing track of new material.

This kind of problem never occurs in the comb model because users always see the headers of every new item generated in a conference. In comb systems, navigation through a rapidly expanding list of items is facilitated by support for manipulating item header texts separate from the comments that follow them—for example, the ability to read, browse, or search a new item's starting text without reading its comments. Of all the products based on the comb model, only Confer supports this ability to treat item openers separate from their comments. Nevertheless, all comb-based systems will at least inform users that new items exist, and all permit examination of their titles.

A default display of *all* new conferences could be effected in Parti. It is an impractical solution, however, because the structure of the system fosters a geometric growth in the number of conferences. By contrast, new items in the comb model increase arithmetically. Furthermore, in the comb model, new items are at least theoretically related to the conference under which they appear and are made available to users on a conference-by-conference basis. Because every branch in Participate is a conference in its own right, there is no inherent structure within which to limit the default display of new material.

6.8.6 Limiting the Structure to Two Dimensions

Parti's flexibility permits it an easy escape from this dilemma. Conference organizers can limit the total branch depth to three. Every record in branch 1 is a branch that represents a conference. Each of these branches splits off in another line of pure branch headers, branch 2, that assume a Confer-like *topic* role. All the text of the conversation takes place under these headers in branch 3. The effect is a pure comb model. Coupled with Parti's excellent system-wide navigation and reasonable search facilities, such a deliberately restricted system would support many formal and informal activities without fragmenting conversational streams.

Other developers have attempted to deal with both problems—topic drift and availability of new items—without losing the advantages of natural conversational branching. The most successful of these, in this author's opinion, are Alastair Mayer, developer of CoSy, and Steve Manes, author of Magpie. We shall have more to say about these systems and their models in Chapter 8.

■ 6.9 THE SIGNIFICANCE OF NAVIGATION AND SELECTION

What is repeatedly apparent in using these systems is that to a significant degree, system facilities for searching, filtering, gathering, and displaying records are more important than the overall structure of the message base. Good navigation and selection facilities can impose a virtual structure on an almost structureless environment. The good news is that such structures can be customized from the individual user's viewpoint; the bad news is that it requires some expertise, frequently with a programming language (script), to achieve the effect. Simple structures like the comb model can be very helpful because they provide a context for the operation of navigation and selection utilities. Users also benefit from an ability to visualize the organization of conversation.

Elaborate structures like an unrestricted Parti conversation can be more fragmenting than illuminating. The deliberate promotion of all threads to the status of a conference effectively disconnects them from one another until a user assembles the relationships with a PROFILE command. There are domains, however, in which this structure functions very well; *distance learning* is a good example. Educational situations benefit from several layers of distinction in discussions. New themes can be opened class-wide on one level, while small ad hoc student groups pursue things at another. Students need not be constantly aware of this internal structure, because their own inboxes will reflect all activities related to them specifically. The domain itself, an electronic classroom, ensures an adequate association among activities thanks to the restricted nature of the application.

To succeed, such systems require ever-more sophisticated navigation, selection and association capabilities. The Participate *inbox*, for example, is a powerful interface aid, but it fails as a malleable association device. Parti's PROFILE command is a powerful association tool, provided that the total structure being profiled is not overwhelming; however, limiting a PROFILE's depth will result in information loss. To a point, good structuring makes it easier to avoid learning much about system navigation and selection facilities. No structure however, no matter how flexible, can ever substitute for good navigation and selection tools when conference volume increases. Without the power to pick their way through a virtual structure of their own choosing, users are forced to ignore the vast proportion of material in high-volume systems.

6.9.1 Virtual Two-Dimensional Structures in Three-Dimensional Models

An example of a control mechanism that eliminates the problems associated with pure branching systems is a filter that permits user creation of a virtual two-level structure starting at a specified branch. This kind of user facility is not yet supported and would require some additions to the Participate data structures (see Chapter 7) as well as added computational complexity. Users would perceive their starting point as a conference with a string of comments to the original conference branch point — a topic 0. All other branches under this conference would appear as separate topics under the original conference. If a user "forgot" a particular topic, the system would have to ensure that branches generated under this level in the physical system would still be mapped to new topics from the user's viewpoint. The effect would be identical to that achieved by restricting the branching of the conference; yet the real conference (and other users) could continue to operate in normal branching mode.

Two other requirements immediately arise. One is the need for a mechanism that prevents users from seeing a message more than once. If, for example, one conference is nested inside another one, the appearance of a given note should be associated with the lowest-level conference. The second problem is more complex and involves mechanisms that permit users to add new branches to the system when they perceive them to be new topics under a single conference. One possibility is to make the new topic a branch off the thread-level chosen as the starting point—the conference level. The new topic may, however, be closely related to a sub-branch of that thread in the physical system, something that appears as another topic to this user. This suggests an option for this user to associate the new topic (at its creation) with another topic. The system then treats the virtual topic header as a branch header attached to the appropriate branch in the physical system.

This level of user control, the imposition of a virtual structure, is mostly unknown in commercial systems. Ironically, it exists to some degree in EIES, one of the earliest group communications applications systems. In EIES, users must construct their virtual structures piece by piece using a complex script language, and they must know what they are looking for before the fact. In high-volume systems, such control mechanisms would permit designers to have the best of both worlds. Internally, a finely branching system could be mapped to any virtual structure less finely divided. If accomplished efficiently, such a product would function in many domains equally well at the same time.

■ 6.10 PHILOSOPHICAL IMPLICATIONS OF CONFERENCE STRUCTURE

All the systems previously discussed share a common philosophy of text organization within a given conference, topic, or branch. User replies are not linked directly to a single record, other than their link to the topic or conference header; rather, they are replies to the stream of discussion as a whole. Of course, such replies may semantically be comments to a specific previously posted record. However, the comment header does not signal this link. Some developers have viewed this structure as problematic, and not adequately representative of the intentions of the participants. This led to the elaboration of an alternate philosophy which supports direct connections between comments and the earlier records they comment upon. CoSy, Magpie, and many other software systems exemplify this alternate approach (see Chapter 8).

Participate and COM first suggested the comment-in-context, or comment-oriented, approach. Yet Participate is still a conference-oriented system because the branch headers are not specifically associated with any particular comment, but with the branch as a whole. Parti's logical structure is branching, but conceptually, since each branch has the status of a conference, it can be flattened into a linear structure like that of EIES. Parti affirms its conference orientation because new branches are always appended to the end of an existing thread.

As one might expect, such philosophical differences have led to heated debates. Supporters of the comment-oriented approach claim that it is more responsive to user intentions and the real flow of human conversation. Proponents of the conference-oriented structures claim that the other approach leads to confusion, because a single subject is fragmented into many miniconferences, and the overall topic is easily forgotten. To them, such systems are not conferencing systems at all, but rather glorified electronic mail. This, because they act to disperse the collective energies of the group by encouraging (or at least supporting) responses to individual records before the entire stream of discussion is read.

In the view of this author, both types are legitimately conferencing applications. The first type represents the format of a formal meeting, while the second suggests the atmosphere of an informal gathering. Each has its place and best supports different communications requirements. Ultimately, the second form is more flexible because it can, theoretically, be constrained to emulate the first. Practically, however, the developers of the second structural form have not made the effort to support such constraints. As a result, software reflecting the first philosophy has become far more popular in corporate and other institutional settings, while the second approach is more commonly seen on informal public systems.

■ 6.11 GRAPHICS IN CMC SYSTEMS

All of the software and user interfaces reviewed thus far are limited to text. In the United States, this typically means the lower 127 bytes of the ASCII character code set. Critics deride these interfaces for their lack of support for modern graphics and sound capabilities.

If text manipulation was often inconvenient in the past, the prospects for managing binary information that might, for example, drive graphics displays is much worse now. No standards for this existed through most of the 1970s and even today, one cannot be sure that connecting terminals have graphics capability, let alone software support for image display. Development of facilities for widely exchanging graphics is, therefore, both technically and economically complex.

Some developers submit to these restrictions and build systems whose terminal links must support a graphics protocol. If proprietary protocols are involved, the system vendor must supply proprietary terminal software. Submitting to this restriction may be perfectly acceptable from the viewpoint of some corporate requirements; such systems are evolving in LAN environments. There are also a few commercial systems available for public exploration. One example is Coconet, but by far the most visible is the Prodigy venture of the Sears and IBM corporations.

Picture description instructions (PDIs) like those used by Prodigy and Coconet are an alternative to direct image transfer. In North America, the most widely accepted PDI standard is the North American presentation level protocol syntax (NAPLPS). In Britain, it is PRESTEL, and in France, MINTEL. NAPLPS is a description language that does not convey an image directly, but instead conveys instructions for building it on the remote computer. For example, a sequence of only a few bytes would convey the instruction "draw a circle of 20-pixel radius with center at pixel 100,100 and color it red." Standard PDIs still require users to have hardware or software capable of interpreting this information. They broaden the reach of the host because third parties can supply products to meet this requirement.

More than anything else, PDIs have failed in the marketplace because they do not satisfy a perceived requirement for image transmission. Much of the graphic data users want to exchange consists of scanned images. PDIs would, however, support a great deal of business information exchange in graphic form. Charts, diagrams, and other business or technical presentations can be assembled and exchanged using PDIs.

6.11.1 Limitations of Graphical Systems: The Need for Coupled Interfaces

The trade-off between graphical interfaces and severe restriction in potential user populations has worked to put conferencing software designed for public use at a tremendous disadvantage compared to other application domains. By the end of this decade, graphics of many kinds will be available in every applications context imaginable. Computer conferencing has taken steps in this direction. Some systems in the United States and Canada have experimented with NAPLPS—based applications, and systems elsewhere use other PDIs. Each requires callers to have personal computers with communications software that supports the PDI used by the host. Those systems that wish to maintain contact with the widest possible range of devices (and therefore users) must either eschew use of these protocols or support them on top of text-based interfaces. Either way, their job is complicated by support for incompatible display modes from one data structure or support for multiple sets of structures.

If the data structures of the system as a whole are oriented around graphics information (as they are, for example, in the IBM/Sears Prodigy product), supporting a nongraphical interface results in, at best, an inelegant contrivance. If graphic support is added to data structures optimized for text, facilities for manipulation of the graphics data may be difficult to produce or may require extensive CPU resources. One can design a system with even-handed support for multiple interfaces, but few such commercial products exist.

Software developers recognized early on that support for graphics and even voice-to-text and text-to-voice translation would be valuable adjuncts to text-based communications. They are only now, however, becoming a practical possibility with the advent of fast microprocessors, powerful compression systems, and the glimmerings of recognition for graphics transmission standards. It will probably be the next century, however, before there is enough penetration of protocols and protocol emulators in the majority of telecommunications products to implement a widely marketable communications mediator that depends upon support for one or more protocols in the user population. One also presumes that the telecommunications landscape of the twenty-first century will be considerably changed.

■ 6.12 WIDESPREAD VERSUS RESTRICTED ACCESS AND THE ROLE OF THE MICROCOMPUTER

Until the time of the aforementioned standards development, developers and users will have to accept the trade-offs involved. Widespread access and availability will depend upon interaction between user and system in a pure text mode or with a minimum of other requirements. Work with such interfaces, however, has been ongoing for more than 20 years. There are well-established design principles that produce highly serviceable user control features. It is unfortunate that making general use of these systems requires some motivation and learning; because of this, the market most often expected to adopt this technology for the sake of enhanced communications, the corporate sector, has mostly resisted it.

Reasons for this resistance are numerous, including the learning curve and the commitment, as a result of learning, to a radically altered corporate communications environment. Somewhat unexpectedly, the public at large, whose computer awareness is steadily growing, has discovered this medium, and the result has been economic support for literally thousands of small BBSs supporting file exchange and a great variety of lively conference-like discussions. Medium-sized systems are growing rapidly in popularity as well. On many of these, the public is being introduced to more sophisticated text-based communications.

In the educational sector, students are being exposed to large-scale conference communities and experimental systems. As these people enter the private sector, they bring their experience with them and may recognize opportunities for the technology as they emerge in their professional lives. These same people may also contribute to the ranks of those who spend time or money (or both) using public conference facilities in their nonprofessional lives. For some, computer communications are an adjunct to a hobby; to others, they become the hobby.

In the last 20 years, there has been a great deal of expansion in the number of system configurations. Smaller computers with faster processors and far more power on a user-by-user basis continue to develop. Telecommunications systems have increased in speed and complexity; conferencing and electronic mail systems have also evolved. Many remain rooted in centralized environments similar to those of the last two decades, but they have grown in features, or have been modified to operate in an environment of relatively high-speed communications. Command stacking and script customization as supported on EIES were astonishing in 1973. Even now, few systems are as flexible. Today, however, the model of optimum communications relies on the presence of a microcomputer at the remote node.

Given the processing power of the micro, even simple—one might say simplistic—interfaces having few features can be enhanced by the local facilities of the microprocessor and its software. The combination has, in the end, more flexibility than is possible in any dumb-terminal-to-host configuration. What makes the use of microcomputer interfaces so interesting is their ability to add enhanced navigation and selection features to the host software. The microcomputer can use primitive navigation facilities on the host and translate them into elaborate, customized interface systems. This principle has been applied to information retrieval systems like Dialog, and to some extent on conference systems (see Chapters 8 and 10). To reach its full potential, both the host and the connection between the host and user must be very fast.

The trade-off, as usual, is access. There are now more microcomputers than terminals worldwide, not counting the IBM-dominated mainframe arena. Terminals, however, have been around longer. Systems like EIES, Confer, Participate, and many others have long since been able to take advantage of special terminal characteristics. Microcomputers emulating terminals have even broader range, but the *microcomputer-enhanced* interface must be customized for each computer or operating system on one side, and for every host on the other. Simple user support interfaces can be developed in many terminal software script languages, and there are a number of these in the public domain and shareware marketplace. More complex assistant systems, especially those involving graphics, are fewer in number. In Chapter 8 we shall discuss some of the existing systems and their relationships.

7

IMPLEMENTING COMMUNICATIONS MODELS

■ 7.1 COMMUNICATIONS DATA

At the physical level, the design of a computer mediated communication system must address the structure of the data to be exchanged, and the processes to which it is subject. In a text-oriented communications system, the data includes letters and numbers, words, punctuation, sentences, paragraphs, documents, tables, and so on. Processes must manipulate structures filled with instances of these data types. They must add new instances, retrieve instances, modify and delete them, and recombine them. They must also exchange data with processes operating on behalf of other users, possibly on other machines.

One might also include one or more graphic representations, from simple structures like lines and circles composing charts to bit-mapped images. Processes for converting voice to text and vice versa could also be included. Graphics display technology has been widely available since the mid 1980s. The problem, however, lies not in reliably transmitting and delivering graphics information, but in *displaying* this information to the user. The developers of text-based communications systems rely on the ubiquity of the ASCII character set. Displaying *text* on a remote console comes down to translating a stream of bits as ASCII characters, something almost every terminal in the world is capable of doing. By contrast, there are many competing graphics representation schemes, and many users do not have either the hardware or the software to use any of them.

■ 7.2 PHYSICAL TEXT STRUCTURES

The physical starting point was, historically, the structure of the text record as supported by a particular machine architecture. The software tools of the early to mid 1970s did not easily permit more flexible arrangements. Early implementations were very dependent on facilities provided by the operating system to the application software. This was especially true concerning operating system support for file manipulation and user I/O. Many early operating systems lacked native support for random access to records of a text file. Without this, the facilities required to provide users with control over the way in which conversations are delivered to them had to be built into the applications software. Yet no matter what the application software did to transform data for the user, the operating system read files sequentially. Performance was therefore abysmal in an age when people counted CPU cycles, and seconds were precious.

This dependency of the application software on the operating system is nowhere better illustrated than with Confer. When the University of Michigan received its spanking new mainframe in 1974, IBM had neglected to provide an operating system! Computer science students at U. of M. knew an opportunity when they saw one, and promptly set out to produce one. The result, the Michigan Terminal System (MTS) was one of the few operating systems of the time to support random access to text records that were not of fixed length.

7.2.1 Structure of Confer Records on MTS

Bob Parnes used this very feature to construct the basic record structures and file management components of Confer. When Dr. Parnes implemented the first version of the system, MTS supported only *single-line* records of up to 256 bytes! Proposals and votes were therefore placed in separate files. Proposals could be of any length (any number of records, one record per line), but each individual vote could occupy at most one record (one line) in the vote file. By the time Bob got around to supporting a debate on the proposals, developers had extended the MTS text features to handle units of 999 lines as a single logical record. Confer made immediate use of this extension without a change in its underlying file system strategy.

The 999-line limit, while an improvement over the original one-line restriction, is still a limitation the software must partly circumvent. Item headers of any length are no problem because the header can occupy any number of 999-line records. In the response file, the limit requires the conference software either to restrict a single response to 999 lines, or to split a long response automatically over two or more records. The first approach, while generous, still represents an arbitrary restriction. Dr. Parnes opted for the second method. In addition, he limited individual responses to considerably fewer than 999 lines for the sake of keeping individual responses to an easily readable length. This last decision was a constraint based on the psychology of users, rather than the capabilities of the operating system.

■ 7.3 PROGRAM STRUCTURES

Early programming tools and environments lent themselves to monolithic programs. In monolithic systems, most, if not all, of the application services provided the user are coded in a single executing program. These services include its user interface, editors, conference and directory handling mechanisms, search parsers, navigation aids, file I/O, and so on.

Multitasking environments like UNIX, and tools like the C language, appearing in the early to mid 1970s, suggested an alternate organizational style. Separate programs handle various service functions with a kernel channeling the selection of modules, passing parameters, and interpreting results (user output and error messages) as illustrated in Figure 7.1.

7.3.1 The Influence of UNIX Philosophy

UNIX is a popular environment in which to experiment with this technique. Picospan, a product of Marcus Watts during the mid 1970s, illustrates this style. Picospan itself is a very large kernel. Its roles encompass the maintenance of conference files and the connection between users, conferences, items, and notes. Many related services, however, are supported by executing programs external to Picospan, passing them data, and passing results to users.

Services provided by external programs include editing, file transfers, operating system shells, the user directory, electronic mail, and any other services operating on the host: databases, bibliographic retrieval systems, news feeds, or other communications systems. Picospan allows system administrators and users to control the behavior of the software by incorporating switches in files located in the user's home directory, the conference directory, and the Picospan system directory. These settings control not only the appearance of the Picospan interface, but also the operation of programs outside of the Picospan software.

Standard UNIX redirection and piping facilities provide the connection between Picospan and external programs. Picospan loads user control files into memory. It uses the definitions and settings in these files when it hands user requests and parameters off to other programs. This strategy results in one of the most flexible user interfaces of all the products on the market in this genre. EIES, EIES2, and TEIES are among the few products that also provide this much control over the user interface. They achieve it through support for script languages; and in the case of EIES2, through the Smalltalk object-oriented programming language. Picospan's capabilities are impressive given the relative simplicity of its concept.

■ 7.4 PICOSPAN AND THE UNIX FILE SYSTEM

Picospan relies heavily on the UNIX file system. When a conference is created, a corresponding subdirectory is generated. The conference subdirectory contains a file of switch settings for the conference, and another with host information. Conferences may have multiple administrators. Their names and privileges are shared by inclusion in the conference host file. Still other files control password access to the conference, the conference introduction and sign-off messages, a summary file that lists topic (item) headers, and the number of responses for each item.

These files are ordinary ASCII files. A topic's opening text is stored in the same file with all of its responses. It is treated specially only in that its message number is 0, and therefore contains the name (ID) of the item's originator. Just ahead of message 0, other records are prepended to the file conveying the title of the item, and other information (see Figure 7.2). Since UNIX does not support random access

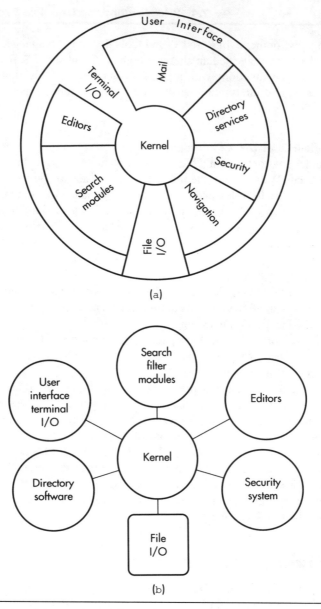

Figure 7.1 Monolithic and modular architectures. Applications may be monolithic, or modular. The latter architecture may take a number of forms [see Fig. 7.4(b)]. In a monolithic system (a), the whole program is a part of one executable module. In an extreme case, this may include all file and terminal device drivers, along with the user interface code. The system *kernel* may be responsible for multitasking operations, and/or may serve as a single point through which other modules are activated. In a modular system (b), different, stand-alone programs, will take responsibility for separate system functions. These will often communicate between themselves by passing messages and tokens through the software kernel. Some remote programs may communicate directly with others, and each to the file system through their own calls to the file management software.

```
!<ps02>
,H[item title]
,R0000
,U[temporary user reference number],[userID]
,A[pseudonym]
,D[coded date/time stamp]
,T
[body of item header text]

    .

    .

    .

,E       ← signals start of first comment
,R0000        ← flag field

,U[temporary user reference number],[userID]
,A[pseudonym if any]
,D[coded date/time stamp]
,T
[text of comment]

    .

    .

    .

,E      ← signals start of next comment

etc.
```

Figure 7.2 Structure of Picospan conference files.

to ordinary, variable length, text files, Picospan simply reads them sequentially. Each response record (response to message 0) is delineated from the prior one by a comma in column one of a line, followed by the uppercase letter E. The software counts ,E sequences as it reads through an item until it encounters one higher than the last message number recorded for that user.

The text (comment) record contains other fields, variable-length sets of bytes, whose meaning is signaled by a significant character in the first column following a comma. These contain coded date and time stamps, comment author's ID, and pseudonym used when creating the comment. The body of the text itself is the last such field. Each user's home directory contains a file for every conference that user has joined at some point. The contents of this file are a list of conference items, the date and time when they were last seen, and the highest message number read.

It is through this file's counters that Picospan knows how far a user has progressed through the conference. Picospan's `fixseen` command executes an external program that reads the conference summary file, and sets all the item markers for this user to the number of the last response for each item.

UNIX was designed to facilitate the scanning and manipulation of large numbers of small files. Facilitation here means it is relatively easy for a software developer to do these things, but the process is anything but fast. Over-reliance on the UNIX file system couples the software very closely to the efficiency of the file system implementation. Picospan's performance also depends very much on the efficiency of operating system utilities. Consider that the Picospan user interface can be configured to display the number of lines and or characters in each response, but the item/response file does not store this data explicitly as a field. Picospan actually computes these values as it reads the files.

On the positive side, use of this technique in an operating system like UNIX allows a developer to provide more features per line of code than is possible otherwise. For example, Picospan has no inherent user directory system, but UNIX itself does. System-wide directory services are provided to all conference participants without adding a single line of code to Picospan.

■ 7.5 DECOUPLING INTERNAL STRUCTURES FROM THE OPERATING SYSTEM

The facilities of both Confer and Picospan are strongly flavored by their underlying operating systems. Participate, the software product of Harry Stevens and George Reinhart, handles all services independently of the host's operating system. Confer has a hierarchical control structure coupled with a fragmented file strategy. Fragmentation of file systems is common, and used by many conference designers. Participate's developers chose instead to add another level of abstraction to the file system and couple the conference software itself to this logical schema, leaving the details of physical file manipulation to utilities optimized for the task. This allows Participate to be transported to any hardware/operating system environment for which the necessary low level file-handling utilities exist.

7.5.1 Participate's Logical File Structure

The Participate conference software recognizes three basic file types: text, users, and pointers, as illustrated in Figure 7.3. Each is essentially a separate section of a related database. Each supports a complex record type with data content, key-values signifying the record's type as well as identifying it in relation to other records. Each logical type is shadowed by a corresponding index file. Index maintenance is entirely in the hands of the file manager outside of Participate. All Participate file requests are made through a single interface to the file management software. Given a found record in a thread, the next is retrieved with a simple request because the file system provides such services to the application. It knows what index it is currently following, and what record was recovered by the system's *last* file request.

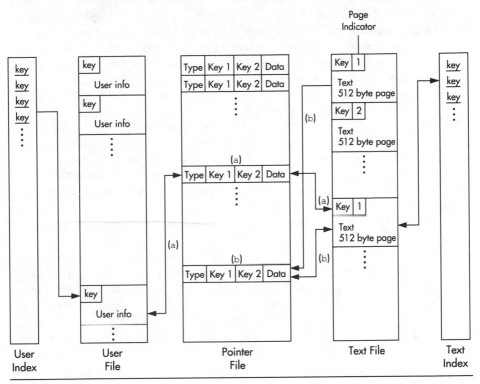

Figure 7.3 Participate file structure. Participate has three main files. Two of these, the *user file* and the *text file* have associated index files as well. The third file consists of *pointers* that connect users to texts they have written (a), texts to their conference threads (b), and other kinds of connections. There are 15 pointer types in all.

The text file contains all the texts supported by the system. This file stores every thread header, comment, vote, or private mail. The user file contains user information. It is the basis of Participate's searchable directory and contains, in addition, information about a user's global permissions. If, for example, a user is allowed to begin a new thread, that right is reflected by setting a bit flag in the user's record. Such broad privileges can be overridden by other switches set up for the conference. These are maintained in the header record for the conference in the text file, and also in the pointer file if the information relates to specific users.

The pointer file *relates* data in the other two files. It has a diverse set of record types mapped to a logical structure that is a superset of all their requirements. In total there are 15 different pointer types. For example, a set of records might map addressees (users) to a particular message in the text file. Another pointer type connects users to topics they have joined, with switches showing which user is the originator of the thread, and any special (non-default) access permissions between named users and that thread. Yet another pointer type connects conferences to sub-threads contained within them.

Given a thread with child threads and grandchild threads, a single relationship can be traced between the branches until the top or bottom of a chain is reached. Each pointer record relates one entity to one other. The overall relationship between many text records and many users must be determined by analyzing the content of many individual records in the pointer file, but the system typically operates from the perspective of a single user. The use of indexes permits the software to gather together each user's relationships relatively quickly.

The Participate software uses these relationships to determine a user's access privileges at any juncture in a thread's structure. When a user asks to join a new thread, that user's permissions are examined to determine if he or she is permitted to join threads in general. Next, the thread's default permissions are examined. If it is a public thread, the user is allowed to join. If not, records relating specific users to the private thread are read to see if this user is listed. The software performs such checks only when required, that is, when the user reads the header record of a new thread and asks to join it, or attempts to create a thread.

Participate's designers did their best to reduce the number of checks performed. Once given access to a given thread, no further checks are made in reading subsequent notes, including the header records of new branches. However, because every Participate thread has equal status as a unique conference, such tests are performed often because specific permissions can vary by thread, by user, by system (global defaults), or all three in any combination. As a consequence, Participate does more processing to keep up with user permissions than do other, more simply structured systems.

7.5.2 Relationship between Participate's File and Command Structures

The Participate logical file system supports its flat command structure. Texts can be posted to one or more users and conferences at the same time because they are easily identified by their key types in the text and pointer files. For example, one key identifies the record as a note to a conference, and another as a private note to one or more individuals. Participate builds each of the required records and sends them to the appropriate physical files with a call to its file system entry point. From there, the independent file utility handles the physical creation of the records and their associated index entries. Participate pays a price for its flexibility, however. Compared to more hierarchically organized systems, Participate is a slow performer. Other relevant parameters being equal, a string search through just a few branch levels takes longer than searching through an equivalent amount of text in other systems.

■ 7.6 FILE ABSTRACTION IN THE COM FAMILY

Another variation on the one-file-fits-all approach is found in COM, PortaCom, and SuperCom, by Jacob Palme at Stockholm University. In these systems, conference texts and private mail are managed in one logical file along with links between associated records. Conferences in the COM software family are, in effect, shared mailboxes with which users are associated through pointers contained in a *user* file (see below). A single text may have any number of links. That is, it may be linked to any of the following:

1. Another text on which it comments
2. Other texts containing comments
3. One or more conferences
4. User mailboxes as well as conferences

When a new text is created and linked to a previously existing record, any links between the earlier text, conferences, and mailboxes are automatically established for the new text as well. The link list of the earlier note is updated to reflect the relation to the new comment. In this way, links can be traversed in any direction. New links between existing texts, conferences, and/or mailboxes can be established or removed at any time by persons with appropriate authority.

A *user* file contains a list of all users on the system, their links to private mailboxes and conferences, and their access authority. Using this mechanism, users may ask to see all texts associated with a given entry, but will see only those for which they have at least read authority. For example, suppose a user makes a suggestion for a software enhancement in a conference designed for that purpose. The software developers may open another conference to discuss the recommendation, and link it to the suggestion in the user conference. If the software developers ask to see all the texts associated with the initial user comment, they will see all the associated texts in the developers' conference, plus the original user suggestion, and subsequent comments on that text by users. The users, by contrast, would see only the comments in their user conference. They are not permitted to see the developer conference; that is, their names in the user file do not contain the necessary links.

■ **7.7 SOFTWARE MODULARIZATION**

In Confer, Picospan, COM, and Participate, the application kernel handles most of the basic processing and manipulation of the communications model and the user interface. Each uses external programs to manage peripheral services. Modularization of such programs is achieved at the source or object level with source libraries or linkable service routines. A second kind of modularization involves separate programs, acting as requesters of actions, and servers of results. A single program may be a requester to one part of the system and a server to another. Programs communicate through messages, pipelines, or calls to procedures residing in other programs running concurrently. Each separate program has a prescribed means of address, an interface protocol. It performs a limited function and returns results in a standardized manner. Functional modularization of this kind is the basis of most international standards efforts.

The first form of modularization has the necessary properties to satisfy portability and maintenance requirements. New developments in interface, file, or process technology, can be incorporated into the software, provided vendors make connection libraries available. It is sufficient when the system configuration is purely centralized, with the host controlling the user interface, as well as the internal data representation. It is the only kind of modularity supported in hosts with single tasking operating systems like MS-DOS.

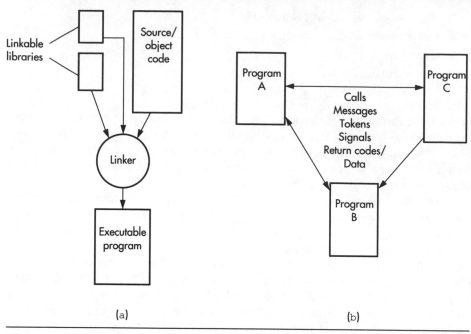

(a)   (b)

Figure 7.4 Modularization. Modularization of code (a) is achieved by linking object code to preexisting modules, resulting in a single executable program. While object-level modularization is shown here, source-level modularization is also common, and represented by `#include` files, and other techniques for combining original code with preexisting modules. Modularization of executable programs (b) is achieved by establishing communications links between separate executing programs. Such programs may communicate through a central clearinghouse program, as they do in Figure 7.1, or may communicate directly with one another, as illustrated here.

The second, illustrated in Figure 7.4, has the benefits of the first, and in addition, the capacity to support distributed hosts, distributed interfaces, and/or communications between otherwise centralized systems. The approach may be fruitfully used in centralized applications as well when the operating system supports multitasking with communications between separate tasks. Contemporary software tools permit many variations in between the two types. This kind of modularization can be achieved in single tasking environments with the use of an application-level, multitasking shell. It can be simulated with Terminate and Stay Resident (TSR) programs. These last are very much like device drivers, though they are often larger, perform a wider variety of tasks, and may communicate with more than one device at a time.

■ 7.8 SOURCE MODULARIZATION WITH PROGRAM LIBRARIES

Modern software tools designed to manage disk and communications I/O have greatly aided the development of modular code. Traditional applications use these tools to optimize their screen, keyboard, and file management operations, leaving developers free to focus on an application's internal processes. These tools most often take the form of libraries; collections of algorithms and data structures that provide a narrowly defined set of services commonly required by application software.

Applications use these services by making calls to routines defined in these libraries, and passing them appropriate parameters. Many libraries contain both source code and object code for their services. The source code may be included in an application and compiled along with the rest of it. Alternately, the resolution of the calls may be postponed until the application object code is linked into an executable module. The latter approach keeps object modules relatively small, and permits inclusion of some types of enhanced services without a complete recompilation of the entire program source.

7.8.1 File and Communications Management Libraries

Screen/keyboard I/O libraries are of little use in communications applications unless the developer intends to distribute a portion of the software's functionality to remote connection equipment. This strategy and its disadvantages were covered, in principle, in the last chapter. File management and communications libraries, however, are used extensively in the development of both MS-DOS and UNIX/Xenix conference software. The former provide elaborate data and index management capabilities. Using these libraries, developers can add and delete records without concern for data or index management and optimization. Participate uses the CBTREE B+ Tree ISAM file manager from Peacock systems of Vienna, Virginia, in both its MS-DOS and UNIX/Xenix versions. Appendix A contains a list of some popular libraries.

Incorporation of communications library products in conference and electronic mail software is also common. MS-DOS's native communications services are very weak (see Chapter 4). Many third parties have produced collections of routines that address the communications hardware (the UART) directly on one side, and provide appropriate services to the application software on the other. Libraries provide programmers with the ability to construct their own customized interfaces between the application and the communication hardware. Such interfaces become a part of the application execution module. Alternatively, these same communications libraries could be used to write customized device drivers like the FOSSIL driver discussed in Chapter 4.

▪ 7.9 REQUESTERS AND SERVERS

The second, and more dramatic, form of modularization is implicit in the seven-layer separation of protocols and services in the ISO's OSI model. The run-time integration of modularized systems on the execution level demands multitasking capabilities in the underlying operating system, or some other mechanism (like an application shell) satisfying these requirements. MS-DOS and the Macintosh Operating System are probably the only well known and heavily used operating systems that are *not* multitasking. Most other operating systems will support radical modularization without third-party add-ons.

In this architectural style, one program may act as a database server, recovering and inserting records in the local text base on request from another module. A second module might handle establishing a connection to a remote machine and transferring data. Yet another handles the chores of the user interface and hands data off to a local administrator program, which communicates with the module making remote connections, and so on. Each of these modules are separate programs running independently of one another. Their services are integrated by message passing.

In centralized configurations, modularization of this kind is not often seen, because of the added overhead imposed by message passing. An exception is the use of pipelines to establish permanent communication channels between modules. Where multiple copies of a communications application are running in a single system (say one copy per user), a reflection of this architecture is seen in message exchanges between users. Data moved to and from storage devices may also pass through messages to an independent DBMS engine. Another use of this technique in centralized systems may involve programs that connect one machine to others in a network. The intersystem communications programs may service other applications besides the interpersonal communications software. System auditing software may also execute independently of the application providing the communications services.

This kind of program modularity is more common in the world of distributed systems. The communications kernel, as represented in most centralized systems, is too large and generalized to be practical in existing distributed environments. This restriction stems primarily from the need in large-scale distributed configurations to communicate with a computer and application that are likely produced by different vendors.

Rather than try to support many services from a single kernel, services can be mixed and matched, as required by the needs and restrictions of the individual environments. Different user interfaces are commonly supported in this way, but the greatest difficulty arises from transformations of physical and logical record structures from one implementation to another. From one vendor to another, the file structures are different enough to prevent establishing convenient and efficient exchange tools. Given a sufficiently generic set of data structures, a process used to transform them from one representation to another can be developed. Yet it is no accident that many of the richer distributed conferencing systems rely on an underlying, standard, record structure throughout the network.

7.9.1 Locating Server Programs

Server programs can have very specific functions. Clients are optimally served by different placements depending on network load and server function. Mail routing servers, for example, might be run separately on each node of a campus network. At the same time, a server providing translation services to a separate network might run on only one node of that campus net. The individual mail servers must have a means of recognizing records destined for the gateway node. For mail services, some convention specifying the alternate network in the address of a message is servicable. For other services, particularly conference distribution, this may not be adequate. Instead, some local directory may serve to determine which conferences are transported across the gateway.

Depending on such matters as the size of the local network, its traffic patterns, or local bandwidth, a single conference server might be more efficient than storing many copies of the conference on individual nodes of the network. If the network is large, and/or slow, distributing server functions to individual nodes is worth considering. The size of these nodes, how many users they support, is another factor to consider.

■ 7.10 DATA TRANSFORMATION FROM ONE STRUCTURE TO ANOTHER

There is a generic process through which data is transformed and/or enveloped for the transition from symbols comprehensible to humans to electronic or fiber-optic data streams, and back again. If this transformation is defined in small enough chunks, then the services provided by each chunk, really layer, can be defined in isolation from the others. Just as importantly, interfaces between the layers can be defined, allowing a two-tiered differentiation of product types. Products can compete *within* a layer, and a given product can communicate with products of more than one vendor at levels adjacent to it. This is exactly what OSI provides for. By dividing up tasks and deliverable services, the OSI model encourages interprogram modularization.

The client-server model is an abstraction superimposed on collections of cooperating software modules across the network. Each element, the client, and the server, are implemented as separate programs. Clients make requests of servers who, in turn, return results and/or error codes to the clients. Servers may also make request of other servers.

There may be other programs operating between clients and servers, and even between clients and users, but the fundamental OSI idea is preserved; each module provides known services and behavior to the other. Client programs typically act in behalf of a single user, though they could service a collection (another network) appearing as one user to the host-server (see Figure 7.5). Multiuser systems may run many client programs at the same time. Where operating systems support re-entrancy, they may automatically share a single copy of a client among many users. Shared clients may or may not make use of control files to tailor operation to each user's preferences.

The client-server model has figured prominently in the development of standards supporting distributed message passing, including conference texts. This model was the essence of the ARPANET when it first became available in 1969. Subsequent developments in document standardization reflected in the Simple Mail Transfer Protocol (SMTP) RFC821, the Arpa Internet Text Message Standard RFC822, and the Usenet Interchange Standard RFC1036, all relied on the preexisting client-server architecture of the evolving Internet. The ISO/CCITT X.400 application standard embodies a specific client-server model. We explore these standards briefly in the following sections, and then describe extensions designed to support many-to-many communications.

■ 7.11 THE ISO AND X.400 MESSAGING

In 1984, the ISO ratified the first X.400 suite of standards, its Red book. In 1988, it extended this suite and modified some earlier components in its Blue book. In 1992, it is expected to extend X.400 further, particularly in the area of conferencing,

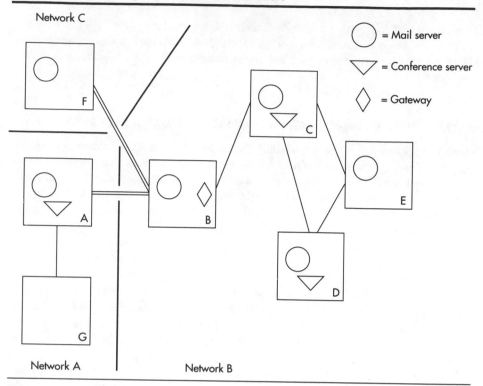

Figure 7.5 Possible server configurations. Servers may be placed wherever convenient, depending on system loads and other factors. Clients (not shown explicitly) act in behalf of individual users associated with each of the nodes represented on the diagram. Associated with each conference and mail server is a local store of text records. In this configuration, users on nodes A, C, and D, have their own conference server, and conferences can be read locally. Users on machines E, F, and G cannot read conferences locally. Accounts on node G cannot even read mail locally. Though the connection may be automatic and transparent, these users receive their conference or mail records from a remote machine. Node B is an internet gateway. It may or may not have local users. It serves to route mail to one network, and both mail and conference data to another. Notice that node B does not have a conference server of its own. Conference requests made by or through node A must be passed through to node C. The same would be true for node F, though it may be that the exchange of conference data between network C and B is not supported.

electronic data interchange, file transfer (independent of messages), voice messaging, access units (see Section 7.11.1), and conformance testing. Appendix C contains a list of the X.400 Red and Blue book specifications, along with related standards.

The purpose of the X.400 standard is to provide capability for user defined messages of any *content* to be transparently encapsulated in a standard envelope for delivery to any defined network mail destination. An X.400 system is a collection of separately executing elements functioning on the highest layer of the ISO seven-layer OSI. One of these elements is the user. The other is the message handling system (MHS).

7.11.1 The X.400 Message Handling System

The MHS is a conceptual entity, a relationship between several discrete elements, and standardized protocols for interelement communication (see Figures 7.6 and 7.7). MHS itself is divided into two parts, the message transfer system (MTS), and the interpersonal messaging system (IPM). A given messaging system is an X.400 system if its own internal elements conform to the specifications of the standard, and it respects the interadministration X.400 protocols. The elements of a full X.400 IPM could be implemented in any number of ways. A system supports X.400 if it *looks* like an X.400 system to a remote network. It does not have to support X.400 internally.

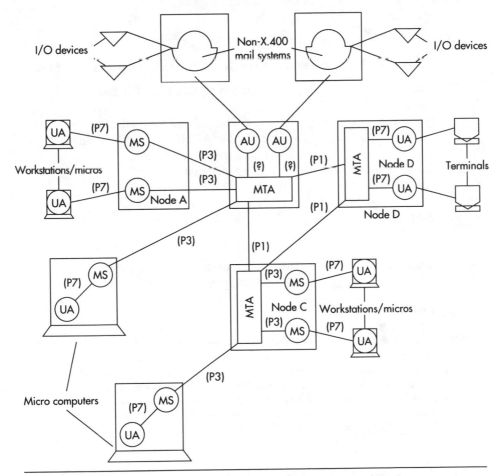

Figure 7.6 Possible configurations of user agents, message transfer agents, message stores, and access units. There are any number of ways that the separate modules of the CCITT X.400 proposal may fit together. Protocol numbers are shown in parentheses. Message stores (MS) communicate with message transfer agents (MTA) through the P3 protocol, user agents (UA) communicate with MSs and MTAs via P7, while MTAs communicate with one another through P1. The protocol for communication between access units (AUs) has not yet been defined.

Recipient Name	O/R name of recipient
Content type	Type, list of types, pointer to another object (e.g. an executable program).
Conversion signal	"YES" means no downstream conversion
Submission/delivery time	
Intended recipient name	O/R name
Converted EITs*	
Original EITs*	
MTS Identifier	
Originator Name	O/R name of originator
Other recipient names	
Priority	

The O/R name buried in the envelope consists itself of the following attributes:

ADMD Name	Administration Management Domain
Country Name	
Domain Types	Classes of information. Allowed values are assigned by the ADMD (of PRMD if any)
Domain Values	Instances of the domain types
Generation	The user's generation, e.g. "jr."
Given Name	
Initials	
Network Address	
Numeric user ID	
Organization Name	
Organization Unit	The division or dept. of the organization
PRMD	Private Management Domain
Surname	
Terminal Identifier	

*EITs are specifications for the message's original and resulting encoding type; they are required if conversion between types might have taken place (if not prohibited). These include various telex, Fax, and ASCII translations. It may also show that a message containing NAPLPS graphics controls had been stripped of them by the receiving MTA, or translated to Prestel protocols. EITs are an example of information in the UA envelope that supports the activity of external programs on the message base.

Figure 7.7 Attributes of an X.400 delivery envelope.

The first component of the MHS encountered by a user is either a user agent (UA), or indirectly, an access unit (AU). The primary difference between them is that UAs are interactive programs executing on behalf of each user individually, one per user. AUs were included, and will be extended further in X.400 to permit attachment to otherwise self-contained e-mail systems that are not X.400-compliant. Users on non-X.400 systems do not interact with AUs; Instead, their software makes such connections to AUs on their behalf if the vendor has enabled it to do so.

7.11.2 X.400 User Agents

UAs provide the interface between the user and the message delivery system. As an interface, they can appear in a variety of forms, text-based or graphical, menu or command-driven, or with internal or external editors. They can provide input forms and output formatting along with text-searching and message-filtering capabilities. None of these services are limited by X.400. Most vendors do not support elaborate search/filtering capabilities, but input and output formatting is reasonably common.

The UA is also a conceptual user mailbox. It must support storage services that allow users to read messages at any time after delivery, keep them for re-reading, file them, and so on. Outgoing messages must be stored and queued for delivery to the next step in the X.400 chain. Services required of the UA as a part of basic read and write facilities in X.400 include:

1. Message identification: Assignment of a universally unique ID to each message, and corresponding display/recovery of that ID for recipients. Message identification also includes the originator/recipient (O/R) name, an individual's full identification. See Figure 7.7 for details.

2. Nondelivery notification: Conveying to a user the fact of the system's inability to deliver a previously written message.

3. Submission time and date stamps.

4. Delivery time and date stamps.

5. Content type indication (text or binary).

The UA wraps a message in an envelope of associated information. The originating user supplies some of this information. Other components are generated by the UA and/or the local MTA. The UA's envelope conveys information about the message to human users directly, or to external programs (external to the mail system) that act for the user.

In the SMTP and RFC822 message protocols used by the Internet, the message contains its own envelope. While the services of the UA are commonly provided by analogous agents in the Internet system, there is no requirement that they be so. As long as the message itself complies with the appropriate Internet structures, the network's exchange software can successfully manage it. The X.400 system is more complicated, but it more clearly delineates the processes managing message exchange. Specifically, the UA must service a user by constructing a suitable envelope for delivery. This envelope may include substantial information pertaining to advanced services. A small portion of this information is shown in Figure 7.7.

7.11.3 X.400 Message Transfer Agents

The message transfer agent (MTA) is the next step in the X.400 module chain. While the UA is associated with a single user, MTAs typically service many users, or even many machines with multiple users. In the MHS model, the UA is the client, the MTA is the server. MTAs receive messages from UAs or possibly from message stores (files or database records) managed by the MTA. These holding bins may or may not be under the jurisdiction of the UA as well. UA messages are sent directly to the local MTA storage area.

Messages entering the system from the outside are sent to other MTAs or individual UA file areas. They may also be left in an outgoing MTA storage area for a UA to find when it starts up. The collection of MTAs in a network or internet comprise the message transfer system (MTS). The X.400 naming scheme permits each MTA to know the local MTA of a message's recipient. The originating MTA is responsible for contacting the remote server either directly, or via intermediate MTAs with automatic forwarding. MTAs may also *create* messages in a limited sense. They determine if a message is to be copied to multiple users in the MTA's domain. If so, they generate a separate copy of the message for each recipient.

The MTA surrounds the UA envelope with another layer of information. For example, this may include a flag indicating that message copying is or is not allowed. This flag may override UA instructions to copy the message. It also contains trace fields used to audit a message's trail of connections within the MHS. There is a recipient descriptor field which might be used to route messages to shared text pools (conferences), programs, or individuals by interest, rather than by name. Support for any of these last features is not specifically required by X.400 at this time.

7.11.4 Cooperation between MTAs and UAs

UAs and MTAs must cooperate in an assortment of tasks. For example, an MTA may by default submit messages to special compression or other encoding schemes for security or efficiency reasons. UAs and MTAs must signal one another to prohibit such actions if necessary. Other kinds of conversions could include support for ASCII to Fax or telex conversions and vice versa. UAs and MTAs also communicate to support recovery of cross references, the automatic recovery of one message referenced by another. Many of the more advanced services described here were not addressed in the 1984 Red Book, but only in the later 1988 version.

Depending on implementation levels (1984, 1988, 1992), other UA or UA/IPM services include:

1. Multipriority delivery: a user's ability to specify special presumably faster but more expensive handling of priority messages. The corresponding service on the recipient side is notification and message categorization by priority signal.
2. Multidestination delivery: multiple recipients, with control over disclosure of those recipients to any one or all of the others, blind copies, and so on.
3. Deferred delivery and deferred delivery cancellation.
4. Delivery notification—as contrasted with nondelivery notification.
5. Message forwarding capabilities, along with notification regarding forwarded messages.
6. Expiration date indication: automatic deletion of expired messages whether or not all intended recipients have read them.
7. Probe activity: a probe is a message with no body. Its task is to provide an originating user with a report indicating a message's deliverability to a remote system and/or user.

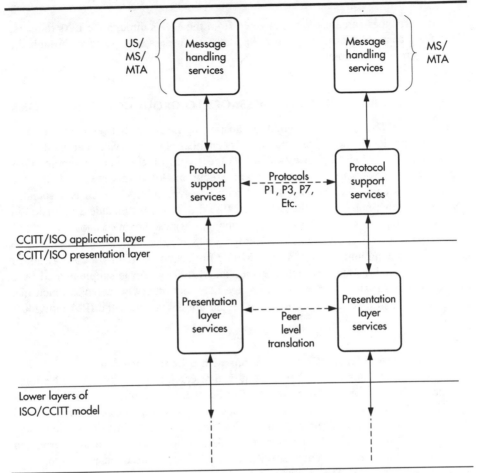

Figure 7.8 Various configurations of X.400 MHS components. Message handling services in the UA or MS include the message submission service element, message delivery service element, and the message administration service element. The UA, in addition, contains a message retrieval service element. In the MTA, a message transfer service element replaces the retrieval services of the UA. For the UA, these services control such things as the disposition, selection, creation, prioritization, auditing, and reporting of messages. It also services user requests for audit reports regarding message delivery or errors. In the MS, storage control is included, while the MTA services provide for the establishment of communications and exchange of stored messages between nodes of the X.400 network. Protocol support services include such things as surrounding messages in appropriate envelopes (P1, P3, P7, . . .), determinations about the most efficient routes between MTAs (using internal directory services), along with matching intersystem security requirements, and migration support between systems using different levels of the X.400 standard (1984/1988/1992). The presentation layer may be used to reformat data between different application-level devices. For example, reformatting text data generated electronically for presentation as a Fax message.

8. Reports: these are messages delivered from the MTAs through the UAs to users. They contain information about the status of a message's passage through the system to its recipient.

■ **7.12 EXTENDING PERSONAL MESSAGES TO GROUP COMMUNICATIONS**

Note that the MTS itself is not limited to transporting messages between persons. It is a generic, high-level, intersystem transport mechanism. Other services can be derived directly from the MTS system by defining other types of UAs. For example, UAs defined for Fax exchange, remote program execution, login services, or batch file exchange. Currently, the ISO has defined only one type of UA, which is associated with interpersonal messaging, the IPM. The ISO did, however, include a provision in the IPM UA type to support binary files exchange disguised as messages.

Two parallel projects underway in Europe seek to extend the X.400 standard to support group communications. In the AMIGO project sponsored by a consortium of European universities and research agencies the X.400 system is supplemented by a special directory system that handles message lists, but otherwise behaves much like the X.400 IPM in that messages originate in and are delivered by the IPM individual user agent.

7.12.1 Supporting Group Communications with a Conference Agent

The "special agent" approach is being taken by a research group at the Centre National d'Etudes des Telecommunications (CNET) in France. This group is developing user agent models for file transfer, remote job submission, computer conferencing, and remote database access. Their experimental system is called SMARTIX, illustrated in Figure 7.9. In this model, conferencing is defined as "a collection of interrelated messages or *transactions* about a specific theme." Each transaction is composed of *contents* and *attributes*. The attributes are:

1. Global unique identifier
2. Author name
3. Submission date
4. Transaction object (the nature of the content)
5. Expiration date
6. Key words
7. Links

Links define the relationship between one transaction and others in a single conference. Examples include: "in reply to," "continuation of," "new version of," and "comment on." When a conference is created, appropriate links are specified by its administrator.

The SMARTIX model defines a new class of UA called a bulletin board user agent (BBUA). This UA continues to act on behalf of an individual user, and contains attributes that represent that user's role in relation to any given conference on the

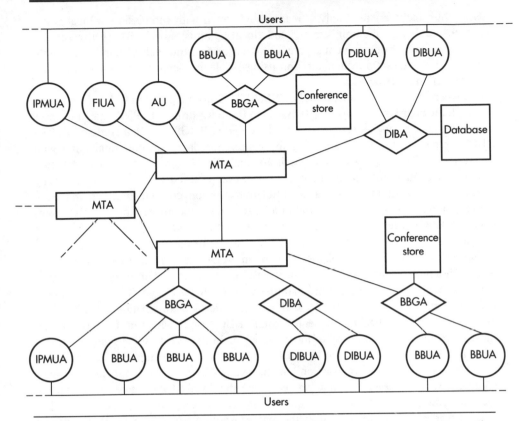

Figure 7.9 SMARTIX proposal for extending X.400 to group communications. The bulletin board user agent (BBUA) and the distributed information base user agent (DIBUA) are added to the X.400 model, which currently defines only the interpersonal user agent (IPUA), and is working on both the file transfer user agent (FTUA) and the access unit (AU) supporting connections to non-X.400 systems. Between the BBUA and DIBUA, SMARTIX proposes another level of agency, the *group agent*, bulletin board group agent (BBGA), and distributed information base agent (DIBA), respectively. Each of these communicates with the MTA on behalf of their respective user agents, conferences and/or databases. For each *conference* or *database* represented on a system, there is *one* BBGA and one DIBA. A given system may have many hundreds of these group agents. Each is responsible for the appropriate conversion of conference messages or database queries/results and delivery/receipt of these communications to/from the local MTA. They also handle message security and distribution to the appropriate list of individual user agents as necessary. A given BBGA and DIBA must also know when it is appropriate to access local storage, and interact with it appropriately. The BBGAs and DIBAs may or may not be connected to their own local conference or database stores. That is, the model does not limit the possible architectures of either conferencing or database access. Both may be distributed either by replication or using the local machine/distributed-access approach, or a mixture of the two. Some nodes supporting the group communications and distributed database systems may not have any local stores at all. They may also support any mix of the other kinds of UAs, or none at all.

MHS. Roles include: "read-only," "read-write," "read with submission to local editor for inclusion," "global administrator," and "local administrator." BBUAs also support services like transaction content suppression (censoring), transaction marking for rapid retrieval, and transaction filter/selection using Boolean operators in conjunction with the transaction's attributes.

Between the BBUA and the MTA, SMARTIX introduces a new level of agent, the bulletin board group agent (BBGA), and a new protocol, P30, that addresses peer communications between BBGAs. There is one BBGA for each conference. The BBGA is responsible for maintaining the conference database, communicating with the system MTA on one side, and the individual BBUAs on the other. The database is maintained in replicated form, in theory, a complete copy for each participating BBGA. This requirement avoids potential transmission complications arising from nonreplication of conference material in a large heterogeneous network. Furthermore, since reading conference records is far more common than writing new ones, the maintenance of a local database improves access performance.

Yet because of delay problems inherent in MTA message distribution, coupled with differential storage abilities of local BBGAs, there is a chance that a reply to a comment will arrive before the original message, or that a reply will reference a note that has been removed from the local BBGA. Problems of this nature are minimized by imposing yet another requirement: a single BBGA somewhere in the network that must maintain a *complete* copy of the conference. In the event of a system crash, this reference BBGA can reload the local BBGA. Another interesting technique involves the creation of a *virtual* transaction. In the event that a given comment references another already removed or not yet received, the local BBGA generates a virtual record representing that referenced transaction. At the same time, the BBGA makes request of the local MTA to recover the real transaction from the network's reference BBGA for that conference.

The SMARTIX model is due for consideration by the ISO/CCITT in their 1990–1992 cycle. For now, it is only an experiment and a suggestion. It should receive a reasonable hearing because the concept of the BBGA is an elegant extension of the interpersonal messaging system. By imposing an entity between the BBUA and the system-wide MTS, SMARTIX supports the basic concept of a user agent (an entity acting on behalf of a single user), and it imposes no added burden on the MTAs.

■ 7.13 DISTRIBUTING INFORMATION RETRIEVAL

7.13.1 Remote login as a Distribution Technique

Requests of bibliographic or other databases, as well as the returned results can both be encapsulated in X.400 or RFC822 messages. Distributing an information retrieval system is well within the capacity of current technology, although the size of many collections makes this impractical. Not only the data, but elaborate index systems imperative for access performance, must also be stored. One alternative, distributed remote access, is commonly used by large research and educational networks like the Internet. Local telephone companies are also assessing this delivery approach. Gateway services provided by the regional phone companies can link users to specialized databases running on many computers, large or small. US West, headquartered in Omaha, Nebraska, has the most ambitious experiment underway at the time of this writing.

7.13.2 Remote Query Execution

Another form of distribution involves distributed, remote, query execution. Technologically, this is related to remote program execution services found on some networks. The primary problem with distributed query execution is that no standards for bibliographic citation structures, report formatting, query services, or submission are widely supported. The National Information Standards Organization (NISO) and the ISO have developed competing standards addressing some of these needs. Adequate batch and interactive submission standards have been around for a long time, but they are not typically supported *between* networks (the Internet being an exception). In addition, databases may contain records that are not bibliographic. Any number of record formats might require support.

7.13.3 Distributed Query Languages

Finally, although proposals and specialized experiments exist, no widely distributed network has implemented anything like a universal distributed query language. Both the National Information Standards Organization (NISO) and the ISO have developed proposals for a universal *command* language, of which database queries are a natural subset. Both recommendations include reasonably intuitive commands for finding records and displaying them in various formats.

Neither standard has gained much acceptance. In the end, administrative difficulties with distributed remote program or query execution have effectively suppressed widespread acceptance of these standards. These same problems, including financial arrangements and security concerns, have slowed acceptance of message standards as well. The cost of transporting messages is relatively easy to measure and predict for any given user population. Remote query execution can result in extended use of CPU resources yet result in very low message traffic. Performance requirements impose a further burden of maintaining real-time or near real-time links between a user and distant host through multiple intermediate nodes.

7.13.4 Distributed Directory Services for Information Retrieval

Even if a query language or a standard for query services existed, users would still have to *apply* queries to databases of widely varying structure. This imposes a need for a standardized database directory service. This directory must show the fields in the database available to the user, their relationship (if relevant to the query process), and what specific set of query services each database supports. At some point, the database purveyors must agree on some universal means of informing the network of what is available in their database and how it will respond to generic network queries. Distributed database capability of any kind is only moderately supported in the major academic and research networks. DBMS directory standards are now evolving, but they have not been implemented on networks spanning administrative domains.

■ **7.14 OBJECT-ORIENTED PROGRAMMING AND COMMUNICATIONS SOFTWARE**

In addition to the modularization techniques discussed, development of software for interpersonal communications systems is ideally suited to an altogether different programming paradigm—object-oriented programming (OOP).

The variety of text-based communications are semantically infinite but there is, generally speaking, a well-defined set of communications types. Reports may take many forms, but they have something in common. The same is true of business memos, periodical articles, conference comments, and bibliographic citations. Many formal structures share common data attributes and behaviors. For example, many have dates and author/originator names. Most can be copied or in some way passed through a network at the discretion of an individual reader. Other characteristics may not be shared. Reports, for example, might have graphics data associated with them, while essays do not. Multiple sorts make sense on some structures, say phone lists, but not others, like book chapters.

It is quite natural to think of each structural variation as an object class, sharing properties of a super class or many classes. Corporate reports and articles may share the properties of the class "individually-filed-documents." Management bulletins and electronic-mail could be members of the class "personal-transmissions." Each might have properties the other has not. The first, for example, might support very long texts, while the latter is limited to a few thousand bytes. Yet they may share properties as well, for example the capacity to be forwarded to another person.

Most of the text transport and delivery models of distributed systems consist of programs, operating as independent entities, communicating with one another through the procedure calling and data passing rules of well-behaved interfaces. These programs are also natural "objects" from the viewpoint of the whole system. They have characteristic behavior, manipulate certain types of data structures, and so on.

7.14.1 EIES2, an Object Experiment

The OOP model applies equally well to centralized systems, or systems designed to run in multiple nodes. The most significant experiment in this area is M. Turoff and J. Whitescarver's Electronic Information Exchange System II or EIES2, illustrated in Figure 7.10. While maintaining the EIES name, this second product bears little resemblance to the former software. Its lowest level routines are written in C. Above the driver level are a series of abstractions, a database, user agents, terminal interface, development (customization) environment, application entities, reliable transport service interface, and remote operations server. Elements are tied together by a communications processor whose native language is an extension of SmallTalk, the first full object-oriented programming language, created by the Xerox Palo Alto Research Center in the early 1980s.

An application entity (AE) is a program or collection of programs that support some one narrowly defined part of the communications system. For example, useful work on the system requires at minimum, a database AE, and a user agent AE. Other AEs are common, including message transfer agents (MTAEs), directory service agents

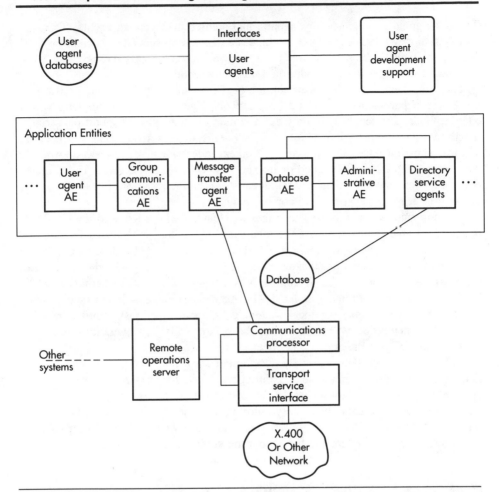

Figure 7.10 The EIES2 environment. The EIES2 system has many application entities, only a few of which are shown here. These govern all system functions and capabilities. At the heart of the system is a database that contains not only the message base itself, but the definitions and protocols for all intra- and intersystem communications. This database may reside on one machine, but it is designed to be distributed. This is also true for the application entities. In general, each of the components shown in the diagram may reside (within reason), on a different machine. Similarly, components may be replicated across machine boundaries.

(DSAEs), group communications agents, and archive management agents. The AEs of a system may all reside on one machine, be resident on separate systems, or both; that is, individual AEs may communicate with their counterparts through a network by sending messages to one another and receiving replies.

These messages are called operation protocol data units (OPDUs), and conform to the X.409 requirements for P1 and P3 protocols. They consist of type, length, and content fields. The length field provides a simple mechanism for supporting variable length messages. Type is divided into three subfields, class, format, and ID. The class, in turn, shows whether the message is context-independent, or context-dependent, conforming to the X.400 standard or interpretable only by the receiver. The contents may be a command and associated parameters, a returned result or error code, or one or more nested sets of type/length/content fields.

The communications processor is a message handler whose job is to route OPDUs between the objects that comprise the total system. It is also responsible for defining new classes of objects to the application's database. Database objects are both record types and methods, operations that can be legally performed on or with the data. When a message is sent from one AE to another, what happens depends on whether or not the intended recipient is a remote or local AE. Access to remote AEs is asynchronous. Once a message is sent, the local system goes about other tasks until a reply is received. It then recovers the context of the message from its operations stack and forwards the reply to the appropriate local entity.

EIES2 is therefore both vertically decentralized and horizontally distributed. Vertical decentralization is implemented through a layered interface between systems, applications, and users. Horizontal distribution is achieved through support of remote operations on remote data objects. By tailoring the objects and classes that comprise the EIES2 distributed database, programmers and users can produce any structures and interaction rules imaginable for supporting communications.

■ **7.15   ARCHITECTURES AND TAILORABILITY**

In the end, many kinds of interfaces and internal conference structures can be supported in one or more architectural styles. Which style a developer chooses depends on his or her goals for the software. If one hopes to port the application to many different machine/operating system architectures, the approach taken by Participate and Caucus seems best: monolithic programs operating on file and interface abstractions connected to real file systems and interfaces through single-point software interfaces. If one is content to remain within a single operating system family, then the multiple program approach of Picospan contributes to ease of development and maintenance of the software. If the system must support elaborate tailoring of the communications structures by users, then a centralized configuration makes sense. Achieving a high degree of tailorability in distributed systems is next to impossible unless the same application software is running on all nodes of the network.

This is the case with both EIES2 and VaxNotes. Usenet, by contrast, is impossible to tailor because the nodes supporting it may run all manner of independently produced interface and communications programs. There is no guarantee that a specific structure supported by one group's software would be intelligible to another, in fact it almost certainly wouldn't be. Such systems rely on standardized exchange protocols, and relatively simple data structures, manipulated by interface programs. Even the X.400 Interpersonal Messaging System, and conferencing extensions based on it, will be limited to such simple structures. Alternate structures are, generally speaking, the product of individual creative imagination. One cannot permit such innovations to corrupt a network. Standardizing all possible structural alternatives and requiring some support for them is an impossible task.

8

COMMUNICATIONS SERVICES AND SOFTWARE

In this chapter we will examine some publicly accessible conferencing systems and a few medium-sized software products for group communications.

■ 8.1 CONFERENCING IN THE PUBLIC ARENA

8.1.1 The Byte Information Exchange

In terms of user base, the three largest public services supporting conference functions are CompuServe, GEnie, and BIX. Of the three, only BIX, the Byte Information Exchange of Byte Inc., is fundamentally oriented around a true computer conferencing package. CoSy, developed at the University of Guelph in Ontario, Canada by Alistair Mayer, has a somewhat novel high-level conference model. Although heretofore used in sites other than BIX, it is only now being put in a form suitable for widespread commercialization by Softwords Inc. of Victoria, British Columbia, Canada, which purchased the commercialization rights from the University of Guelph in 1989.

The CoSy model, illustrated in Figure 8.1, is a hybridization of the comb architecture and the infinite branching capabilities of comment-oriented software. As of early 1990, there were over 350 conferences on BIX. Like those of its competitors, these conferences span a wide range of human interests, with a concentration in computer and telecommunications technology that is denser than on either of the other two systems. Besides its employment of CoSy, BIX distinguishes itself by being a premiere arena for technical information exchange, and it is rapidly becoming an important system for third party support services.

In January 1990 there were over 50 companies represented on BIX with their own conferences dedicated to product support and user interaction. BIX technical conferences are unparalleled in depth of information, and this is particularly true for subjects in which computers play a direct role. Most machines in the microcomputer

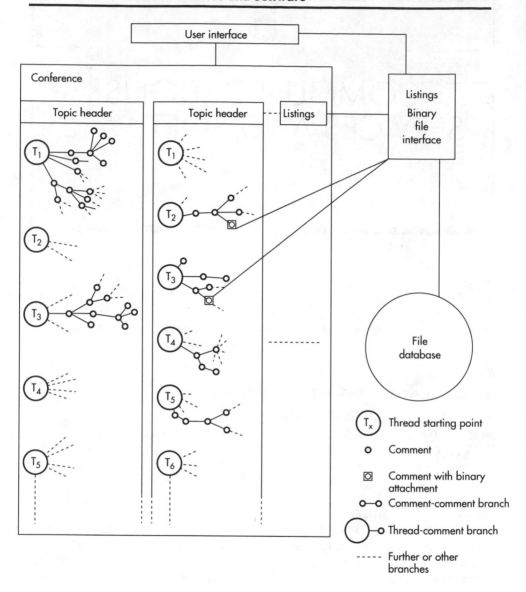

Figure 8.1 CoSy communications structure. Conferences enclose a set of topics which cannot be created by ordinary users. One of these topics is the listing area. When a user selects this topic, he or she is connected to a special file interface program which prompts for further action. The same process takes place when a user reads a message to which a binary file has been attached. Under the regular topics, users can create new threads on which comments can be associated. Comments can also be addressed to comments, and so forth, leading to a branch structure. Thread starters are not themselves connected to one another in any way. One cannot, for example, read only the thread openers in a topic. The software does support moving an entire thread, starting with its originating message, to another subtopic of the conference.

arena are represented, including long-discontinued models, as are most operating systems, computer languages, BBS and telecommunications software, database engines, and other software. BIX has extensive file libraries, but it is the technical excellence of the information available from knowledgeable persons in many fields that is most impressive.

BIX conferences are divided into 5 to 10 subareas; this is an average, and is not limited by the software. There may be many subconferences, or none. Only the conference administrator can create or remove areas. Within these subareas, users can create new conversation threads. These original entries are somewhat analogous to the items created under conferences in the comb model; any number of comments can be attached to these starting points. CoSy is among the few systems that melds the comment-in-context philosophy with a conference orientation. Comments can have comments explicitly attached to them, producing a branch effect; however, at the same time, CoSy avoids the "hidden branch" problem of Participate by embedding the branch system in a conference or topic shell (see Section 8.1.1.2).

8.1.1.1 CoSy File Structure

CoSy's file structure is straightforward; messages, whether comments or originals, are stored in a single file—one per conference subarea. The header portion of each record contains a number of fixed-length fields that contain time, date, and author information along with either the title or subject of an original message, or a pointer to a message on which the current one is a comment. There is also a field containing the length of the text portion of the record. CoSy records are thus delimited by length offsets—the length of the fixed portion of the record—plus the length of the text part. Associated with this file is an index file that contains offset pointers to each message in the main file and is used to provide random access capability thereto. If, for example, a user connects to a conference subarea and his or her last-read pointer shows that message 200 was the last read, the system reads the index file for message 201 and uses the offset present to find that record in the message file.

Because CoSy knows the length of the text part of each record, there is no limit to the size of any given message. CoSy also has the potential for supporting the North American presentation level protocol syntax (NAPLPS) for graphics (see Chapter 10). BIX does not at this time contain areas or files with picture information, but users can embed this information in their own comments. One of the options under user control (see Section 8.1.1.2) tells BIX to filter out this information as it transmits comments.

8.1.1.2 Navigation and Control in CoSy

CoSy's file design is simple yet provides a foundation for unusually powerful features. Unfortunately, CoSy does not live up to its own potential in many ways. For example, users can choose to read messages in time or reference sequence. Time sequence flattens out the structure essentially making the subconference areas like *items*. Reading in this manner allows one to distinguish original entries from comments only by the presence of a title in the former, and a backwards pointer (for example, "this is a comment to message 200") in the latter. It is this feature that gives CoSy its hybrid comment-conference orientation. However, ordinary users cannot *create* new item-level entries, so they behave more like EIES conferences subsumed by a super-conference.

When reading by reference, entries are arranged so originals are succeeded by their comments. Branches are automatically displayed in depth order. Consider the following example:

A. Original message 200 entered at 12:01

B. message 201, comment on 200 entered at 12:02

C. message 202, comment on 200 entered at 12:03

D. message 203, comment on 201 entered at 12:04

E. message 204, comment on 200 entered at 12:05

F. message 205, comment on 203 entered at 12:06

A read reference command would retrieve the messages in the order A, B, D, F, C, E. If a user encounters a comment to a message he or she does not recall, entering *original* will redisplay that message. CoSy will not, however, permit users to read only original messages and skip the comments. Nor will it permit them to read comments breadth first; in other words, across one generation of replies. To use the example above, this would be A, B, C, E, D, F. Ironically, both of these facilities would be easy to support given the data present in the two CoSy files. Reading original messages without comments allows users to determine which hold the most interest for them. Breadth-first reading gives users the opportunity of selecting which comment branches to pursue further. Both facilities add enormously to the overall filtering potential of a communications system. It is the lack of such facilities that hobbles most comment-in-context systems and makes them difficult to use in formal settings.

CoSy's search support is on par with those of other conferencing systems. Within a given subarea (and not between them), users can search for records by date, string, or both. The latter scans both message headers and their texts. Searches can be limited to a range of messages by number or pointer. For example, "search 100 to 200 'string,'" and "search current to last 'string.'" BIX also sports a special conference called the *index*. Joining the index conference executes a process that permits users to search for strings across all BIX conferences. The results of a search are displayed as a list of subtopics by conference along with the message numbers in those subareas containing the target string. The normal search facility within a subtopic simply displays the message number, along with the line or lines containing the target. The system does not support Boolean connectors between strings: for example, one cannot search for "string A" *and* "string B."

8.1.1.3 Binary Exchange Support

CoSy does support one feature, somewhat rare in conferencing systems, reflecting its post-microcomputer BBS origins. Users may attach binary files to any original message or comment, including private electronic mail. If, for example, a user posts a message containing a reference to a long document or an executable program, that document or code can be *attached* directly to the message. The existence of attachments is signaled by a pointer to a file name present in one of the fixed fields of the message header. If a comment is attached, a reader is invited to download it. On accepting this invitation, the reader activates a process that prompts for the download protocol to use (X-on X-off, Kermit, X-modem, Y-modem, and Z-modem are supported) and begins the process of transmitting the file.

Each conference also contains a subarea called *listings* where binary files (programs, compressed documents, and so forth) are also stored. This area is not associated with any specific message of the conference. On entering a conference's listing area, a program that presents users with a menu is activated. From this menu, participants can search for files, read descriptions entered by the files' authors, select a protocol, and download or transmit one or more files.

8.1.1.4 User Customization
BIX can be user-customized by storing commands and option settings in a file associated with each user. This permits users to customize both the commands and, to some extent, the format of BIX output. Though not as flexible as Picospan in this regard, the options file can be used, among other things, to turn menu mode on or off, control the interface of the text editor, and otherwise tailor some of the actions that BIX takes when a user logs in. For example, the *order* option tells BIX in what order to display conferences. Default upload and download protocols can be set here as well. Options can be used to select a specific editor, set default prompts, filter out control or NAPLPS characters, produce aliases for any BIX commands, and so forth.

8.1.2 CompuServe Information Service
CompuServe Information Service (CIS) is the Pacific Ocean of public information services. Conferencing, information retrieval, extensive electronic mail facilities, dozens of games, synchronous many-to-many chat facilities, and on-line shopping are available in one system. The information retrieval aspects of the system include a gateway to dozens of external bibliographic, legal, business, scientific, and engineering databases, as well as local databases and file libraries. Inside CIS itself there are an on-line encyclopedia, stock and commodities information, airline flight and price information, weather and climatographic data, UPI and AP news feeds, and the full text of several national newspapers.

8.1.2.1 Navigation, Structure, Search and Selection on CIS
CompuServe's store-and-forward conferencing takes the form of independent special interest groups (SIGs). Like BIX, there is a wide-ranging coverage of computer and technology topics. Several technology vendors—generally the larger ones—also use CIS for customer support and interaction. The range of CIS SIG subjects is, however, much broader than it is on BIX. Religion, politics, social issues, economics, education, philosophy, psychology, and the arts (music, painting, dance, film, theater, photography, fiction, poetry, cooking, and so forth) and sciences are represented. Several multiplayer games have their own SIGs for learning, strategic and tactical development, and general camaraderie among the players. The wine SIG maintains an extraordinary database of wines, prices, and availability.

CIS SIGs, like BIX conferences, are divided into an average of 6 to 12 subsections, each dealing with a different aspect of the conference topic. Users may post original messages under these subtopics or attach comments to existing messages, including other comments. Superficially, this is like the structure of CoSy conferences; messages may be read in time-sequential order or by *thread,* which functions like the CoSy *read reference* command. Beneath the surface, however, there are marked differences (see Figure 8.2 for a demonstration of CIS SIG record structures).

First, CIS SIG subsections are not as clearly separated from one another as are CoSy subconferences. Users can elect to read messages from all, or a select subset of, the SIG sections at the same time. Second, messages are not posted to the conference itself, but to individuals. When entering a thread-starting message, the author is prompted for the name or ID (or both) of the person to whom it is directed. A user may here designate "all" or "persons interested in X" instead of a real person; all messages not posted *privately* are available for all to read whether or not a real person is named.

If an individual's ID is included, the CIS software automatically *marks* that message for the appointed participant. When this person next checks the SIG, he or she may read messages marked directly, without working through all the new messages in the SIG. Replies to messages are automatically *marked* for the author of the message to which the reply is directed. This feature facilitates some conversations, but information can be lost if a participant reads only messages marked for him or her.

Suppose, for example, that Adam posts a message to Beth. Beth, Charles, and Doug post replies to Adam's message. Doug also replies to the message posted by Charles, and Ellen replies to messages posted by Charles and the second message posted by Doug to Charles. When Adam visits the SIG, he will see three messages marked for him, namely the first three replies from Beth, Charles, and Doug. If he reads only the marked messages, he will miss the second message from Doug to Charles and the messages from Ellen to Doug and Charles. It is this strong "message orientation" to which so many proponents of conference-oriented software object in CIS and other such systems. The marked message feature encourages people to avoid the totality of what has transpired in a thread of discussion, stripping it of its conversational value.

Yet the marked message feature is a useful information filter if one is not interested in related messages (replies to replies). Using this feature does reduce the many-to-many function of the conference medium to a many-to-one–like structure similar to electronic mail. CIS does, however, provide other filtering mechanisms that may

```
#:  [msg. #] [section #]/[section title]
      DD-Mon-YY  HH:MM:SS     ← posting date/time
Sb: [subject msg. # - title]    ← blank if original message
Fm: [Author's name] [Author's ID]
To: [Recipient Name] [Recipient ID]     ← may be "all", a specific person,
                                           or another recipient

Text..........
    .
    .
    .
```

Figure 8.2 CIS SIG record structure.

be used in place of the marked message function. All the messages in the previous example will retain the subject field of the original message posted by Adam. Adam could therefore recover all the messages by reading messages posted to this subject, and he would see all his marked messages at the same time.

Perhaps the biggest difference between CIS SIGs and CoSy conferences is that there is no mechanism analogous to the CoSy show new command. That is, users cannot determine which SIGS have new messages and in what sections they appear without checking each SIG individually. CIS does have a find command that functions somewhat like the BIX *index* conference. Users can search for subjects of interest, but the CIS command displays only the *names* of SIGs that encompass the subject area, not individual message numbers.

When a SIG is entered, the software tells a participant what message numbers are now active in the SIG (see the following discussion about the scroll problem) and the highest message number read by the user. The user is left to perform a mental calculation to ascertain how many new messages there are to read. Complicating the problem further, the information given pertains to the SIG as a whole; the user has no way to tell how many new messages there are in each subsection.

The command scan quick new will display the message number and subject field of each original message in a SIG, followed by the number of responses not yet seen by a user. Users can restrict the SIG sections to which this or any other command applies with the set section command. Along with these filter mechanisms, CIS supports reading by thread which is similar to BIX's read reference, and a limited search facility. SIG messages may be searched for entries from or to a certain person, dates, and strings contained in their subject field. No searching of the message text itself is supported.

8.1.2.2 Binary Exchange Support

CompuServe does not support binary attachments to message texts. Each text line must be no more than 80 bytes in length and must end with a carriage return; entries are restricted to about 2KB in length, or about 24 lines. This occasions some rather inelegant workarounds for users when messages must exceed this length. The most common practice is to divide longer messages into separate sections and send sections beyond the first as replies to the original message. This can be especially disconcerting when such messages are replies to someone else's message, because the subsequent attachments are not marked for the author of the note to which the replies are directed.

For binary file support, each SIG contains a number of data libraries (DLs)—one associated with each message section. Users must switch from the message section to the appropriate DL to upload or download binary files. CIS supports several common file exchange protocols, including its own high-speed cserve-binary protocol. The management of CIS has released the specification for this protocol into the public domain, and it is supported by many, but not all, terminal emulation programs. One interesting experiment on CIS points out the emphasis placed on binary file libraries over conferencing itself. Among the five SIGs dedicated to IBM-PC-like systems (systems programming, applications, hardware, communications, and bulletin boards), there is a program that will allow users to search for files in all their DLs from one place. Files can be searched by name, keyword, date, and author. The software displays the name of a program, a description if requested, and a list of IBM SIG data libraries that hold it. An identical service exists for Apple Computer owners.

8.1.2.3 User Customization

User-setable options are not as flexible as those of BIX, but will serve to customize the system interface to some degree. Menus can be turned on or off, one of two editors can be selected, and SIG last-read markers can be set forward or backward. The options command can also determine whether or not an author's own messages will be redisplayed to him or her, or automatically skipped if a read command would otherwise recover them.

CompuServe's greatest conferencing weakness is its scroll rate. Each SIG is given limited disk space on the host, and the number of people active on the system, especially in heavily used SIGs, causes messages to scroll off the system at a prodigious rate. Messages on the less active SIGs may remain for up to two or three weeks, but only two or three days in heavily trafficked areas. CompuServe's ability to function as a true conferencing system in most domains is thus nullified. Much of the convenience and value of store-and-forward conferencing is destroyed when users are forced to check conferences every few days so as not to miss possible replies to questions, or continue an interesting discussion. Often the same questions must be asked repeatedly by users because there is no long-term message base to search. Despite their popularity and relatively high volume of information exchange, both of CIS's main competitors manage to retain their message bases for much longer periods, typically several years!

Many CIS users are aware of this acute deficiency, yet the system remains popular because of the availability of many other services besides the SIG conferences. CIS's electronic mail facilities support not only mail among CIS users, but also two-way connections with MCI Mail and the entire Internet. CompuServe's news databases are comparable to competitive systems, and many other sources are accessible as well through its EasyNet gateway. CompuStore is among the largest and most diversified electronic stores in existence, and the system supports more games than most of its competitors combined.

8.1.3 General Electric Information Service

GEnie covers much the same ground as CIS. It is comparable in news, travel, financial services, and electronic shopping. It has a similar synchronous many-to-many chat capability and an extensive collection of files. On the whole its prices are a bit lower, but so is its overall volume because there are fewer people generating new material. GEnie's conferencing facility is the Roundtable. Each is a stand-alone conference disconnected from the others, exactly analogous to CompuServe's SIGs. Like CIS, GEnie's Roundtables encompass many subjects. There are not as many as on CIS— about 65 in early 1990—but there is no extraordinary concentration around technical subjects as exists on BIX.

8.1.3.1 Navigation, Structure, Search, and Selection in GEnie

Internally, the Roundtables are different from SIGs; the Genie message structure is illustrated in Figure 8.3. Each is divided into categories analogous to SIG sections,

A. Topic header structure

```
CATEGORY    [category #] [category title]
*********
TOPIC  [topic #] Date: [day] [month], [year]     ← topic creation date
[name] [forum handle]          at HH:MM EST    ← topic creation
Sub: [subject]


Subject Text ....
   .

   .

   .


[NN] message(s) total
******


B. Comment structure


------------------
CATEGORY    [category #]    TOPIC [topic #]
Message     [message #]     Date: [day] [month], [year]
[name] [forum handle]       at HH:MM EST


Text of comment...
   .

   .

   .
```

Figure 8.3 Structure of GEnie messages.

but there are more of them, sometimes a few dozen. Ordinary users are not permitted to create or destroy *categories* (really subconferences). Below this level, users can create *topics*. The topic headers behave much more like item-level records on Confer or Picospan. Below this level are linear strings of comments resulting in a pure comb structure beneath the category level. Certain operations can be performed across categories, such as setting the last-read pointer to mark all new messages as read. Most other commands work only within categories, but across all or any subset of its topics. Unlike CIS's set section command, GEnie's set category command will permit examination of only one category at a time.

Inside a *topic*, messages are arranged in a linear time sequence. There are no distinctions between a statement or a question and the messages that comment upon it; even the first message of a topic is not treated in any special way. The topic itself is stamped with the time, date, title, and user ID of the person who created it, but its first message could conceivably be entered by someone else. In CIS, BIX, and most other systems, topic initiators include some textual introduction, yet few systems permit users to scan or read topic headers independently of their comments. GEnie does, however, because it happens to support user-specified message numbers along with ranges of topic numbers in its read command.

Messages are numbered sequentially under each topic. This is the reason that topics in GEnie behave like *items* of the comb model. For example, the command read 1- 10 1 will read the first message (most of the time a "topic starter text") of topics 1 through 10. Other than this mechanism, GEnie supports filtering by author, date, and strings appearing in a topic title. It can also display a numeric breakdown of the new messages posted under each topic, a feature that some otherwise comb-structured systems do not support.

Two interesting association and selection commands are describe and index. The former provides a short description of each forum category—a kind of subconference header—and the latter displays the topics within each forum category and their descriptive headers. Topics can be forgotten and avoided or marked, and followed as a group with the read command.

8.1.3.2 Binary Exchange

File libraries are associated with each Roundtable. On selecting the library section, a user is presented with a control menu much like that of BIX or CompuServe. Users can search or browse for files by author, date, filename, keyword in description, or other criteria. The facilities available for file exchange match those of CIS and BIX very closely. All three vendors are very much aware of the importance of file exchange in their markets, so each strives to provide reasonably convenient access to file libraries, and each achieves about the same measure of it. BIX allows a user to review the subjects of all the file listings areas on the system from one place. The sheer volume of material on CIS is prompting to experiment with utilities that will search collections of SIG libraries for files. GEnie permits searching all libraries on the system with one command, provided that either a string or a user ID is used to filter the results at the same time.

8.1.4 Delphi and P-Link

There are two other companies that operate large public CMC and information systems. One is the General Videotex Corporation, with Delphi. The other is American People Link corporation, with P-Link. The first does not have the extensive SIG or Roundtable collections of CIS and GEnie, but it contains even more in the way of financial and news services. Delphi is the second-oldest such service still on line. It began a few years after CompuServe and the Source (now subsumed by CIS), and long before BIX, GEnie, and P-Link. Its price is about the same as CIS, but, for one reason or another, it has not grown as rapidly as the three systems previously discussed.

P-Link provides a less expensive version of CIS SIG and synchronous chat facilities while foregoing news, financial, database, and other such services. P-Link's Forums are functionally identical to CIS SIGs, and they suffer from the same scroll-off problem. The turnover rate is not nearly as high as CIS. However, the activity volume—the number of new entries per day—is correspondingly lower.

Delphi has the potential to compete with CIS in every aspect of its business. P-Link does not. Delphi's user directory and system-wide communications facilities are superior to those of its competitors. Its conference software is not as powerful as Confer or Participate, but much better than that of CIS and GEnie. Yet growth in these services has been primarily influenced not by who has the better technology, but rather by the volume of activity in conferences, chats, and games. The transaction rate for news, financial, and other services is more or less constant for each of the systems. Stock prices may be updated to the minute and news wires refreshed daily or hourly. Delphi has more detailed financial news than either GEnie or CIS, yet that part of its user population subscribing for this information has many other competing sources from which to draw, and Delphi is not delivering it any faster than its direct competition.

8.1.5 Conversations and the Snowball Effect
CompuServe's SIG, chat, and game activity volume was always greater than that of its competitors. This fact gave CompuServe an edge that attracted more than an even share of new users, which has a snowball effect. Over the decade of the 1980s, CIS SIG transaction volume continued to grow at a faster rate than that of the competition. It now far exceeds the growth of its competitors except for BIX conferences in the computer science arena. Higher activity means more people with which to communicate. Having more users increases the likelihood of real expertise or authority in any given realm. This in turn increases the value of the ongoing discussions and increases the probability of timely answers to questions.

8.1.6 Regional Systems
As the 1990s begin, there are a growing number of people with communications capabilities, microcomputers, modems, and telecommunications software. Many of these are politically opposed or economically unable to support a subscription to CompuServe, and may not care for the big corporate image of a GEnie or BIX either. Prices are often lower on smaller *regional* systems with novel means of supporting high activity rates. The group communications software employed by the regionals is usually superior to that of the bigger systems (except BIX), and their retention periods are very high—sometimes years. Coupled with a specific focus—for example, especially good music or science fiction discussions or access to an interesting database—this fact helps draw and keep users. The regional systems are absorbing much of the market that might otherwise go to Delphi and P-Link.

8.1.6.1 Coupled versus Open Interfaces
Two broad types of regional systems have emerged; one is based on traditional communications software and interface architectures, and the other uses coupled software running on the user's machine to provide graphical interface and data facilities. The second type has only recently appeared, and many of these lack adequate support for binary file exchange or otherwise popular conversational facilities. Travel facilities, some news, a few games, and possibly a database or two are commonly available on these systems. Regional systems employing coupled software (see Chapter 10 for a discussion of coupling), are less focused on communications per se or on achiev-

ing recognition as major file library centers. Most try to achieve a regionally dense mix of services analogous to those present on CIS, GEnie, or Delphi. These may also include gateway services to other networks, for example, the international FIDONet, uucp, or MCI Mail.

Users are attracted by charging schedules resulting in lower prices for heavy (presumably local) use, and the value inherent in geographic concentration. For example, local news or restaurant reviews would be more complete and more accurate than those found on CIS for the same geographic region. Users are also interested in the features of graphical user interfaces supported by these systems. These systems are both easier to use than their more conventional brethren, and potentially even more versatile with respect to supporting novel communications structures. Although this potential is undoubtedly real (see Chapter 11), it has not yet materialized in a commercial product.

Ironically, this particular feature is not being ignored by the large vendors. CompuServe has recently introduced a coupled system interface, the CompuServe interface manager (CIM). CIM uses ordinary ANSI graphics and not NAPLPS. It supports graphic exchange via its own Graphics Interchange Format (GIF) protocol and includes a GIF interpreter in the CIM interface software that runs on the caller's machine. Despite the use of ANSI graphics, CIM provides most of the features available on the better regional systems. These include a top-of-screen light-bar menu, pop-down windows, and a very smooth entry into and use of CIS's file libraries. By early 1990, the required software was available for IBM and Apple Macintosh systems. It will undoubtedly be made available on more hardware platforms as time goes on.

8.1.7 The Well

The Coconet of San Diego, California, is a good example of the new generation of regional systems. The Whole Earth Lectronic Link (WELL) in Sausalito, California, is a well-known example of the first type. The Well is probably the country's premier regional system where computer mediated communications are emphasized. Its local market is the wider San Francisco Bay area, including Silicon Valley. As of this writing, the Well's hardware platform is a Sequent Balance with eight CPUs acting in parallel. This gives the system very fast response time, even under heavy load. Disk capacity is on the order of 2 gigabytes. There are currently 64 lines attached to the system, including a number of lines connected to the CompuServe packet network, giving the system a national—even international—reach. The Well's operating system is a version of Berkeley UNIX. The conferencing software has been Picospan since the system's startup in 1985, though other software is being investigated.

Picospan's close relationship to the UNIX operating system, and the Well's relation to the much of the UNIX community, have done much to boost the credibility of the system in the technical arena. Inside the Well there are a broad range of discussion groups. Computer and telecommunications-related subjects are covered in depth. The technical quality of the UNIX conference in particular exceeds that of BIX's counterpart. The telecommunications conferences play host to some of the most respected thinkers and doers in the public access communications arena nationwide. The conference on information covers the subject from numerous angles—logical, economic, psychological, and metaphysical. The arts—especially music—social and political science, politics, philosophy, religion, and business are represented, as are subjects like raising children, sex, staying healthy, and finding or keeping a job.

8.1.7.1 Well Conferences and Community

Each conference may have from 20 to 2000 topics, with 100 to 300 being common. Volume may range from only a few messages a day, conference-wide, to many hundreds of new messages. There is, however, no scroll rate. Material is kept essentially forever, though topics having no activity in them for many months or years are removed from time to time. Picospan is fully adequate for the task of supporting user filtering of this data. Picospan's abilities as a message base manipulator are on par with those of other large conference packages. It lacks some of the features of Confer, Caucus, or Participate, but it supports operations that these lack. It permits easy access to the underlying UNIX operating system and its wealth of utility software.

One of the objections leveled against Picospan is the need to operate these utilities to gain access to electronic mail, user directories, editors, and other features that in other systems are an integral part of the conference software itself. Such objections have some basis if only for the reason that executing interactive utilities or software outside the conference system requires more learning. Using advanced features of any system, however, requires some willingness to acquire new skills. On the Well, an extensive support network is readily available for any user requiring assistance with any of the facilities of Picospan or UNIX.

The Well is a for-profit business, and it is one of the few medium-sized systems that does make a profit. Users connecting through locally available telephone service pay only two dollars per connect hour at any time of the day at any supported connect speed. This is less than one quarter the price of CompuServe or Delphi. Those reaching the system through the CPN network must pay an additional surcharge for this service, bringing their cost about as high as CIS, Delphi, or any of the large systems. Yet people continue to use the Well from the far Northwest to the East coast because its underlying sense of purpose and value is very strong. Using the Well is much like living in a small town populated by artists, writers, engineers, philosophers, and telecommunications specialists. On systems like CompuServe, this talent is equally present, but it is scattered among the neighborhoods of a big city. The professional profile of the Well's user population is one of the factors contributing to its early success.

8.1.7.2 The Well and Usenet

The Well is also an internationally recognized Usenet site, one of a number of systems that provides public access points to the international conferencing network (see Appendix D for a list), along with electronic mail connections to many other large-scale networks worldwide. Usenet news groups and Well conferences are not integrated into one software system, but the very presence of the Usenet connection means that the small town has an open channel to the rest of the world. This conduit contributes significantly to the intellectual and technical scope of the Well's activities.

Another of the factors contributing to the Well's success was the willingness of the Well's management to grant free accounts to a significant number of early users. All conference managers have free access to the Well, as well as others who contributed in some significant way to its early history. These people contribute a significant amount of material to each other's conferences, and the result was early high-volume, high-quality activity. Coupled with good software, low prices, long retention periods, and a Usenet connection, the Well achieved rapid recognition and respect, leading to its current bustling atmosphere.

8.1.8 Other Open-Interface Regional Systems
There are a number of regional systems appearing throughout the country. Appendix D contains a list of such systems, many of which support conference activities. None of them have achieved the activity levels present on the Well. M-Net in Ann Arbor, Michigan and Fishnet in Miami Beach, Florida also use Picospan. Others, like Echo in New York City and the Meta Systems Design Group of Arlington, Virgina run Caucus. The NWI in Conneticut uses Participate. Many smaller software systems, such as Magpie, TBBS, RBBS, PC-Board, AKCS, Chairman, Major BBS, and others are found on both hobbyist and corporate communications platforms. All of these, including the Well, support binary file exchange and maintain program libraries, but their focus is on conversational activities. The Portal system in Palo Alto, California exists solely to support public access to Usenet. One of its salient features is its proprietary Usenet interface software.

8.1.9 Games, Files, and Other Services
Other regional systems emphasize file libraries, games, news services, and a crop of newly appearing on-line magazines. These systems employ the same overall centralized-host communications software as do systems focused on conferencing. Their conference software usually derives from BBS roots rather than the mainframe or mini lineage of conversationally focused systems, and there are crossovers in both directions. Exec-PC, operating out of Elm Grove, Wisconsin sports over six gigabytes of disk space, 90,000 files, and more than 100 phone lines. The Medcom BBS in Anaheim Hills, California has games, files, and news with connections to more than 80 lines. The File Cabinet BBS in Bethlehem, Pennsylvania is one of several systems connected to a worldwide conference echo network called the Interlink (see Chapter 11). It boasts 80,000 files in its libraries and 100 internationally echoed conferences. Few of these systems see significant conference activity compared to CIS, BIX, or the Well, but they do represent a growing volume of use for on-line services of various kinds.

Each of these systems shares a common philosophy of being contactable by the widest possible range of remote terminal equipment. This precludes the use of graphical interfaces for now, forcing these systems to distinguish themselves by narrowing their concentration. This focus may take the form of geographic emphasis, types of services, volume of material, depth of coverage, or other criteria. Any or all of these factors may be influential at the same time.

The most important effect on geographic influence is the cost of a connection. Regional systems always have subscription fees associated with them, and such fees, whatever their schedules, are almost always lower than the cost of a corresponding connection to CIS for local callers. As longer distances are bridged, connection costs always rise to levels equal to or higher than the large services. To make long-distance connections to these systems, users must also factor in the cost of long-distance calls, a subscription to a local gateway or access network providing a connection to the distant host (an example is PC pursuit), or surcharges for third-party connection services (such as Tymnet, Telenet, or CPN). This forces the regional net either to accept a geographic focus and attempt to exploit it, or to specialize in some market niche—files, specialized information, or unusual services, for example—and find geographically dispersed users who value that specialty enough to maintain long-distance relationships.

8.1.10   Coupled Interfaces

8.1.10.1   Coconet

Coconet Computing is one of the companies pioneering the use of coupled software and graphics interfaces specifically intended for computer mediated communications. The software is Xenix-based, and runs on any hardware supporting that operating system. There are no inherent limits to the number or type of communications lines supported, and the software, written by Brian L. Dear, is intended for the public and corporate marketplaces. There is currently one system running in San Diego, California with seven lines and 500 megabytes of disk space mostly occupied by extensive libraries of binary files.

The Coconet Communications Model.   The Coconet message model is similar to that of CoSy, except that comments cannot be attached to other comments, but only to *base notes*. Conferences are divided into two levels—the discussion or conference level, and the topic or subconference. Users cannot create topics, but they can create original notes—base notes—within them. Other users comment on these notes, and these threads can be followed much as in any other system. Because the system is graphically oriented, notes are divided into 80-column by 24-line pages. A single note must fit on one page. At the time of this writing, users themselves must arrange to break longer notes up on separate pages, but the next release of the software will do this automatically, supporting text uploads as a side benefit.

Navigation and Control.   It is the graphical nature of the software that distinguishes it from other systems and suggests some alternatives to traditional means of informing users of conference status and activity. For example, there is no equivalent to a system-wide topical index, but the titles of discussions, topics, and even notes for the entire system can be instantly displayed on a user's screen. Users need only page back and forth around this display to find items of interest. Once found, placing the cursor over the item and pressing enter will instantly take the user to the discussion, topic, or even note. Inside a discussion area, each topic is displayed along with the number of notes attached to it.

Base notes are similarly displayed inside the topic categories. New base notes (never seen before by the user) appear in a different color from material already seen. As notes are read, comments attached to them are highlighted. To follow a discussion thread, one merely picks comments from the list—some, all, or none of them. Information, supplied on other systems in the form of a text report, is thus

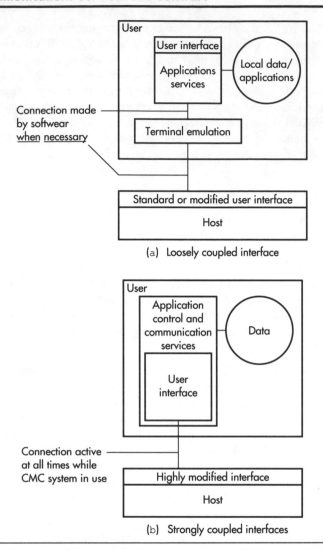

(a) Loosely coupled interface

(b) Strongly coupled interfaces

Figure 8.4 Loose and strong coupling. Loosely coupled systems (a) interact with the host on an occasional basis. Typically they emulate a fast typist, using the same host interface as a user would without any coupled software, though the host may have a special interface for coupled systems. Local databases are used for most tasks and updated as necessary upon the user's request. Local user programs perform most of the interface control work. Strongly coupled systems (b) are always communicating with the host. There is always cooperatively interacting software on both ends of the connection. Applications control, data, and all other user related processes are controlled as much by the host as they are by local resources. There is no a priori way of distinguishing activities controlled by the host from those governed by the local software.

conveyed by the graphic relationship of note titles. Users can, for example, elect to read only the opening messages of threads and ignore their comments (something otherwise supported by few systems), just by selecting the base notes from their display screens.

The Coconet software is now gaining more sophisticated conferencing features. Keyword searches are being added, as is a user directory. Users may soon be able to associate system operations with function keys on IBM-style keyboards and execute sequences of operations with a single key. A many-to-many synchronous "meeting facility" will be added in the near future. Those responsible for establishing a meeting will be able to record it and move its transcript to a discussion, where others can read and comment upon it. One feature now supported is unique among even the most powerful conference systems. Users can mark messages for later retrieval; however, what is unusual about this facility is that lists of marked messages can be attached to other messages sent to conferences or electronic mail. Upon encountering one of these lists, a user can place his or her cursor on a particular reference and instantly recover the note. The user's context is also preserved. After reading the reference and possibly replying to it, users are returned to their prior activity.

8.1.10.2 *IBM-Sears Prodigy Experiment*
The IBM-Sears Corporation Prodigy experiment is by now the nations best-known graphics-oriented communications service. We will not dwell on it here because its conferencing features are notable only for their absence. Electronic mail is available, and there are a few bulletin boards, but they are not at all suited to serious interpersonal communications. These boards have no internal structure other than a linear collection of notes, which can be marked for specific users. This facility is functionally similar to that found on CIS SIGs, but there are otherwise no selection or filtering capabilities. Users cannot even capture notes to disk, let alone upload them, and there are no file libraries whatsoever.

Like the Coconet software, Prodigy is a closely coupled system. Coupling is close when the remote console software and the host are constantly communicating behind the scenes (see Figure 8.4), while from the user's perspective, all activity is taking place on the local system. Unlike Coconet, however, the remote console software does not maintain any data locally. All actions on the part of the user require some response from the host, albeit this exchange activity is transparent. The remote Prodigy software is little more than a graphics generator and input handler. This makes the system seem slow compared to Coconet; although the system is strongly connected to its host as well, it makes much use of locally stored data.

8.1.11   Distributed Public Systems

8.1.11.1   *Prodigy as a Distributed System*
Prodigy is interesting from a technical perspective. It is both a coupled and a distributed system. Each of the cities serving as Prodigy centers is also the physical site of a network node. Regional information density is achieved by storing local data only at the host site. Shoppers' catalog information is replicated across the node space, so most of the system's information retrieval requirements can be satisfied locally.

Conversational data is not replicated. Some hosts serve as the local repository of one or more of Prodigy's bulletin boards, and if read or write commands are issued at a node that does not host the addressed board, a network connection is made to the proper node.

IBM and Sears jointly operate a private network for this purpose. Data paths between nodes are always open and operate at speeds sufficient to ensure completion of user transactions in a reasonable time. Local transactions may take three to four seconds, not including the time it takes to paint the resulting graphic. Remote transfers can require from a few seconds to half a minute depending upon network load at the time. Internodal links may range from fully dedicated T1 (1.54 Mbps) trunks or satellite links to fractional channels in the 56 Kbps range. In theory, there is no reason why the remote transaction time need ever exceed twice the local delay. If internodal traffic ever becomes heavy enough, T3 44 Mbps pipes are available. A hundred percent monomode fiber network would make remote transactions indistinguishable from local ones. Like others do, IBM and Sears must balance the need for wider channels with the cost of providing them.

Other publicly accessible distributed communication services include Usenet and FIDONet. There are a number of public access points to Usenet (see Appendix D). In terms of numbers of users, this system is already the largest conference-oriented service in the world. For now, most of these persons are in school or were exposed to the technology at school. The breadth of newsgroup subjects is vast, but it is still firmly controlled by academic administrations. Public access points as yet represent but a small fraction of the Usenet user community; as a result, they have little influence over the creation or subject matter of Usenet conferences. This will probably change because public access points can serve more users. The average Usenet node has dozens—possibly hundreds—of users but regional systems can play host to thousands. As these systems multiply, their usage volumes will give them influence. They can and should also assume a greater responsibility for wide-bandwidth backbone exchanges of Usenet material. Their share of the costs must remain at least proportional to their degree of activity.

8.1.11.2 The FIDO Network

In terms of node numbers, the international FIDO network may actually be larger than Usenet. Most FIDO nodes, however, are single-line BBSs or small machines supporting only the console operator. A typical FIDO node may have many dozens of regular users and always provides an E-mail connection to any other FIDO node. Conference activity can be regional, reflected in a geographically unified set of machines, or international. In the second case, conference records are not automatically echoed to every machine in the FIDONet; rather, there are regional centers—usually the largest machine in any given area—that serve as bearers of these worldwide distributed conferences. Smaller nodes can make arrangements to subscribe to echofeeds from these centers; however, they are not required to do so, nor must they feed every conference. There are now hundreds of conferences that echo nationally or internationally in this way.

The FIDO network consists mostly of dial-up connections with voice-grade phone lines operating until recently at a maximum speed of 2400 bps. Though even this speed has become common only in the last two years of the 1980s, 9600 bps links are beginning to make their appearance. Most of the large regional centers are connected at even higher—14.4 Kbps—speeds. Growth in FIDO conference and mail volume has so far been adequately absorbed by the recent availability of 9600 bps and higher-speed asynchronous modems.

The public nature of the FIDO file architecture and transmission protocols like those of Usenet make it possible for third-party products to provide applications-level services. The original FIDO software provides only primitive search and selection facilities for electronic conferencing, but many third-party products have features equivalent to the Usenet conferencing software. Significantly, the FIDO network is itself a public access point to the Usenet news and uucp mail networks. At the present, a single machine provides gateway services to and from Usenet. This node echoes activity onto FIDO conferences and relays it to the rest of the FIDONet. Entries from FIDO nodes are translated at the FIDO gateway into Usenet records and passed to a nearby Usenet node.

The FIDO network could become, in effect, a distributed gateway to many other national and international networks. So far, only Usenet is connected. Most other large networks are not accessible to the public; UUNET of Washington, D.C. is a commercial service supplying interconnections to the Internet. Most of this service is designed to provide Internet-wide electronic mail and file transfer capabilities and another gateway to Usenet.

Many powerful mid-range regional systems are beginning to emerge. In 1985 there were but a handful of bulletin board systems nationwide that supported more than two telephone lines; by 1990, there were dozens. Most of these systems run MS-DOS or UNIX. Products like Caucus, AKCS (pronounced "access"), TBBS (The Bread Board System), XBBS, Wildcat, Galacticom, Magpie, and PCBoard are commonly employed.

■ 8.2 OTHER CMC SOFTWARE

8.2.1 Caucus

Charles Roth, the author of Caucus, set out to duplicate as much of Confer—its initial inspiration—as possible. His goal was to do it in such a way as to ease the porting of the software to many environments. While UNIX was its first target environment, Roth did not connect the user facilities of Caucus to the toolset of UNIX as Marcus Watts did with Picospan. Giving up UNIX tools meant incorporating more of the required facilities into the applications software itself. This job was made more difficult because many of Confer's text manipulation features rely on the MTS operating system. Achieving the functionality of Confer without using the special features of its operating system required a complete redesigning of the software file structure. By maintaining as much system independence as possible, Roth was able to port the Caucus system to more environments than any other software in this genre. More continue to be added, but there is a price to pay for portability.

The Caucus software is internally more complex than either Confer or Picospan on a feature-by-feature basis. That is, it takes more code to support a given feature in Caucus than it does in the other two software systems. Though Caucus looks much like Confer, there are facilities of the older system that it does not attempt to replicate. These include the vote and survey facilities, synchronous conferencing, Confer operations over collections or sets of records, many of the Confer command options, and binary attachments to electronic mail. Caucus also lacks Picospan's item-linking abilities, but it does include a provision for reading and writing files directly from and to the underlying operating system, thus supporting binary exchange capability.

8.2.1.1 Caucus Tailorability

The Caucus user interface is flexible, much like that of Picospan. Caucus supports macros and dedicated user-selectable dictionaries of command translations that permit customization of commands, language translations, help messages, and system output formats similar to Picospan's user control files. A system will support as many as 999 active dictionaries from which users can choose one appropriate to their experience and activity.

Macros allow system administrators to build complex operations, producing some variations in the communications model. Caucus's macros can incorporate mixtures of Caucus and operating system instructions in a single stream. They can also receive instruction streams from a file outside the Caucus system. Macros can be executed from inside the Caucus dictionaries. Uses for these capabilities include enhanced directory services or sophisticated filter devices.

In Caucus terminology, the user's active dictionary is a mask imposing various forms on system prompts, and the format of returned responses. The facility is flexible enough to support interface variations ranging from complete menu navigation to a quick, stackable, command mode. In theory, users can build and employ their own dictionaries, but most often, system administrators produce masks of varying kinds and allow users to choose from among them. Supportable variations are the same, no matter what the underlying operating system or hardware. The dictionary script language also behaves identically across all supported environments, which opens the door for third parties to produce dictionaries and market them to Caucus administrators without regard to their hardware and operating system environment.

Compared to competing systems, Caucus is both powerful and limited. For example, its user and conference directory capabilities are more powerful than those of most competing small systems; it is one of the few systems that reports not only who users are, but also on the conferences they have visited and the notes they have read. On the other hand, a simple display of the number of characters or lines in a given note is not supported.

8.2.2 MS-DOS based Multitasking Software

TBBS—The Bread Board System—is an example of an MS-DOS-based multiuser conferencing product commonly encountered on a growing number of regional hosts. It is a comment-oriented system written entirely in assembly language for performance reasons. Like Caucus, it addresses multiuser requirements by assuming the burden of multitasking itself. Some advantages of this approach include the folowing:

1. *Performance*. The system can be optimized for its high-level tasks. For example, the software can lock data at the record level.

2. *Superior status and statistics monitoring.* The application kernel is aware of all activity system-wide, making statistical and status displays of such activity a relatively easy task.

3. *Synchronous communications.* They are easily supported because the software kernel controls all user activity from one place.

4. *System tuning.* The system can be tuned based on known maximum system load. These packages are sold by the number of ports they support. The software is much more expensive at the 64- or 128-port level than it is for eight ports. The developers can incorporate performance-enhancing services into the software when such loading is anticipated—for example, special drivers for intelligent buffered ports.

5. *Security.* These systems are inherently aware of all users logged in to the host. A single entry point governs user entry, and no caller can bypass the software to reach the computer's operating system. File systems are addressed through one application interface. The file system is either completely governed by the applications software or by some third-party file management system. A third-party file manager functions exclusively on behalf of the communications application.

There are two fundamental disadvantages to this approach. One is the system's inflexibility with respect to connecting with outside applications and operating system utilities. MS-DOS may be natively weak in this area, but the number of high-powered utility programs available from third parties is legion. Not only utility programs, but larger applications like database managers are also precluded from interaction with these conference systems unless provision is made for these external programs in the software. For example, TDBS is a special version of TBBS that functions on top of Ashton Tate's Dbase DBMS.

The second disadvantage stems from the same feature as advantage number 4. As systems grow in size, they cost more. Of course, administrators can upgrade from one level to another, but doing so incurs a capital cost in addition to that for expanded hardware. This is an accepted fact of software marketing in the mainframe and mini-computer worlds, but it can, and sometimes must, be avoided in the microcomputer arena, where many shops or departmental systems must subsist on small budgets.

Chairman is another representative system in this marketplace. It is special in that it was written in Ascom IV (from Dynamic Microprocessor Associates), an applications language designed to support communications activities. The Ascom language runs under an interpretive shell normally supplied with the purchase of DMA's language and terminal emulation software. In the case of Chairman, developed by DMA itself, the shell is a special multitasking program.

8.2.3 Multitasking Shells
Multitasking shells have been adopted by several communications software developers; they simplify the cost of software implementation. The Chairman shell is proprietary and is optimized to its support role for the Chairman software. The result is a fast

and robust conferencing applications package. Functionally, it behaves much as does TBBS. Other systems rely on conforming to the protocols of a commercial shell, the most popular being Quarterdeck's Desqview. Wildcat and Magpie are two examples of this software architecture.

Desqview is a popular shell for communications systems because it is text-oriented, nongraphical, and therefore fast. It also requires less memory for its own operations than does its main competitor, Microsoft Windows. It provides options for memory and session optimization and can be tuned to the software that runs under it. It also has a protocol for intertask communications. Conference software developers have written to this protocol, making possible much the same synchronous communications features as those supported by systems that perform their own multitasking.

Software running under a shell like Desqview must still operate its own record-level contention scheme, or be content with the file-level locking operations provided by the shell. Most choose the second option, simplifying file handling in exchange for a record queuing subsystem that makes potential "file is locked" problems invisible to the user. This constraint tends to force file design strategies toward the use of many small files, rather than a few big ones (see Chapter 10 for a discussion of file strategies). Statistical reporting on system activity in real time is difficult to achieve because the shell knows about all processes running under it at a given time, but the communications software is isolated, each running copy knowing about only its own session's activities. Statistical services would therefore have to run independently of the communications software and communicate with both the shell and all processes running in it.

Shell-based systems are somewhat less robust than their dedicated multitasking counterparts, because complex software from multiple vendors must operate cooperatively. There are security and administration complications as well. Because the shell performs the multitasking chores, users can be allowed to exit the communications application and run other programs. While doing so, any user accounting—for example, tracking user time on the system—is held in abeyance. Another problem is illustrated by what occurs if a user hangs up the phone while outside the conference application. The software will not be able to re-ready the port for another caller except by timing the user out after some period of inactivity. Most of these problems can be handled by not giving users unrestricted access to the host operating system.

Shell-based systems are wonderfully flexible with respect to the operation of software outside the conference system. Under this architecture, the communications software becomes a gateway to any number of programs and services available on the host. Databases, spreadsheets, utility software, and even other communications services (such as a Usenet connection) can be associated with the conference activities of the host.

Communications between the conference application and external software can be completely automated. Users need not know they are being connected with another program. Alternatively, users may be allowed to deliberately exit the conference application and interact with the host at its operating system level. Either way, system administrators are not so constrained by limits imposed in the software's design. Careful planning on the part of system administrators is required, however, to minimize some of the aforementioned problems.

8.2.4   Magpie: High Power at a Low Price

One package—Magpie, written by Steven Manes—is interesting because it is an un-usually powerful conference-oriented package at a very low price. Magpie's initial target environment was UNIX. Its porting to MS-DOS was facilitated by the avail-ability of Desqview. The DOS version is distributed as shareware for but $120. An ordinary 80286-based PC can support eight simultaneous sessions, while an 80386 platform can handle as many as 40 sessions given enough memory.

8.2.4.1   Magpie Communications Structure

The Magpie message and mail architecture is deceptively simple (see Figure 8.5). Messages, including private mail, are numbered sequentially system-wide, reminiscent of CompuServe's SIG system. Message numbers 0 through 199 are reserved: these are the header records—some may be empty—for each of Magpie's 200 supportable conferences. All Magpie messages are replies to other messages; either they are replies to the conference header records, or replies to these replies, and so on. Since Magpie messages can be formally associated with other messages (comment chains) at any level, the system takes on the kind of branching structure found in CoSy. Unlike CoSy, however, the entire message system is connected to message 0.

Users can enter this branchlike structure at any point along the set of replies from 1 to 199, the conference headers. Private mail is attached to the first spine of replies associated with the first message. That is, the replies to this message are the names of and other information about system users. Mail, in Magpie terms, is simply a reply chain associated with each of these users' root messages in turn connected to the first message. These "root messages" are mailboxes. The default security mask for all of the first message's replies allows the creator of the mailbox to *read* comments associated with his or her mailbox, but everyone else can *write* to that mailbox. Sending E-mail to a user amounts to sending a reply to his or her root message under the first board. User names are automatically associated with a unique message number when they create their mailboxes. Mail sent to a user name is automatically translated into a reply to that user's unique number.

8.2.4.2   Navigation and Control

Magpie's record display technique is among its more innovative features. Magpie is a comment-in-context–oriented system that solves the lost thread problem and permits users to flatten the communications structure in a way that suits their purposes and generate new topic-level threads at the same time. It achieves this by associating each message with an explicit list of pointers to messages written in direct reply to it. As a user displays a message, reply numbers are also displayed along with the first line of text in the form of a menu attached to the message being read.

Users may elect to read threads by reply chain, topic introduction sequence, or by direct replies to a message at any level of a branch. Single keystroke commands navigate the user forward or back one or more steps in a discussion thread. Magpie is the only system, in which users can read messages breadth or depth first and switch between them at any level of the reply chain. Of course, one *presumes* that a comment, which may start a new level of the reply chain, is really related to the record upon which it comments. If not, the structure becomes unfocused and begins to work against the smooth development of coherent discussion.

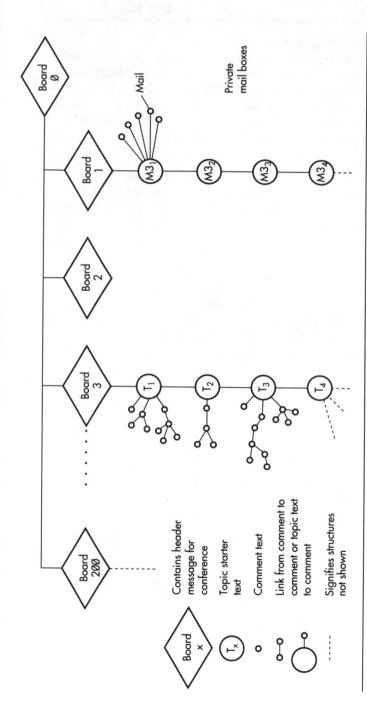

Figure 8.5 Magpie communications structure. The Magpie system is divided into boards numbered zero through 199. Every Magpie conference can trace a path back to board zero. Board zero is special in that it is the root of all other boards (conferences). Board 1 is also special in that each of its starting messages is private in the sense that anyone can `write` to it (comment on it), but only its owner can read the comments. This constitutes Magpie's mail system. Other boards store messages for the more common kind of conferences. Users may start an original thread, and people can comment on these messages. Comments can be attached to comments and so forth. This structure is similar to that of CoSy (Figure 8.1), except that the original messages under a board are also threaded together so that users can read the original (topic) message headers without having to read the comments. The mail board (number 1) is special in that there is only one branch level from each thread starting point (a user mailbox). Direct replies to mail are attached to another starting message—the recipient's mail box.

8.2.4.3   Binary Exchange

The X-modem and Y-modem error checking protocols are included with the package, and any number of other exchange drivers may be added. The software also contains direct support for the execution of file compression and decompression software. Board #2 serves as a file library by default. Files, text or binary, can also be attached to any other message on the system. When a user reads a message with attached files, he or she is informed of their presence and asked about downloading them.

8.2.4.4   Search Capabilities and Other Unusual Features

Magpie is an unusually powerful piece of software, especially considering its price. It has, for example, a more versatile message search capability than almost any other package. Searches can be conducted on any combination of author, recipient, date, and text fields. It supports the Boolean opperators *and, or,* and *not.* A search returns results as a series of connected messages. Users have only to execute their normal read commands to step through the collected set as though it were a discussion thread. There are similarly powerful user directory services, and two overlapping security subsystems. Finally, Magpie uses the FOSSIL driver to hook itself to a computer's serial communication facilities. As new drivers emerge using the FOSSIL-application interface, packages like Magpie will be able to take advantage of new communications technologies—for example, built-in X.25 boards—without modification of the software.

8.2.5   TEAMate, Proprietary Communications Structure, and Full Screen Display

TEAMate is a computer conferencing package from MMB Development Corporation in Manhattan Beach, California. It runs on number of hardware platforms that support either UNIX or Xenix operating systems. The product relies on a full-screen display, insisting that callers use terminal software that emulates DEC's VT100 terminal control codes. Many other systems support full-screen displays with VT100 or other terminal control standards. These include the Usenet, Compuserve, Caucus, and others, but the full-screen display is so integral to TEAMate's interface that users must support VT100 in order to use the system. The product is discussed briefly here because it is one of the few computer mediated communications products packages that experiments with an unconventional conference structure.

The TEAMate interface is a hierarchically organized system of screens that produce an outline of substructures to which messages, binary files, or executable programs are attached. The entire database thus appears as a single logical file. It is conceptually like Participate if the latter's branch headers are viewed as parent nodes to yet other headers that contain comments of their own. Like Participate, TEAMate is essentially a conference-oriented system because new levels of the hierarchy are directly connected to the parent records of those above it, and not to comments. In effect, they behave like topic headers branching from encompassing topics, rather than as comments to topics or other comments. In Participate, only one branch can start at any single point in the reply chain. TEAMate supports multiple branches from the same point. Even so, users can stop at and respond to any message individually. Those replies are, however, added to the end of the message reply chain at its current level in the hierarchy.

On entering the system, users see a screen of items much like a menu. By moving the cursor to an item of interest and pressing the ENTER key, one navigates down or up the levels of the hierarchy. A "+" character next to a menu line denotes other substructures below the present level. A "#" signals attached messages or other data. At any given level, there may be both substructures and data at the same time. For example, a discussion topic "all about modems" may have many messages attached. At the same time, there may be separate structures (other topics) below the topic like "high-speed modems," "modem standards," "internal and external modems," and so forth. Any of these may have messages or other structures below them.

The system displays lists of messages attached to the current level of the structure, much as in Magpie. Users can navigate by cursor keys to any message and read it, or display all or some of the messages one after another. At the end of each message, the software appends a list of the persons who have seen it. This display is TEAMate's substitute for more conventional user-to-conference directory services. This list can be read, searched, or ignored at a user's option.

Users can page through messages—there is no indication of how long they are—or navigate back to higher levels of the structure from any point in the system. There is no distinction between *conferences* and *topics* or *replies* as on other systems. Messages are attachments to hierarchical levels of the system that are called *topics,* but bear only functional resemblance to such things in other systems. For example, a conference may take place (have messages attached) on level 3 of a given structure and also at levels 5 and 9. If a discussion drifts off the topic, the system administrator may move the entire structure (including substructures) to which it belongs to another level of the hierarchy.

TEAMate avoids the hidden branch problem to some degree, because the software signals the presence of sub-branches immediately, as each level of the hierarchy is traversed. In Participate, the presence of a sub-branch is not revealed until a user reaches the branch point in a record-by-record examination of the current branch. The TEAMate solution, however, reveals only one level deeper than the one being viewed.

Some parts of the system are very "forms-oriented." One can understand the need for full-screen cursor control, though MMB is restricting itself unnecessarily by supporting only the VT100 protocol. For example, a user may search the entire text base—all topics—for a given string of characters, or for responses by a given author, date, subject, or keywords. Searches are initiated through a form that the user fills out. Once complete, TEAMate executes the search and displays a screen showing the specific topic hierarchies or messages that contain the results. Its search capabilities are reasonably good, but not great. Multiple strings in a search are automatically *or'd* together, while searches across fields (such as author-subject), are automatically *and'ed.*

TEAMate is particularly strong in supporting exits to external programs. Its abilities in this area are reminiscent of hypertext systems. For example, delphic voting is not natively supported, but a given message can actually be a pointer to an external program that automatically runs when the user reads the message. This program may take a user's vote on some subject or other and then return the user to the conversation stream. Another message can automatically execute a program that compiles and displays vote results to date, and so forth. Any kind of external software can be associated with the product in this manner.

8.2.6 Other BBS Software

Besides Magpie, TEAMate, and the others previously discussed, there are dozens of other small interpersonal communications systems. Some, like Wildcat, PCBoard, RBBS, and XBBS, may be suitable in more than a few application domains. The best of these packages have 80 percent of the functionality of large-scale systems like Participate, Confer, and Notepad. Others require careful investigation. They often have limitations that, while not terribly burdensome in a small system, may not be flexible and robust enough for a commercial application. Good, flexible communications structures, directory services, and so forth, are not enough in commercial applications. System administrators must also be able to track activity as and after it occurs; the system must be auditable. They must also be able to conveniently manipulate data and control system operations while applications activity continues.

Some of the competing products are better than the others, but "better" here refers to the number of usage domains they can fully or almost fully address, along with their auditability and performance. Technically speaking, the majority of available software in this genre is of very high quality. This is all the more noteworthy because the cost of this software is lower than that of any other large applications domain.

8.2.7 VaxNotes

We should not leave this chapter without a short discussion of VaxNotes from Digital Equipment Corporation (DEC). In terms of corporate sites, there are more VaxNotes installations in the United States (more than 1000), than all other conference products combined (about 500). This figure is somewhat misleading, however, because DEC now bundles VaxNotes with sales and upgrades of its All-In-One office automation software. It is not at all clear how much of this software is being used.

VaxNotes is a comb-structured system. Under normal circumstances, only moderators can create conferences, but users can both add notes to topics and create topics under a conference as necessary. A special conference structure called the Bulletin Board by DEC is essentially a read-only conference. Other controls permit conference organizers to restrict user entries to reply to existing topics. VaxNotes is a potentially distributed, but not replicated, conferencing system. Users may join conferences whose home-node is somewhere other than their local system without needing to be aware of that fact. Organizers can associate conferences running on different DEC machines with a centralized domain naming service (DNS). Use of the DNS permits conference administrators to shift conferences around to different machines as necessary without users having to know where on the network a conference resides.

Users can find conferences of interest with a "directory/conference" command. Once inside a conference, they can display topics with yet another "directory" command. A user-maintained "notebook" file lists conferences of interest to a given user. These may be grouped into *classes* that can be made active or inactive as the user desires. It is through the notebook mechanism that VaxNotes keeps track of a user's last-read pointer in any given conference. That is, users may enter any public conference and read or write notes, whether or not their notebook lists it. Unless it is listed, however, the system will not know how far they have read in any of the conference's topics. Other user controls permit establishing default settings for printing conference records and control of the behavior of the system when they first enter a conference. For example, a user can elect to have the software automatically display the list of topics and the number of replies to each, or begin by showing them the first unread message of the conference.

Most products can scroll messages past the screen without pausing between them if the user desires this. VaxNotes does not, primarily because it relies on the presence of DEC terminals or workstations at user desks and automatically makes use of their ability to segregate a screen into different regions. The top line of the screen is always a command line on which a user can issue instructions to read and write notes, move to different topics, conferences, and so on. The next two lines display status information such as the name of the conference, the title of the current topic, the current note's number, author, its number of lines, or the creation date. Notes may be of any length and are displayed one page at a time. The system's default action is to display the next page of a note (if it exists) when the user presses the ENTER key. Otherwise, it moves to the next note of the topic, the next topic, or the next conference in the conference class currently active in the notebook.

Searching and filtering are accomplished through keywords associated with each note. These keywords are entered by conference administrators and sometimes users. Users may search for notes containing a keyword, or search for strings present in the title or text of the notes. These searches may be restricted to a range of topics or notes or applied to an entire conference. Author and date searches are also supported. Other than the display of topic titles, there is no support for browsing notes or replies. Users can elect to skip subsequent note pages by issuing appropriate commands— for example, *next* on the screen's command line. Individual notes can be marked by users for subsequent retrieval or sent as electronic mail to other users with comments appended by the sender.

On the whole, VaxNotes is a good product with a few glaring omissions. Users have a great deal of control over the editors they employ to write notes, the use of VMS E-mail facilities from inside the VaxNotes software, and the execution of external programs. If a user has a DEC workstation running DEC Windows, the communications software may be displayed independently of, and concurrently with, the output of other programs. The package is also integrated with DEC's All-In-One office automation software so that, for example, notes may be embedded in word processing documents. VaxNotes' facilities for controlling the structure of displayed notes is weak compared to Caucus and Picospan, for example, and its searching and filtering capabilities are inferior to those of Confer, Notepad, Participate, and Magpie. The product has no internal user directory facilities whatsoever, and there is no provision to *forget* a conference topic.

VaxNotes' greatest strength is its distributed but nonreplicated architecture. This permits small and medium-sized Vax hosts to support large numbers of very active conferences, provided that they are well-connected to one another by dedicated circuits or by high-speed dial-up links. The software will initiate required connections to remote hosts automatically without any user intervention. This architecture melds the advantages of both distributed and centralized conferencing, which provides an excellent foundation for associated services, especially distributed database and information retrieval applications.

9

DOMAINS, CHARACTERISTICS, AND IMPLEMENTATION OBJECTIVES

Implementing a computer conferencing, electronic mail, or information retrieval system is, first, an exercise in decision analysis. The first step is determining what the system will be used for. Second, the implementation team must determine what specific features will be needed in the software to support those uses. Third, a search is conducted to find existing software that meets requirements within budget constraints. Finally, a decision is made to (a) purchase a system, (b) use an external system operated by a third party, or (c) build a system or modify an existing system. If developing a proprietary system is within the realm of possibility, further analysis must determine whether:

1. The system could be built by extending an existing system for which source code is available.
2. The system can be written using various special purpose, high-level languages and tools developed specifically for supporting communications software development.
3. The system must be written in its entirety using general purpose computer languages coupled with low-level support tools such as libraries of file and communications routines.

At some junctures in this decision process, more than one option will probably be viable. Conversely, factors external to application considerations, such as budgets or existing hardware/operating systems, may constrain choices at any given point.

Table 9.1 Computer conferencing usage domains and application priorities

Domain	High	Medium	Low
Coauthoring/Joint document editing			
Decision support[a]			
Implementation planning			
Project management			
Interagency activity coordination			
Technology scanning[a]			
Technology transfer			
Product development coordination			
Vendor support/coordination[ab]			
Sales staff coordination[b]			
Customer support[ab]			
Management/employee communications[b]			
Team building			
Professional development			
Strategic development			
Crisis/diaster resolution[a]			
Public relations			
Political action[a]			
Entertainment			
Education/distance learning			

[a] May also involve information retrieval technology.
[b] May possibly be achieved with electronic mail technology.

■ **9.1 CLARIFYING INTENDED USES**

Step one involves clarifying the use or uses to which the application will be put. Chapter 2 contains a list of domains to which group communications software has been applied. That list is duplicated in summary form in Table 9.1. Check off those domains that apply to your requirements, along with the priorities of expected usage.

■ **9.2 GENERIC FEATURES OF IDEALIZED CMC SOFTWARE**

Once the target domains are identified, we address specific features. The following list of features is taken from a recent paper by Jacob Palme, developer of the COM family of group communications software.* Note that features specific to electronic mail and information retrieval systems are not included. This list is divided into 11 categories. My own comments on additions to the list are given in summary after each subsection.

* J. Palme, "Group Communications Facilities," A working paper, unpublished.

1. Group communication activities — the "general" category.
   a. Group communication activities have names by which they can be identified.
   b. Users can find, join, and withdraw from the named activities.
   c. There is a mechanism to announce new named activities to prospective members.
   d. Users can easily create new activities.
   e. There is a directory system of both *activities* and *users*.
   f. Activities are, by some means, divided into some system of subactivities.

All group communications systems support the first three items in this list. Item (1.d) is often supported for subactivities, but not named conferences themselves. Typically, this level of the model is initialized by someone with special authority. Most contemporary systems support item (1.f). People associate this feature more than any other with "conferencing systems." Item (1.e) is often supported in a rudimentary way; there is room for much improvement in contemporary systems. At the least, the user directory should be searchable by user ID, name, city, state, and keyword (usually a list of personal interests), and it should provide all this information if so requested.

Conference directories are often manifested in the form of menus of named conference categories or specific conferences. A hierarchy of (category → conference) serves to help users find things of interest. A few systems support indexes of conferences, searchable by name or subject matter. Few systems provide detailed information about the conference, its subject, date of creation, activity volume, number of participants, sysops, and so on. All would make useful additions to most contemporary directory systems. The developers of EIES and Confer recognized the value of these services.

2. Data within activities.
   a. Conversation.
   b. Support for conversion of conversations into activities.
   c. Variable expiration times for texts and activities.
   d. Use of geographic constraints to control text distribution.
   e. Use of organizational structure to control text distribution.

Conversations refer to any set of contributions implicitly or explicitly linked. Such sets can be chains of replies, links from other conversations, or copies from E-mail systems, and so on. A conversation may happen to be the same as a conference *subactivity*, but it may happen to be more than that. All systems support implicit linking of reply chains if only by associating new records with the activity that inspired them. Support for easy elevation of conversations to activities or subactivities (2.b) is not typically available. Participate, TEAMate, and the COM family are exceptions.

Item (2.c) is often supported, although some of the smaller systems require some work on the part of the system operator (sysop). The need to expire older texts, for performance or disk capacity limitations, is a limiting factor in some usage domains.

Items (2.d) and (2.e) are related. Geographic restrictions on distribution apply mostly to distributed systems such as Usenet or FIDOnet and are largely meaningless in centralized configurations. In distributed architectures, message restriction by geographic location is an efficiency consideration more than anything else. It unburdens the net of some traffic and conserves disk space on excluded machines. Feature (2.e) amounts to the same thing, but the restriction is based on job role or suborganization (division, department, and so on). This feature, which can be very important to corporate applications, applies equally well to distributed and centralized system types. Support often takes the form of provision for private conferences using lists of eligible participants. Such lists may contain other lists or overlap in many ways. The idea of named classes of users is not often supported; users might belong to many classes. Conference access would be controlled by membership in a *class* named by the conference. As it is, most sysops must go through the work of maintaining private conference lists manually.

3. Sharable, logical file system.
   a. Old contributions are available for retrieval by new members
   b. Previously written contributions are available to new participants.
   c. Joint databases of contributions, available to many.
   d. Archiving capabilities
   e. Search and retrieval facilities in the contribution text base.
   f. Directory of text items (item or comment texts).
   g. DBMS facilities—integrity and serialization of transactions, recovery support, and so on.
   h. Distributability of the text-base and other related databases, retaining all functionality of the stand-alone version.

Items (3.a) through (3.c) are supported by all systems that purport to do "conferencing." Along with (1.f), they are central to the very notion of text-based conferencing. Systems always provide some means of storing older data in some recoverable form (3.d), but not always at the convenience of conference users. Item (3.e) is also supported everywhere, at least to some minimal degree. Commercial and shareware packages vary widely on this. In general, the more expensive systems have better retrieval facilities, but none of them come close to dedicated information retrieval systems in this area.

Directories for text items (3.f) are supported by indexes to keywords appearing in texts. Even this support is rare. Items (3.g) and (3.h) should be transparent to the user. The availability of DBMS services and the ability of the software to run in a distributed architecture depend altogether on the original design and target environment.

4. User data.
   a. Supports informing users of database changes.
   b. Individual priority ordering of activities.

Item (4.a) is supported in one way or another by all systems. This support may take the form of bulletins associated with each conference individually or the system as a whole. Electronic mail may also be employed for this. Item (4.b) is supported in most systems. That is, users can establish lists of activities they wish to visit in turn, along with specifying what action the system should take in entering each new conference—for example, to display all new comments in items previously seen, then new items, and so on.

5. Access control.
   a. Access control in the creation of activities.
   b. Access control on group communications activities.
   c. Roles used for access control.
   d. Use of geographical structure of user population for access control.
   e. Use of organizational structure of user population for access control.
   f. Activity suspension.

All systems support controls over who can create new activities (5.a) or eliminate them (5.f). Item (5.b) refers to authority over user read or read/write privileges, user control over their own conference participation, administrative control over private conferences, and so on. These three are supported by almost all conference systems. Item (5.c) refers to a privilege classification scheme, meaning that user privileges are derived from the class to which they belong. Examples might be "ordinary user," "auditor (read only)," "conference organizer," "moderator," and "sysop." Items (5.d) and (5.e) are exactly parallel to (2.d) and (2.e), respectively. They are analogously significant as well.

6. News control.
   a. Ability to lead user to and through unread material.
   b. Automatically prevent the user from seeing the same message twice (for example, if the message is linked to two conferences).
   c. Unread material is grouped by activity.
   d. Users can read new contributions in "conversational thread" order.
   e. Users can select unread contributions directly from a list, at least across activities within a conference, and possibly across conferences.
   f. Support for personal, automatic, filters.
   g. Support for group filters.
   h. Query facility limitable by new material.
   i. Users may move from activity to activity, and conference to conference, at their discretion.

This category refers specifically to support for finding new, and only new, material not seen before by a given user. Items (6.a), (6.c), and (6.i) are universally supported. Most systems will not automatically suppress displays of messages appearing more than once to users (6.b). Support for (6.d) was one of the rationales for developing branching structures below the conference/item hierarchy of the comb model, and is supported only in branching systems. Feature (6.e) is supported in some products, for example, Participate, but not most.

Filters, (6.f) and (6.g), are user-settable conditions that automatically serve to limit receipt of new material to that which passes the filter. Constraints might operate on the existence of a string in the subject or text, the author's name, or the organizational division to which the author belongs. When filters are positive, they are, in effect, automatic selection devices. They can also be negative—for example, "do not display messages from John Doe," or "show no messages less than five words long." There are few systems that support automatic negative filtering, except in the form of forgetting whole topics when displaying new material in a conference. Query facilities, (6.h), are often limitable to new material only by specifying an origin date as a part of the query specification. Otherwise, this feature is mostly unsupported.

7. Moderator control.
   a. Moderator pre- and/or post-control over contribution inclusion in an activity.

This category refers to the ability of a moderator (or someone in an equivalent role) to preempt a comment or remove it after posting. Some systems support the latter style by permitting removal of a comment, while leaving a marker in its place signifying the deletion. In general, preemptive control makes for a more controlled conference but may disrupt the dynamic of conversation flow. Removing undesirable messages after the fact may cause some confusion (some participants may have read and responded to the particular entry), but it does maintain conference flow.

8. Conference record I/O controls.
   a. Replies are easily sent to all who read a previous contribution.
   b. Users can elect not to read replies, even if they haven't seen them.
   c. Support for activity-level encryption and decryption (users must have keys).
   d. Ability to send messages and/or screen them by role.
   e. Deferred contributions.
   f. Support for author and/or moderator editing of entries after their inclusion in the text base.

Feature (8.a) is the essence of group communications. It is the fundamental property of communications structures in these products. Item (8.b) is supported in many different forms. Most systems provide a means for a user to move his or her last-read marker to include new entries even though they have not been seen. Selective avoidance is also supported in many, but not all, packages. Items (8.c) through (8.e) are not commonly supported. Support for (8.d) is rare.

Feature (8.f) is not on Dr. Palme's original list. There exists a considerable difference of opinion on the propriety of allowing record editing (as distinct from removal) after inclusion in the text base. This is absolutely required in joint document editing. In ordinary conferences, however, the practice has a potential for generating confusion as new readers encounter edited texts and then read replies issued before the edits were applied.

9. Specially customized group procedures.
   a. Specially customized group procedures exist.
   b. Roles used for customized group procedure control.
   c. Forms-handling support.
   d. Joint text editing.
   e. Voting support.
   f. Support for binary attachments and/or a shared binary file area.

The term *customized group procedures* refers to variations on existing communications structures and message flow among participants. An example would be a document approval system that routes documents to different individuals, or departments, in a prescribed order. This area may be addressed by some of the tailorability features present in some software.

Item (9.b) refers to the ability to link customizations to roles such as conference organizer and sysop. Forms, (9.c), are templates that constrain text entry to a prescribed format. They also contain required fields such as to/from and subject. Although such fields will normally be stored as a part of the text portion of the record, the forms facility may restrict access to certain parts of the form by name, role, and so on.

Joint text editing (9.d) implies the ability to edit records after they have been entered into the text base. More importantly, it implies that many persons may have such editing authority, and that multiple edits will be handled properly by the file mechanism. Although joint document editing is supported in a number of systems, none support editing by more than one person at the same time.

Voting, (9.e), is supported mostly on the larger systems, Confer, Notepad, Participate, and the COM and EIES families. It is useful in such domains as crisis resolution and decision support when the participant population is knowledgeable regarding the problem arena. Using various voting techniques helps solidify recommendations more rapidly than conversational discourse alone. Those systems that support voting do so in various forms: Yes/No/Abstain, choice of alternatives, essay answers, numerical range, and numerical interval. Voting support also includes facilities for setting up a vote and the ability to tabulate and display the results.

Support for binary attachments, (9.f), was not on Dr. Palme's original list. Most systems support uploading and downloading of binary files stored in a separate part of the system from the text base. Attaching binaries directly to text messages is something different. Binary attachments permit users to exchange long text files by including them in a compressed format. One must assume that recipients can decompress them after receipt. Support in this context implies some means of informing readers that a binary is attached and allowing them to decide to receive it or not. It also implies an automatic invocation of the file download utility on the host side.

10. Roles.
    a. Roles exist.
    b. Management of roles supported.

Roles have already been discussed. This category exists only to identify system support for roles as a thing-in-itself. All systems support at least two roles: sysop and user. Users acting in connection with conferences to which they belong can read, write comments, start new items or branches, and so on. More sophisticated role support may involve such things as a distinction between sysops and conference organizers or moderators. The latter have sysop-like powers, but only for those conferences they manage. Distinctions among user roles are also found (though these are rare). One user level, for example, may add comments and start new items, while another is allowed to enter comments to existing items but not begin new ones, while a third can only read and not write at all.

Another kind of role involves the association of a person with a role outside the context of the system. Company president, chairperson, department manager, and secretary are examples. Operations may be keyed to these external roles. For example, a memo sent by J.D., who happens to be the chairman of a committee, would be displayed to recipients as "from the chair." If J.D. goes on vacation, some other person might assume that role temporarily, and her memos would then carry the "chair" designator on the originator line.

Management of roles implies some system facility for assigning roles, changing roles, nesting one role within others, associating names and/or user IDs with roles, reporting on existing roles and users that occupy them, and so on. It may also imply the ability to form new roles and associate them with a variety of privileges. These management functions apply equally to roles taken in either of their contexts above.

11. Compatibility.
   a. Integrated conferencing and electronic mail facilities.
   b. Support for X.400/MOTIS.
   c. X.400 users can participate in group communications activities.

Integrated conferencing and electronic mail, (11.a), first means that comments to conferences and letters to individuals can be both read and written by facilities internal to the communications software package. It also implies the ability to send conference comments as mail, and receive mail in conferences for all participants to see. Of the well-known products, Participate probably has the most integrated E-mail and conferencing features because both services are accessible through an identical interface. Letters or comments can be posted to multiple places at the same time.

Support for X.400/MOTIS (MOTIS being the name given to the X.400 1988 extensions) is included here as a reminder that the X.400 standard is being rapidly adopted as a means of facilitating worldwide Inter-Personal Messaging, electronic mail. As the 1990s begin, only SuperCom and EIES2 inherently support the X.400 standard alongside conferencing. Other systems such as VaxNotes will shortly support it. Most of the current support for X.400 is limited to pure electronic mail systems. The CCITT is now addressing the need for extensions to X.400 in support of group communications activities. Its preliminary recommendations will be forwarded in 1992.

Feature (11.c) means that users having only access to X.400 mail facilities can nevertheless participate in group communications activities (see Figure 9.1). This would be accomplished by posting conference comments to distribution lists on the mail side of the bridge. Mail sent the other way would be collected for a single user, "the conference." The generation of distribution lists and the transformations in data format (from X.400 to conference, and conference to X.400) would take place automatically and would be difficult to implement. This feature is made possible by the flexibility of the X.400 standard, but it is not supported in current software.

The matrix of Table 9.2 describes several of the software products mentioned in this book crossed with a few of their characteristics. Some features are not mentioned because they are universal. For example, all of these products have a private electronic mail component. The column "Private messages in conference" refers to the product's support for private messages inside the context of a conference. "Format" refers to the product's ability to support user customizable output formats. Security provisions are not mentioned because they are so varied. Similarly, many of the PC-oriented products have extensive user accounting facilities designed to support billing of subscribers and these are not mentioned. "User control of subconference" refers to the ordinary user's ability to create a new thread at the level immediately below that of the conference.

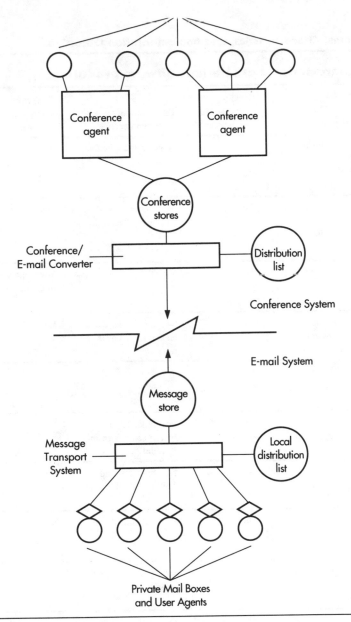

Figure 9.1 Possible architecture for a conference/E-mail hybrid system. This illustration takes as its starting point the SMARTIX proposal for a distributed conference system illustrated in Figure 7.9. A new entity, the *conference/electronic mail* converter, is introduced. The converter is responsible for taking conference data and formatting it compatibly with some (presumably X.400) electronic mail system, along with handling the distribution of the outgoing texts based on local distribution list data. On the incoming side, the converter merges mail messages into conferences, again based on the distribution list, along with the subject (possibly) of the messages. On the other side of the system, the electronic mail software perceives messages properly marked for their intended recipients, arriving as though another E-mail host. Outgoing mail is treated as mail with a single destination (the conference system). At the present time, the only products supporting this kind of service are EIES2 and SuperCom.

Table 9.2 Characteristics of selected software products

	Structure	Private messages in conference	User control of subconference	Real-time/ store and forward
EIES	Linear	No	None, not applicable	Yes
EIES2	Variable customizable	Yes	Yes, depends on structure selected	Yes
ConFer II	Comb	Yes	Yes	Yes, separate structure from standard conference
Participate	Conference-oriented branching	No	Not applicable; users create conferences	No
Picospan	Comb	No	Yes	No
TEAMate	Branch/ hierarchy	No	No, depends on switch settings in individual branches	No
Magpie	Branch, comment-oriented	No	Yes, branches and threads	No
CoSy	Branch/ comb hybrid	No	No, new threads only	No
Notepad	Linear/ comb	Yes	No	Yes
Caucus	Comb	No	Yes	No
TBBS	Branch, comment-oriented	Yes	Yes, new threads	No
AKCS	Comb	No	Yes	No
PC-Board	Branch, comment-oriented	Yes	Yes	No

Table 9.2 *(Continued)*

Role support	Field addressability	Joint document editing	Binary file support	Control and navigation
By ID; many names per role	Yes, for any number of defined fields per conference	Yes, multiuser notebooks	Yes, as attachments to E-mail	Command with stacking and script language
By ID, class, etc.; many options	Yes, any number of fields	Yes, many kinds	Yes, various techniques	Many kinds, customizable by general purpose object-oriented language
By ID, many names per role	No	Yes	Yes, as attachments to E-mail	Command with stacking
By ID, system wide or per conference	No	No	Yes, one attachment per thread	Inbox directory and command
By ID, per conference; many names per role	No	No	No, controlled by utilities at OS level	Command
By ID and class	Yes	Yes, through external programs	Yes, by branch or message	Control keys, menu, and command
Systemwide only	No	No	Yes, attachments to messages or special circumstances	By picking messages from display and command
Limited to conference level	No	No	Yes, attachments to messages or special file area	Various menu levels and command
Customizable as required	Yes, if so customized	Yes	None	Single key commands using numbers
By conference ID per administrator role	No	No	Limited in DOS version; uses OS in UNIX	By customized menus or command
Several administrators per conference	No	No	Yes, to special file areas	Highly customizable menus or command
Multiple administrators per conference	No	No	Yes, through OS	Customizable menus and command
At conference level, multiple administrators per conference	No	No	Yes, extensive	By menu, pick-list, or command

Table 9.2 *(Continued)*

	Format	User directory	User status reports	Filter support	Search support
EIES	Full text, headers, summaries	Yes, ID only	Yes	Time/date, author	Full text, keyword-defined fields, subsets searchable
EIES II	Customizable; reports at field level	System-wide distributed	Yes	Customizable by field	Extensive, system-wide
Confer II	Fixed, but with many options	Yes	Yes	At item level (forget) and high-priority get	Extensive, full text, keyword, index, searchable subsets
Participate	Full text or summary only	Yes	No	At inbox level only	Single-term only, branch level control
Picospan	Under full user control via files in user log-in directory	No, uses OS facilities	No	At item level only	Sigle term in subject lines or full text
TEAMate	Highly customizable, but not by ordinary user	Yes	As part of record display	By branch and message	Full text field-selectable
Magpie	No	Yes	No	By message selection	Extensive, systemwide
CoSy	No, headers or whole messages only	Yes	No	By thread or time sequence; can forget sub-conference level	Single term, conference subtopic at a time
Notepad	Full-text or user-specified subset	Yes	Yes	By subconference, choosing from display of new items/comments	Multiple term, Boolean support
Caucus	No	Yes	Yes	By ITEM-FORGET	Single term, conference level
TBBS	No	No	No	By message marking	Single term, keyword or full text
AKCS	No	Yes, through OS	No	Subconference FORGET	Single term, full text
PC Board	No	No	No	By message marking	

Table 9.2 *(Continued)*

External program access	Decision support	Notes
Through OS	Yes, votes, tables, projections	Searches are systemwide; proves that linear format is capable of flexible manipulation by software
Through hooks built into system interface	Yes, many variations	Most extensive and elaborate software on market; requires extensive system experience to install and operate; operates in centralized and distributed modes and any combination
Through OS	Yes, in context of special structures	Most elaborate built-in output formats; best sub-setting search capabilities; good record cross-indexing; only comb system that permits item header texts to be treated independently of comments
Through OS	Yes, in special structures	Easiest command structure; only system (besides EISS and COM family) that permits messages sent to two or more places simultaneously; very flexible structure
Through OS	No	Most flexible output formatting; performance is *very* hardware dependent
Yes, through links to messages	Yes, through external programs	Best external program hooks; searches between fields automatically ANDed, within fields automatically ORed
Through OS	No	Best search capability; only product to support Boolean NOT operator; very smooth interface; best price/performance ratio
No	No	Very smooth interface; easy to use; only comment-oriented system that directly supports conference-level integrity at same time
No	Yes	Extensive decision support; most integrated asynchronous/synchronous conference modes; available only as third-party provision
None in DOS; good in UNIX	No	Solid system; runs in many environments, but not nearly as flexible as ConFer, from which it is derived
Only to specially supported software	No	Good multiuser DOS-only system; wide support
Through OS	No	Good cost/performance ratio for UNIX system; easier to use than Picospan, but not as powerful in format controls
Through "DOORS" programs	No	Very widely distributed system; many third-party add-ons; requires network, network cards, or multitasking shell for multiuser operation

All of the features described in this section apply equally to formal and informal (conference versus record) structural philosophies (see Chapter 6). Given sufficient selection, filtering, and navigation control mechanisms, both types may be effectively applied to institutional domains. Formally structured systems, in which responses are solicited after a reader has seen all new material in a topic or branch, are best suited to decision support, crisis resolution, strategic development, project management/development, and interagency coordination. In contrast, customer and vendor support, employee communications, and technology transfer may be best served by the more informal type of structure, in which questions and comments are directly attached to the records that prompted them. Technology scanning and other applications can be equally well served by either approach.

As it is, the more formally oriented systems are more mature. All of the models developed through 1980 embodied a philosophical orientation toward the conference/topic as a whole. Even Participate, which suggested the comment-in-context approach, is fundamentally a conference-oriented model. These systems generally contain better search, filtering, selection, navigation, directory, and decision support features than the later-appearing comment-oriented systems. At least this is true of the bigger, more expensive versions such as Confer, Participate, Caucus, Notepad, and a few others.

Many smaller systems have also adopted this philosophical model, but they lack some or most of the extended features. There is nothing to prevent their developers from adding these features; the cost is software size and/or development time. The same is true for the systems that reflect comment orientation. In their case, the development effort is even more pronounced because such systems must support user navigation through arbitrary chains of conversation. The current generation of these systems does not support levels of user control over the varying threads of conversation analogous to that provided by the better conference-oriented systems. Magpie and TEAMate are exceptions.

Part of the problem is conceptually insurmountable. If conferences are very active, trying to keep up with more than a few threads at a time is like trying to follow many simultaneous conversations in the social atmosphere of a large convention. It is possible to do so, given the asynchronous nature of the medium, but it requires a significant amount of time on the part of the user. That many of these systems have achieved the popularity they have is due in part to the general audience that most often uses such systems in the public arena.

This is not to say that these systems shouldn't be used in corporate or other institutional environments. The metaphor of the boardroom suggested by conference orientation can be achieved in comment-oriented systems by tailoring the environment with controls available to conference organizers, and even with customized interfaces applicable by users. Except for EIES2 (an expensive, delicate, and unusually large system), such controls do not exist to a great extent in the systems of the early 1990s.

■ 9.3 HUMAN FACTORS IMPACTING REQUIRED FEATURES

Although all of the features detailed above are desirable, no contemporary software contains all of them. In succeeding evaluation steps, as real software is examined, a product's mix of features will contribute to its realistic candidacy. When examining Table 9.2, corporate users should consider the following generic concerns.

1. What part of the employee population will be permitted access to the software? Remember that the overall utility of communications systems increases in proportion to its availability. Although not everyone needs access, it is imperative that employees who must interact within a particular domain have such access. If, for example, technology transfer in a manufacturing corporation is the domain of primary use, all engineers must have access to the system, or the software will prove valueless.

2. With respect to computer use generally, what is the typical skill level of the persons who will use the system? Do the intended users have access to microcomputers or terminals as a regular part of their work, or will participation in computer conferences, electronic mail, or information retrieval be their only purpose in using computer facilities?

3. How often will the typical user use the system? Put another way, during what part of the working day will users be actively engaged in group communication activities? If system use is a regular part of an employee's daily work, the individual can be expected to become reasonably proficient with even complex software in a relatively short time. If they use it only occasionally, users may never become fully comfortable with command-driven software. In this case, a system that provides users with a menu-driven front end will be imperative. Because some users will grow tired of menus, the software should enable those persons to bypass the menus and use a more efficient command mode if they so choose.

4. How will users be trained? How many hours of training will be provided? Will training be individual, conducted in classes, or both? Even the most complex conferencing, E-mail or information retrieval software can be used in a rudimentary way with but a few hours of training. Mastering the system, however, may take much longer if the particular software chosen is "facility rich."

5. How many persons will be appointed to act as on-line helpers, conference organizers, and so on? What special training will these persons receive? Ordinary users may become familiar enough with the software to use it in a very few hours, but the persons charged with maintaining conferences and helping other users reach intermediate and expert levels must become expert users themselves.

6. Will synchronous conference facilities be required, or will store-and-forward, asynchronous capabilities be sufficient for all requirements? None of the domains listed above entail synchronous facilities in and of themselves, with the possible exception of crisis/disaster resolution. All researchers and developers in the field agree that most real work is accomplished asynchronously, where the store-and-forward capabilities of the software increase the communications potential of the medium across time zones and personal schedules.

7. What requirements are there for system and conference security? Presumably there will be both public and private conferences present on the system. Public conferences, in the context of a corporate system, are those that any employee

of the corporation with the necessary equipment can join. Private conferences are those restricted to a group of persons invited to participate. Persons not invited to a private conference should not even be aware of its existence, although they might know as a matter of course that private conferences exist. If users are permitted to dial into the system from outside the company, or if this is a publicly accessible system, then the identity of remote users must be verified. The security requirements of the system will also help determine whether a distributed or centralized system is more appropriate.

8. What is the geographic distribution of the user population? The answer to this question will help determine to some extent whether it makes sense to lease time on conference facilities run by a third party, especially if the user population or the company is relatively small, but widely dispersed nationally or internationally.

■ 9.4 A PLACE FOR ELECTRONIC MAIL

Electronic mail systems should receive first consideration if they satisfy all requirements. E-mail has grown more and more common in corporations worldwide. The metaphor of the mailbox is easy for users to grasp. Electronic mail systems can be more or less complex to operate, but once proficient, users can pretty much get along by themselves with a system overseer handling routine maintenance chores (backups, disk optimizations, adding and deleting users, and so on.) on a periodic basis. Electronic mail does not require facilitation as do conferences. Like conferencing, it must be available to every employee who might be involved in a given usage domain, or it will be ineffective.

9.4.1 Electronic Mail and Group Communications Merged

The primary disadvantage of electronic mail is its lack of flexibility with respect to some features common in most conferencing systems. Few mail systems permit the user to sort and select mail for reading by subject or the presence of a character string *before* reading the mail. Some such systems are beginning to appear.

Another general problem with pure E-mail systems employed as group communications devices is their lack of user status reporting facilities. In a group communications environment, it is sometimes important to know who has seen what messages, and when a given person was last present (reading) in a conference. Electronic mail is inherently private and cannot provide such reporting for the members of a given mailing list without violating the privacy of other communications.

Two other problems with electronic mail are the current lack of standardized directory services and the fact that E-mail systems do not scale well as users attempt to use mailing lists to simulate conference capabilities. As conferences grow in size and participant population, it quickly becomes impractical to "catch people up" to previous activity by shipping them copies of the conference transcript.

9.4.2 Importance of Standardized Directory Services

If the system is localized to a single company, network, or collection of networks, the lack of standardized international directory services may not be so large a problem.

Directories have their most immediate impact on users by allowing them to send mail to a person or persons without knowing their machine/node address on a given network. Most electronic mail software designed for local area networks, and even larger metropolitan area networks, provide such directory facilities. The lack of standardized directories is felt primarily when multiple E-mail packages are linked via bridges or gateways between dissimilar networks or where the network or collection of networks is expected to exchange mail with remote systems and users. The CCITT X.400 and TCP/IP RFC822 mail protocols are now widely enough accepted to permit dissimilar systems to exchange mail, but directing that mail to the proper recipients becomes a significant problem as mail networks become very large.

9.4.3 Extending Electronic Mail to Group Communications

As with many kinds of software, initial projections for use of an E-mail system, specifically its domain set, are often rendered obsolete when users begin to work with the software and find new, unanticipated ways to use it. Users begin to apply the software to inappropriate domains. Electronic mail, frequently exchanged between groups of users, becomes something of a simulated conference without the facilities required to support group conversations. Because electronic mail is an open-ended application, it is often subject to this kind of distortion. The resulting inefficiencies may result in lost opportunities and reduced productivity because there are no graceful extensions for conferencing.

9.4.4 Attaching Users to Electronic Mail Systems

Remote users can attach to corporate electronic mail systems in one of two ways. They may be empowered to dial into the local system through a special communications server or a modem attached to a local workstation. In this configuration, the user's mailbox is located on the host system, and the user manipulates the system mail software to deliver and receive mail. The advantage to this approach is that the remote site requires no special mail software. The disadvantage is that the user must become familiar not only with the mail system running at the home office, but also with some terminal emulation package used to make the connection between remote and central systems. The user must also go to the trouble of making a phone call periodically to see if he or she has any mail waiting, or to send mail to other users. All of these disadvantages can be circumvented with script programs designed to place appropriate calls and to exchange mail with the central host. Of course, someone must write these scripts.

Another approach is to put mail software on the remote user's computer, permitting him or her to read and send mail at his or her own workstation. The second approach is analogous to distributed versus centralized conferencing. The analogy is not complete, however, because the remote software is aware of but one private mailbox for each system to which it is connected.

Remote mail packages must be purchased separately from the same vendor that produced the mail software running at the home office. These remote mail packages are like terminal emulation software with appropriate scripts built into them. They appear to the user exactly like the centralized system would if the user were directly connected to it. Often they have enhanced features, as well: for example, background mail checks and scheduled transmission. This is their primary advantage. Their primary disadvantage is the cost for a package that performs what are essentially terminal emulation plus script services without the open-ended flexibility of other communications software. If the remote package merely emulates a user communicating through the host's standard interface, the result will be less efficient, but easier to implement, than a separate interface handler run on the host side.

■ 9.5 INFORMATION RETRIEVAL IN COMMUNICATION DOMAINS

Information retrieval technology impinges on computer conferencing in several domains. The two technologies can be related in two ways. First, the conference itself is a searchable database. Second, external databases may be scanned for information that is included in the conference for all to see. Inclusion is typically by import to the conference communications structure. A more sophisticated approach would embed pointers in the conference record and automatically retrieve the referenced records at a reader's discretion. The first relationship is supported primarily by good search and filtering facilities inside the conferencing software. The second may involve databases on or external to the machine or machines on which the conference takes place.

All of the conferencing domains with information retrieval implications can benefit from data available in databases outside the conference system itself. For example, customer or vendor support conferences or electronic mail systems can permit users to access information on company products, lead-time requirements for ordering, prices, parts substitution information, and so on. Such a database would likely be internal because such data is usually proprietary.

Technology scanning, decision support, and crisis management can also benefit from internal, proprietary databases, but these domains may also profit from available links to external databases maintained by third parties. Engineering productivity is enhanced by access to information respecting problem solutions achieved both inside and outside the corporation. Management decision support benefits from the widest possible access to information not only about the activities of the company, but of the industry as a whole. Crisis resolution frequently involves multiple agencies or companies that must all have access to a common pool of background information in the crisis arena. A connection to Usenet is of value to almost any corporation involved in technology or research of any kind because the universities of the world, most of whom are connected to this system, form a rich pool of potential information and research skill.

9.5.1 Information Retrieval in Customer Support Systems

Customer support systems benefit from the ability to scan conference records because many customers have similar problems. Solutions, work-arounds, and new documentation remain available to other customers with similar questions at a later time. This use of information retrieval clearly illustrates the value of performing this support in the context of a conference as opposed to electronic mail. The latter provides no database to the customer, thus requiring support staff to re-answer the same question again and again.

Crisis management is another area where the conference-as-database serves well. Like customer problems, some crises have repetitive characteristics. Oil spills, earthquakes, nuclear accidents, and chemical mishaps reoccur in much the same form. As each is handled with the support of a computer conferencing system, the recommendations of experts, actions taken, and results achieved remain as a valuable database to apply to the next occurrence.

■ 9.6 IN-HOUSE OPERATION VERSUS OUT-SOURCING

9.6.1 Advantages to Out-Sourcing

Except for some information retrieval demands, any given set of corporate requirements for conferencing or electronic mail could likely be satisfied either by a number of products internally or by third parties maintaining systems outside the corporation. Electronic mail and conferencing systems are both well represented by third parties who sell services to corporations or individuals (see Appendix D for a list). The best-known electronic mail services include MCI, Western Union's EasyLink, Sprint-Mail, and AT&T mail. Third-party conferencing systems include the Notepad, run by Notepad International; Confer II from Advertel Corp.; and others such as Unison, NWI, the Well, and Point Information Network, Inc. Advantages to out-sourcing (contracting with third parties to maintain corporate conference facilities outside the corporation) include the following:

1. *Experimentation.* Companies looking to try services, particularly computer conferencing, may contract for outside services for a time so that users and management may experiment with the technology before bringing it in-house.

2. *Third party maintenance, training, and user assistance.* When support is contracted, it is the responsibility of the vendor to maintain the software, keep the system available, and provide user training and ongoing assistance. This relieves the corporation of these chores, although such services do not typically extend to facilitation of specific conferences that are private to the contracting corporation. In this same vein, the vendor is also responsible for maintaining the security of the conference and for customizing the application software to meet users' specific requirements.

3. *System quality.* Third-party software is typically of the highest quality, with rich feature sets, and is tailorable to specific requirements. Although it is possible to purchase most of these application packages for use in-house, they tend to be quite expensive.

4. *Global connectivity.* Third-party systems are well connected nationally, and some worldwide, thus saving individual corporations the cost of establishing such connections if their users are geographically distributed. All four of the best-known electronic mail vendors have a global presence and are already establishing connections to other international networks via X.400 protocols.

By the mid 1990s it should be possible to send electronic mail to anyone on any network in the world from any other network. Establishing international directory services and resolving the problem of network cost sharing remain the primary obstacles to global connectivity at this time. The CCITT X.500 directory standard will cover the first problem in a very few years, and user pressure to come to costing agreements will drive solutions to the more political problems. The largest third-party conference vendors are also accessible from just about any point on the globe having telephone service. The Notepad is outstanding in this arena, having established connections with more communications vendors (including national telephone and telegraph companies) than any other conference provider.

5. *Accessibility.* Third-party systems provide connections, and sometimes specialized interfaces, for virtually all types of terminal and terminal emulation equipment. This can be a great advantage to corporations that wish to link users with a wide variety of terminal equipment. The larger systems either maintain their own national or international network of connection points, or contract with other parties (such as Tymnet or Telenet corporations) to provide such networks. This allows most users to reach the vendor's central facilities with a local or almost local call from almost anywhere in the world.

6. *Cost distribution.* This is of particular advantage to widely dispersed users who may be managers or employees of government agencies or nonprofit corporations and who must coordinate operations with departments or agencies. Users or their agencies may contract to pay just their share of the costs associated with the conferences. These costs include not only the conference or mail vendor's charges for use of the system's facilities, but also the cost of using global telecommunications networks to reach the conference or mail system. Since the electronic mail or conference provider handles accounting and billing, any single agency is relieved of the task of charging other agencies for their use and collecting the payments.

Items 4 through 6 account for the popularity of third-party systems such as the Well and others that serve not only the public, but also many widely dispersed groups with common economic, political, and social interests. Other than these common interests, the members of such groups have no formal relationship as do employees of a single corporation. The use of third-party systems is ideal for these groups because they would otherwise have to make long-distance calls to a central system maintained by some member of the group or maintain a complex network of small distributed systems.

9.6.2 Out-Sourced Systems for Technical Support

Technology companies also make extensive use of public services to provide customer support. By using such services as CompuServe, BIX, and GEnie, many corporations maintain relations with their customers, providing rapid service, marketing new products, and acquiring valuable feedback without the cost of maintaining in-house systems. Many of the customers of these companies are already subscribers to one or more of the major public conference vendors. Thus, the corporation, at relatively little cost to itself, gains access to a large segment of its customer community.

9.6.3 Third-Party Pricing

There are relatively few companies whose primary business is maintaining communications facilities for corporations and other organizations. These companies are competing for business in a relatively small market. As a result, there is no median service cost around which most of the competitors cluster their pricing. Many different and widely varying pricing strategies result. Most of these companies charge either a flat rate per user per month, bill per hour of use, or both. Fees range from $40.00/month flat rate to $30.00/hour. Mixed arrangements—for example $15.00/month, with hourly charges ranging from $3.00 to $20.00—are common.

Most of these companies will negotiate pricing arrangements to some extent, and all distinguish between profit and nonprofit accounts, the latter receiving anywhere from 25 to 50 percent discount over corporate rates. In some cases, telecommunications costs (the use of packet networks to reach the facility) are folded into the overall price of the service, whereas others pass these costs directly on to the users.

Organizations whose primary business is providing group communication services to the public will also provide private accounts. These tend to be less expensive than the examples given above. The Well, for example, charges $10.00/month flat rate plus $2.00/hour, with telecommunications costs passed on to the user. Lower prices do not always mean less capable facilities, but they do entail competition between private and public accounts who must use the same bank of telephone or packet circuits to reach the provider.

Notepad Systems International is unique in this market, preferring to price its services on a problem-resolution basis. Rather than charging for time on a machine, the Notepad staff consults with a client about the nature of the client's communications requirements. If the use of Notepad software and facilities is to figure in the resolution of a problem, that use is priced as a unit, for the duration of the project. This approach is much like that of a construction contractor who bids a fixed price on a project. Using Notepad can cost a corporation anywhere from $500 to $2500 a month, with prices averaging about $1500.

Notepad Systems has had more experience in this field than most other organizations and has made a living by pricing appropriately most of the time. This one price approach includes all telecommunications costs (worldwide), consulting fees, and ongoing customer training and support, something for which most of their competitors charge extra. The result tends to be a little higher price than much of the competition for short duration projects involving few people. Notepad prices, however, are typically much lower than its competitors when a project has many participants and a longer duration.

9.6.4 Cost and Benefits of Operations In-House

In general, there are more reasons for out-sourcing a corporatewide conferencing facility than not doing so. For conferencing to be successful, some terminal device (terminal or microcomputer) must be immediately accessible to each user. This requirement applies whether the system is run in-house or out-sourced. Given this need, and the existing worldwide connectivity of third-party vendors, there are only four conditions under which running in-house is substantially less expensive than out-sourcing.

1. There is a limited domain of use, for example, a customer support BBS. In this case, customer support and possibly engineering will require access to the system. The latter group may need to communicate with the former through (possibly existing) electronic or voice mail channels on only an "as required" basis. Few phone lines are required, and a simple, inexpensive group communications system will be adequate.

2. The company is so small that it cannot afford to out-source the system, and a very small, simple system will suffice. If such a company or its personnel are geographically distributed over a very wide territory, it will have to factor the cost of telephone usage into its financial considerations very carefully. If it is not distributed at all, it may not really need a conference or electronic mail system in the first place.

3. The company is very large—national or international in distribution—and already has an interconnected set of computer systems nationally or worldwide, all of which can support a single, available communication package. In this case, the hardware cost is already being borne, and the cost of software and support becomes the primary consideration. Similar considerations might apply if the software is used *exclusively* by a large or small work group already connected through a dedicated network of some kind. Such restrictions on participation, however, typically result in less than optimum value from the communications system.

4. There is some feature, required by a specific application that cannot be found in, or built into, the services of any third-party system at an acceptable price. If this is the case, it is unlikely that the need will be met by existing software for purchase and use in-house, either. Some customization will be necessary. Sometimes the "missing feature" is related to corporate security policy and requirements. For example, the use of modems that exchange interlinked access codes is precluded in third-party systems because many clients must use the same modems.

Third-party systems prove cost-effective when the system's use is time delimited; that is, there is a reasonable expectation that the project concerned will end at some time in the not too distant future. If the system's use is ongoing—for example, as with technology scanning and management decision support applications—it will often prove less expensive to bring the system in-house, particularly if a reasonably small one will serve. There are, however, exceptions to this general rule. Much depends on the nature of the entities connected, their number, and their geographic distribution. Customer/vendor relations are an obvious exception, especially if the persons or companies involved already use public communications services. Even ongoing connections between separate entities (corporations, government offices, nonprofit organizations, and so on) may favor out-sourcing over an indefinite period of time.

■ 9.7 IN-HOUSE SYSTEMS

9.7.1 Variety of Electronic Mail and Group Communications Software

Although there are a number of vendors and a variety of software to choose from if a company decides to out-source its conference facilities, there is even more software available for in-house use. Most major local area network operating systems now support one or more electronic mail packages written by the LAN vendor or some third party. Systems range from those completely resident in and dependent upon a particular local area network or family of networks, to products like Alethic Software's Backmail, which supports an entirely distributed collection of stand-alone microcomputers by automatically generating calls (local or long-distance) to remote machines for mail delivery. Systems from mainframes to microcomputers all support connectable electronic mail software.

If there is variety to be had in choosing electronic mail packages, the choices available for computer conferencing are even more expansive. As an additional bonus, one need not face the problem of having to purchase two packages for conferencing and electronic mail. Virtually all conferencing systems also support electronic mail. The reason for this assortment is historical and accidental. Electronic mail seems now to have the greater commercial potential, but its historical development did not challenge so many people as did the potential inherent in the group dynamics of conferencing and bulletin board systems.

As a result, there is a tremendous variety of software for asynchronous conferences. Many of these systems are not suitable for serious activities in most of the domains to which conferencing is applied in corporations. Customer and vendor support operations are exceptions. These domains require very simple structures and usually do not require support for many conferences, user directory facilities, and other features associated with more sophisticated packages. These two domains do require good search and selection facilities, however, and possibly also a means of accessing local databases for information the company wishes to make available to its customers or vendors. This is not too severe a restriction, however. Many of the simplest BBSs provide exits that permit users to operate other software on the system, including DBMS applications.

None of the smaller systems support such things as joint document editing, delphic voting, or linking of threads between separate conferences. Support for most features related to group communications, aside from text exchanges proper, is found only in systems that evolved in the 1970s on mainframe platforms. Their designers aimed at both conference abilities and group communications support in general. Such was not the case with the smaller systems that emerged in the 1980s. Early microcomputers were too limited to support such features, and system designers were not aware of the overall value of other adjuncts to group communications.

The same is true for systems that evolved in the minicomputer universe of the mid to late 1970s. Their designers were, for the most part, trying to demonstrate principles illustrated by a limited set of group communications facilities. There are exceptions, however. In the mid to late 1980s, a few systems appeared that support extended communications functions by integrating the conference arena with external programs.

9.7.2 The Need for Alternate Communications Structures

Other domains require more sophisticated systems. Decision support and crisis management in particular are best facilitated by software that supports delphic voting and sophisticated navigation through conference texts, as well as facilities for synchronous communications. Corporate systems used by many users with widely varying computer skills must also support various levels of customization. Users must be able to perform their work through various levels of menu support and command customization. This customization should be easy to perform either by the user or support staff acting in the user's behalf. Ideally, the system should be transportable to a variety of hardware and operating system platforms. This allows the corporation to expand the system as it becomes necessary to do so, without losing the data already present in the conferences.

As more domains become involved in a given application, a wider variety of communications structures will prove desirable. Different conferences may be best reflected in conference or comment-oriented structures. Bulletin areas (read-only conferences) are useful for general distribution of technical or management information. Joint document editing services should have their own structures, and electronic mail and conference facilities should be well integrated. Support for fine discrimination among user and administrative roles also becomes more valuable as systems expand into more domains.

As a general rule, the less expensive software will be appropriate for a more restricted domain set and smaller overall systems. This is to be expected, but it is somewhat unfortunate because many of the more interesting interfaces are found in small systems produced primarily with the small operator or public market in mind.

■ 9.8 CONFIGURATION

There are two basic issues involved in system configuration. The first, external to the conference or electronic mail software itself, concerns the telecommunications environment used to link users to the system. This issue relates both to systems used in-house and to systems out-sourced to a third party. The second issue concerns software customization for individual users. The customization potential of any given package should be one of the primary considerations in selecting conferencing software, whether out-sourced or purchased for in-house use.

Electronic mail and conferencing systems are marvelously flexible with respect to their telecommunications environment (see Figure 9.2). Available software ranges from microcomputer to mainframe environments. No matter what a corporation's primary system environment, however, a communication system may run in an altogether different setting, with channels connecting it to other corporate computing systems.

To take an extreme example, a corporation with 1000 users connected to a large mainframe running MVS can elect to establish a conference system on a microcomputer, transparently switching users, through the mainframe's communication controller, to the microcomputer via SNA or X.25 links. Corporations operating many dissimilar local area networks may find no single conference or E-mail package that

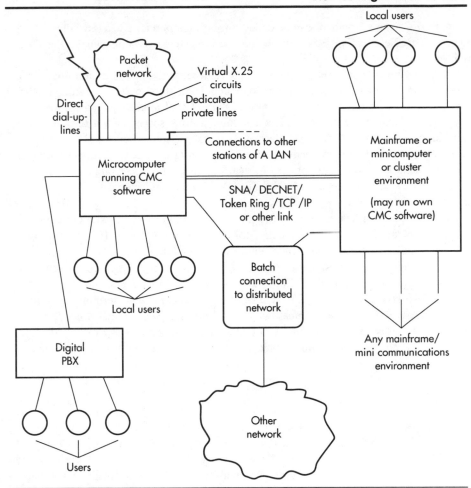

Figure 9.2 CMC telecommunications environment. This figure illustrates the possible variety of telecommuncations in which a CMC system may be embedded. In this case, the CMC software is running on a multiuser microcomputer, but it might just as easily be resident on a mainframe or minicomputer, or distributed across multiple hosts. As the diagram suggests, the possible variety of telecommunications environments to which a CMC system can be connected is virtually endless, but no systems come with ready-made drivers supporting all these connections at the same time.

runs on all of them. They may purchase a system that runs on one of these networks and gateway all the others to it through asynchronous communications servers. Alternatively, they may run their conferences on a micro- or minicomputer and gateway all networks to this system.

Conference systems can be reached via PBX facilities as well. Drivers may be purchased or written to make use of any number of network protocols, transparently to the conference software. For example, a DEC VaxNotes system running in a distributed DECNet environment can be called through telephone, packet-switched X.25 lines, or DECNet's native Ethernet network from systems running outside the DEC environment.

The problem of connecting employee and remote workstations or terminals to a conferencing or electronic mail system operated by a third party is similar to that of establishing connections to an in-house system. Local area networks can be connected to the outside world through a communications server or via the corporate mainframe/minicomputer. Another alternative is to use an in-house PBX system to reach systems outside the company. If the service being used has a contract with one or more packet-switching vendors (as most do), the contracting company can bring an X.25 packet assembler/disassembler (PAD) in-house and connect directly to the packet network.

This last approach has the virtue of requiring little in the way of extra communications equipment. If a corporation wishes, for example, to establish 16 outgoing lines for communications with a conference vendor using the telephone network, then some communications server must somewhere have 16 ports connected to 16 modems. In contrast, a product such as OST Corporation's Xnet X.25 card fits into a single PC slot and will service as many as 256 X.25 circuits. The company's terminal emulation software must recognize the X.25 card instead of the usual serial ports. Some terminal emulation software, such as Digital Communications Associates' Crosstalk Mark 4, is delivered with options for connecting the software to user-defined drivers for this purpose.

■ 9.9 THE SIGNIFICANCE OF TAILORABILITY

The telecommunications environment is the external side of a system configuration strategy. The internal side is the customization potential of the application software itself. If conference facilities are run by a third party, the contracting parties must settle on an appropriately customized environment within the limits of the available software. Some of this customization may be done by the contractor, some by employees of the contracting corporation trained by the contractor to do this work. Users may also customize their personal environments to some extent when they become proficient enough to do so.

If the system is run in-house, all customization must be performed by operators trained in this work or by users, possibly subject to limitations established by internal corporate standards. User customizations are not, however, typically subject to standards limitations. Ordinary users are often given authority to customize their own input and output commands or formats. Users may, for example, create their own synonyms for commands, choose between a menu and a command mode, or customize the system's output format. Such changes will be effective only under their personal IDs, and will not interfere with the activities of other users.

Developers have established a number of mechanisms for system customization. Some of these were discussed in previous chapters. EIES, for example, has a flat and simple communications structure, but this open-ended form can be highly tailored by the development of specialized commands and filter systems using the software's sophisticated command/programming language. Caucus provides for customization through its "command dictionaries." Users are free to select the system style they prefer based on the available dictionary sets. Picospan provides individual users with similar powers, using a control/display language available to each user. The Notepad is customized by being rewritten (if necessary) to each individual client's specification. At the time of this writing, it is possibly the only conference software that cannot be purchased for in-house operation.

Tailorability refers not only to the interface issues outlined above, but also to a number of mechanisms built into the software to support group communications of different kinds. Some of the mechanisms elaborated in support of group work are delphic voting and automatic results tabulation, joint document authoring, synchronous conferences, facilities for editing records already entered, variable restrictions on length of user entries, addressable fields, support for numerous role distinctions, user and conference directory services, high-quality search and filtering facilities, and convenient association between conference comments and individual messages (E-mail) coupled with the ability of conference administrators to easily alter various switches controlling these characteristics. As a rule, only the largest (most expensive) software supports all of these features. EIES descendants, TEIES and EIES2, have an extraordinary amount of tailorability in this area.

Tailorability may also refer to the number of operating environments in which the software will run and the ease of moving from one environment to another. This also includes the software's capacity to run centralized or distributed. Picospan is powerful, but is limited to operations in a UNIX environment. TBBS is easy to use, but operates only in the MS-DOS world. In contrast, Caucus and Participate run in environments ranging from MVS- and VM-based mainframes through VMS-based minicomputers to UNIX and DOS. Their developers have focused, among other things, on the software's ability to migrate to whatever environments are present in a given shop.

Customization, therefore, has many facets. Vendors strive to make their software appear highly tailorable because their perception of the market suggests that flexibility of one or more kinds is what customers want. Although this is probably an accurate perception, it is also true that the nature of what is supported, *group communications,* demands flexible mechanisms for human expression. It is for this reason that most of the developers of larger, more expensive, and more flexible systems eschew the smaller systems as too rigid or as being tailorable in only one or few dimensions. This is also, generally speaking, a valid perception. Vendors of smaller systems have concentrated on *interface* tailorability and to some extent cross-environment operation. Flexibility of communications structures themselves has been largely ignored by these developers.

Yet many of these smaller products are succeeding at least as well, in fact better, than the larger systems. One reason is price. Coupled with this is the corporate recognition that a tool may be right for one job without having to contain the world. One need not purchase a system with support for polling and delphic voting (for example) if that tool is not used for decision support. A system dedicated to customer support and vendor communications may require sophisticated database access and search capabilities, but it is well served by the simplest communications structures. Electronic mail alone, with but rudimentary features supporting group communications, may be all that some corporations require.

In the next chapter we will explore some of the areas in which customization may prove useful and the impact of customization on system services.

10

ADVANCED FEATURES AND IMPLICATIONS

Given the availability and variety of text-based communications software now on the market, it is almost inconceivable that a corporation that was not in the business of producing such software would tackle the job of generating such complex systems from scratch. It is possible, however, that corporations might want to customize existing systems to add specialized features not included in the original package. Such additions might include the following:

1. *Graphics support*. Companies might standardize around one of the available graphics protocols, for example, the North American Presentation Level Protocol Syntax (NAPLPS). Their conferencing system and all local and remote workstations expected to interact with that system might be required to support this graphics standard. It may not be the conference software, but the terminal emulation software used in individual workstations, that requires customization.

2. *Special database access*. Many available communication packages contain provisions for user exits to external software of many kinds. Such exit facilities may not be, however, an acceptable solution as they require users to be proficient in the use of a particular DBMS or other application interface. Allowing users easy access to data in databases outside the conference software may require some source code customization. Conversely, a company strongly committed to using a particular DBMS may consider adding communications facilities to its DBMS software if the project could be kept to a reasonable size.

3. *Conference text-base search and retrieval facilities*. Despite the importance of good search and retrieval features in several domains, the facilities provided in support of such services are relatively primitive in many otherwise good conferencing systems. A customization effort might strive to improve such facilities.

235

4. *Automated user interfaces.* Given the flexibility of many of today's communications systems, this is not so much a matter of customizing the software's code, as of using the tailorability features of the system interface coupled with terminal emulation scripts that permit a user to send and retrieve messages off-line, as a background task, while simultaneously performing other work.

5. *Special features and communications structures.* A company may require special communications structures not provided by a chosen package. These may be added with a code customization effort. They include such things as adding binary file support, enhanced directory or security services, voting facilities, joint document editing, field addressable records, and so on.

6. *Special device access.* Companies may wish to customize those parts of a package, and/or the device drivers they use, to take advantage of special communications devices.

Each of these reasons for customization is discussed in the following sections, along with a brief description of the factors involved.

■ 10.1 GRAPHICS SUPPORT

Graphics can certainly be a useful adjunct to text-based communications. To date, few systems directly support graphics as a part of the conference stream. The primary reason is the lack of widespread acceptance and use of any one graphics control standard. As a result, few terminal emulation packages contain support for graphics display. If a conference participant is not using terminal emulation software, but a real terminal, then support for a particular graphics standard would have to be built into the terminal itself. Such devices, while available, are expensive and not widely used outside engineering circles.

In the United States and Canada, the North American Presentation Level Protocol Syntax (NAPLPS) has been accepted as a basic graphics control standard; this standard offers advantages to systems that adopt it. In their text streams, these systems can embed control characters that are interpreted by terminal software at remote nodes. Users of NAPLPS-supportive terminal software can construct pictures or transmit control instructions automatically to a host as a part of a text record. The host passes the control information on to other nodes during their receipt of text information.

NAPLPS information can be encoded in seven- or eight-bit bytes. Although eight-bit encoding is more efficient, seven-bit encoding is far more common because it is easier to support in text-oriented record structures. NAPLPS uses several sets of control characters to substitute Picture Description Information (PDI) into a portion of the space normally occupied by the 127 characters of the ASCII seven-bit character set. These control codes typically begin with an ESCAPE character (ASCII character 27) followed by one byte indicating which PDI is to be shifted in. These sequences may be the same as those used by many terminals to perform various screen functions like clearing, erasing a line, setting a scroll region, and so on. The standard includes several PDI sets, and more can be added, including such things as codes describing audio tones, characters of a pictographic language, or the statements of a programming language.

Enhancing a system to make the transferral of graphics information transparent and selective is mostly a matter of getting support for the graphics protocol in use into the terminal emulation software employed by the users. This is true provided the file management and user interface portions of the software can pass ASCII information mixed with PDIs, without mistaking them for end-of-record delimiters or other significant characters. The most significant factor determining the ease with which a given system can support such embedded codes is that the record management system be able to recognize the beginning and end of the text part of a record without line or other delimiters. This is usually accomplished by encoding the length of the record's text part in one field of the record header (see the following text).

In addition to the data management functions of the host system, the user interface routines will also have to properly handle this mixed data. For example, the interface processes may have to filter such characters from the outgoing data stream. This need arises if the remote terminals are not required to support the graphics controls transmitted by the host.

■ **10.2 CUSTOMIZED ACCESS TO EXTERNAL DATABASES**

Linking conference systems to information retrieval systems and extensive databases is becoming more common. Such links may take place through special gateways that connect the user to databases residing on other machines, though they can provide access to local databases available as well. Notepad is beginning to differentiate its timesharing communications service by providing specialized databases to its users. At the time of this writing, Notepad Systems International has specialized databases in the areas of earth, nuclear, and space sciences. The New York City Board of Education runs a 16-line Magpie conferencing system that also provides databases on educational activities in and around New York City. Compuserve, through IQuest, its name for Telebase Incorporated's Easynet gateway service, makes a large number of external bibliographic, scientific, and business databases available to its users (Figure 10.1).

External database operations are most commonly supported in the form of exits from the communications software. That is, a user's communications operations are temporarily suspended while system control is passed to a DBMS program of some kind. When the user is finished with the DBMS, usually he or she is automatically returned to the communications environment. In single-user environments it may be necessary to redirect the output of the DBMS application to the communications port rather than to the local console. Similarly, the application must recognize some telecommunications link as the source of user input. Some MS-DOS configurations (for example Magpie running under Desqview) performs this I/O redirection automatically. Others require special programs, called *doors* to perform these functions.

If the communications software is written around a kernel that controls all system multitasking as well as communications operations (for example, TBBS), there may not be a way to operate a program external to the communications software. In this case, exits must be added to the application code, along with all necessary provisions to operate the external program as one of the processes recognized by the multitasking

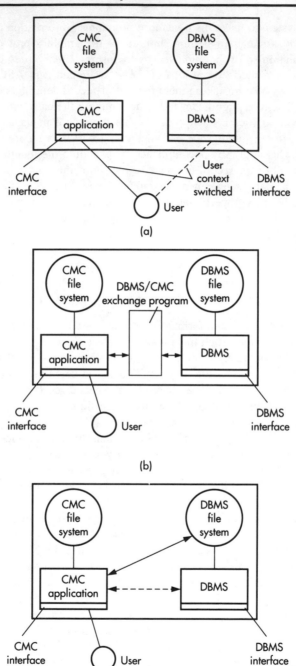

Figure 10.1 Strategies connecting CMC to external programs. The most common approach is represented in (a) where control is passed from the CMC application to the external program (in the illustration a DBMS), and the user is connected to its interface. The external software is completely independent of the CMC application. If the users wish to incorporate output from the external system into the CMC database, they must do so manually. In (b), an intermediary program is interfaced directly with the CMC application on one side and the external software on the other. Users continue to interact with the CMC application interface, while the exchange program passes their commands to the external software and returns results directly to the CMC application. In (c), the CMC program itself is capable of reading and writing directly to the DBMS file system. This kind of connection is usually specific to DBMS systems, and impractical with most other kinds of applications, though word processors, spreadsheets, and other external software may be addressed in this manner. Alternatively, the CMC software may address the external file system through the DBMS (or other external) engine without the mediation of an intermediary program. Phil Becker's TDBS is an example of this form.

kernel. Each specific application available to users in these systems must be supported by its own handling code in the communications package.

In either case, the output of the DBMS or other application is not usually coordinated with the message database and I/O facilities. A user may receive output from the external program, but redirection to a host file or local capture must intervene between the DBMS search and inclusion of the results in a message stream.

A more versatile facility would permit users to communicate with external programs directly through the communications software interface. Data requests might be translated directly into searches on the files of an external application. Returned results can be automatically formatted for inclusion in the text base if desired by the user. Ideally, the DBMS and communications products should be so closely integrated that records in the former are made available to the latter through pointers included in the conversation stream. If a user finds a DBMS record of value to a discussion, he or she should be able to embed that record's key, invisibly, in the text stream. On encountering one of these pointers, the conference software might automatically retrieve the DBMS record (or records) and display it.

Users may add interproduct integration to communications software provided they have access to the underlying file system of all the applications involved. If the software is its own multitasking shell, then integrated external operations can be added along with all of the other code written to support external operations generally. If the system runs under an external shell (for example, Desqview), integration can be achieved with a third program that communicates with the external application on one side, and the communication software interface on the other.

■ **10.3 IMPROVED INFORMATION RETRIEVAL FOR CONFERENCE TEXTS**

Problems resolved, decisions reached, and technology reviewed in conference streams can be a valuable source of information for those who review these discussions long after they have concluded. In bringing together a communications package and a separate DBMS, the facilities of the database system are immediately available for support of operations on the text data. Such features include its index management system, table and record manipulation abilities, query language, and so on. Each of these features has its parallels in computer mediated communications, but they are often poorly developed, particularly with respect to query operations on the text base.

Historically, conferencing systems were developed to facilitate discussions between groups of people. Although they were aware of the value of good search and retrieval capabilities, their developers did not want to involve themselves in many of the costs and complexities of implementing elaborate search facilities. Many computer mediated communications systems provide convenient support for retrieval formulations like the following:

1. Display the last N messages (where N is a number).
2. Display message M through N.
3. Display the previous/next message in time sequence.
4. Display messages in-reply-to message N, or in-reply-to the current message.
5. Display the message to which message N, or the current message, is a reply.
6. Display messages containing string X in their subject or text.
7. Display messages by person Y.
8. Display messages written after Z date.

A few systems support limited boolean or cross-field queries such as the following:

1. Display messages written by person Y *and* containing string X in their subject.
2. Display messages containing string $X1$ *or* $X2$ in their text, and so on.

Some systems also support limited formatting of query results, such as the following: *show only the subject lines of messages found,* or *show only the first N lines of text.* A few also support nested queries, the ability to gather a group of records into a set, and perform another query on that set.

Another important set level operation, however, the ability to form two sets and subtract one set from another, for example "find those messages in set 1 that are *NOT* in set 2", is not supported by any current communications software. Nor did any of the systems researched for this book support nested parenthetical grouping of terms, for example: "find A *and* ($(B$ *or* $C)$ *and* $(D$ *or* E))." Another important use of the *not* operator, "find A *not* $(A$ *and* $B)$," which allows for tuning of query precision by excluding irrelevant uses of term A, is also unsupported. Support for wild-card or truncation operators, for example "find wom?n" to find both *woman* and *women*, is also unsupported in this software. By contrast, systems specializing in information retrieval tasks support all of the above query forms.

Hypertext-like connections between conference records can also be useful both to the individual user and the participating community. The Coconet's ability to include references in a text, and then permit users to jump immediately to the referenced texts is a step in this direction. Future systems may include the ability to mark words or phrases of a record and then search automatically for other records containing those words.

Such a feature might permit users to search across topics or even conferences for items of interest, and would constitute a new tool for both navigation and data filtering.

The potential value of complex query support is indisputable in domains like technology scanning or crisis resolution, although probably of more limited value in most others. Users of the more complex information retrieval systems are often experienced and motivated to get the most precise results. Their research has a high value, and the retrieval systems are expensive. By contrast, many users of group communications software never progress beyond the more basic functions of the system because their needs are satisfied at that level. Many users require only the ability to find simple text strings or to gather together texts written by a certain person.

Complex search support has a high price in CPU cycles. The specialized systems have elaborate file index schemes and specialized hardware to facilitate both the interpretation of complex query formulations as well as the recovery of the data itself. Writing software to support elaborate queries is also a difficult task. To get respectable performance with large databases, the job must be done in assembly language, effectively frustrating the general goal of making software easily transportable between different hardware and operating systems.

10.3.1   A Comparison between Dialog Citations and Usenet Message Structure

It is these difficulties, coupled with a questionable need for elaborate search support in many domains, that have prevented many developers from doing more in this area. If, however, a specific requirement for such support is identified, there is no reason why it cannot be added to existing software. Consider, for example, the structure of a typical Dialog bibliographic citation (Figure 10.2), compared to a Usenet message defined by the RFC1036 standard (Figure 10.3).

Although the Usenet message format seems more complex than that of the Dialog record, both record types are composed of distinct fields. Some of the fields in either record type may contain repeating groups. The Dialog ID field always contains two numbers, and the Identifier and Descriptor fields both contain an arbitrary number of terms separated by semicolons. In the Usenet record, many fields may contain a variable number of elements. These include newsgroups, reply to, follow-up, dis-

Message-ID	(Dialog database ID followed by database provider ID)
Title	
Author	
Journal Name, Pub. Date,	
Volume, Page numbers,	
Library of Congress number	
Language	(for example, English, Spanish, German)
Document type	(for example, Review, Article, Time series)
Abstract or full text of article	
Descriptors	(keywords)
Identifiers	(general reference concepts)

Figure 10.2   Representative Dialog citation.

Message Originator	
Date	
Newsgroups	(conferences to which this message is sent)
Subject	
Unique ID	
Path	(the node list this message traversed to reach this host)
Reply to	(ID of message to which this is a reply)
Follow-up	(conferences to which replies will be posted)
Expiration Date	(date message, if any, should be deleted)
References	(other message IDs to which this message relates)
Control	(if present the message is a probe between hosts, not intended for users to read)
Distribution list	(tunes the distribution by geographic area)
Organization	(the sender's organization)
Keywords	
Summary	(a short summary of the following text)
Approved	(ID of moderator approving this message if the conference requires such approval)
Lines	(number of lines in the comment body)
Xref	(used by machines only, this line crossreferences the message's ID in each of the conferences to which it is posted)
blank line	
Text of comment	

Note: All fields from *reply to* through *Xref* are optional, except the *Approved* line which must be present if the message is posted to a *moderated* conference. Messages are not posted directly to moderated conferences, but to a person, the moderator, who must release the message to the conference. Each of the above fields has a specified format, as well as its place in the field list.

Figure 10.3 Usenet message defined by RFC1036.

tribution lists, and references. Dialog searches are not hindered by the presence of such repeating values, because each field is treated as a string to which match requests may be applied. The same can be done for the Usenet records, or for any other communications software record.

There are costs associated with support for sophisticated searches. Even with the limited search support provided by most communications systems, searches can be terribly slow. To speed them up, text records may have to be indexed automatically, trading increased storage requirements for search efficiency. Indexing text records takes some time during input. Bibliographic systems update their databases only periodically, but communications software can receive input at any time.

A compromise solution is to allow text records to be inserted with a marker on unindexed records. Indexing can take place later when the machine or the particular record base is idle. To alleviate the storage burden imposed by indexes, compression systems may be added either to the index, the text base, or both. These compression systems may operate within the software, as they do in Notepad, or external to it. Within the next few years, hardware-based compression systems will be commonly available. These fast peripherals can triple disk capacity and increase disk throughput as a side benefit.

Keyword indexing and searching is an alternative or supplement to full text searches. Specific fields will contain words descriptive of a comment as a whole. It will prove easier to index and search this field than the text of the record itself. Some systems already contain support for keyword fields (Confer and EIES, for example). Keywords must, however, be added by the message's author or the conference organizer. Building keyword lists automatically, based on semantic analysis of the record, is within the realm of possibility, but not yet available in commercial software.

10.3.2 Retrieval Languages: The Application of SQL to Messaging Systems

There is also the matter of retrieval languages. Both American National Standards Institute (ANSI), and the National Information Standards Organization (NISO), have proposed standard information retrieval languages. One of the unusual efforts in this area is an attempt to apply ANSI standard Structured Query Language (SQL) to message retrieval tasks in an X.400 message system. The X.400 Message Handling Structure is defined as a series of possibly repeating and recursive elements of the following form:

```
<message>               := envelope <content>
<content>               := heading <body-part> [<body-part>]
<body-part>             := text | <forwarded-message-ID>
<forwarded-message-ID   := Previous-delivery-information <content>
```

This information may be carried in a single file. Each sub-component, especially the envelope, is itself a complex structure (see Chapter 6). However, it is the repeating groups of the content part of the message, along with the recursive definition of the forwarded-message-ID, that violate the fundamental rules of relational databases (note that RFC1036 for Usenet messages contains repeating groups, but no recursive definitions). Because SQL was formulated to build and manipulate relational structures, its syntax does not apply directly to an unmodified X.400 message.

What follows is a description of the approach taken by a Spanish/German research group to cast X.400 messages in relational form. The description is complex because the X.400 message specification is complicated (more so than the Usenet RFC1036 specification). In the following discussion, many attributes are described only as categories, (for example, fixed versus repeating attributes). This blurs details, but may make the results easier to grasp.

Relational tables must be *flat*. Their individual fields (attributes, or columns) cannot contain other fields within them. Also, they cannot be defined in terms of other fields; that is, they cannot contain recursive definitions. Each row of a relation must have a unique, *primary key*. This key may be composed of subcomponents so long as the following conditions hold:

1. Each subcomponent is a separate field with its own independent meaning.
2. All the subcomponents of the key are really necessary to uniquely identify every record.
3. No subcomponent of a key is ever null (though other attributes of the record may be null).

X.400 messages, by contrast, contain fields with multiple values that, in general, specify relations between separate messages or between messages and names. The message-message relations include such things as message-obsoletes-message, and message-crossreferences-message. Message-name relations include links between the message and its primary or copy-to recipients. Message envelopes also contain protocol information. The P1 protocol information standardizes the transfer of messages between message transfer agents (MTAs) operating on behalf of an Administrative Domain. The P2 information standardizes the format of the InterPersonal Messages (IPMs) and the Interpersonal Notifications (IPNs). The IPM is the message itself, while the IPN is an acknowledgment of the message's receipt by one of its intended recipients. The IPN is, of course, itself another IPM.

In the relational model, foreign keys provide the connection between one table and another, possibly several others (see Figure 10.4). Foreign keys are attributes in one or more tables whose values occupy the same domain as elements of the primary key in another table. Domains are essentially a type of value. Fields in different domains may have values represented by the same kind of data, but their *meaning* is different. For example, *weights* and *dollars* are both represented by digits and decimal values, but they are not the same domain. Foreign keys must be in the same domain as the primary keys they reference.

The first objective in casting the X.400 structure in a relational form is to identify an appropriate set of primary keys. One field of the P2 information in the envelope is the Message-ID. This, in turn, consists of a combination of Administration Management Domain name (ADMD), Country name, a Local ID, and a Private Management

---

Figure 10.4 Foreign key types. There are basically three kinds of foreign keys. The first is a regular attribute in one table that references all or part of a primary key of another table (a). The second is a regular attribute of a table that references all or part of a primary key of another row in its own table (b). An example of this might be an employee table whose primary key is an employee number, and which contains a field *manager* which contains the employee number of an employee's manager. The third kind (c) is a primary key (or part of a primary key) in one table that is also a foreign key at the same time. The first two types of foreign keys may be either *essential*, *assigned*, or *descriptive*. An *essential* key is one that must be present due to the nature of the relationship. For example, you cannot have an invoice line without an invoice. An *assigned* foreign key is one that MUST have a value because a business rule demands it. For example, "all employees must have a manager." The *descriptive* type may or may not be present in the table for which it is a foreign key (that is, it can be null), but if it is present, it must be represented in the primary key table. The third type of foreign key must be *essential* because it is also a primary key, and no primary key (or any component of it) may be null.

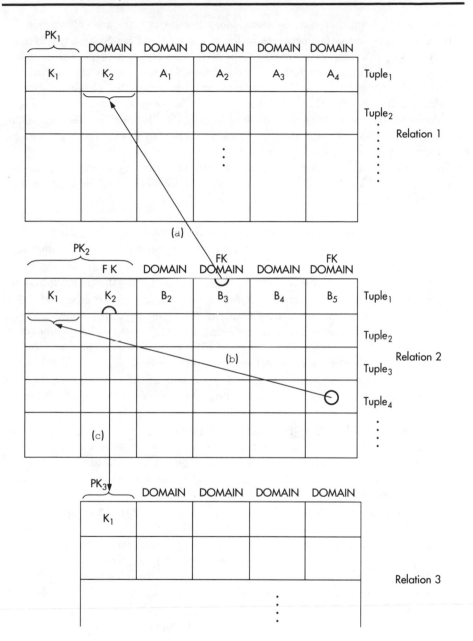

Domain name (if any). X.400, by itself, does not insist that such information be absolutely unique across all messages in the Message Handling System (MHS). To identify messages uniquely anywhere in the MHS, the SQL group used three components of the P2 envelope attributes and combined them into one key called the Unique-IPM-Identifier (U-IPM-ID). The three attributes were the Originator-Name, the Message-ID, and the Delivery Time. They further assumed that no UA would ever duplicate the local component of the Message-ID. Because the Message-ID is itself composed of four components, this means that the key to each message consists of six separate fields.

The group determined that four tables would be necessary to compose X.400 messages in a relational scheme. The four tables are as follows and are illustrated in Figure 10.5:

1. The Message Table, consisting of the U-IPM-ID (the key), the fixed (nonrepeating) parts of the envelope, and the fixed (nonrepeating) parts of the message heading.

2. The Message Links Table, consisting of the U-IPM-ID, and the U-IPM-ID of the other message to which this message is a link. These first two groups of fields (twelve separate attributes) are the key to this table. This allows any message to have many rows in this relation because it may be linked to many other messages. This separation of recursive information into separate rows satisfies the requirements of the relational form. Besides the key information, this table contains another field which describes the nature of the link between the two key groups. Some possible values of this field are: *obsoletes, crossreferences,* and *in-reply-to.*

3. The Names Links Table. The structure of this table is exactly the same as the Message Links Table, except that the second key is the name of the person to whom the message is linked. The third field group in this table also describes the nature of the link between the message and the name. Possible values include: *primary recipient, copy recipient,* and *reply to users.*

4. The Bodypart table. This table consists of the U-IPM-ID, its key, and a second field, the text of the message itself. A third field contains a forwarded U-IPM-ID, signifying that this message was forwarded by some other user. If forwarded, the message itself need not be stored a second time. Only a reference to the previous message is stored. New information about forwarded messages includes the U-IPM-ID of the envelope in which the forwarded message is embedded. Because the envelope of the original message is contained within the message content of the forwarded message, a single three part ID is required to reference the original message from the one forwarded. Note that if the bodypart of the message is a forwarded-pointer, the text part of that row of the table will be empty. If the text part is not empty, then the message is original, and not forwarded, so the forwarded group of fields will be null.

This structure permits a general query against an X.400 message system to be converted into an SQL query against the relational message database. A query like:

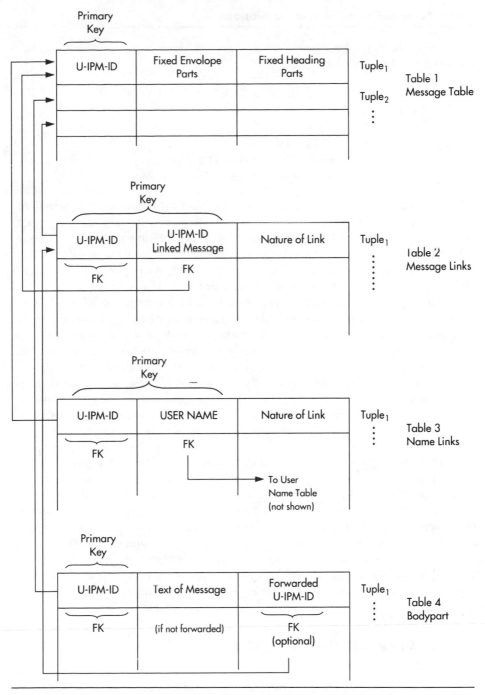

Figure 10.5 Four relational tables for X.400 messages. Four tables are used to resolve the X.400 message specification in relational form. A fifth table (user names) is not shown. The message table is the starting point, and each of the other tables contain foreign keys that point to its primary key. Each of these foreign keys is of the types represented by (c) in Figure 10.4, with the exception of the forwarded U-IPM-ID in the body part table, which is of type (a) in Figure 10.4.

"Retrieve the heading of all messages that have the string X within their subjects," becomes an SQL query of the form:

```
Select message
From message-links
Where
(message-subject LIKE X) and
(message-U-IPM-ID = message-links-U-IPM-ID) and
(message-links-relation-type = "crossreferences")
```

This example shows only a selection on the subject field, but extended selections can be achieved by boolean combinations of fields and/or subqueries inside the main query. The *subject* field is one of the fixed attributes of the heading parts of the message table, while *message* in the select line is a column name in the message-links table.

Of course there may be other tables involved as well, for example, a user names table. For the scheme to work, it is assumed that there is a software translator to convert the user query into SQL format, as well as a transparent way of dividing up incoming X.400 messages into their tables, and conversely, building X.400 messages from messages created by local users. This example merely serves to demonstrate that it is possible (though perhaps not practical) to convert X.400 messages into another specification for the purpose of applying an existing retrieval language.

Conference records and bibliographic citations can avoid the recursive requirements in the X.400 mail specification because the records involved are inherently shared. Any cross reference information can be supplied innately as a part of the conference record structure. It does not have to be recovered as an independent entity, but only as a record in the same file, or a file in the same directory. Only two or three table types need commonly be used to store conferences in a relational structure.

The first would store the fixed-header information and foreign keys. These keys would point to a second table with many rows, one for each header field with repeating groups. The first table could contain the body of comment text as one of its fields. The structure of the body, however, is different enough to warrant its own table. This would facilitate support for nontext body types. Of course, as with the X.400 relational mapping above, other tables are required for the system to work in a real application. All manner of information regarding authors, security, cross references to mail, comments in other conferences, supplemental (DBMS based) data, and so on, could be connected to the header table, and possibly the body table, via foreign key links.

■ 10.4 AUTOMATED USER INTERFACES

This aspect of software customization has the least to do with the internal workings of the conferencing, E-mail, or information retrieval package, and relies the most on the product's inherent interface flexibility. The other component involved in the automation of user interfaces is the terminal software used at the remote end of the connection. Most terminal emulation programs contain script languages. Using these languages, programs can submit commands to the host system while receiving output and storing it on the user's behalf.

If a company standardizes on one or a few such terminal programs, the MIS department can produce one or more customized scripts permitting the user to manipulate conferences while off-line, disconnected from the host system. On their local systems alone, users may read new messages and reply to them. When they have completed their work, the terminal program can call the host, properly enter the users' contributions, collect new material, and then disconnect. Figure 10.6 illustrates a simple module that permits a user to interact with a remote system, and yet automatically respond to certain host conditions.

```
# Start of Script Demonstrating interactive loop
# Variable initialization
    cr = chr(13) : lf = chr(10)
    blank_line = cr + lf + cr + lf
    control_state = 0

# Terminal initialization
terminal "DEC"
CURSOR = "_"

# Script procedures

PROC P1
  IF control_state = 0 THEN control_state = 1
    ELSE
      REPLY "next" : control_state = 0
ENDPROC

PROC P2
. . . Procedure definition (not shown)

ENDPROC

PROC P3
. . . Procedure definition (not shown)

ENDPROC

PROC inside_loop
while online
    z = inkey
    watch 1 tick for
        blank_line + "Do What?" : PERFORM P1
        "string-a" : PERFORM P2
```

```
            "string-b" : PERFORM P3
            key 27    : END
      endwatch
      if z then reply chr(z);
wend
   ENDPROC


# Window initialization
WINDOW #1, AT 1,61, SIZE 1,17
TITLE #1 "Script Active"
PRINT #1, "  ESC=Kill" ;


PERFORM inside_loop


END
```

Figure 10.6 This short script, written in Crosstalk Mark 4 CASL control language, is an interactive loop that responds automatically to certain prompts from the host system. The loop defined in the procedure "inside_loop" allows users to interact with the host system as they normally would. At the same time, the loop watches for the occurrence of various strings (only the first of which is shown in detail), and performs various procedures as these are received. For example, if a blank line followed by the prompt "Do What?" is encountered, procedure P1 is performed. This procedure checks a variable *control_state*. If its value is 0, then the prompt was received upon entering a conference, and its value is set to 1. The next time this prompt is seen, it will be at the end of activities in a given conference. In this case, the value of the *control_state* variable will be 1. If this is the case, the script issues the command "next" to the host (perhaps taking the user to a next conference on a list) and resets the variable to 0, and so on. Before executing the "inside_loop" procedure, the script creates a small window in the upper right hand corner of the user's screen. This reminds the user that a script is active and posts the message: "ESC = KILL" in the window. Pressing the ESCAPE key (ASCII character 27) will end the procedure. This is not a robust script by any means. The "watch" mechanism is good for checking on *expected* responses from the host. Another CASL verb, "TRAP", can be used to perform error handling for unexpected events in conjunction with the built-in functions "error," "errclass," and "errno."

System interfaces for conferencing, electronic mail, and information retrieval may also be automated and customized in this manner. Such tailoring saves money if there is a telephone charge associated with the connection because the user is connected to the host for a minimal time. In addition, the remote interface can be tailored to a greater extent than the host system because the local terminal software can add features and perform functions that may not be available in the host package.

The combination of such terminal software and host facilities is a loosely coupled system. The two are coupled because the terminal script communicates with the host software, as compared to a user communicating with the host. This communication may be far more terse and efficient than any that can be achieved when users interact directly with the host system. It may also be performed in the local system's background, leaving the user free to perform other tasks while communications with the host are under way. The coupling is loose because the connection is intermittent. The terminal software can reflect the host *to* the user without being connected to the host at all times.

Input and output customization is normally reflected in formatting menus, commands, and output that give the user the most comfortable working relationship with the system. Factors that enter into this comfort level include the user's experience, the particular domain or domains to which the system is being applied, and the volume of activity managed from day to day. Although more experienced participants will opt for command interfaces because they are faster and usually more powerful, inexperienced or moderately experienced users will often elect to use menus.

Even when menu interfaces are not available, the majority of repetitive activities performed by most users can be accomplished with as few as six easy-to-learn commands. This is because communications software, whether conferencing or electronic mail, is designed to facilitate the most commonly repeated tasks. For example, CoSy, as implemented in Byte's BIX, will permit a user to jump from one joined conference to another and read all unread material by entering nothing but a succession of carriage returns at each system prompt.

Desirable output formats are as much a matter of taste as experience. These are often less configurable than are the commands and prompts used to recover results. In designing loosely coupled software, the goal is to minimize the information transmitted from the host. The local coupled software does not require host-based menus, and it can recompute output information locally, saving both time and money.

For example, for each response received from the host, a user may wish to see the response number, the response's position in the text stream (for example, response 25 of 30), the number of lines in the response, and the title of the topic to which this response is posted. If the host software can be so configured, this information need be transmitted only *once* for each topic. For example, host might be configured to supply the following information as each new topic is encountered:

Topic number
Title
Total responses in topic

Given this information and the number of each new response (responses not seen by this user) as it is displayed, the script can compute the information desired by the user as a header line on each separate response. This could include the number of lines or characters in a response, counted either as the information is received, or when the response is displayed.

10.4.1 Formatting Facilities in Picospan

Picospan is probably the most versatile software on the market when it comes to this kind of customization. As discussed in Chapter 6, an organizer may customize a conference's output in a variety of ways. Alternatively, each user may elect to override the customization set up by the organizer and establish his or her own output format. Picospan supports the following output variables for each item and response of a given conference:

```
%a  Response author
%h  Item header
%i  Item number
%l  Response author's login ID
%L  Defines the line output for lines containing a string found
    in searches.
%n  Number of responses in the item
%N  Prepends line numbers to each line of the response.
%r  Response number of current response
%s  Number of lines in this response
%k  Number of characters in kilobytes in this response
%q  Number of characters in this response
%K  Number of characters in kilobytes in this ITEM
%Q  Number of characters in this ITEM
%u  Response author's UID (the numeric ID assigned by the
    system)
%d  date format 1, e.g. Mon. Feb. 23, 1990 (13:45)
%t  date format 2, e.g. Mon. Feb. 23 13:45:20 1990
    (elements of date/time displays can be controlled individu-
    ally as well)
```

To format Picospan's display at the start of each item in the manner described above, the conference control file (or the user's control file) need only contain the following line:

```
"isep '%i\n %h\n %n\n'"
```

"Isep" is the control flag that governs what happens between each new item. Similarly, "rsep" governs the format of each individual response; "nsep" is for special controls between the item header and the first response; "zsep" handles what happens after the last response in the item; and "fsep" controls the output format for lines found in string searches. The '\n' is a UNIX convention for displaying a "new line," putting a carriage-return/line-feed at the end of each field.

Not only can Picospan format output in this way, but it also employs conditional controls. For example, the line

%(b new items %y !%(b no new items %(r new responses %r !%(r no
new responses\n

will display the number of new ITEMS in a conference *and* the number of new
responses (total) in the conference only if there are new items or new responses. If not,
the strings "no new items" and/or "no new responses" will appear instead. Altogether,
there are 16-item level conditional controls, 14 conference-level conditionals, and
19 conference-level format variables similar to the item/response variables detailed
above. These may be used at any point in the chain of events, from entering a new
conference to seeing its items and responses (or summaries of them), through leaving
the conference. Conditionals can be combined in simple Boolean expressions. For
example, "%(X ¦ Z string" will print the string if an item is either retired *or* frozen,
while "%(I&D %h" will print an item's header if it is a new item (to this user) *and*
it was entered in a specified date range. All of Picospan's command prompts can be
changed as well.

10.4.2 Value Added Input Features of Customized Terminal Programs

The local node's terminal programs can create input formats otherwise unavailable on
the host. For example, a host program may be purchased for features relating to various
advanced uses, though it is difficult for beginners to use. It may not, for example,
support a menu mode, or it may require that intermittent users remember too many
commands for effective use. Rather than sacrificing such a package for a simpler one
that may not satisfy other requirements, the purchasing company may provide its users
with the needed beginners features through a microcomputer interface script. This
may include a menu interface, special help screens, and even connections to multiple
communications environments. For example, suppose a corporation maintained an in-
house conferencing system, MCI mail accounts for international correspondence, and
a separate system supporting Electronic Document Interchange (EDI) with its vendors.
All of these separate systems could be operated through a single, consistent interface,
written in a terminal control script language.

Strictly speaking, it is not necessary to fine-tune the commands and output formats
of a given communications product in order to build a custom interface. The terminal
control program can communicate with any interface, including a pure menu system.
One of the goals of producing loosely coupled software, however, is to minimize
the information exchanged between the terminal program and the host. Because it is
possible to customize the user interface at the local level, it is desirable to generate a
host interface that is as terse as possible.

Early but powerful systems like EIES used cryptic command structures in the
interest of minimizing commands exchanged over low speed dial-up connections. In
exchange, EIES provided internal script languages and macro facilities permitting
users to execute complex commands built up from many simple instructions with a
single command word. Now the microcomputer and the script languages available with
many terminal emulation packages allow the local system to become the intelligent
center of communications operations.

10.4.3 Semicoupled Systems

Semicoupling is an approach to host-microcomputer relations that does not involve any interaction with the host interface. Mark Graham of Pandora Systems in San Francisco has pioneered this approach using the Usenet RFC1036 message structure standard. Basically, the host becomes a special file server. The host maintains a file for each user that consists of new material from conferences translated to RFC1036 format. Each file is customized, containing only material from conferences and topics of interest to each individual user. When the microcomputer logs in to the host, the customized file is automatically downloaded.

Once on the local storage device, the file could be interpreted by any number of software interfaces. Because the message format would be standardized to RFC1036 specifications, third parties could produce a variety of "conference readers." The messages themselves could be grouped and threaded together in many ways at the discretion of each individual user. For example, topics might be ordered and grouped according to the user's interests. There is no need to follow the conference/topic-number organization as it appears on the host. Having read through the messages, users can respond to conversations at their leisure. User responses are gathered into a file on the user's local system, and then uploaded to the host which would reverse-translate the file into the host format and add the texts to its conference base.

The beauty of this scheme, from the user's viewpoint, is that no special terminal emulation software is required. The link between microcomputer and host can be made by any software. Secondly, individuals are not locked into a single, local, conference reader, because the standardized message format will enable many parties to provide alternatives. Because many vendors are already supporting, or planning to support the RFC1036 specification, the only technical barrier to widespread availability of this system is the demand that developers add facilities to produce the user session files, and automate their transfer to user machines.

▪ 10.5 STRUCTURAL ENHANCEMENTS FOR SPECIALIZED FUNCTIONS

As discussed in the preceding paragraphs, there are a number of enhancements to group communications systems that do not require customization of the host software code. It may turn out, however, that customizing the overall communications environment may not be practical. For example, the organization running the conference system may not have the power to standardize on one, or a few, terminal emulation packages that have the needed script language facilities. Other kinds of enhancements may not be amenable to handling through interface modifications and coupled software. Examples include such things as the following:

1. Adding forms processing services.
2. Electronic Document Exchange (EDI) features.
3. Author verification or other security facilities.
4. Implementing joint document editing features.

5. Incorporating store-and-forward enhancements in synchronous conference services.

6. Adding support for binary attachments, and soon.

7. Enhanced directory services.

8. Adding flexibility to output formats like record summarization, menus, and so on.

All but the last of the above list require extensions and/or modifications to data structures, the software that manipulates those structures, and the basic I/O facilities. What must be modified, and how it must be modified, depends on the existing structures, software, and facilities, the needed changes, and the overall goals governing the software extension. If the software is portable among different environments, and one of the goals is to maintain this portability, then design of the new extensions must bear this in mind. If, by contrast, maintaining portability is not a prerequisite, then the design team is free to take advantage of the target hardware or operating system in formulating its plans.

■ 10.6 CUSTOMIZATION OF THE SYSTEM'S INTERFACE

Changes or enhancements to user interface features, like eight in the preceding list, do not usually require modifications to data structures. One knows that the data required is: (a) available, and (b) accessible through existing retrieval functions of the software. A good general principle to follow is to pass a minimum of information through the fewest possible levels of the software's module hierarchy. This usually means adding new facilities as close to the display and user input function(s) as possible.

For example, a *browse* function permits users to view the first N lines of each item or comment entry, where N is a number of lines specified by the user. A more sophisticated utility might also permit recovering the item text for all items, all new items, and all items containing a certain string in their title or text, without reading the comments on the item. Confer, Participate, and EIES support all these features. Most others support only the first set if anything. Adding these features requires no changes in the software file structures, but would require additions to that part of the code that (a) validates commands from users—the browse command will have to be added to its set—and (b) controls the reading of items and comments from the text base.

If the text itself is stored as lines (see the following text for a further discussion of storage architectures), then the file management code can know when it has read the needed number of lines. It may still need to read through the rest in order to find the next record, however. In a case where texts are stored as a single, possibly long, field of a multifield structure, line numbers will have to be determined when the display module (or something below it) inserts delimiters in appropriate locations. It may seem efficient to put counters in low level modules and pass the counts upward, but this also requires that the low level routine be aware of the need to maintain and pass a count, adding more than a minimal amount of complexity to the software.

It may turn out, however, that the display routine, of itself, does not have the power to stop the process feeding it text for a single record. Nor may it have the power to suppress display of whatever it receives. In this case, some module below the display process must have the power to end the text stream fed to the display (that is, if it gets to the end of a comment sequence). The required line count must now pass downward from the user input area. A counter must be maintained (even when not needed) at the lower level, and the appropriate text passed upwards. Note that if text is stored as an undelimited stream of some maximum (but large) length, this low level routine must also perform the formatting computations (though not the actual insert of delimiters, and so on) of the display routine. Besides complicating the logic of the lower process, we now require additional data, the display requirements, to be passed downwards.

The second part of the browse command is similar, but requires instead that the high level logic knows when it has gotten the desired text of the ITEM, and can discard the comments. Since the software itself has some way of distinguishing them, the user I/O routines probably contain code for displaying this information along with signals that govern *when* to display it. It is at this point, where the signals are set, that the additional token controlling the suppression of the comment display should be added. This data will have to be passed further along to the process that interprets these signals, so they in-turn will have to be aware of their meaning.

10.6.1 Error and Status Handling

Error handling is a broad, complicated area, that does not involve data structures per se. Error handling involves graceful software recoveries following a system problem. For example, a user command fails for an unexpected reason. The software must not only keep running, but users and system administrators must receive appropriate information, security must not be compromised, and so on. The Error-handling system should be able to inform the Status-reporting system with enough information to permit the latter to suggest, to the user, a temporary workaround. This level of service is as yet unknown in most software domains.

Status reporting involves informing users of any results of commands. This can refer to the normal process of reporting a user's progress through the system, for example, "No new items to read," or "you are not authorized to write in this conference." It also refers to the process of making system errors intelligible, so that the user can work around the problem if that is possible. "Bad index, DATES not supported in select criterion," gives the user a clue as to what went wrong and why. Ultimately, all error messages should be mapped to status reports with enough information so that the appropriate person (user, sysop, or someone else) can fix or work around the problem.

It is a complicated arena because the lowest levels of the system generate the most detailed error codes. These become masked by error handling routines at higher levels, but might contain just the information required to enhance the status reporting part of the system. In the example given above, the corrupt *date* index is detected at the lowest levels of the file system. The name of the bad index, or probably an encoded signal (flag, digit, and so on), and not just the fact that there is a bad index, must now be passed all the way up the module hierarchy to the level that maps error messages to status reports. Many modules can be affected by enhancements to the error and status-reporting parts of an application's code. Modifying error and status reporting capabilities can be a daunting task. This is most likely why these capabilities are uncommunicative in most software, communications systems being no exception.

■ 10.7 MODIFICATIONS REQUIRING FILE SYSTEM ENHANCEMENTS

All of the other modification types require an understanding of, and modification to, the structure of the conference records. This may include adding new record (and possibly file) types or possibly new fields to existing records.

10.7.1 Logical Strategies

There are two general record handling strategies used in group communications systems (not to be confused with the file strategies discussed in Chapter 7 and following). One stores records sequentially as lines in a file, and delimits logical records and fields by special characters or character sequences. If the operating system permits sufficiently long file lines, then it is possible to form separate fields from a single line or incorporate an entire record in it. A minimal length for storing a reasonably rich header with some room to spare is usually 256 bytes. It also means that text bodies will likely span multiple lines. MVS permits single disk records of up to a single track, about 44KB in length. It is often easier to distinguish each field from the next with the same delimiter used for the physical records comprising the item/comment body. The separate fields (not including the body) may then be distinguished by their order in the record, or by a special leading/ending character sequence, or both (as in Picospan).

The other strategy is to interpret records as collections of virtual fields that may or may not be mapped one-for-one as physical file records. Such fields may be interpreted by position, length, pointers, or special sequences of characters associated with the physical data before the operating system gains control of them. This association is performed by the communications software, a file manager, or a DBMS engine. A single field might be many thousands of characters long, and map to many disk records.

The primary delimiting mechanism is usually a length pointer that permits the file handling software to reconstruct the virtual record from the physical one. This is especially true of the body of the text. Conversely, many fields, some thousands of characters long, may map to a single disk record and be delimited only by position and length. Such characteristics will be either buried in the record structures of the software, or abstracted from it by a third party file manager. Modifying the latter system requires a licensed copy of the library or management engine development package, as well as the communication software's source code.

Some file handlers permit the existence of one or more fields of essentially infinite length. Such systems prepend a length signal to the beginning of such fields that permits the file handling mechanism to identify the field's end point. One unusual operating system, PICK, permits single field lengths of up to 64KB, provided no single record (the total length of all its fields) exceeds this value. In PICK, all fields may be of variable length subject only to the total 64KB limitation. They are delimited by special character sequences, not by length. This makes it difficult to store binary information (like NAPLPS codes) without special handling, but it is a very efficient way to manage disk space for pure text records.

Systems that use the logical record approach often have more restrictive field length limitations. For example, a comment can contain no more than 4K characters. Most systems of this type store the text portion of their records as a single field of the item or comment header record. Often, the text body of a record is stored as a ribbon of text, that is, without line delimiters. On input, delimiters entered by the remote system are stripped off. On output, this structure facilitates the process of displaying the line in different formats. For example, the remote system may request a display width of 48 or 132 characters instead of the usual 80. It may employ a special terminal or communications convention that requires an unusual delimiter for its own display or file system.

One of the ways that output format capabilities are supported is to use this format free body structure, and implement sophisticated formatters in the output process of the user interface, for example, the *browse* function described in the preceding text. Delimiters can be stored with their lines in this format, but it makes no sense to do so, even when maximum field lengths are very generous. The biggest advantage to this approach is the ability to retrieve records randomly in conjunction with an offset file.

In reading records new to a given user, Picospan must read sequentially through the comment stream until it reaches a comment number one higher than the user's read-through marker. Given a command like "read last 10," the system takes the total number of comments (which it stores in the item header information) and subtracts 10 from that number. It arrives at a comment number that it finds either by forward or backward processing over the comment file. If records are stored as text ribbons with length offsets, a file containing record numbers and their offsets can be used to jump directly to a desired record in the main file. Suppose, for example, that the offset file contains two fields in each of its records, a record number (4 bytes), and the offset value for the start of that record (8 bytes). If a user's last-read marker contains the value "100," the retrieval software has only to jump 1204 bytes down in the offset file to find the offset for record 101 in the main text file.

The value of random retrieval is obvious here, as much sequential processing is avoided in the most common retrieval tasks. Coupled with the addition of index support on some other fields of the item or comment header (for example, the date of entry, author name/ID, subject, and so on) the performance of many retrieval tasks can be further accelerated. The system could be sure to select subsets of qualifying records based on date and other criterion (if they exist) using the indexes, and perform the final string search (if any) as a sequential pass through the subset's body fields.

Other systems allow, or even require a standard line terminator (usually a Carriage Return, possibly followed by a line feed), at least every 80 or 256 characters. This reflects either the use of underlying operating system for record handling, or the use of a file handler, or DBMS with restrictive field length limitations. These systems will truncate longer lines, and replace the delimiter on output by counting characters for nonstandard line widths.

Sometimes the text record contains a length counter for the record as a whole or the body portion. If for the record, the beginning of the text is identified with an offset byte signifying the length of the nonbody material, or a constant offset based on the field lengths of the nonvariable portion of the record. In MTS, the operating system itself supplies a line numbering system, and Confer uses ranges in these number values to offset different portions of the records. This allows any record in the system, down to the line, to be retrieved randomly. Adding line counters to other systems is rarely useful, so long as random retrieval, at least by record is supported.

10.7.2   Physical Strategies.

There are four fundamental file system architectures that can be superimposed on the strategies above.

1. Every item and each comment on it (or comments on comments) consists of a separate file.
2. Each ITEM and its comments is stored as a separate file, possibly in its own subdirectory.
3. An entire conference is stored in a single file.
4. The Conference housekeeping information, and the housekeeping information of its items and comments is stored in one file, while the body of text for those items or comments is stored in another. This may apply not only to an individual conference, but to the system as a whole.

10.7.2.1   Each Record a Separate File

The first strategy permits random retrieval of records even when the system stores information with operating system facilities that support only sequential access. DOS is a good example of such an operating system, but unfortunately, it becomes very inefficient when the number of files in a given subdirectory exceeds 255. If each ITEM along with its comments can be stored in a separate directory, processing efficiency dictates that items are limited to 256 comments. This may or may not be a problem depending on the structure of the conference model (comb, branching, linear), and the system usage pattern. The latter factor will depend on the service domains to which the software is applied, the number of users, and so on. UNIX permits some tuning of the directory system to provide reasonable performance even with thousands of files per subdirectory at the expense of disk space for directory information.

Random processing is achieved by splitting a record's header information from its body and storing the header data along with other record headers in a single file. A pointer in the header record allows the file software to recover the text body randomly from the directory. If every field in the header is indexed, then the header record can be eliminated because it can always be reconstructed from the index files. This structure is called an inverted list and works well if there are not too many separate fields in the header portion of the records. It will not work if the header contains a field (or fields) with repeating groups unless the each element within the field is broken out and indexed separately.

Adding fields to this type of header structure means modifying the file system in some way. The headers may be stored in a file managed by a DBMS or file manager above the level of the operating system, as in options (3) and (4) in the preceding list, or as a sequential list, as in (2). Special body types, for example, binary files, vote records, or other additions, can be handled conveniently provided their header records do not require special fields. Special codes containing the pointer to the body may be placed in the header field to signal the body type being referenced.

10.7.2.2   *Items and Comments Together in One File*

The second strategy is generally used in systems that process text records sequentially. There are two variations. In the Confer approach, the item header and its text are stored in their own file, and all associated comments are stored in another file. In Picospan, item and comments are associated in a single file. This results in a relatively simple file system that can be manipulated by the operating system alone.

Splitting the item and comments provides some flexibility in processing them separately; for example, this arrangement supports commands that recover new items without reading their comments. It also helps to distinguish field types in item records from field types in comment records by allowing, for example, binary attachments directly in the item record. The field can begin with a length specifier. If necessary, it can even be stored as delimited lines (for sequential processing), provided that the retrieving software knows where to strip the delimiters to reconstruct the original attachment.

If item headers and comments are associated in the same file, binary attachments would almost certainly be stored as separate files. There would be pointers in the item header, the comment records, or both, signifying the existence, name, and so on, of these attachments.

In both the Confer and the Picospan methods, if new fields or new record types are added to the system, sequential file processing entails a modification of the file handling portion of the communications software. This is because the software employs operating system level services to do the physical file handling. Adding a new field may require a change to the software's method of recognizing field boundaries. There is a problem, for example, if the record handlers expect the third delimited line to be the beginning of the text portion of a comment. Either the new field is placed inside the first two fields (with attendant consequences for the process that extracts those subfields), or a new line is added. In the latter case the record I/O mechanisms must write and count four lines to the beginning of the body. A new record type may entail changing the file-handling mechanism for reading and writing those records and some way for the software to recognize which method to employ in any given instance.

10.7.2.3   *The Conference as a File*

Conferencing software using a DBMS for file management may adopt the third approach: storing an entire conference in a single file. Most contemporary DBMS systems support logical file sizes in the gigabyte range and record numbers in the millions, at least. Storing conference items and any comments in one logical file facilitates many different ways of ordering record retrieval and many different ways of displaying records or portions of them. Of course, the DBMS engine may map the logical conference file to physical files in any number of ways. Random retrieval is always supported, but individual record lengths are generally limited. Usually, the limits are generous enough not to cause problems if at least one large and variable length field is permitted per record. If not, and if the DBMS transparently recovers files that contain the physical text of the conversation, the conference may *appear* as one logical file to the communications software. The DBMS maintains pointers to the files and uses the pointers to return them to the communications system. This approach can result in many thousands of *physical* files in a given directory. Designers must carefully consider potential performance problems.

Using an underlying DBMS or file manager adds an abstraction layer between the physical files and the communications software. It permits the creation of new structures (for example, for supporting vote or joint editing facilities) and does not interfere with the operation of the system's file handling logic. Interface logic needs to be developed or modified to communicate user I/O to and from these new structures, but the record retrieval and insert logic will not be affected. Other advantages of the approach include the following:

1. Direct recovery support—Transaction logs can be used to recover information lost (due to a crash) since the last backup or other problem.

2. Handling of storage I/O integrity and serialization of transactions—Updates to multiple tables will take place in an appropriate order and can be committed or aborted in a single operation.

This technique can be a problem if the facilities of the DBMS do not permit convenient access to repeating fields. For example, a field containing numbers that cross-reference other items or comments may have to be stored in a single DBMS field. Lack of support for repeating groups complicates the software logic used to recover these fields individually (perhaps for subsequent recovery of those records), because two processes must be employed, one to recover a field, and another to distinguish instances of repeating references within it. Without direct repeating field support, this approach either collapses into a form of file strategy (1), mentioned at the beginning of the section, above, or the repeating instances are broken out into a separate structure (see the following text).

There will also be storage inefficiencies if the single field must have a fixed length—how many cross references per record will the designer permit? PICK and PICK-like DBMS (for example, Revelation Technology's REVELATION AND AREV products) permit easy distinction between values of a naturally repeating group and do not use excess storage. Most DBMS systems based on the Relational Model will not permit such structures. The alternative is to divide the repeating group into separate logical tables that are nevertheless gathered transparently by the DBMS and handed to the communications software. Using a relational model permits flexibility in data access, though it invariably costs something in storage and performance for two reasons:

1. Foreign keys connecting the instances of repeating-value to their records must be stored.

2. An extra set of logical accesses is required when a record is recovered. The repeating-value table must be scanned to see if there are instances of cross reference information for this record. The repeating-value table itself may be stored as an inverted list for this purpose.

Repeating groups may be illegal in the Relational Model, but they are a natural way to express some information in the structure of a conference record. This is not to say that a Relational DBMS cannot encompass the data requirements of a good communications system. The DBMS itself should be able to *resolve* relations between different tables and make them transparent to the rest of the application.

Using a high-powered DBMS engine in an appropriate environment, can make a lot of sense, though it always results in some degree of performance degradation.

The practice of using this type of engine is not much employed with communications software, because developers cannot rely on their customer base to have a particular DBMS to support the application. Run-time versions of DBMS engines are available but may add substantially to the cost of the software. If these engines are not used, connections need to be written for a wide range of DBMS packages, which complicates the initial development task. A data manager or DBMS that supports repeating groups would simplify software development. The PICK operating system and Revelation for MS-DOS would make excellent file system managers for this purpose. However, developers can expect customers no more to have or purchase these environments than to have or purchase relational products.

10.7.2.4   File Division by Function

Systems employing a sophisticated third-party file management system often take the fourth approach. Participate is an example. This approach has most of the abstraction advantages of the third method, along with a balance between the number of logical files and their sizes. One loses some of the integrity features associated with DBMSs, and the communications software may have to do more work itself when requesting associated records from different logical files if the management system does not automatically relate them. This organization can suffer from the same potential problem with repeating values as does (3), though many file managers contain built-in support for repeating fields.

The advantage of the fourth approach is the ability to optimize both the physical file type and logical access techniques to the file type. Header record fields can be indexed to maximize performance in recovering them, and the text bodies can use a different random recovery support system like hashing. Decisions regarding the use of subdirectories will need to be made by designers when implementing data structures, but, in normal operations, subdirectory use will remain completely transparent to the application.

■ 10.8 EFFECT OF FILE STRATEGIES ON IMPLEMENTING DIRECTORY SERVICES

What follows is an example of the effect of the above logical and physical strategies on an enhancement task: providing support for enhanced directory services. Suppose our package supports user directories containing area-of-interest information and searchable by area of interest. It also provides lists of conferences that can be searched by subject or keyword. What we seek to add is the ability to retrieve lists of conference participants, along with information like the number of records they have entered, their last-read record, the date of their last visit in the conference, and so on. Finally, we want to cross-reference the two list types. That is, given a conference, we want to get user information for its participants, or given a user interest, find all conferences (and their users) related to it.

We associate (logically) the conference participation list either with the user information, or with the conference. If with the user information, we must have a repeating structure that points to each conference of which the user has been a participant. Each of these conference pointers will itself be composed of a repeating structure that must carry a number of fields, including the date of last visit, last-read marker, and so on. This data structure could be attached directly to the existing user-file structure or maintained in a separate file. The best way to do this depends on how the existing system maintains its user information. Picospan already does this implicitly by storing user data, and the conference participation data for that user, in each user's own subdirectory. This makes adding our extra fields (if any) an easy task, but the scattering of user files in many subdirectories makes assembling this information very expensive in CPU terms.

If the underlying file system is relational-like, then a hierarchy of files can be built from the basic user information by adding foreign keys to it. These keys would, in turn, point to tables holding the conference participation data. Note that information such as the number of entries a user has posted to a conference can be determined directly by scanning the conference record headers (or an index) for the user's name/ID in the author/ID field. An alternative, less time-consuming method is to keep counters for such things in the participation file.

If the conference user list is stored with the conference, we complicate the conference file structure. There must already be a logical file or files somewhere that store conference level information, for example, the keyword list. If this list is one file consisting of conference/keyword-list fields, it can be modified to hold, or relate directly to, participant information for each conference. If there is a separate file storing housekeeping information for each conference, then this file might be usable as a repository of participant information. Otherwise, the mechanism for handling conference housekeeping files must be present in the software, so we could add another such file to each conference with user information.

If we associate conference information with the user lists, we must change the software to recognize and interpret this new information. This may occur within the communications environment, that is, a new command, or be the product of some utility program executed seperately. If we associate participant information with the conference, we must be able to relate the two areas in response to a user request.

Processes searching through the conference key-word information must now be made to search the user data as well, and acquire user information based on the names recovered.

All of the approaches will necessitate the addition of logic to that part of the software that first recognizes user actions, such as joining a conference or reading and writing records. As users progress through conferences, the directory processes will have to use this information to update the user or conference directory information. These updates should occur only when users move from conference to conference, or the directory processes will consume a disproportionate amount of system time.

This means that the software must monitor user progress through a given conference. Virtually all systems do this, at least with respect to rewriting a last-read marker. If stored counters (for example, number of records written) are used to speed the process of directory operations, then appropriate devices will have to be added to the control loops that exist to follow a user through a conference. Whether or not this process is modified, the information must be passed to the directory update processes.

■ 10.9 TAKING ADVANTAGE OF SPECIALIZED DEVICES

This kind of customization applies mostly to low-level device access. Its ease or difficulty depends as much on the nature of the host environment as on the particulars of the application implementation. Examples of such enhancements include the following:

1. Adding drivers for access to specialized storage devices like CD-ROM, WORM, or other optical drives.
2. Supporting packet or HAM radio data transmission protocols and associated hardware.
3. Taking advantage of large memory spaces available to each individual user, or the system as a whole.
4. Supporting new developments in communications hardware such as buffered UARTs, "intelligent" serial devices, or communications between application code and internal X.25 packet assemblers/disassemblers.

These modifications may merely entail writing custom device drivers, or modifying existing ones. If the general environment supports such development (for example UNIX), then the process is relatively straightforward. Other such enhancements may require modification of application file handling routines, internal buffers, and communications I/O modules, as well as the addition of other ancillary support code.

All such modifications will be made for reasons of performance, extending system storage capacity, and other considerations that have little to do with the communications model or the user interface. There are many sources of information on writing device drivers. The practicality and difficulty of other modifications of this type depend on the way in which the application software communicates with the host operating system and hardware environment.

■ 10.10 DEVELOPING A SYSTEM FROM SCRATCH

There is a wide variety of group communications software on the market, a great deal of it including source-code at a price. Given all this, if a company still felt it must write its own CMC system, then all of the foregoing considerations about locating control logic and logical/physical data structures will still apply. Other higher-level decisions come first, however.

Computer mediated communications is first a set of structures that instantiate some model of inter-personal communications. Examples include mail, telephone calls, meetings, parties, and interactive games. Besides simulating these environments, the medium is yet another category in its own right. The first design principle in communications software for proprietary use is to consider strongly the requirements respecting these two aspects of the application class. The more expensive commercial systems invariably strive to expand upon the second aspect. However this approach may make the system more complex than required for use in a limited domain.

10.10.1 Characteristic Operations of Computer Mediated Communications Systems

Communications software is typically I/O intensive, and process light. It spends most of its time getting instructions, displaying results, and reading and writing text records in response to user input (see Figures 10.7 and 10.8). Attention to the user interface is therefore critically important. This in itself is a big job. Will the interface be menu-driven, or command-oriented, or both? Will it use graphics, or include them as an alternative only? Processing operations involve security features, output formatting, maintaining data for user directory and conference directory updates, and search-retrieval operations of many kinds. Constructing these processes can be a time-consuming job. Their difficulty, performance, or both, is strongly affected by the following:

1. The target operating environment—distributed or central.
2. The file/record structure recognized by the application.
3. The target operating system or systems.
4. The development language used.
5. The number of users, and data throughput required.

A computer-mediated communications system is, at its heart, a transaction center. User commands, in the form of strings or menu selections, are interpreted in the context of a user's activity. Their legitimacy in that context must be established, and security verifications must be made. Following that, a module, or set of modules, is activated that performs the requested operation. Possible operations include navigation to another part of the system, reads, writes, searches, setting filters and so on. Some display to the user is always required. These may be simple messages regarding the completion of a command, or a return of results. Results consist of user or text records (from the system's data stores) that are appropriately formatted

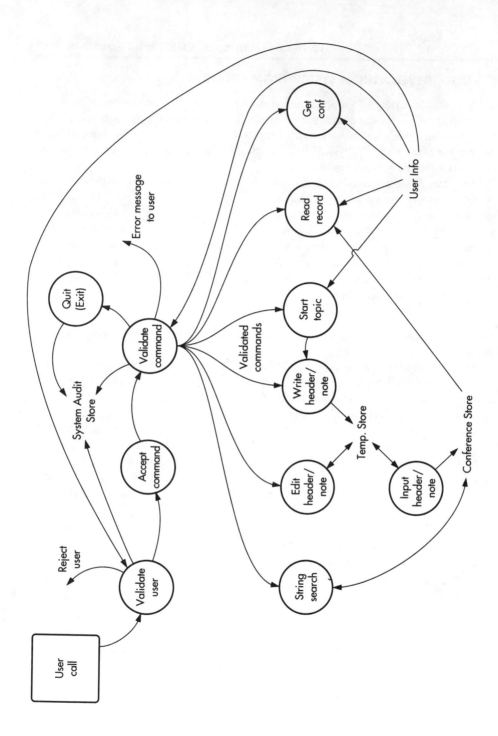

Figure 10.7 Data flow diagram for a portion of a CMC system. This figure illustrates a part of a CMC system data flow. Not shown are operations involving files, mail, or details within the operations of reading and writing notes, string searching services, and so on. When a user logs on to the system his/her ID and password is validated. The validation routine reads information from the user information store. If the user is validated, information like the login time, date, etc. is added to the system audit store, and the user is prompted for commands. Commands are also validated, and possibly added to the audit information. Once validated, commands activate one of many operations available to the user. What constitutes a valid command may (and probably will) change depending on what the user is doing at any given time, along with the users permissions, etc. (read from the user information store). After acting on each command, the user is returned to the accept command process for the next command. If the user exits the system, the logout time is recorded in the system audit store.

given the context and specifics of the user command. For example, a request to find a specific string in a conference may result in any of the following:

1. The display of the topic titles and numbers containing that string.
2. A display of the lines of comments and topic header texts containing that string.
3. A display of the body of the comments and/or header texts containing that string.
4. The production of a named set that becomes the user's context for his or her next command(s).
5. Any of the above filtered by some specific criterion, for example, "show only header texts for any topic whose header or comments contain the string."
6. A "string not found" message.

Possibly the operating environment for the software is already known. Even within the constraints of a given environment (if widely used) there are a wide range of design and implementation possibilities. If the application is distributed over multiple environments, features tend to be limited by what can conveniently be communicated between them. Distributed systems tend also to be limited to those structures that can be comfortably supported in all the target environments involved.

If the application domain is limited enough, then one might make do with a skeleton system, hastily assembled. Even here, volume considerations by users and data will always intrude to complicate the situation. With large numbers of users, performance and security considerations always arise. Filter mechanisms and conversation models adequate for a few dozen or a hundred users processing dozens or hundreds of messages a day may be utterly overwhelmed when the user base numbers in the thousands or higher. Large volume considerations always complicate software. Communications systems are no exception to the rule. Any of this is further complicated by a distributed environment.

Thus even a system intended for use in a very limited set of domains that are not themselves complex may yet become a very involved software development project.

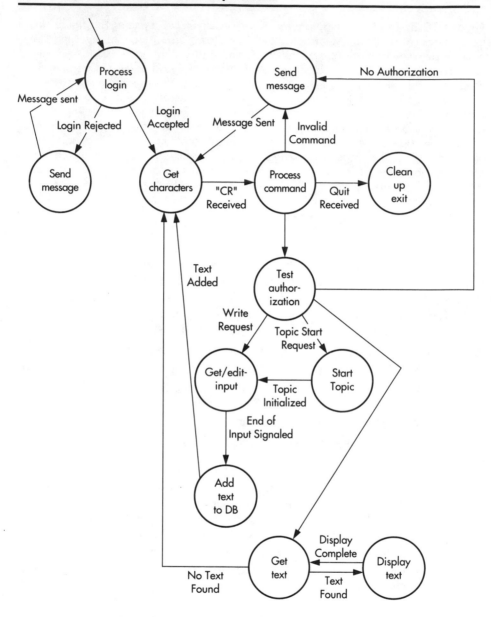

Not the least of a designers problems here is heightened user expectation regarding software interfaces, including the handling of error conditions. If users are to communicate with the system through terminals, then all the interface logic must be built into the host. Even a limited system will have to provide a clean, consistent, and adequately powerful user interface if it is going to be used at all. To support such development, there are screen handling management systems and function libraries. Even using these packages, system interface logic can comprise the largest single

Figure 10.8 State transition diagram of a CMC system. This figure illustrates some of the state transition possibilities for a portion of the system modeled in Figure 10.7. Its initial state is the login process, which is either accepted or rejected with a message passed to the user. Next the system presents a prompt and gets characters until a 'CR,' *carriage return*, is received. At this point, the system moves to processing the command received. If the command is invalid, a message is sent to the user. If the command is to *quit* or *exit*, the system terminates, the final state. Once a command has been validated, the user's authority to issue the command is tested (if necessary). If the user is not authorized to issue this command, a message is sent. Note that the validity of a command, as well as the user's authorization to issue it, will vary depending on what the user is doing. Only *read* and *write* text commands, along with topic initialization, are illustrated. If the command concerns a write, the system moves to getting user input. Once input is complete, the text is added to the system's data base. Note that the add may not be automatic as displayed here. Instead, the system may return to *get characters* and wait for the user to issue the add request, which is then processed. If the command is a request to start a topic, then the topic process is initialized, text is requested, and so on. If the command is a read request, the state changes to *getting text*. If there is no text, the system returns to *getting characters*. If there is text to display, the system cycles between *displaying text* and *getting text* until there is no more text to get. Note that *reading* here may apply to conference texts, mail, directory displays, and so on. There are, of course, many operational levels below that shown in this diagram. The bubble *Get Text* may be processing a conference string or directory search, a navigation command, or a comment read command.

segment of the application code, vying for this honor with the code's error/status mechanisms.

Just below the application domain and environment levels, other design considerations involve the general division of functions between interface, processing, and storage code. Where will different operations be controlled? If developers are to allow for alternative interfaces produced by users, administrators, or third parties, how will the software manage the association between a user and his or her chosen interface? What parts of the application kernel will have to be aware of the interface in use and its capabilities? Will the software have to recognize PDIs embedded in text records, and so on? Extended features are always purchased at the price of more logic or more complex data structures. Where will the communications hardware be managed? Will a device driver arrangement be used? If so do available drivers have the required functionality? For the most part, the answer to this last question will be yes. Alternatively, a daemon could field all data originating at or bound for a port. In the MS-DOS world, there are a number of Terminate-and-Stay-Resident (TSR) programs available to support communications hardware. What about security? At what level of service will modules require no authorization information from the modules above them?

10.10.2 Language Choices
What language will be used for application development? It may be that the needed functions can be added to an existing application environment. There exist any number of communications libraries designed to facilitate such development. Such libraries

exist for most C compilers, and some Pascal, Fourth, Modula2, Assembler, Cobol, and BASIC systems as well. Of the DBMS and DBMS-like systems, dBase, and some systems similar to it are supported by such libraries, and Revelation or PICK's application development languages are rich enough to support communications development.

Developers might want to consider a specialty language, one designed for communications and usually associated with some terminal emulation software. A number of commercial products, Digital Communication Associates' Chairman being the best known, have been developed using these products. At least two products, Crosstalk Communications' Crosstalk Mark 4 and Microcom's Relay Gold, are distributed with integrated multitasking capabilities where communications are concerned. Such languages can reduce the development time for a simple group or E-mail communications system from months or years to weeks. One problem with these languages is their lack of support for various PDI standards (this may change soon). They are also limited in the number of file structures and arrangements they will conveniently support. Indexing and other performance-enhancing file management strategies are not easily implemented. Few file management libraries or databases support connections to these languages.

More complex systems should have the benefit of a multitasking environment. The current state of the art in multitasking shells for MS-DOS–based systems will support a greater variety of capabilities in application software, but there is no adequate substitute for a real multitasking operating system. In the first environment, language choice will be constrained to products that have libraries supporting communications between the application code and shell product employed. At this time, these include a variety of the better known general purpose languages, so this may not prove too large a constraint.

■ **10.11 CONCLUSIONS**

All in all, it is probably not going to be worth the effort for a company to write its own system most of the time! At the very worst, something reasonably close to what it needs will be available in source-code form (at a price) and can be modified. This is true in environments from microcomputers to mainframes, though it is more true at the microcomputer level. The cost of mainframe software, by contrast, sometimes leaves room for specific site customizations as a part of the contract. Again, at the worst if the required modifications are at all extensive from the software engineering view-point, the vendor can probably do them less expensively than the buyer. For a large system, such special arrangements could well be less expensive than the source code alone.

11

TRENDS AND SOCIAL ISSUES

There are some identifiable forces shaping the use of computer mediated communications services in the private and public sectors. One is the continuing, rapid expansion in available communications bandwidth. Corporations routinely own or lease channels passing data at 1.44 Mbps. Some have dozens of them. Subsections of this bandwidth are available to smaller organizations that do not need entire T1 trunks. Single lines with capacities of 44 Mbps (T3 trunks) are already available. Possibly 10 or 20 years from now, if monomode optical fiber is available from customer premises through the local and long distance carriers to customer premises on the other end, bandwidths supporting from 100 to 500 Mbps will be common. Researchers have already demonstrated transmission in the gigabit per second range. Even faster technology is being developed.

■ 11.1 BANDWIDTH EXPANSION IN TELECOMMUNICATIONS

Sudden jumps in the effective bandwidth of the ordinary voice telephone network are dramatically affecting communications in educational, corporate and public communications sectors. The 1989 establishment of the V.32/V.42 CCITT standards for 9600 bps asynchronous transmission on voice grade lines, resulted in supportive products from most modem manufacturers by early 1990! The price of this technology has dropped from nearly $2000 per modem in 1986, to about $500 in 1990. The presence of a standard, a fourfold drop in price, and a fourfold increase in speed over now common 2400 bps modems has dramatically expanded the small business and public use of the new technology. Dial-up modems operating at 19,200 bps are even now becoming available.

271

In the corporate sector, these asynchronous speeds demand more of high capacity trunk lines, and so are helping to push corporations into acquisition of still more capacity. A T1 line can support the activities of almost six hundred 2400 bps modems, but only one hundred fifty 9600 bps devices. The research networks serving educational institutions are being pushed even faster than corporations, because they cannot control the increase in high-speed devices demanding connections to the nets.

11.1.1 Implications of Short-Term Bandwidth Expansion

As bandwidth grows, previously impractical applications become cost-effective. Information retrieval and remote computing applications will quickly benefit from such growth. High-capacity trunks coupled with 9600 bps service at a user site can facilitate remote login on distant network nodes. For example, users may attach themselves to database repositories thousands of miles distant. The user's commands and the results returned by the server may pass through several machines at such speeds that the user will notice only a small delay. Virtual, and not physical, circuits will enhance the efficiency with which the whole transaction takes place. Even so, some connection must be constantly at the service of the user.

Alternatively, internodal connections can be established only long enough to pass a user request from one machine to another. Similar connections are made as data makes a return trip through the network. This technique has been used since near the inception of long distance networks. In 1975, however, requests were passed from one machine to another at intervals throughout the day. Round trip delays of up to several days were not uncommon, and responses within hours were very good. By the late 1980s, a lucky few experienced reply delays of minutes because high-volume nodes would make connections immediately as new data arrived. With a digital network in place nationwide, such connections can be made and broken in seconds. Return responses in minutes should be the rule throughout the network.

If the bandwidth grows large and inexpensive enough, even this ad hoc network traffic could further be curtailed with database distribution. The primary barrier to distribution, besides the speed of transfer of commands and results, is the quantity of traffic generated by intermediate results and the coordination among systems necessary to achieve them. From the user's viewpoint, distribution permits support of a variety of database interface tools. Users can choose those they prefer and avoid dealing with the syntax of different servers. If the database in question is updated on a periodic and not too frequent basis (say hourly, daily, or weekly), the bandwidth available (particularly in corporate networks) may make large-scale database distribution economically feasible.

Bibliographic and Management Information databases are likely first candidates. It takes only 100 seconds to transmit a 1 gigabyte file update at 100 Mbps. Most applications could tolerate this update delay, even on an hourly basis if necessary. Fully distributed databases will always be limited to corporate, government, or educational entities that control the overall network and the distributed data. In a widely accessible worldwide network, some databases will always be remote relative to some users.

In the public arena, the advent of inexpensive 9600 bps services means that users can exchange files of up to four times their previous sizes at a constant cost, or at four times lower cost for constant file sizes. It also permits hosts to establish networks over greater distances with other hosts. The public telephone system can support more and larger ad hoc networks. A nightly 500 KB conference relay from New York to London is four times less expensive at 9600 bps than at 2400 bps. Both kinds of growth are occurring, along with increases in data volumes on existing dial-up networks. In general, the short term effect of the 9600 bps V.32 standard has been an expansion in point-to-point long-distance services. Point-to-point connections are easier to establish than multinode network data transfers. Higher-speed dial-up modems make a larger number of them cost-effective.

■ 11.2 INCREASING DESK-TOP COMPUTING POWER

Along with the acceleration in available bandwidth, there has been an increase in the power of desktop computers. One effect of this has been the spread of graphics capabilities. The average desktop user has a built-in means of displaying graphics if his or her communications software will interpret one or more of the competing graphics transmission protocols. Graphics have an impact on the way users interact with their computers, and therefore have an impact on the way users interact with each other.

11.2.1 Modern Hardware/Software Compression Technology

For transparent, or at least acceptable operation, contemporary hardware and software compression technologies assume growing CPU speed. File compression before transmission is well known in the public BBS community. Higher CPU speeds merely serve to make this a little more convenient. There are, however, applications that perform constant compression/decompression in the background between a local computer's disk drives and memory. There are hardware devices that perform the same job. Both effectively increase the capacity of storage devices at relatively low cost.

Efficient compression is another feature of modern modems. V.42bis and MNP compression schemes are implemented in the modem hardware, and dedicate a CPU to the task. These achieve the same overall compression ratios as the best software-based compression systems. Interestingly, transmitting a software-compressed file through one of these modems will not achieve more throughput than sending the uncompressed file. There is only so much compression to be achieved—until CPUs become still more powerful.

11.2.2 Graphics and the Rise of Coupled Software

Modem-based compression systems bring a dramatic improvement in the responsiveness of text interfaces such as menus. At 2400 bps with MNP level 5 compression, a full screen menu will paint itself on a local screen in about one second. Compression also permits more efficient use of graphics technologies. Hosts can pass more instructions and/or graphics data to remote systems in an acceptable time. Locally stored data (screen formats, menus, background images) can be updated more quickly and more frequently.

Using the processing power of the caller's CPU in this way means coupling the software operating at both ends of a connection. The trend towards the use of strong coupling between caller and host is unmistakable. In theory, this permits the host/caller combination to provide a greater variety of flexible communications structures and tailorability features. To date, however, experiments and commercial ventures with such systems have focused exclusively on the potentials of the graphical interface. The interface has a dramatic effect on the versatility and power of a communications system. Because it is the place where the user meets the system, and through it other users, the interface is the final expression of features available to the user.

A hypertext organization of conversation streams, executable programs, and other binary files can be achieved, to a degree, without graphics. A graphical interface, however, permits facilities to be greatly expanded internally. Hosts, though, must first support such organizations beneath the interface. A few systems, like the Coconet, are moving in this direction. Yet it remains true that, with few exceptions, the most flexible communications structures, selection, filtering, and tailorability controls are still to be found in software developed from the mid 1970s through the early 1980s.

▪ 11.3 RECENT GROWTH IN THE POPULARITY OF ELECTRONIC MAIL

In the corporate sector, the use of conferencing software to tie groups of people together is hardly evident at the opening of the 1990s. Electronic mail usage, however, is growing rapidly. It is text-based, and both conversational- and document-oriented. Most of the major electronic mail products support binary and/or textual file attachments, and grouplike conversations can take place through the management of mailing lists. A growing number of local E-mail products can now be interconnected

Table 11.1 Impact of various CMC technologies

	Technology				
Effects	**V-mail**	**E-mail**	**FAX**	**EDI**	**Text conf.**
Conversational	yes	yes	no	no	yes
Document	no	yes	yes	yes	yes
Effect on corporate communication channels	low	low–medium	none	none	medium–high
Training required	low	medium	low	low–medium	medium–high
Special equipment for each user	no[a]	yes[b]	no	yes[c]	yes[b]

[a] Usually, some special corporate or area-wide PBX may be required, or such services may be provided by the local Bell Operating Company. Either way, users require only their phones
[b] Access point, either terminal, or microcomputer/workstation is required on each user's desk.
[c] Special hardware and/or software is required, but the number of direct users may be very low.

with each other and with international E-mail systems. Voice mail, a conversational medium, and Fax, a document-oriented medium, are both gaining ground even more rapidly than E-mail. All three are telecommunications technologies that address a part of the market for which computer conferencing was developed.

11.3.1 A Place for Electronic Mail

These technologies are not always better than conferencing as they are now applied. Conversely, there are many applications for which they are well adapted. Significantly, they impose less pressure for changes to established corporate communication channels (see Table 11.1). Phone mail requires no special equipment in the immediate user's hands. Most people can learn to use it in a few minutes. It adds the element of asynchronicity to ordinarily synchronous phone conversations and the ability to broadcast messages to a group—one-to-many communication.

Voice mail, in effect, extends the power of the telephone in time. A call can now be more consistently effective at a time after it was made. Modern voice mail and voice conferencing systems are very flexible. Synchronous conversations among any number of people can be conveniently established at any time. By adding store-and-forward capabilities, along with message broadcast features to one-to-one telephone conversations, this technology is addressing a significant number of communications needs in the corporate arena. Coupled with Fax, which adds value to documents by minimizing the time it takes to move them from one place to another, communications based primarily on voice become still more efficient. Fax, in addition, supports the transmission of pictures, provided one is not too demanding about resolution. Add E-mail to this mix, to handle much of the need for store-and-forward text, file exchange, and so on, and there are not too many applications remaining that truly require the facilities of a group-oriented text communication system.

■ 11.4 NICHES FOR GROUP-ORIENTED COMMUNICATIONS

There are, of course, applications that are particularly suited to the group support features of text-based conferencing systems, but they are small in number, considering the effort that must be made to user such products effectively. The need for group-oriented supporting features rises in proportion to the number of people collaborating in some effort that benefits from general knowledge about the effort as a whole. Some characteristic features of these applications include the following:

1. There is a wide geographic distribution among participants, a very large number of participants, or both. The wider the geographic dispersion of the group, the more inconvenient is group coordination by E-mail. The most advanced group coordination features of modern E-mail software are usually limited to a work group sharing the same, usually local, network.

2. The group involved and the data being exchanged benefit from its general dispersion (subject to security or other administrative requirements) among the group.

3. The data is subject to a wide range of interpretation, with important insights often emerging from peripherally related domains. Without group-oriented communications products, such demands often result in an unusually high number of face-to-face meetings.

4. The application benefits from a user's ability to search records of previous conversations and meetings for material relevant to a current discussion.

5. There is a need to supply all or most participants with data from external sources: databases, news feeds, and so on.

6. The group benefits from the recording of synchronous communications (real-time, text-oriented meetings) for later review and comment. The need for and advantages of real-time group support are particularly evident in crisis management situations.

7. The application *demands* a circumvention of normally hierarchical communications channels. Disaster mitigation is the domain that typically manifests this requirement.

8. A part of the requirements for a particular application is the ability to know what each participant has accomplished or been apprised of during the course of the project.

9. The products of the project involved require the coordinated efforts and approval of many individuals. Such products may be specific deliverables such as reports, programs, or product specifications. They may also include products without specific "completion dates," such as daily reports, analysis, or coordination of some on-going effort.

Note that many of these requirements are to be found, to some degree, in a wide variety of communications tasks. What is at issue is not that group-supporting text communications are helpful in many domains, but that their particular advantages are absolutely required, and worth their cost. As it turns out, while there are many applications in which such features are "nice to haves," there are relatively few in which they are "must-haves."

11.4.1   Social/Political Implications of Group Communications in the Corporate Sector

These costs reflect much more than the hardware and software alone. Extensive E-mail or voice mail systems each cost as much as a group communications product. Employing group-oriented communications technology for any application requires a substantial commitment to training, ongoing support in social and technical contexts, and, so on. It also entails some risk that traditional corporate communications channels will be circumvented at inappropriate times, though this is avoidable given proper, attentive administration of the system.

All organizations develop an internal politics, because employees, although pursuing their jobs, are also seeking to further their own self-interests (careers, personal interests, and so on). There are not enough resources or time to satisfy everyone's self-interests to their fullest extent, and politics is the institutional mechanism that emerges to mediate the resulting conflicts. Conference systems have been seen as a threat to various self-interests, especially those of higher management. The existence of an audit trail for every decision, suggestion, and policy established by corporate management can be very threatening. The immediate availability of such records is a potential political problem and may be the primary reason for the resistance to this form of communications.

■ 11.5 BANDWIDTH PLUS CPU POWER: THE DEMISE OF TEXT-BASED CONFERENCING?

Vast bandwidth increases and expanded CPU power promise to remove most of the technical disadvantages mentioned in the preceding paragraphs. For example, video teleconferencing can acquire asynchronicity through the use of fast optical storage and high-bandwidth connections between conference sites. Combined with even-current voice-to-text and text-to-voice conversion technology, this could allow users to have asynchronous face-to-face meetings.

Synchronous video conferences could be stored and later rewound and replayed by any subsequent participant anywhere in the world. Text transcripts could be generated as desired. The comments of this participant (text, voice, video, or any combination) could then be transmitted to all sites participating in the conference. The participant would appear, to still later viewers, to be stepping in and joining the conference. Each participant would see a video image of any persons actually in the conference with him or her at that time. Users could conveniently switch between the synchronous meeting (if any) and material previously recorded for review or reference. Synchronous meetings and asynchronous reviews could be easily displayed in separate windows of each participant's view screen. If a pair of display goggles were substituted for the view screen, the meeting could appear to be virtually anywhere. There is no reason why the participants must be displayed in the settings in which the recording takes place. One user might choose to see the others sitting in a well-appointed corporate boardroom, another might choose to see them sitting in a circle on a beach in Fiji.

If the technology were extended just a little farther, it should not even be necessary to transmit real pictures of anybody. The machines could generate appropriate images from instructions stored locally or transmitted in real time. Simultaneously, an executive could appear in three-piece suit to his peers in New York and in casual clothes to participants in Los Angeles. Working out some of the other potentials arising from this level of technology is left as an exercise for the reader.

The "at the desk top" advantage of current text-based communications systems could accrue to wider forms of teleconferencing if equipment becomes available at a reasonable cost and intracorporate communications channels have enough capacity. Where information is best exchanged as text, this can be accomplished through the same audio/video distribution channels. The result is that the benefits of asynchronous text-based group communication can be extended to other technologies. These technologies can augment corporate communications potentials without requiring all users to adopt the same input and output devices and formats, or even compose text. As vendors follow standards developed for high-bandwidth multimedia communications, many of which have not yet been proposed, inter-corporate, international communications may also be aided through these combined communications technologies.

■ **11.6   TRENDS IN PUBLIC SECTOR GROUP COMMUNICATIONS**

In the public sector there is already adequate bandwidth for current use of available text- and graphics-based communications services. There is already far more going on in the wider electronic meeting place than any person can reasonably assimilate. Only a small part of the problem lies with the existing technology. Most group communication *services* now available to many people *lack* the more sophisticated navigation, filtering, and selection *tools* needed to use high volume systems effectively.

Most of the vendors argue, however, that the majority of their users would never bother to learn to use such facilities anyway, and that their mere presence will scare some people away. This latter argument is ineffective, given the organization potential in on-line documentation. The vendors, for their part, think users want more intuitive interfaces and graphics, and are not so concerned with better search facilities or finer control over navigation through conversations. They have, therefore, focused their efforts on the interface, and left experienced users to flounder with weak support for advanced communication structures and control facilities.

Undoubtedly, there is some truth to vendors' claims regarding menu interfaces and graphics. Most users are unaware of what more advanced search features, for example, could do for them. It is also true that most users would not bother to learn them. Much of the cash flow generated by the largest vendors is not from asynchronous communications activity anyway. Regional systems often try to focus their efforts on interpersonal communications. Frequently they have better software than the largest public vendors, but they still lack many important control features built into the earliest group communications products. Ironically, in the absence of a widespread interconnection between regional systems, it is the largest services that have the most potential for serious international conference activity. They could garner some of this market if they improved their software, and, in CompuServe's case, reduced its scroll rate. It may be, however, that this market is not very big after all.

In 1990, some estimates put the number of bulletin board systems operating in the United States at 14,000! The majority of these support only one phone line. At the same time, the number of small (2 to 8 lines) and medium (8 to 50 lines) multiline systems accessible to the public is now in the hundreds. Only five years ago, there were but a few dozen. Almost all of these systems provide one or more communication functions. This usually includes electronic mail and at least minimal conferencing support. Many of the medium-sized systems provide gateways to the Usenet, which facilitates the transfer of ideas between public and education sectors. The largest systems have not grown so much in numbers, but their user populations continue to expand. All of this suggests an emerging public awareness of the value of on-line communications.

Colleges and universities are exposing more and more people to group communication technology. Between 1985 and 1990, there has been a significant expansion in the number of Usenet news groups in fields not directly related to computer science. Most of these are in natural, social, political, and psychological sciences. The arts, particularly music and literature, are represented, as are sports and other recreational activities. Outside the educational arena, there appears to be growing awareness of existing services.

11.6.1 Legal and Ethical Issues

The growth in public use of BBSs has spawned its share of criminal activity and put some new twists on privacy and civil rights issues. In 1985 the FBI impounded backup tapes produced by the Source as evidence in an investigation of drug trafficking between Florida and California. Two paying subscribers of the Source were using its electronic mail services to set up drug transfers. The Source, claiming that its private mail system should be given the same protection as mail carried by the U.S. Postal Service, went to court to block the seizure of the tapes. The courts disagreed.

More recently, several Federal justice agencies were involved in the outright seizure of BBS hardware and software from operators who were not accused or even suspected of any crime. Subscribers used their systems to pass stolen credit card information, credit authorization information, passwords, and proprietary corporate data. The implications of these actions on the part of government agencies are serious because BBS operators cannot possibly monitor all correspondence passing through their systems. If they tried, the nominal privacy of electronic mail transactions would be compromised, and they would quickly lose the trust of their subscribers, honest and otherwise.

Most BBS operators conduct a careful, daily examination of new files placed on their systems. Files containing material of questionable legality are deleted immediately. Most of the time such files consist of copyrighted software. Sometimes, when the content of these files is more sensitive and potentially dangerous, these operators inform local, state, or federal authorities of their existence. The reaction of law enforcement agencies is to take hardware and software that is necessary to keep the system functioning. Most sysops maintain excellent backup copies of data on their system disks as a precaution against system failure. Such backup disks or tapes would serve perfectly well as evidence in the event some crime, or conspiracy to commit crime, was really taking place through these systems.

Unfortunately, there are a few small BBSs that are established for the purpose of fostering criminal activity of one kind or another. Federal agencies charged with policing such crimes have shown themselves both unable and unwilling to make distinctions in these matters. Many legitimate BBSs represent substantial investments on the part of their operators. Yet sysops attempting to recover their seized equipment have met with judicial resistance at every level. In many cases, the systems are held for as long as six months or a year, effectively putting these operators out of business.

Aside from the problems associated with criminal activity on BBSs, the medium has opened other ethical issues. Who owns the text placed in an open forum on a BBS or publicly accessible computer conferencing system? What rights do the system owner/operators have with respect to editing or deleting offensive material posted by a paying subscriber? In dealing with such questions, operators have adopted policies ranging from absolute noninterference to censoring any material deemed inappropriate by the system operators. In most cases, nominal ownership and copyright of text records is explicitly awarded to their authors. CompuServe, for example, claims a "compilation copyright," a right to the combination of texts and files present on line, but gives individual authors copyright over their own entries. The Well has explicitly declared authors the "owners of their own words." There has been no end of debate on that system respecting the limits, rights, and responsibilities implied by that declaration.

On the University of Michigan's Confer system there was a long debate over the propriety of archiving conference records for historical purposes. Some students felt that such archives might be used against them, for example, dashing political aspirations with revelations of attitudes recorded 20 or 30 years earlier. Such issues and questions highlight the social and community nature of many public conference arenas. Like issues and controversies arising in real, physical communities, these questions have no easy answers. Questions and problems are resolved, if any resolution is possible, on a case-by-case basis.

■ 11.7 MASS MARKETS FOR GROUP TELECOMMUNICATIONS

Although the number of people using on-line utility services (for communications and other reasons) is undoubtedly growing, that growth may not be as fast as some estimates suggest. A casual survey reveals that people who use the services very frequently have accounts on two or more systems. The growth of the public access on-line industry is therefore, disproportionately supported by a relatively small number of people.

There has never been any evidence of a mass market for group, text-based, asynchronous communication per se. The availability of high-speed modems has not caused a large increase in the number of people using modems for conference activities but has rather translated into higher levels of activity for those already participating. Existing services do not sufficiently motivate the mass market to participate. Larger communications channels expand receive-only services (for example, television) whose content is also dominated by the mass market. This process is self-feeding. The more there is to watch, the more it will take to motivate people to do more than watch. This trend is divisive in a social sense, because the growing availability of passive communications services is channeled into narrower special interests.

11.7.1 The Demand for Personal Commitment

Computer conferencing has the potential to counter this trend in two ways. First it provides new channels for competing interests to communicate directly and efficiently. Of course, these interests can as easily remain isolated even when using this technology. Secondly, it can provide new outlets for those who wish to do more than receive information. Use of these services depends on how much people want to act, and on how easy or inexpensive it is for them to do so. Vendors have focused almost exclusively on making the task easier, but even they presuppose that users have some basic working knowledge of a terminal or microcomputer. Vendors can put effort into making their products more powerful, but they cannot motivate users. Only the issues, and/or other services provided can do that.

The cost of using an on-line system for any reason is three-fold. First there are direct financial costs (the telephone, vendor subscription, packet carriers, and so on). Second there is the time and energy cost of learning to use both the services and the connection equipment. Third, there is the ongoing time required to use the system and gain value from it. If a user is completely new to computer or terminal equipment, this becomes a multilevel learning experience requiring some hours of practice, no matter how "easy" it is to use the related hardware and software. If a user is already familiar with computers, the task is that much easier, amounting to learning another application or two. Once the user is on-line, the particular system or systems in use may require him or her to practice to develop and keep skills sufficient for typical use. If transaction volumes grow, or are already large, beginner-level skills will not prove adequate.

Where group communications products are employed, decisions are often reached faster and implementation activities coordinated more effectively. This has been true in both the public and private sectors. It remains true, however, that participation in these undertakings requires some effort on the part of the individual. In the public arena, the number of individuals willing to make the effort depends on a number of factors including the cost and convenience of participation, the appeal of the interests being discussed, and the eventual influence of the communications process on a technical, social, political, or economic arena. In any event, the number of people involved will be a relatively small proportion of the population.

Communication software designers took motivation for granted. They assumed that where text-based communications produced noticeable productivity gains, or resulted in better decisions in less time, or required less energy to coordinate the parties involved, that people would voluntarily accept responsibility to learn to use the software effectively. Very much has been published on the importance of on-line help facilities. These facilities come in the form of software self-help systems, and users appointed to the role of helper. Even so, some effort on the part of the users was presupposed. Technical people, typically MIS or DP persons, engineers, and so on, adapt to it readily. Among business units, employees perceive it as just another tool to learn and one that is at best only tangentially related to their jobs.

Research with corporate users suggests that when a system is seeded with interesting discussions, these discussions stimulate people's interest in using a communications system and motivate them to practice to become efficient users. These discussions should be of interest to a variety of employees, even if they have little to do with work. Office politics is another good motivator, especially because the forum itself provides a mechanism for addressing political issues. Yet management has been the biggest stumbling block to leveraging the potential gains of computer conferences.

The technology simply cannot achieve its potential in the day-to-day business activity of any corporation until every employee involved in strategic corporate operations, from the president down to order entry clerks, has access to the available forums. At the very least, all employees encompassed by a particular project or work group must be able to use the system. No matter what this domain, there is management involvement. Managers must take the system seriously if it is going to work to everyone's advantage. Managers, however, have achieved their stations largely on the basis of verbal skills. Altering the basic communications landscape to make writing skills paramount has dramatic political overtones. In the end, this very fact may prevent text conferencing from ever achieving a significant impact on American corporate communications.

■ 11.8 MASS MARKET MOTIVATORS

In contrast to factors slowing growth in group communications activity, the promise of vast jumps in publicly accessible telephone channel capacity cries out for applications. Some variations on popular synchronous communications services may supply some mass market momentum. Synchronous "chatting" with others for the fun of it has become an entertaining activity and occupies hundreds of people for hours on CIS, GEnie, and P-Link.

11.8.1 Synchronous Conversations Without a Keyboard

Suppose that you did not have to type at all, but actually sat, talking to others, at least their computer generated personas, and listened to them talk with you. Your setting could be anywhere in the world. It could vary by user, or all could agree to share a background environment. This experience is virtual reality, what some have called cyberspace. If the real world is not a stage, the virtual one most certainly is. Participants are all actors and spectators at the same time. If contemporary experience with synchronous facilities is any guide, the personas (not to mention the physical images) we project to others sharing the virtual world will be less inhibited than our personalities in the real world.

The success of current endeavors in this area is utterly dependent on the number of people involved, the more the better. The attractiveness of synchronous communication for entertainment alone depends very much on a variety of new people with whom to talk. CompuServe, GEnie, P-Link, and Delphi all provide for synchronous chats among any number of people. All four systems use the mechanism to host interactive talks by celebrities, captains of industry, political figures, and so on. As pure entertainment, however, these facilities are used by people, calling themselves some very strange names, to babble in a friendly fashion with other people about anything that comes to mind. These parties come together spontaneously, just because the facility is there.

It is quite probable that the technologies required for the logical fulfillment of this possibility will remain beyond the public reach for a while longer. The potentials, however, are enormous, because other services could then be marketed and used by many different participants. Electronic shopping is a good example. People could stroll together through electronic malls, seeing the same merchandise and discussing it in real time no matter where they really live. Reunions of all kinds could be conducted electronically. Even virtual foreign travel could be experienced by groups of people and this could include travel in time as well as space. Classes could be conducted in all manner of surroundings, including virtual laboratory, or simulated historical settings. Binocular displays have been demonstrated and will soon appear in small game units.

11.8.2 High-Technology Games

Quite possibly, however, much of the momentum supporting mass market use of on-line systems will not come from interpersonal communications, or shopping, or news services of various kinds, but through the availability of exotic on-line games. While unwilling to report exact figures, CompuServe has said that some of its games are among its most heavily used services. People have purportedly spent as much as $600 a month playing Megawars on CIS. Given a continued acceleration in CPU power, the emergence of a widely accepted graphics standard, and as much expansion in accessible telephone bandwidth as seems likely in the next ten years, there will be games that the most fanatical Megawars player now only dreams about. The technology is already available. It must only become inexpensive enough to be worth its entertainment value.

Along with the expansion of group games will come the need for various levels of organization and communication *about* the games. Local, regional, national, and international tournaments may be held. Players will have ratings. There will be classes (informal and formal), ad hoc conclaves of players, and discussions of all kinds. All of this activity can be conducted on-line from anywhere in the world. Group communications will support the ancillary activities spun off from widespread public gaming. As more and more people become used to the medium in this way, they may begin to turn to it for other information and social communication needs.

If the games are to be truly internationalized, then some reliable network must exist and operate beneath the user's view of the system. The rise of such networks is also predicated on the promises inherent in expanded, inexpensive, bandwidth. It is possible that networks of regional, or small-sized systems will supersede centrally organized, very large, systems. Another, perhaps more likely, possibility is that the large systems will become nodes on networks populated with systems of all sizes. Many of these systems might specialize in the dissemination of particular types of data or in the presence of special communications activities. Either way, group communication activities will be pulled along by the growth of the primary mass market service.

11.8.3 A New Political Arena

Politics, and political organization may further enhance the use and awareness of group communications services. Most people will continue to give financial support to the politics of their choice. The organization of fundraising efforts, issue debates, and platform establishment can be dramatically broadened in scope if the organization's administrators and other active participants coordinate their efforts with group communication tools worldwide.

Political organization is even more dependent on the widespread network interconnections than is the entertainment domain. Games, after all, are artificial constructs. If a pool of game players is restricted to the population of a regional system, they can still improve their skills against one another. Games between regional populations can be prearranged, special connections established, and so on. In the political arena, local issues often benefit from exposure to persons at higher levels of the political organization. Similarly, actions of higher bodies can, and often do, have a great deal of influence on the options available to more local interests.

It is impossible to predict when events with import across organization levels will occur in most real life situations, including politics. For this reason, widespread connectivity is more important in real world applications than it is in games. Local and regional systems can support regional political activity, but even here it is likely that a number of hosts and networks may be involved. Although interconnectivity is required, there is no strong pressure for real-time links. Gaming situations change by the second. Update frequencies ranging from a few minutes to an hour will usually be adequate in the political arena.

■ 11.9 THE GROWTH OF AD HOC NETWORKS AND DISTRIBUTED CONFERENCES

Interconnected communications systems are appearing in greater numbers, thanks to the plummeting price of 9600 bps modems. These networks often rely on common use of a particular application package. This approach is somewhat restrictive but insures the maximum amount of trans-system compatibility for the minimum amount of implementation effort. One or more times per day, these systems poll one another to exchange E-mail and conference data. Each maintains a full record of each conference.

As with other replicated, distributed systems, these systems will receive responses that are somewhat out of phase with one another. This is because original notes and their responses will be differentially delayed both to and from remote hosts. Record numbers on comments will not match across systems because of local activity combined with transnetwork periodic updates. Local interfaces, however, are always able to display activity in date and time sequence. If the update process preserves the original, local date and time stamps conversational threads can be reconstructed in their proper sequence. This continuity is sufficient, eventually, to reconstruct the entire sense of a distributed conversation.

The FIDO network is probably the best known of these ad hoc networks. The FIDO network originated in the days when 1200 bps was a heady dial-up speed, but the advent of 9600 bps service has accelerated its expansion. The Interlink network is a loose federation of IBM-type microcomputers running PCBoard software. It is hierarchically organized, like the FIDO net, but more formally so in the sense that all communication, whether private mail or echoed conferences, passes through hierarchical channels. Whereas the FIDO net is mostly composed of single user nodes, the-

Interlink machines are all multiuser hosts. The existence of the network, its ability to carry its traffic economically, depends on the availability of 9600 bps dial-up service. Other such networks include Canada Remote Systems, The RelayNet (with over 600 hosts), and the SmartNet. These last three are composed of machines running a variety of BBS software packages and sharing a common message exchange format. Each host translates echoed messages into its own local form.

■ **11.10   THE ELECTRONIC TOWER OF BABEL**

There is a growing number of group communication products available and no standards for communications structures, data structures, or navigation and selection. Standards for group communications are in the early development stages. The NISO and ISO have both made recommendations regarding filtering and display standards for information retrieval. If their developers incorporate them into the search facilities of their software, these standards could help users of communications systems. Many of the navigation text manipulation requirements of conferencing software, however, are only distantly related to search operations. Neither the ISO or the NISO have addressed these requirements specifically.

In 1992, both the ISO and CCITT will issue joint recommendations on a standard for intersystem or internetwork group communications. Like the X.400 personal messaging standard, the group standard will probably cover the behaviors expected of modules communicating between systems and the data structures being communicated. It will also include some recommendations respecting the basic text manipulation and navigation facilities available to individual users. Prior experience suggests that complex software standards will not be commonly supported for three to seven years after their appearance. CCITT/ISO standards for electronic mail have been around since 1984 but are just now being supported by commercial products. Few if any of these are BBS or group-oriented communications systems. All of this suggests that a global conference network, supporting local applications from many vendors and accessible to the public, will not be possible before the late 1990s. At least this will be true if the resulting internetwork is based on a CCITT/ISO standard suite.

Until that time, there continues to be a need for some communications between dissimilar systems and networks. Following existing standards for electronic mail exchange is proving difficult enough. Larger vendors of E-mail products and services have made an effort to produce compliant applications. The smaller developers of microcomputer-based conference and BBS software have not had the resources to make their mail features operate in an X.400 environment.

11.10.1   Intersystem Exchange Standards
Even the smaller vendors have recognized a need for a mutually agreed upon structure through which to translate the conference streams of disparate systems. In the Internet collection of research, government, and educational networks, such a standard, RFC1036, was formulated in late 1987. Provided vendors were willing to support it

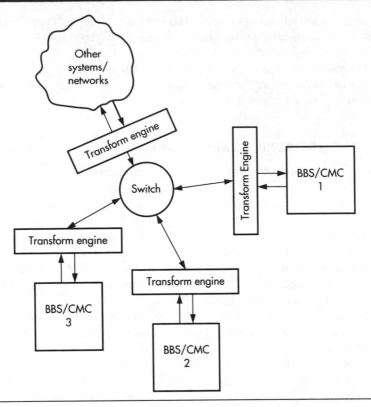

Figure 11.1 An intersystem transform engine. One proposal for a transform engine would require each CMC system participating in conference exchange to transform its outgoing messages into the standard format. These would then be sent to a switching node that would distribute the texts to other participating hosts and/or network. Incoming messages would be converted from the standard form to the proprietary format of its own CMC database. Another possibility is to locate the transform engines at the switch node, but this would require different agreements between the participating systems. In this case, the individual CMC systems would not have to be aware of the standard format, but they would have to agree to permit the administrators of the switching center to transform data into their possibly proprietary formats. The individual systems might also lose some control over the division of material into conferences, topics, notes, and so on.

with conversion routines, the RFC1036 standard could support the information needed to map complying records back and forth between most existing communications data structures.

There are any number of problems standing in the way of widespread implementation of such translators. Technically, the conference models of the Internet are one- or two-dimensional, either linear, or comb-structured like Usenet. Two-dimensional records can always be mapped to three-dimensional structures, but this is not always true the other way around. A branching system like that of CoSy, Magpie, and Compu-

Serve can be mapped two-dimensionally because its separate threads are derived from a relatively nearby record that starts a given conversation.

In a system like Participate, however, it is impossible to assimilate a collection of branches into a two-dimensional structure, because in a two-dimensional system each branch has the same status as a conference. The structure of Parti, and systems in the Com family, deliberately blur the distinction between a conversation and the context in which it takes place. This makes it impossible to tell if a branch is a response to a specific preceding record or a general topic divergence. The only mapping choice one can make is to turn each branch into a separate conference with a linear format.

Such technical problems can be resolved only if all or most product developers participate in a standards effort, and only if their participation is active and long-term. In fact, this is being done using the RFC1036 format. Some vendors that already support the standard include the developers of Caucus, AKCS, FIDO, and of course, the entire Usenet. Others are considering conversion engines that will translate their data structures to and from the RFC1036 format. Figure 11.1 illustrates where such conversions might take place. The process will take time. Most developers are focusing their energies on the further extension and internal flexibility of their own products.

Other problems are political and economic. Vendors still hope to replace other products in the market. This gives them little incentive to support features that permit communications with users of competing products. Third parties cannot develop the necessary translation tools because some nuances of a vendor's file design are often proprietary. The most intransigent vendors are those that maintain the largest systems. Smaller vendors are beginning to recognize the inherent value of supporting interconnections between systems, even those running different software. By the mid-1990s we can expect that many of these products will support RFC1036, which is rapidly becoming the de facto standard for intersystem exchange.

11.10.2   MetaSystems: Systems Connecting Systems

Some interconnection of E-mail networks is taking place. CompuServe has forged a connection with British Telecom's MCI, and MCI with Sprint's Telemail. Each of these, and AT&T, are busy forging X.400 connections between themselves. CompuServe subscribers can exchange mail with any MCI, Telemail, or EasyLink subscriber or communicate with any telex machine in the world. There is also a CIS gateway to the Internet mail service. Users may communicate with people on any Internet node. CompuServe does not, however, serve as a forwarding point for messages passing through it. Internet messages must either start or end on CIS.

The DASnet is another third-party product created to ease the automatic exchange of mail between disparate systems. Operated by DA Systems Inc. of Campbell, CA, DASnet allows subscribers to specify an existing account on a commercial system (for example, CompuServe, Delphi, The Well) as their home mailbox. Each subscriber pays a monthly connection fee and a per message fee. DASnet polls commercial and noncommercial hosts and networks for messages addressed to users on other hosts linked via DASnet. DA Systems downloads messages from one host, and uploads them to others. It avoids any translation requirement by behaving, essentially, as a user of each system, recovering or sending text messages.

11.10.3 Gateway Services

Gateway services represent another attempt to interconnect different systems. Their purpose, however, is not to achieve cross system conferencing or personal message exchange but rather to make real-time connections between a user and one of many remote hosts. DASnet and intersystem message connections permit users to reach others who do not have accounts on their host systems. Gateways, by contrast, provide remote login services to distant hosts from a single point. They permit users to reach many hosts without having separate accounts. In some cases, the user is not put in direct communication with a host. The gateway server may act for the user, making the connection with a remote system and soliciting data in response to queries. This is how Telebase Systems (IQuest on CompuServe), enables users to submit the same search on multiple information retrieval systems.

At the time of this writing, gateway services are in a state of flux. Most experiments of this kind are being conducted by the regional Bell Operating Companies (BOCs). (See Figure 11.2.) These organizations are in the best position to supply such services because they already own the required switching technology. US West, in Omaha, Nebraska, and NYNEX are the only two experiments still going on, Bell South having dropped its test project, and Pacific Telephone deciding to cancel before it even began.

Local telephone companies have a strong interest in these services because they generate more phone usage. Users make a local call to the gateway service, that presents them with a menu of participating services. Some of these may be local BBS/conferencing systems, Information Providers, or news, game, and shopping services. Others may not be local at all, but participating users are connected to any of them for the same local phone call. Although the phone call is local, however, charges for use of the external services range from nothing at all to several dollars a minute. Payments are collected by the gateway provider, and surcharges are passed along to the individual participating service providers.

11.10.3.1 Economics of Gateways

The economics of these ventures is somewhat confused. Should information providers expand their market reach by buying connections to gateway servers, or in order to generate more traffic through the gateway should gateway businesses pay information providers to connect to them? Much of this depends on the size and existing market reach of the information provider. Much also depends on the overall attractiveness and market reach of the gateway. Most gateways ask users to subscribe to them. In addition to levying applicable surcharges for connection to other systems, they may impose a flat monthly fee, a per minute charge, or both. Others attract users by waiving per minute charges or any subscription fee and by obtaining some percentage of remote system surcharges instead. Most try to collect fees both ways in addition to imposing a high cost barrier to providers who would otherwise sign on.

To date, the gateway experiments have not been terribly successful. Part of the problem is the need to motivate large numbers of people to use the services when they require information, want to make a purchase, want to play a game, and so on. From the individual's viewpoint, success at this endeavor still entails a substantial amount of learning. Success also depends on enough information, socialization, and enter-

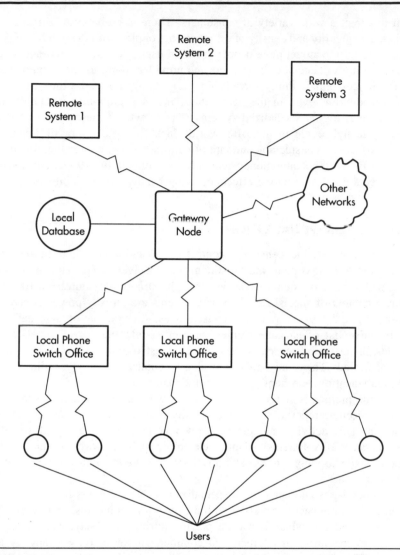

Figure 11.2 Gateway architecture. This figure illustrates one possible gateway architecture, much like the experiments being run by some of the Regional Bell Operating Companies (RBOCs). Users are connected to the gateway service through their local telephone company switching offices. From there, they are connected to remote systems that may or may not reside in the RBOC area. These connections most often take the form of remote logins, though batch connections are also possible. An example of the latter is the Telebase gateway (IQuest) available through CompuServe. The gateway node typically has a local database that contains descriptions and other information (surcharges, for example) about the remote services to which it is connected.

tainment to attract a wide variety of consumers. There is probably a critical mass, a point where the quantity and density of information, coupled with the number of people involved will begin to attract more people in and of itself. To date this has not occured. Observers cite high financial cost, to users and providers both, as the primary reason.

So far, services remain thinly spread. Yet the gateways portend a time when rising telephone bandwidth, even in the near future, meets a growing number of small- to medium-sized, highly specialized systems. The growth of these systems has been observed by many people in the BBS world. Jack Rickard, editor of *Boardwatch* magazine, has used a considerable amount of editorial space, contending that it is the only way for BBSs to become money generating ventures in the 1990s. His assertions are predicated a great deal on the effects of rising bandwidth availability.

■ 11.11 SYSTEM SPECIALIZATION

If it becomes relatively inexpensive to contact any machine anywhere in the country (or world) at 9600 bps, systems must distinguish themselves by specialization. Almost everyone will be able to mount lots of files, though extraordinary numbers, 100,000+, will remain an area of specialization. Small systems are already powerful enough to mount some large databases, or small, unusual ones. An example of "unusual" would be the definitive list of pancake recipes, or a cross-reference of all hotels and the kind of telephone wall connectors they use in guest rooms. Many systems are far more sophisticated. There are BBSs dedicated to botany, zoology, satellite tracking, bacterial classification, job hunting, and many, many more.

Also in the picture is the U.S. government, with BBS systems specializing in earthquake epicenter reports, solar flare activity, manned space launches, shipping manifests and port activity, and others (Appendix D contains a list of some government operated BBS systems). Games, electronic mail gateways, weather and tide information, and shopping, dating, and travel services are examples of other potential specialization areas.

Regional density is another kind of specialization. New Yorkers traveling to Houston might want to connect themselves with a Houston regional system to make travel arrangements, find out what shows are playing during their stay, and so on. Systems may also specialize in interpersonal communications activity. Many try to attract groups of people with related interests. Examples include a writers' BBS, a lawyers' BBS, and political interest BBSs. A horticultural BBS could support extensive databases of information on seed and growing techniques, climatological forecasts, subterranean water supplies, and disease prevention. At the same time, there might be a wide variety of discussions occurring about growing conditions locally and worldwide, economics of the industry, and grower/seller/buyer relations. Trades and purchases might be arranged, equipment and supplies sold, and so on. There will always be room for a number of technical systems, such as those specializing in particular hardware, software, or communications data and discussions.

The success of specialty systems depends on the availability of inexpensive, high-speed connections between the subscriber and the host. It also depends on it being reasonably easy for users to find all these systems. Some users will regularly use only one or a few services. Others will regularly use many. Eventually, there will be enough information in widely scattered places to support commercialization of search, retrieval, and reporting skills in this environment. Success in this context refers to the market as it exists today and may exist in the near future, without the benefit of present telephone channel capacity increasing by one or two orders of magnitude.

11.11.1 Gateways as Portals to Specialized Systems

The most consistent way to put all these services together is through a locally available gateway, whose native services include, at least, a good directory facility to help users find systems specializing in what they require at the time. The gateway server adds value to the data and services of the participating specialized systems. For hosts, it coordinates the links between the gateway user and the service, and it can select the best of possibly several connection options at a given time. Economies of scale may enable a provider to take advantage of connection options that might otherwise be unavailable. Gateway providers also audit the connections between themselves and the remote providers. This in theory, simplifies the provider's billing chores. For the user, the gateway provides a convenient home base from which to connect to a world of information, discussion, and entertainment. Multiple vendor bills are condensed in one, we hope, well-documented statement.

The gateway soaks up available telephone bandwidth by connecting users, in real time, to the services they choose. The gateway itself may require some special software such as a coupled system to handle its graphics displays and other special features. By using these same protocols, each of the services connected to the gateway must be able to deliver information to the gateway service, or the gateway must appropriately transform the data for presentation to the user. If the gateway is a coupled system, then connections to services of various kinds, for example, real-time remote login, and batch, can be made completely transparent to the user.

When enough gateways exist, and their user populations become large enough, gateway vendors themselves may begin providing services like intergateway electronic mail, and user directories. In total, the electronic world accessible through any gateway should be larger than even the largest centralized on-line system, though these too might be available through the gates. Most providers should be available from most gateways, and there is no reason why gateways cannot service competing providers.

The merging of information retrieval and communications technologies is evident in the association of these systems on gateway projects. Information retrieval has diversified enormously during the 1980s and will continue to do so. Many systems serve very specialized needs. Systems containing information on the census, the climate, government contracts, the yellow and white pages, specialized news, and industrial equipment and supplies for specific industries are examples. They are used, primarily, by people whose business requires such information, but there are others who would like to have access to such things occasionally. Many of the government-sponsored systems are free but hard to find. Most of the commercial services are expensive. Their availability through a gateway would make them more accessible and permit users to pay on an as-used basis and only to buy the more expensive offerings as a last resort.

▪ 11.12 SMALL SYSTEMS AS DATABASE SERVERS

Increased CPU and disk capacity has made it practical to mount medium-sized databases (up to a few million records) on desk-top machines. Only a limited number of simultaneous connections need to be maintained. Information retrieval systems must provide fast response. To do this with a small system means limiting the number of users on-line at one time. Specialized information repositories would not expect to see the demand for access or time on-line that is experienced by more general providers. Twelve or sixteen lines is enough to service a dozen or more gateway connections and satisfy demand for years.

The same CPU/storage capacity growth means that communication application vendors could begin to place more emphasis on integrating databases with conversational software *and* on improving the search/retrieval, navigation, and filtering features of their systems. To date, this has not taken place because operators have used greater CPU power and speed to support more lines rather than more facilities. In the public sector, especially where file exchange is the principle reason for using BBS systems, this makes economic sense. More lines translates, potentially, into more users per minute or hour, and therefore, a higher income. The same economies are true for corporate systems where a relatively small investment in hardware can be used to mount a BBS supporting dozens, and even hundreds of users.

Unfortunately the corporate environment is also the one place where more money could provide more facilities and fewer lines per CPU. In a LAN-based system like PCBoard, for example, one very powerful CPU could be dedicated to search tasks, and less expensive workstations could support conversational activities. Developers have been slow to incorporate such features into their products, because users, particularly corporate users, have not shown enough interest in the technology as a whole. Only dedicated third-party service providers, like Notepad International, have been able to incorporate more advanced search techniques into versions of their software that are customized for particular applications.

▪ 11.13 THE PROMISE OF A BROADBAND INTEGRATED SERVICES DIGITAL NETWORK

The eventual emergence of A Broadband Integrated Services Digital Network (B-ISDN) will rewrite all the rules and economies of communications. Distinctions between carriers and users will blur because "user equipment" will be as much a part of the network as the telephone office hub. No single connection between two endpoints need ever be established independently of the data being transferred, a true "connectionless service". It will become difficult to differentiate information providers from carriers. Providers will become information pools, repositories holding networkwide data for a longer or shorter period and releasing it to the network on demand.

The difference between private and public carriers and networks will be similarly obscure. The network will resemble a web rather than current trunk-and-branch topologies. The concept of a "network backbone" becomes meaningless when every node can establish identical, virtual connections to every other node as required. The concept of a private line becomes meaningless in an environment where connections can be made and broken in microseconds. Data packets will be self-routing, and the current generation of network equipment dedicated to insuring the accurate delivery of data between two endpoints will give way to a network of machines dedicated to making and breaking short-lived connections and to ultra-fast switching.

Users will have enormous control over the services they use at any moment. Users need not contract with carriers for private data pipelines of known bandwidth. Instead, requirements will be stated in terms of dynamic demand for variable bandwidth and delays. The potential capacity of the network will be so large that many users will need to limit the bandwidth used at any given time so as not to overwhelm their ability to receive and process the data. The network itself becomes a huge processor, a virtual processor/bus system with its own high-speed storage, dynamically moving, replicating, and modifying data, and adding or deleting control and accounting information as it passes from connection to connection. New theories of charging and cost allocation will be required. Costs may be related to the number of connections generated by a call, rather than to the traffic volume or bandwidth used. From the viewpoint of the network, there are no users or circuits per se, only self-routing, variable packets of data.

11.13.1 Some Implications of B-ISDN for Communications Services

The impact of all of this on computer mediated communications can be dramatic. The B-ISDN network is analogous to a massively parallel computer. A single user request may impact many machines. Individual records of a conference, for example, might be stored on their originating nodes. A user request to "read all new comments", might involve data gathering requests to dozens of machines. Contemporary systems like the Coconet are experimenting with hypertext-like interfaces. A particular message might reference a diagram or two, a program that computes the current values of some data at the time of reference, a taped High Definition Television (HDTV) program, and a news clipping service maintaining a database of wire stories related to the subject of the message. Users could point at any of these references and recover them, though each might be stored on some other node of the network. As far as the user is concerned, the distinction between local and remote services utterly collapses.

To achieve all of this will require some agreements regarding the decoupling of application interfaces from the data being read or written by them. There is no need, nor would it be desirable, to standardize either interfaces or data storage architectures. Because the B-ISDN itself is, in effect, a virtual computer, data can be manipulated and transformed enroute, based on the requirements of the requesting node. Some set of agreeable standards for queries must emerge. Request syntax employed by users can be translated into various forms depending on the nature of the data sought and its location. So long as the network is aware of all the variations they can remain completely transparent to end users.

If the user prefers, interfaces may not be text-based at all. The B-ISDN network can carry HDTV images, graphics of many kinds, and voice, as easily as text. By the time a B-ISDN network arrives, technology for voice-to-text and text-to-voice conversion may be reasonably inexpensive. Such conversion could be yet another service provided by the network itself.

Jerry Pournelle, science fiction author and computer columnist, once observed that the ultimate goal of an information-based society is to enable any person to find the answer to any answerable question. Although we are still not quite there, much has been achieved since the advent of the first on- line information services. The number of systems catering to special information needs or communications requirements is growing rapidly. Already the primary problem is finding services that already exist. In the next 15 years, we can expect the number of specialized systems to grow by an order of magnitude or more. By the end of the first decade of the 21st century, the problem of discovering the whereabouts of these systems may be solved with the general availability of local on-line directory services that cross-reference specialized information providers worldwide.

The problem of overcoming political and economic barriers to access will be more difficult than the technical problem of providing connections to these systems. At the present time, political and economic hurdles are the primary stumbling blocks to worldwide electronic mail interconnection. Information providers suffer from these problems not only with respect to the cost of transporting information across national boundaries and the question of who pays and how, but also because the information itself may be politically sensitive. That sensitivity depends a great deal on changing national administrations. It is not likely that universal access to a global information network will be a reality before the emergence of a world government. It is likely that technical achievements needed to satisfy such a vision will be available long before the political agreements are attained.

12

EPILOGUE

On March 24, 1989, the oil tanker Exxon Valdez slammed into a rocky reef in Prince William Sound, Alaska, precipitating the worst oil spill disaster in United States history. Subsequent communications between Exxon Corporation's headquarters in New York, the U.S. Coast Guard, and Valdez, Alaska, were conducted through a single Fax machine in Valdez. Public telephone lines, although available, were jammed with calls in and out of the disaster area.

Exxon set up an emergency office in Houston to coordinate the work of agencies willing to help with disaster recovery. Exxon's head of strategic planning asked Notepad International Inc. to submit a proposal for aiding communications and operations between all parties concerned in the recovery effort; this about a week after the spill. Notepad's proposal emphasized not only the communications capabilities, but the auditability of a computer mediated communications system. A short while after Exxon received the proposal, the principles of Notepad received a short communication from Exxon saying, in effect, "thanks, but no thanks. . . . " According to Ren Breck of Notepad International, in a few hours the Notepad system could have been on-line, supporting the cleanup effort.

Sometime in June, a computer operator at Exxon claimed he had inadvertently destroyed tapes containing copies of existing communications about the crisis received to that point. Exxon assured authorities that it was cooperating with all investigations, and nothing of substance had been lost. At the same time, however, the Alaska Attorney General charged that Exxon was not being very cooperative, having missed a deadline for delivery of communications about the accident to the office of the Attorney General. Perhaps the erased tapes were just redundant backups as Exxon claimed. On the other hand, as with the Nixon Whitehouse tapes and the documents destroyed by Oliver North's secretary in the opening days of the Iran-Contra scandal, it is unlikely that all parties involved will ever know the whole truth.

When making (or not making) decisions and committing actions that may or may not turn out appropriately in any given circumstance, high-level corporate managers share the ability to show that everything they have done is "by the book" or "by accident." This is perhaps their single most significant, if undocumented, skill. Not only corporate management, but also presidents and other high-level government officials (elected or otherwise) share this skill. Indeed, one might argue that reaching the heady levels of the corporate boardroom, presidential residence, or other national government chambers is in itself proof that such skills have been gained.

In discussing the reasons why group communications technologies have not been more readily adopted by American corporations, we have focused on the technical skills (typing) required, along with the costs, and the pressure that this technology exerts on established communications channels. Quite possibly the biggest problem, however, is the unspoken realization that the use of text-based teleconferencing technology has a highly undesirable side effect in the eyes of corporate management: an uncompromising audit trail of every decision, judgment, and piece of information made by, or available to, every manager of the corporation from the CEO on down.

Without accidental (sic) or deliberate destruction of information, the existence and widespread use of a group communications system makes it much more difficult to sidestep errors in judgment or lack of attention. Communications software and potential revelation of culpability go hand in hand. To be sure, the use of this software can also insure that credit is given where it is due. The text record reveals who really was the first person to suggest a new, money saving technique, a winning product, or perform some other action with highly visible and positive after-effects. The threat to management, however, comes not from proper recognition of the positive so much as from unquestionable documentation of the negative, the bad judgment, or the decision unnecessarily delayed.

At the present time, there is a rising tide of sentiment in the public sector for accountability. More and more, the public is putting pressure on corporations and the government to make themselves and their personnel accountable for their actions. Government regulations and red tape going back more than a half a century are directed, primarily, at establishing accountability, something that has been and continues to be avoided by both the government's own agencies *and* the corporate sector.

At the same time, there are those corporations who have embraced the concept of accountability. Some, like Hewlet-Packard and Proctor and Gamble, are American corporations. Not coincidentally, both of these companies have also embraced group-oriented communications technology, and both have gained in productivity as a result. There are others in the United States, and many more in Japan and Western Europe. The trade-off is straightforward. When large or geographically dispersed corporations use this technology properly, their productivity, and therefore their competitiveness improves. At the same time, they must accept the possibility that such systems will also reveal their errors in judgment.

A communications system is a two-edged sword. To have its advantages, corporate managers must accept the side effect of full documentation of their judgments. Eventually, there will be enough pressure, economic and political, to impose such accountability with or without the technology. Corporations that develop a reputation for whitewashing their own crises will be less and less trusted by their vendors and customers, both public and corporate. These entities will fall away to be replaced by those that have demonstrated a willingness to stand up for their mistakes as well as their successes.

In 20 years the overall telecommunications and technological environment will be utterly unlike anything existing today. The pioneers who developed group communications technologies in the 1970s felt that its benefits would be quickly recognized and its mass adoption lay only a few years away. Their confidence proved ill-founded, even throughout the 1980s, and will probably remain so until the world has adjusted itself to the new political, economic, and technical changes in which it is now embroiled. It will be, quite possibly, the opening decades of the 21st century before computer mediated communications technologies are readily adopted by the international corporations of the next millennium.

APPENDIXES

APPENDIKES

APPENDIX A

SOURCE AND OBJECT CODE LIBRARIES, STORAGE, AND COMMUNICATIONS PERIPHERALS

■ **COMMUNICATIONS LIBRARIES**

For BASIC

Product(s): QuickComm
   Vendor: Software Interphase
         5 Bradley St., Suite 105
         Providence, RI 02908
         (800) 542-2742
         (401) 274-5465
      Fax: (401) 272-1273

For C

Product(s): C Async Manager
   Vendor: Blaise Computing
         2560 9th St., Suite 316
         Berkeley, CA 94710
         (800) 333-8087
         (415) 540-5441

Product(s): Comm Library
   Vendor: Greenleaf Software
         16479 Dallas Pkwy., Suite 570
         Dallas, TX 75248

```
                    (800) 523-9830
         Fax:       (214) 248-7830
Product(s):         SilverComm C Interface
   Vendor:          SilverWare
                    Box 781143
                    Dallas, TX 75378
                    (214) 247-0131
         Fax:       (214) 406-9999
```

For Clipper, dBase, and compatibles

```
Product(s):         AdComm/AdComm99/Comm Plus
   Vendor:          Pinnacle Publishing
                    Box 8099
                    Federal Way, WA 98003
                    (800) 231-1293
                    (206) 941-2300
         Fax:       (206) 946-1491

Product(s):         Net Lib
   Vendor:          Communications Horizons
                    701 7th Ave. Suite 900
                    New York, NY 10036
                    (212) 840-1555

Product(s):         SilverComm
   Vendor:          SilverWare
                    Box 781143
                    Dallas, TX 75378
                    (214) 247-0131
         Fax:       (214) 406-9999
```

For Turbo Pascal

```
Product(s):         Turbo Asynch Plus
   Vendor:          Blaise Computing
                    2560 9th St., Suite 316
                    Berkeley, CA 94710
                    (800) 333-8087
                    (415) 540-5441
```

■ FILE MAINTENANCE LIBRARIES

For BASIC

```
Product(s):         db/LIB
   Vendor:          AJS Publishing
```

(800) 992-3383
(213) 215-9145—in California

Product(s): QBase
Vendor: Crescent Software
11 Grandview Ave.
Stamford, CT 06905
(203) 846-2500
Fax: (203) 849-1868

For C

Product(s): AccSys & AccSys with Source
Vendor: Copia International
1964 Richton Dr.
Wheaton, IL 60187
(708) 682-8898
Fax: (708) 665-9841

Product(s): B+Tree for C
Vendor: Sterling Castle
702 Washington St., Suite 704
Marina Del Rey, CA 90292
(800) 722-7853
(800) 323-6406—in California
(213) 306-3020
Fax: (213) 821-8122

Product(s): B-Tree
Vendor: SoftFocus
1343 Stanbury Dr.
Oakville, Ontario, Canada L6L 2J5
(416) 825-0903
Fax: (416) 825-1025

Product(s): CBTREE
Vendor: Peacock Systems
2108-C Gallows Rd.
Vienna, VA 22182
(703) 847-1743

Product(s): C-Data Manager and C-Data Manager with Source
Vendor: Database Technologies
54 University Rd.
Brookline, MA 02146
(617) 739-3390

Product(s): C Index and C Index+
Vendor: Trio Systems

          2210 Wilshire Blvd., Suite 289
          Santa Monica, CA 94043
          (213) 394-0796

Product(s):   Code Base 4
    Vendor: Sequiter Software
          9315-70 Ave.
          Edmonton, Alberta Canada T6E 0T8
          (403) 439-8171
       Fax: (403) 433-7460

Product(s):   c-tree and d-tree
    Vendor: FairCom
          4006 W. Broadway
          Columbia, MO 65203
          (800) 234-8180
          (314) 445-6833
       Fax: (314) 445-9698

Product(s):   dBC III & dBC III+ Multi-user
    Vendor: Lattice
          2500 S. Highland Ave., Suite 300
          Lombard, IL 60148
          (800) 444-4309
          (708) 916-1600
       Fax: (708) 916-1190

Product(s):   db_FILE/RETRIEVE and db_FILE/RETRIEVE Multi-user
    Vendor: Raima Corp.
          3245 146th Place SE
          Bellevue, WA 98007
          (206) 747-5570
       Fax: (206) 747-1991

Product(s):   Btrieve and Btrieve network version
    Vendor: Novell
          122 E. 1700 S.
          Provo, UT 84606
          (800) 453-1267
          (801) 379-5900
       Fax: (801) 373-1990

Product(s):   G-ISAM
    Vendor: Ricoh
          5 Dedrick Pl.
          West Caldwell, NJ 07006
          (201) 882-2000
       Fax: (201) 882-2506

■ **CD-ROM DRIVES**

CD-ROMs are "read only" systems. They are therefore useless for the interactive portions of CMC storage systems, but may serve very well for maintaining large databases of information available to CMC users. Drive prices range from $500.00 to $1000.00. There are now many databases available on CD-ROMs, and more are being developed.

Apple Corporation
20525 Mariani Ave.
Cupertino, CA 95014
(408) 436-6570

Denon America Inc.
Box 5370
Parsippany, NJ 07054
(201) 575-7810

Hitachi Corp. of America
401 West Artisia Blvd.
Compton, CA 90220
(800) 262-1502

JVC
41 Slater Dr.
Elmwood Park, NY 07047
(201) 794-3900

Laser Optical Technology
1803 Mission St.
Santa Cruz, CA 95060
(408) 438-7400

NEC Home Electronic
1255 Michael Dr.
Woodale, IL 60191
(708) 860-9500

Panasonic
2 Panasonic Way
Secaucus, NJ 07094
(201) 392-4602

Philips Laser/Magnetic Storage
4425 Arrowswest Dr.
Colorado Springs, CO 80907
(303) 593-4269

Sanyo
200 Riser Rd.
Little Ferry, NJ 07643
(201) 440-9300

Sony Corp. of America
655 River Oaks Pkwy.
San Jose, CA 95134
(408) 930-7071

Toshiba
9740 Irvine Blvd.
Irvine, CA 92718
(714) 583-3117

■ OPTICAL STORAGE SYSTEMS, READ/WRITE (R/W) AND WRITE ONCE READ MANY (WORM) DRIVES

The R/W drives are much more versatile than the CD-ROMs listed above and can be used for interactive CMC storage. The WORM drives, like CD-ROMs, are probably less useful for interactive work, but they can be loaded with proprietary databases, and have much more storage capacity than CD-ROMs. These drive mechanisms are also more expensive. Prices range from a low of $1500 to $23,000.

Product: 650 MB R/W for IBM AT PS/2
Vendor: Advanced Graphic Applications Inc.
90 Fifth Ave.
New York, NY 10011
(212) 337-4200

Product: Inspire Desktop Dual Drive 1300 MB R/W for IBM AT, DEC, and SUN
Vendor: Alphatronics Inc.
Box 13687
Research Triangle Pk.
Durham, NC 27713
(919) 544-0001

Product: Optical Archiving System. 1 TB (Terabyte). For mainframe and minicomputer systems
Vendor: Aquidneck Systems International Inc.
650 Ten Rod Rd.
North Kingston, RI 02852
(401) 295-2691

Product: 5.25 and 12 inch WORM systems with storage from 450 MB to 6 TB for Macintosh, IBM, DEC, SUN, Data General, and others
Vendor: Computer Upgrade Corp.
2910 East La Palma Ave. Suite A
Anahime, CA 92806
(714) 630-3457

Product: Many models for IBM PC/AT, compatibles, and Macintosh, with capacities from 400 MB to 940 MB
Vendor: Corel Systems Corp.
1600 Carling Ave., Suite 190
Ottawa, Ontario, Canada K1Z 8R7
(613) 728-8200

Product: SCSI WORM, 550 MB–2 TB WORM drives for SUN computers
Vendor: Delta Microsystems Inc.
5039 Preston Ave.
Livermore, CA 94550
(415) 449-6881

Product: Optiserver 600 MB R/W SCSI for the Macintosh WORMServer; 1000 MB SCSI WORM for the Macintosh
Vendor: Deltaic Systems
1977 O'Toole Ave. Suite B206
San Jose, CA 95131
(408) 954-1055

Product: ISi 525GB, 1280 MB Internal and External WORM drives for IBM AT and compatibles
Vendor: Information Storage Inc.
2768 Janitell Rd.
Colorado Springs, CO 80906
(719) 579-0460

Product: Model 810 and 820 IBM AT and Macintosh 810 MB WORM drive systems
Vendor: Laserdrive Ltd.
1101 Space Park Dr.
Santa Clara, CA 95054
(408) 970-3600

Product: APX-4200, 760 MB WORM drive for IBM AT and compatible machines
Vendor: Maximum Storage Inc.
5025 Centennial Blvd.
Colorado Springs, CO 80919
(719) 531-6888

Product: LaserBank 400–900 MB WORM and R/W drives for IBM AT and compatibles
Vendor: Micro Design International Inc.
6985 University Blvd.
Winter Park, FL 32792
(407) 677-8333

Product: Internal and External WORM Drives for IBM PC/AT and compatibles
Vendor: Mitsubishi Electronics of America Inc.
Peripherals Division
991 Knox St.
Torrance, CA 90502
(213) 217-5732

Product: 240–1280 MB Internal and External WORM drives for IBM AT and compatibles
Vendor: N/Hance Systems
908 Providence Hwy.
Dedham, MA 02062
(617) 461-1970

Product: MDU, multimedia storage unit including WORM drive, CD-ROM, and streaming tape combination for Macintosh; IBM, and compatibles, OS/2, UNIX, and VMS also supported
Vendor: Online Computer Systems Inc.
20251 Century Blvd.
Germantown, MD 20874
(301) 428-3700

Product: 940 MB Internal and External WORM drives for IBM and Macintosh computers
Vendor: Panasonic Industrial Co.
2 Panasonic Way
Secaucus, NJ 07094
(201) 348-7000

Product: 635–1270 MB R/W optical drives for Macintosh
Vendor: Peripheral Land Inc.
47421 Bayside Pkw.
Fremont, CA 94538
(415) 657-2211

Product: 650 MB WORM drive system for Macintosh, IBM, and compatibles
Vendor: Pioneer Communications of America Inc.
Optical Memory Products Division
600 E. Crescent Ave.
Upper Saddle River, NJ 07458
(201) 327-6400

Product: 600 MB R/W optical disk system for Macintosh, IBM, and compatibles
Vendor: RACET Computes Ltd.
3150 E. Birch St.
Brea, CA 92621
(714) 579-1725

Product: 786–876 MB WORM and R/W optical drives for Macintosh, PS/2, IBM AT, and compatibles
Vendor: Storage Dimensions
2145 Hamilton Ave.
San Jose, CA 95125
(408) 879-0300

Product: 600 MB R/W optical system for Macintosh
Vendor: Sumo Systems
1580 Old Okland Rd., Suite C103
San Jose, CA 95131
(408) 453-5744

Product: 600 MB R/W optical system for Macintosh, IBM AT, and compatibles; also for DEC and SUN systems
Vendor: Summus Computer Systems
17171 Park Row, Suite 300
Houston, TX 77084
(713) 492-6611

Product: 2 GB WORM drive system for IBM AT and compatibles
Vendor: United Systems Co.
14701-B Myford Rd.
Tustin, CA 92680
(714) 832-3613

■ **MULTIPORT SERIAL I/O CARDS FOR IBM AT AND COMPATIBLES, MICRO-CHANNEL, OR APPLE COMPUTERS.**

Companies listed manufacture boards with at least four serial ports.

Product: 4-port serial boards for IBM PS/2 Micro-Channel
Vendor: Advanced Microcomputer Systems
1321 NW 65th Place
Fort Lauderdale, FL 33309
(800) 972-3733
(305) 975-9515
Fax: (305) 975-9698

Product: 8-port serial boards for IBM AT and Micro-Channel
Vendor: Alloy Computer Products

165 Forest St.
Marlboro, MA 01752
(800) 544-7551
(508) 481-8500
Fax: (508) 481-7711

Product: 8-port serial boards for IBM PC/AT
Vendor: American Micronics Inc.
18005 Sky Park Circle Suite A
Irvine, CA 92714
(714) 261-0693
Fax: (714) 261-0780

Product: 4-port serial board for Apple II
Vendor: Applied Engineering
Box 5100
Carrollton, TX 75001
(214) 241-6060

Product: 4-, 8-, and 16-port serial boards for IBM PC/AT and Micro-Channel
Vendor: ARNET
618 Grassmere Park Dr. Suite 6
Nashville, TN 37211
(800) 366-8844
(615) 834-5222
Fax: (615) 834-5399

Product: 4- and 8-port serial boards for IBM PC/AT & Micro-Channel
Vendor: AST Research
2121 Alton Ave.
Irvine, CA 92714
(714) 863-1333
Fax: (714) 863-9478

Product: 5-port serial board for IBM PC/AT
Vendor: Binary Techniques
35 Medford St.
Somerville, MA 02143
(617) 628-7200

Product: 4-port serial board for IBM PC/AT
Vendor: Chaplet Systems
252 N. Wolf Rd
Sunnyvale, CA 94086
(800) 445-3694
(408) 732-7950
Fax: (408) 732-6050

Product:	8-port serial board for IBM PC/AT
Vendor:	Computer Elektronik Infosys of America
	512-A Herndon Pkwy.
	Herndon, VA 22070
	(800) 322-3464
	(703) 435-3800
Fax:	(703) 435-5129

Product:	4- and 8-port serial boards for IBM PC/AT and Micro-Channel
Vendor:	Comtrol Corporation
	2675 Patton Rd.
	St. Paul, MN 55164
	(800) 333-1033
	(612) 631-7654
Fax:	(612) 631-8117

Product:	4- and 8-port serial boards for IBM PC/AT
Vendor:	Connect Tech
	340 Woodlawn Rd. West, Unit 20
	Guelph, Ontario, Canada N1H 7K6
	(519) 836-1291
Fax:	(519) 836-4878

Product:	8-port serial board for IBM AT
Vendor:	Consensys
	250 Shields Ct., Unit 10B
	Markham, Ontario, Canada L3R 9W7
	(416) 940-2900
Fax:	(416) 940-2903

Product:	4-port serial board for IBM PC/AT
Vendor:	Contec Microelectronics USA
	2010 N. First St., Suite 530
	San Jose, CA 95131
	(800) 888-8884
	(408) 436-0340
Fax:	(408) 436-0206

Product:	4-port serial board for Macintosh
Vendor:	Creative Solutions
	4701 Randolph Rd., Suite 12
	Rockville, MD 20852
	(800) 367-8465
	(301) 984-0262

Product:	4-port serial board for IBM PC/AT
Vendor:	Cubix

2800 Lockheed Way
Carson City, NV 89706
(800) 648-7977
(702) 883-7611
Fax: (702) 882-2407

Product: 16-port serial board for IBM PC/AT
Vendor: Dastra America
976 N. Lemon St.
Orange, CA 92667
(800) 843-5087
(714) 633-2275
Fax: (714) 633-1970

Product: 4-port serial boards for IBM PC/AT
Vendor: Diamond Flower Electric Instruments
2544 Port St.
West Sacramento, CA 95691
(916) 373-1234
Fax: (916) 373-0221

Product: 4-, 8-, and 16-port serial boards for IBM PC/AT and Micro-Channel
Vendor: Digiboard
6751 Oxford St.
St. Louis Park, MN 55426
(800) 344-4273
(612) 922-8055
Fax: (612) 922-4287

Product: 4-port serial boards for IBM PC/AT and Micro-Channel
Vendor: Emulex
3545 Harbor Blvd.
Costa Mesa, CA 92926
(800) 854-7112
(714) 662-5600
Fax: (714) 241-0792

Product: 24-port serial board for IBM AT
Vendor: Equinox systems
14260 SW 119th Ave.
Miami, FL 33186
(800) 328-2729
(305) 255-3500
Fax: (305) 253-0003

Product: 4-port serial boards for IBM PC/AT and Micro-Channel
Vendor: ESE technologies
482 Congress St., Suite 101

Portland, ME 04104
(800) 634-4075
(207) 773-7778

Product: 4-port serial board for IBM PC/AT
Vendor: Kimtron
1709 Junction Ct., Bldg. 380
San Jose, CA 95112
(800) 777-8755
(408) 436-6550
Fax: (408) 436-1380

Product: 4-port serial board for IBM PC/AT
Vendor: Leading Technology
10430 SW 5th Ave.
Beaverton, OR 97005
(800) 999-5323
(503) 646-3424
Fax: (503) 626-7845

Product: 8-port serial boards for IBM PC/AT and Micro-Channel
Vendor: Maxspeed
1180 Chess Dr.
Foster City, CA 94404
(415) 345-5447
Fax: (415) 345-6398

Product: 4-port serial board for IBM PC/AT
Vendor: Metacomp
15175 Innovation Dr., Bldg. A
San Diego, CA 92128
(619) 673-0800
Fax: (619) 673-0321

Product: 4- and 8-port serial board for IBM AT; 16-port board for PS/2 Micro-Channel machines
Vendor: Microway
Box 79
Kingston, MA 02364
(508) 746-7341
Fax: (508) 746-4678

Product: 8-port serial board for IBM AT
Vendor: Raritan Computer
10 Ilene Ct., Suite 1
Belle Mead, NJ 08502
(201) 874-4072
Fax: (201) 231-8684

Product: 6-port serial board for IBM PC/AT
Vendor: Server Technology
2332 A Walsh Ave.
Santa Clara, CA 95051
(800) 835-1515
(408) 738-8377
Fax: (408) 738-0247

Product: 4-, 8-, 16-, and 32-port serial boards for IBM PC/AT and Micro-Channel machines
Vendor: Specialix
444 Castro St., Suite 408
Mountain View, CA 94041
(415) 964-0414
Fax: (415) 969-8660

▪ 9600 BPS V.32 COMPLIANT VOICE GRADE MODEMS

AT&T Paradyne
8545 126th Ave.
Largo, FL 34649
(800) 482-3333
(800) 342-1140—in Florida
Fax: (813) 530-2835

Barr Systems
4131 NW 28th Lane
Gainsville, FL 32606
(800) 227-7797
(904) 371-3050
Fax: (904) 371-3018

Best Data Products
5907 Noble Ave.
Van Nuys, CA 91411
(800) 632-2378
(818) 786-2884

BT Datacom
3701 Concord Pkwy. Suite 100
Chantilly, VA 22021
(800) 648-3532
(703) 818-1770
Fax: (703) 818-1776

Bytcom
2169 Francisco Blvd., Suite H

San Rafael, CA 94901
(800) 227-3254
(415) 485-0700

Cardinal Technologies
1827 Freedom Rd.
Lancaster, PA 17601
(800) 722-0094
(717) 293-3000

Case/Datatel
55 Carnegie Plaza
Cherry Hill, NJ 08003
(800) 424-4451
(609) 424-4451
Fax: (609) 424-8065

Cermetek Microelectronics
1308 Borregas Ave.
Sunnyvale, CA 94088
(800) 444-6271
(408) 752-5000
Fax: (408) 752-5004

Compuquest
801 Morse Ave.
Schaumburg, IL 60193
(708) 529-2552
Fax: (708) 894-6048

Computer Friends
14250 NW Science Park Dr.
Portland, OR 97229
(800) 322-3464
(703) 435-3800
Fax: (703) 435-5129

Comsat Datacom
1720 Spectrum Dr. NW
Laurenceville, GA 30243
(800) 248-9496
(404) 822-1962
Fax: (404) 822-4886

Connect
10101 Bubb Rd.
Cupertino, CA 95014
(408) 973-0110
Fax: (408) 973-0497

CXR Telecom
521 Charcot Ave.
San Jose, CA 95131
(408) 435-8520
Fax: (408) 435-1276

Data Race
12758 Cimarron Path Suite 108
San Antonio, TX 78249
(512) 692-3909
Fax: (512) 692-7632

Datalink Ready
1800 Penn St., Suite 8
Melbourne, FL 32901
(800) 223-5465
(407) 676-0500
Fax: 676-0504

Digicom Systems
279 Sinclair Frontage Rd.
Milpitas, CA 95035
(408) 262-1277
Fax: (408) 262-1390

Emucom
225 Stedman St., Suite 27
Lowell, MA 01851
(508) 970-1189
Fax: (508) 970-1295

E-Tech
3333 Bowers Ave., Suite 165
Santa Clara, CA 95054
(408) 982-0270
Fax: (408) 982-0272

Gandalph Data
1020 S. Noel Ave.
Wheeling, IL 60090
(800) 426-3253
(708) 541-6060
Fax: (708) 541-6803

General Datacom
Rte. 63
Middlebury, CT 06762
(800) 432-2228
(800) 826-6565 — in Connecticut

(203) 574-1118
Fax: (203) 758-8507

Hayes Microcomputer Products
705 W. Tech Dr.
Norcross, GA 30092
(404) 441-1617
Fax: (404) 441-1238

Incomm Data Systems
652 S. Wheeling Rd.
Wheeling, IL 60090
(800) 346-2660
(708) 459-8881
Fax: (708) 459-0189

Inmac
2465 Augustine Dr.
Santa Clara, CA 95052
(800) 547-5444
(408) 727-1970

Memotec Datacom
40 High St.
North Andover, MA 01845
(508) 681-0600
Fax: (508) 681-0600 Ext. 2667

Microcomm
500 River Ridge Dr.
Norwood, MA 02062
(617) 551-1000
Fax: (617) 551-1006

Multi-Tech Systems
2205 Woodale Dr.
Mounds View, MN 55112
(800) 328-9717
(612) 785-3500
Fax: (612) 785-9874

NEC America
14040 Park Center Rd.
Herndon, VA 22071
(703) 698-5540

NetQuest
129 H Gaither Dr.
Mt. Laurel, NJ 08054

(609) 866-0505
Fax: (609) 866-2852

Omnitel
3500 W. Warren Ave.
Freemont, CA 94538
(415) 490-2202
Fax: (415) 657-4079

Penril Datacom
207 Perry Pkwy.
Gaithersburg, MD 20877
(800) 638-8905
(301) 921-8600
Fax: (301) 921-8376

Phillips Information
15301 Dallas Pkwy. Suite 300
Dallas, TX 75248
(800) 527-0204
(214) 980-2000
Fax: (214) 991-6572

Prodatel Communications
720 Montgolfier Suite 201
Ville de Laval
Quebec, Canada H7W 4Z2
(514) 686-0232
Fax: (514) 686-0239

Prometheus Products
7225 S.W. Bonita Rd.
Tigard, OR 97223
(503) 624-0571
Fax: (503) 624-0843

Racal-Milgo
1601 N. Harrison Pkw.
Sunrise, FL 33323
(800) 327-4440
(305) 475-1601
Fax: (305) 476-4942

Racal-Vadic
1525 McCarthy Blvd.
Milpitas, CA 95035
(800) 482-3427
(408) 432-8008
Fax: 476-4942

Rockwell International
4311 Jamboree Rd., Station 501-300
Newport Beach, CA 92660
(800) 854-8099
(800) 422-4230—in California
Fax: (714) 833-4078

Telebit
1345 Shorebird Way
Mountain View, CA 94043
(800) 835-3248
(415) 969-3800
Fax: (415) 969-8888

Telenetics
5109 E. LaPalma
Anaheim, CA 92807
(800) 826-6336
(800) 822-4267—in California
Fax: (714) 779-1255

Tri-Data Systems
1450 Kifer Rd.
Sunnyvale, CA 94086
(408) 746-2900
Fax: (408) 746-2074

Universal Data Systems
5000 Bradford Dr.
Huntsville, AL 35805
(800) 451-2369
(205) 721-8000
Fax: (205) 830-5657

U.S. Robotics
8100 McCormick Blvd.
Skokie, IL 60076
(800) 342-5877
(708) 982-5001
Fax: (708) 982-5235

Ven-Tel
2121 Zanker Rd.
San Jose, CA 95131
(408) 436-7400
Fax: (408) 436-7451

APPENDIX B

BBS AND GROUP CMC SOFTWARE PRODUCTS

The following products are electronic mail systems designed to run in stand-alone/long-distance environments. They are not tied to local area network (LAN) environments.

Name:	BackMail
Description:	General purpose TSR automatic electronic mail software for automated point-to-point wide-area mail
Price:	Shareware; can be found on most BBS systems with file libraries, or contact vendor for details
Vendor:	Alethic Software
	52 Parkhill Rd.
	Halifax, Nova Scotia
	Canada B3P 1R2
	(902) 420-0734 voice

Name:	Dialog 400
Description:	Stand-alone distributed X.400 based electronic mail system; runs on proprietary hardware/OS, dedicated to E-mail operations
Price:	
Vendor:	OST Inc.
	14255-F Sullyfield Circle
	Chantilly, VA 22021

(703) 817-0400
Fax: (703) 817-0402

Name:	RamNet
Description:	TSR Electronic mail, uucp connectivity, terminal emulation, and BBS
	MS-DOS based
Price:	$149.00
Vendor:	Software Concepts Design
	594 Third Avenue
	New York, NY 10016
	(212) 889-6431
	Data: (212) 889-6438

The following products are electronic mail systems that run in LAN environments. There are over 25 vendors supplying products in this area. The first product on this list is included because it implements an unusual subject-threading feature not found in other systems. The others all share compliance with the CCITT X.400 messaging standard, mostly via external gateways that are available with the product. For a description of these and other electronic mail products, see the article by Jim Carr listed in the bibliography.

Name:	Brainstorm
Description:	Electronic mail system with subject threading of messages; operates in LAN environments
Price:	$999/MHS Server, $699/non-MHS Server
Vendor:	Mustang Software Inc.
	Box 2264
	Bakersfield, CA 93303
	(805) 395-0223
	Fax: (805) 395-0713

Name:	Dayna Mail
Description:	MS-DOS and MacOS mail system supporting address lists, and built-in links to MCI, and many other gateways
Price:	$295.00 multiuser
Vendor:	Dayna Communications
	50 S. Main St., 5th Floor
	Salt Lake City, UT
	(801) 531-0600
	Fax: (801) 531-9135

Name: Oracle Mail
Description: MS-DOS, MacOS, UNIX, OS/2, and other operating systems supported in LAN environment; gateways to VMS and many other mail systems
Price: $49.00–$299.00 per user
Vendor: Oracle
20 Davis Dr.
Belmont, CA
(800) 345-3267
(415) 598-8000
Fax: (415) 595-0630

Name: Para Mail
Description: MS-DOS in LAN environment; RAM resident, with gateways to MCI and many other systems
Price: $795.00 Multiuser
Vendor: Paradox Development
7544 Trade St.
San Diego, CA
(619) 586-0878

The following products are true group CMC software systems. The larger and better-known CMC products are represented here. There are many others that may be suitable for limited CMC usage domains.

Name: TEIES/EIES2
Description: Tailorable and distributed CMC software; derived from EIES among the larger systems
Price: Depends on configuration; call vendor
Author: Murray Turoff and others
Vendor: New Jersey Institute of Technology
Newark, NJ 07102
(201) 596-3437

Name: Participate
Description: Multiuser centralized CMC software for UNIX, Xenix, VMS, VM/CMS; MS-DOS multiuser operation in LAN environment; definitely one of the more exhaustive packages
Price: Depends on configuration
Author: Harry Stevens and George Reinhart

Vendor: Eventures Limited
2744 Washington St.
Allentown, PA 18104
(215) 770-0650

Name: Confer II
Description: The original comb-structured system; very powerful and full featured; highly tailorable; runs on MTS and VMS operating systems
Price: Contact vendor
Author: Robert Parnes
Vendor: Advertel Communications Inc.
Ann Arbor, MI
(313) 665-2612

Name: Magpie
Description: Single/multiuser CMC software MS-DOS or UNIX; multiuser on DOS requires Quarter Deck's Desqview; unusually powerful search engine combined with a novel interface
Price: $115 for MS-DOS; UNIX prices vary
Author: Steve Manes
Vendor: Roxy Recorders Inc.
648 Broadway
New York, NY 10012
(212) 420-0527 data (8N1)
(212) 533-1692 voice

Name: TEAMate
Description: Multiuser CMC software running in UNIX/Xenix environments
Price: Depends on configuration
Author: Roger Morell
Vendor: MMB Development Corporation
1021 N. Sepulveda Blvd, Suite K
Manhattan Beach, CA 90266
(213) 545-1455
(800) 832-6022—outside CA

Name: RBBS
Description: Single/multiuser CMC software MS-DOS; multiuser on DOS requires Quarter Deck's Desqview
Price: Shareware, $25.00
Author: Tom Mack

Vendor:	Capital PC Users' Group
	Box 6128
	Silver Springs, MD 20906
	(203) 268-9656
	Data: (415) 689-2090

Name:	PCBoard
Description:	Single/multiuser CMC software, MS-DOS; requires LAN (or internal processors-on-a-card) for multiuser operation
Price:	$120.00 to $990.00 depending on options required
Author:	Frank Clark
Vendor:	Clark Development Co. Inc.
	Box 71365
	Salt Lake City, UT 84107
	(801) 261-1686
	Data: (801) 261-8974
	(800) 356-1686

Name:	SuperCom
Description:	Distributed large-scale CMC software
Price:	depends on configuration
Author:	Torgny Tholerus
Vendor:	QZ University Computing Centre
	Linnegatan 89 Box 27322
	S-102 54
	Stockholm, Sweden
	+46-8-665 45 00
	Fax: +46-8-665 40 88

Name:	TBBS
Description:	Multiuser CMC software MS-DOS; a comprehensive package that does its own multitasking; one of the larger and more extensive PC-based systems
Price:	Depends on number of users
Author:	Phil Becker
Vendor:	Esoft Inc.
	15200 E. Girard Ave. Suite 2550
	Aurora, CO 80014
	(303) 699-6565

Name:	TDBS
Description:	Multiuser CMC software MS-DOS integrated with Ashton Tate's

Dbase III+

Price: Depends on number of users

Author: Phil Becker

Vendor: Esoft Inc.

15200 E. Girard Ave. Suite 2550

Aurora, CO 80014

(303) 699-6565

Name: FIDO

Description: Single-line BBS designed to be linked (through FIDONet Transport level software) to established international network

Price: $175.00

Author: Tom Jennings

Vendor: FIDO Software

164 Shipley

San Francisco, CA 94107

(415) 764-1629

Name: AKCS

Description: Multiuser CMC software MS-DOS, UNIX. A very flexible package competing primarily with TBBS and other relatively large-scale PC-based systems

Price: depends on number of users

Author: Karl Denninger

Vendor: Macro Computer Solutions, Inc.

520 N. Seymour Ave. Suite 11

Mundelein, IL 60060

(708) 808-7200

Name: Caucus

Description: Multiuser CMC software, MS-DOS, UNIX, VMS, VM; a Confer "clone," one of the more powerful packages known for the variety of environments it supports

Price: Depends on number of users

Author: Charles Roth

Vendor: Camber-Roth

1223 Peoples Ave.

Troy, NY 12180

(518) 273-0983

Name: The Major BBS

Description: Multiuser CMC software for MS-DOS; uses exotic, proprietary multi-

modem cards for best operation; source code available at low price;
dial-out, Fax connection available; hypertext module under development at this time

Price:	Depends on configuration
Author:	Tim Stryker
Vendor:	Galacticomm Inc.
	4101 S.W. 47th Ave., Suite 101
	Fort Lauderdale, FL 33314
	(305) 583-5990

Name:	Wildcat
Description:	Single/multiuser CMC software, MS-DOS; multiuser operation sup-ported on LANs and via Quarterdeck's Desqview
Price:	$129 to $499 depending on configuration
Author:	Jim Harrer
Vendor:	Mustang Software
	Box 2264
	Bakersfield CA 93303
	(805) 395-0223
	Fax: (805) 395-0713

Name:	Searchlight
Description:	Single/multiuser CMC software, MS-DOS; multiuser operations on LANs or central configurations using Quarterdeck's Desqview or other multitasking shells
Price:	$95.00 for Extended Addition
Author:	Frank LaRosa
Vendor:	Searchlight Software
	PO Box 640
	Stony Brook, NY 11790
	(516) 751-2966

Name:	QuickBBS
Description:	Single/multiuser CMC software, MS-DOS; multiuser operations re-quire Quarterdeck's Desqview
Price:	$60-$150
Author:	Adam Hudson; now owned by Bret Florin and Steve Vickers
Vendor:	Technologies Unlimited Software, Inc.
	497 Blackwood Ave.
	Longwood, Fl 32750
	(407) 767-0053 (voice)
	(407) 831-2359 (data)

Name: Chairman
Description: Multiuser CMC software, MS-DOS; multiuser operation supported by a proprietary shell
Price: $295-$995 depending on configuration
Author: DMA
Vendor: Dynamic Microprocessor Associates
1776 E. Jerico Turnpike
Huntington, NY 11745
(516) 462-0440

Name: CoSy
Description: Multiuser in centralized and distributed configurations; Xenix operating system on many platforms
Price: Contact vendor
Author: Alastair Mayer
Vendor: Softwords Inc.
4252 Commerce Circle
Victoria, BC, Canada V8Z 4N2
(800) 663-7560
(604) 727-6522

Name: Picospan
Description: Multiuser centralized conferencing software for UNIX environments; very configurable
Price: Contact vendor
Author: Marcus Watts
Vendor: UniCon, Inc.
120 Enterprise Drive
Ann Arbor, MI 48103
(313) 996-2663

Name: Coconet
Description: Multiuser centralized system with strongly coupled interface; good graphics support
Price: Contact vendor
Author: Brian L. Dear
Vendor: Coconut Computing Inc.
7946 Ivanhoe Ave. Suite 303
La Jolla, CA 92037
(619) 456-2002

Name:	DCI BBS
Description:	MS-DOS based system, multiuser operation through shell software like Desqview; has 10 different possible conference/message structures depending on purpose of individual conferences
Price:	$90.00
Author:	Marianne Love
Vendor:	930 Lakewood Ave.
	Tampa, FL 33613
	(813) 961-0788—data, demo board, settings 8N1

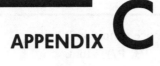

APPENDIX C

STANDARDS

■ X.400 STANDARDS DOCUMENTS

The following specifications constitute the CCITT 1984 Red Book for X.400.

X.400 "System model-service elements," CCITT, *Fascicle VIII.7*, International Telecommunications Union, October 1984, pp. 3–38

X.401 "Basic service elements and optional user facilities," Ibid., pp. 39–45

X.408 "Encoded information type conversion rules," Ibid., pp. 45–61

X.409 "Presentation transfer syntax and notation," Ibid., pp. 62–93

X.410 "Remote operations and reliable transfer service," Ibid., pp. 93–126

X.411 "Message transfer layer," Ibid., pp. 127–182

X.420 "Interpersonal messaging user agent layer," Ibid., pp. 182–219

X.430 "Access protocol for Teletex terminal," Ibid., pp. 219–266

The following specifications constitute the additions and changes in the above standard that make up the CCITT 1988 Blue Book.

X.400 "System and service overview" *Fascicle VIII.7*, International Telecommunications Union, 1988

X.402 "Overall architecture," Ibid.

X.403 "Conformance testing," Ibid.

X.407 "Abstract service definition conventions," Ibid.

X.408 "Encoded information type conversion rules," Ibid.

X.411 "Message transfer system: abstract service definition and procedures," Ibid.

X.413 "Message store: abstract service definition," Ibid.

X.419 "Protocol specifications (P1, P3, P7)," Ibid.

X.420 "Interpersonal messaging system," Ibid.

Related specifications X.208 amd X.209 define the "abstract syntax notation" (ANS.1) used in defining X.400 structures and datatypes, along with the "basic encoding rules" (BER) for that notation, can be found in *Fascicle VIII.4,* International Telecommunications Union, 1988, or published by the ISO as Document 8824.

ISO document 8883 is the ISO equivalent "Message Oriented Text Interchange System" (MOTIS), corresponding to the CCITT X.400 Red Book.

Other related standards for facsimile transmission, international alphabets, and an "International interworking for Videotex services" can be found in *Fascicle VII.3* of the International Telecommunications Union, 1984.

Recommendation X.121 defines an "International numbering plan for public data networks," ITU, *Fascicle VIII.4.*

The X.400 Application Programming Interface Association has developed a standard, object-oriented definition of structures required to connect application software to X.400-based systems. This document may be obtained from:

X.400 API Association

Box 1693

Herndon, VA 22070

■ **INTERNET STANDARDS**

The following list is a short collection of standards developed and supported by the worldwide Internet for message exchange. These documents can be obtained from the Stanford Research Institute at:

333 Ravenswood Avenue

Menlo Park, CA 94025

Alternatively, they may be obtained by Internet electronic mail. Send an electronic message to SERVICE@SRI-NIC.ARPA. In the subject field, write the number of the RFC you wish to receive. For example:

Subject: RFC 1036

The document will be routed to your local uucp or other Internet mailbox. The words "RFC INDEX" in the subject field will result in a description of all RFCs and their numbers. "NETINFO INDEX" will yield a list of other documents produced by Internet standards, administration, and naming bodies.

RFC 821	Simple Mail Transfer Protocol (SMTP)
RFC 822	Internet mail format standard
RFC 987	Mapping between Internet mail standard and X.400
RFC 1026	Addendum to RFC 987
RFC 1036	Usenet message format standard

■ ADDRESS FORMATS FOR SENDING ELECTRONIC MAIL FROM ONE NETWORK TO ANOTHER

The following document is maintained by John J. Chew, Department of Mathematics, University of Toronto, Canada. It is reproduced by permission of its author.*

```
# Inter-Network Mail Guide
#   $Header: netmail,v 1.5 89/12/04 10:45:42 john Exp $
#
# This file documents methods of sending mail from one network
# to another.
# It is maintained by John J. Chew <poslfit@gpu.UTCS.UToronto.
# CA>, and is
# posted monthly to comp.mail.misc and news.newusers.questions.
# Please
# send any corrections or additions to the above address.
#
# Each entry in this file describes how to get from one network
# to
# another.  To keep this file at a reasonable size, methods
# that can
# be generated by transitivity (A->B and B->C gives A->B->C)
# are omitted.
# Entries are sorted first by source network and then by
# destination
# network, and a typical entry looks like:
#
#    #F mynet
#    #T yournet
#    #R youraddress
#    #I send to "youraddress@thegateway"
#
```

*Copyright John L. Chew, Department of Mathematics, University of Toronto, Toronto Canada.

```
# #F (from) and #T (to) lines specify source and destination
# networks.
# These are currently one of:
#
#    applelink    Apple Computer, Inc.'s in-house network
#    bitnet       international academic network
#    bix          Byte Information eXchange: Byte magazine's
#                 commercial BBS
#    bmug         Boston Macintosh Users Group
#    compuserve   commercial time-sharing service
#    connect      Connect Professional Information Network
#                 (commercial)
#    fax          Facsimile document transmission
#    fidonet      PC-based BBS network
#    geonet       commercial information network
#    internet     the Internet
#    mci          MCI's commercial electronic mail service
#    mfenet       Magnetic Fusion Energy Network
#    sinet        Schlumberger Information NETwork
#    span         Space Physics Analysis Network
#    telemail     Telenet's commercial mail service
#
# #R (recipient) gives an example of an address on the
# destination network,
# to make it clear in subsequent lines what text requires
# subsitution.
#
# #I (instructions) lines, of which there may be several,
# give verbal
# instructions to a user of the source network to let them send
# mail
# to a user on the destination network.  Text that needs to be
# typed
# will appear in double quotes, with C-style escapes if
# necessary.

#F applelink
#T bitnet
#R user@site
#I send to "user@site.bitnet@dasnet#"
#F applelink
```

```
#T internet
#R user@site.domain
#I send to "user@site.domain@dasnet#"
#F bitnet
#T applelink
#R user
#I send to "XB.DAS@STANFORD.BITNET"
#I set subject to "user@APPLELINK"

#F compuserve
#T fax
#R +1 415 555 1212
#I send to "FAX 14155551212" (only to U.S.A.)

#F compuserve
#T internet
#R user@site.domain
#I send to ">INTERNET:user@site.domain"

#F compuserve
#T mci
#R 123-4567
#I send to ">MCIMAIL:123-4567"
#F connect
#T internet
#R user@site.domain
#I send to CONNECT id "DASNET"
#I first line of message: "\"user@site.domain\"@DASNET"

#F fidonet
#T internet
#R user@site.domain
#I send to "uucp" at nearest gateway site
#I first line of message: "To: user@site.domain"

#F internet
#T applelink
#R user
#I send to "user@applelink.apple.com"

#F internet
```

```
#T bitnet
#R user@site
#I send to "user%site.bitnet@gateway" where "gateway" is a
#  gateway host that
#I   is on both the internet and bitnet.  Some examples of
#    gateways are:
#I   cunyvm.cuny.edu gpu.utcs.toronto.edu jade.berkeley.edu
#    mitvma.mit.edu.
#I   Check first to see what local policies on inter-network
#    forwarding are.

#F internet
#T bix
#R user
#I send to "user@dcibix.das.net"

#F internet
#T bmug
#R John Smith
#I send to "John.Smith@bmug.fidonet.org"
#F internet
#T compuserve
#R 7xxxx,yyy
#I send to "7xxxx.yyy@compuserve.com"

#F internet
#T connect
#R NAME
#I send to "NAME@dcjcon.das.net"

#F internet
#T fidonet
#R john smith at 1:2/3
#I send to "john.smith@f3.n2.z1.fidonet.org"

#F internet
#T geonet
#R user@host
#I send to "user@host.das.net"

#F internet
```

```
#T mci
#R JSMITH (123-4567)
#I send to "1234567@mcimail.com"
#I or send to "JSMITH@mcimail.com" if "JSMITH" is unique

#F internet
#T mfenet
#R user@mfenode
#I send to "user%mfenode.mfenet@nmfecc.arpa"

#F internet
#T sinet
#R node::user or nodel::node::user
#I send to "user@node.SINet.SLB.COM" or "user%node@nodel.SINet.
#  SLB.COM"

#F internet
#T span
#R user@host
#I send to "user@host.span.NASA.gov"
#I or send to "user%host.span@gateway" where "gateway" is a
#  gateway host
#I    that is on both the internet and SPAN.  Some examples of
#     gateways
#I    are nssdca.gsfc.nasa.gov, longs.ucar.edu, star.stanford.edu,
#I    vlsi.jpl.nasa.gov, io.arc.nasa.gov, hamlet.caltech.edu.
#     Information
#I    is available from NETMGR@nssdca.gsfc.nasa.gov.

#F internet
#T telemail
#R [user/organization]system/country
#I send to "\"[user/organization]system/country%TELEMAIL\"@
#  intermail.isi.edu"
#I further information is available from Intermail-Request@
#  intermail.isi.edu

#F mci
#T bitnet
#R John Smith <user@host>
#I at the "To:" prompt type "John Smith (EMS)"
```

```
#I at the "EMS:" prompt type "internet"
#I at the "Mbx:" prompt type "user@host"

#F mci
#T internet
#R John Smith <user@site.domain>
#I at the "To:" prompt type "John Smith (EMS)"
#I at the "EMS:" prompt type "internet"
#I at the "Mbx:" prompt type "user@site.domain"

#F sinet
#T internet
#R user@site.domain
#I send to "M_MAILNOW::M_INTERNET::\"user@site.domain\""
#I     or "M_MAILNOW::M_INTERNET::site.domain::user"

#F span
#T internet
#R user@site.domain
#I send to "gateway::\"user@host.domain\"" where "gateway" is a
#  gateway host
#I    that is on both SPAN and the internet.  Some examples of
#    gateways are:
#I    AMES, HAMLET, IO, IUE, JPLLSI, NSFGW, NSSDCA, STAR.
#    Information is
#I    available from NETMGR@NSSDCA.

#F telemail
#T internet
#R user@site.domain
#I send to [INTERMAIL/USCISI]TELEMAIL/USA
#I first line of message: "Forward: ARPA"
#I second line of message: "To: user@site.domain"
#I further information is available from Intermail-Request@
#  intermail.isi.edu
----- end netmail -----
Copyright john j. chew, iii   phone: +1 416 425 3818
AppleLink: CDA0329
trigraph, inc., toronto, canada {uunet!utai!utcsri,utgpu,utzoo}
!trigraph!john
dept. of math., u. of toronto  poslfit@{utorgpu.bitnet,gpu.utcs.
utoronto.ca}
```

ON-LINE SERVICES, INFORMATION BROKERS, AND CONFERENCING SYSTEMS

■ **GENERAL SERVICES**

Name:	SUZY
Vendor:	Stratford Software
Requirements:	Coupled Software
Orientation:	Conferencing, synchronous/asynchronous, E-mail, games, shopping, databases
Price:	C$29.95 for the software, C$12.00/hr
Contact:	Terry McDonald, Stratford Software (604) 439-1311
Access:	Datapac Canada

Name:	US West Gateway/Omaha Citinet
Vendor:	US West Communications
Requirements:	Minitel Terminals
Price:	$7.95/month terminal rental; no gateway charge, but surcharges for different services
Access:	US West Communications (402) 422-3587

Name:	CocoNet
Vendor:	Coconut Computing Inc. 7946 Ivanhoe Ave. Suite 303 La Jolla, CA 92037 (619) 456-2002
Requirements:	IBM PC/AT EGA/VGA display and proprietary communications software
Price:	$29.95 set-up (includes software) and $5.00/month

Name: CompuServe Information Service Inc.
Vendor: 5000 Arlington Centre Blvd.
Columbus, OH 43220
(617) 457-8600
(800) 848-8990
Requirements: Any terminal/terminal emulation software
Price: Depends on connect speed and access service

Name: GEnie
Vendor: GE Information Services, Dept. 2B
401 N. Washington St.
Rockville, MD 20850
(301) 340-4000
(800) 638-9636
Requirements: Any terminal/terminal emulation software
Price: Depends on connect time and access service

Name: Delphi
Vendor: General Videotex Corp.
3 Blackstone St.
Cambridge, MA 02139
(617) 491-3393
(800) 544-4005
Requirements: Any terminal/terminal emulation software
Price: Varies with time of day

Name: BIX
Vendor: Byte Information Exchange
1 Phoenix Mill Ln.
Peterborough, NH 03458
(603) 924-9281
(800) 227-2983
Requirements: Any terminal/terminal emulation software
Price: Flat rate or hourly charge plus packet switch costs

Name: P-link
Vendor: American People Link
165 N. Canal St., Suite 950
Chicago, IL 60606
(312) 648-0660
(800) 524-0100
Requirements: Any terminal/terminal emulation software
Price: Varies with time of day; flat fee available

Name: Quantum
Vendor: Quantum Computer Services
8619 Westwood Center Dr.

Vienna, VA 22180

(703) 448-8700

(415) 592-9592—West coast

(800) 782-2278—Apple/Commodore info

(800) 458-8532—IBM compatible info

Requirements: Apple, Commodore, or IBM PC computer with proprietary terminal software

Price: Flat fee + hourly surcharges for most services

Name: Mintel

Vendor: Mintel USA

1700 Broadway

New York, NY 10019

(212) 307-5005

Requirements: Special terminal equipment

Name: Prodigy

Vendor: Prodigy Services Co.

445 Hamilton Ave.

White Plains, NY 10601

(914) 993-8848

Requirements: Proprietary software running on IBM compatibles, Apple Macintosh, Commodore, etc.

∎ **ELECTRONIC MAIL SERVICES**
BY 1991, ALL THESE SERVICES WILL BE INTERCONNECTED VIA X.400 DELIVERY SYSTEMS

AT&T Mail

P.O. Box 3505

New Brunswick, NJ 08903

(800) 624-5672

(201) 668-6548

Electronic registration:

(800) 624-5123

(201) 658-4815

MCI Mail

11900 M. Street, NW

Washington, DC 20036

(800) 444-6245

(202) 833-8484—in Washington DC

Sprint Mail

U.S. Sprint

12490 Sunrise Valley Dr.

Reston, VA 22096

(800) 835-3638
(703) 689-5700

Western Union Easylink
(purchased by AT&T in July 1990)
Western Union Telegraph Corp.
1 Lake St.
Upper Saddle River, NJ 07458
(201) 818-5000

ALANET
American Library Association Network
50 East Huron St.
Chicago, IL 60611
(800) 545-2433
(800) 545-2444—in Illinois

British Telecom—Tymnet Dialcom electronic mail division
6120 Executive Blvd.
Rockville, MD 20852
(800) 435-7342
(301) 881-9020

BITNET Network Information Center
1112 16th St., NW, Suite 600
Washington, DC 20036
(202) 872-4200

DIALMAIL
Dialog Information Services Electronic Mail Division
3460 Hillview Ave.
Palo Alto, CA 94304
(800) 334-2564
(415) 858-3810

■ SPECIALTY SYSTEMS

There are many CMC systems associated with databases catering to all kinds of information requirements. The best single source of information about these systems, along with many other things, is *Boardwatch Magazine*. For a subscription, contact:

Boardwatch
Publisher: Jack Rickard
5970 South Vivian St.
Littleton, CO 80127
(303) 973-6038
(303) 973-4222—data lines

Subscriptions may be obtained on-line or by voice. Subscriptions are $28.00/year. Fifty dollars per year buys not only a subscription to the monthly printed magazine, but also to the Boardwatch BBS (TBBS software), which contains a lot of other news, updated weekly, and information about specialty services.

The DASnet is a specialty system that transfers electronic mail between many different CMC systems. Users establish an account on some home system, and DASnet transfers their mail between that system and others also participating in DASnet's services. At the time of this writing, there were 27 systems participating in DASnet services, including BIX, AT&T mail, Western Union's Easylink, MCI, the entire Internet, uucp, the BITNET, and so on. For information, contact:

> DA Systems Inc.
> 1503 East Campbell Ave.
> Campbell, CA 95008
> (408) 559-7434

The Electronic Networking Association (ENA) is an association of professionals interested in furthering the work of both private and public CMC systems, information retrieval, and all aspects of the developing CMC marketplace. For more information, contact:

> ENA
> 2744 Washington St.
> Allentown, PA 18104-4225
> (215) 821-7777

■ THE PUBLIC ACCESS UNIX LIST

The following list is maintained by Phil Eschallier, who may be reached at the addresses published at the bottom. It is published here by permission of its author. In it are 74 UNIX-based systems accessible to the public by subscription. Many run CMC packages of one kind or another. A large number are public access points to the Usenet and uucp networks.

[April 5, 1990]

Systems listed (74)
Legend: fee/contribution ($), no fee (-$), hours (24), not (-24),
shell (S), USENET news (N), email (M), multiple lines (T)
Telebit PEP speed on main number (+P), Telebit on other line[s] (P)
Courier 9600 bps on main number (+H), Courier on other line[s] (H)
V.32 on main number (+V), V.32 on other line[s] (V)
anonymous uucp (A), archive site ONLY - see long form list (@)
Dialable thru PC Pursuit (^)

Last
Contact

Date	Telephone #	Sys-name	Location		Baud	Legend
08/89	201-846-2460^	althea	New Brunswic	NJ	3/12/24	24 -$ M N S
02/90	206-328-4944	polari	Seattle	WA	3/12	24 $ M N P S T
04/90	209-952-5347	quack	Stockton	CA	3/12/24/96	24 $ M N +P S
12/89	212-420-0527	magpie	NYC		3/12/24/96	24 -$ A T P
03/90	212-447-1522^	dasysl	NYC		3/12/24	24 $ S N M T
02/90	212-675-7059	marob	NYC		3/12/24/96	24 -$ A P T

09/89	213-397-3137^	stb	Santa Monica	CA	3/12/24	24	-$	S A
11/88	213-459-5891	amazing	Pac Palisade	CA	3/12/24	24	$	T
07/88	214-247-2367	ozdaltx	Dallas	TX	3/12/24	24	$	N T
01/90	215-348-9727	lgnpl	Doylestown	PA	3/12/24/96	24	$	A M N +P
01/90	216-582-2460	ncoast	Cleveland	OH	12/24/96	24	$	S N M P T
01/90	217-525-9011	pallas	Springfield	IL	3/12/24/96	24	$	H M S T V
04/90	219-289-0286	nstar	Notre Dame/S	IN	24/96	24	-$	H M N P S T +V
09/90	312-283-0559^	chinet	Chicago	IL	3/12/24/96	24	$	H N P T
10/89	312-338-0632^	point	Chicago	IL	3/12/24/96	24	-$	H N P S T
03/90	313-623-6309	nucleus	Clarkston	MI	12/24	24	-$	M N S
11/88	313-994-6333	m-net	Ann Arbor	MI	3/12	24	$	T
08/89	313-996-4644^	anet	Ann Arbor	MI	3/12	24	$	T
08/89	314-474-4581	gensis	Columbia	MO	3/12/24/96	24	-$	M S
10/89	404-321-5020^	jdyx	Atlanta	GA	12/24	24	$	M N +P S T
05/88	407-380-6228	rtmvax	Orlando	FL	3/12/24	24	-$	N M
09/89	408-245-7726^	uuwest	Sunnyvale	CA	3/12/24	24	-$	N
02/90	408-249-0290^	netcom	San Jose	CA	12/24/96	24	$	M N P S T
02/90	408-423-9995	cruzio	Santa Cruz	CA	12/24	24	$	M T
10/89	408-725-0561^	portal	Cupertino	CA	3/12/24	24	$	-S N M T
02/90	408-996-7358^	zorch	Cupertino	CA	12/24	24	$	M N T

(continued)

Last Contact Date	Telephone #	Sys-name	Location		Baud	Legend
10/89	412-431-8649	eklektik	Pittsburgh	PA	3/12/24	24 $ S N M
11/89	415-332-6106^	well	Sausalito	CA	12/24	24 $ M N S T
06/88	415-582-7691	cpro	Hayward	CA	12/24	24 -$ S
11/89	415-623-8652	jack	Fremont	CA	3/12/24	24 -$ M N T
07/89	415-753-5265^	wet	San Francisc	CA	3/12/24	24 $ M N S T
05/89	415-783-2543	esfenn	Hayward	CA	3/12/24	24 -$ M N S
11/89	416-438-2855	contact	Toronto	ON	3/12/24	24 -$ M N S T
11/89	416-452-0926	telly	Brampton	ON	12/24/96	+P 24 $ M N
12/88	416-461-2608	tmsoft	Toronto	ON	3/12/24/96	24 $ S M N
07/89	416-654-8854	ziebmef	Toronto	ON	3/12/24/96	24 +P M N S T
01/90	502-968-5401	disk	Louisville	KY	3/12	24 $ M N S T
12/88	503-254-0458	bucket	Portland	OR	3/12/24	24 -$ N M S T
12/89	503-297-3211^	m2xenix	Portland	OR	3/12/24	24 -$ M N S
05/89	503-640-4262^	agora	PDX	OR	3/12/24	24 $ M N S T
01/90	512-346-2339	bigtex	Austin	TX	96	24 -$ +P A
10/89	513-779-8209	cinnet	Cincinnati	OH	12/24/96	24 $ M N +P S
01/90	517-487-3356	lunapark	E. Lansing	I	12/24	24 -$
12/88	518-346-8033	sixhub	upstate	NY	3/12/24	24 $ N M S T

09/88	602-941-2005	xroads	Phoenix	AZ	3/12/24	24	$ N T
08/89	605-348-2738	loft386	Rapid City	SD	3/12/24/96	24	$ M N +P S
08/88	608-273-2657	madnix	Madison	WI	3/12/24	24	-$ S N M
08/89	612-473-2295^	pnet51	Minneapolis	MN	3/12/24	24	-$ N M T
01/90	615-288-3957	medsys	Kingsport	TN	12/24/96	24	-$ A N +P
03/90	615-896-8716	raider	Murfreesboro	TN	12/24	24	-$ M N S
02/90	616-457-1964	wybbs	Jenison	MI	3/12/24/96	24	-$ +P M N S T
01/90	617-739-9753	world	Brookline	MA	3/12/24/96	24	$ M N P S T
01/90	619-259-7757	pnet12	Del Mar	CA	3/12/24/96	24	-$ M N P T
07/88	619-444-7006^	pnet01	El Cajon	CA	3/12/24	24	$ N M S T
12/89	703-281-7997^	grebyn	Vienna	VA	3/12/24	24	$ N M T
11/89	708-272-5912^	igloo	Northbrook	IL	12/24/96	24	-$ S N T P
01/90	708-318-7133^	gagme	Niles	IL	12/24	24	$ M N S P T M
08/88	708-566-8911^	ddswl	Mundelein	IL	3/12/24/96	24	$ A S N M P T
11/89	708-833-8126^	vpnet	Villa Park	IL	12/24/96	24	-$ +P M N S
07/89	713-438-5018	sugar	Houston	TX	3/12/24/96	24	-$ N +P
10/89	713-668-7176^	nuchat	Houston	TX	3/12/24/96	24	-$ M N +P S
12/88	714-635-2863	dhw68k	Anaheim	CA	12/24	24	-$ T
05/89	714-662-7450	turnkey	Inglewood	CA	12/24	24	-$
01/90	714-821-9671	alphacm	Cypress	CA	12/24/96	24	-$ A +P T

(continued)

Last
Contact

Date	Telephone #	Sys-name	Location		Baud	Legend
05/89	714-842-5851	conexch	Santa Ana	CA	3/12/24	24 $ A M N S
08/88	714-894-2246	stanton	Irvine	CA	3/12/24	24 $ S N
03/90	717-657-4997	compnect	Harrisburg	PA	3/12/24	24 -$ M N T
12/89	719-632-4111	oldcolo	Colo Spgs	CO	12/24/96	24 $ H M N T
01/90	801-269-0670^	i-core	Salt Lake Ci	UT	3/12/24/96	+P 24 -$ A N
01/90	802-865-3614	tnl	Burlington	VT	3/12/24	24 -$ S N M
08/88	813-952-1981	usource	Sarasota	FL	12/24	-24 -$ A
02/90	814-337-0348	sir-alan	Meadville	PA	3/12/24/96	24 -$ A +H M P T V
09/89	916-649-0161	sactoh0	Sacramento	CA	12/24/96	24 $ M N +P S T
08/89	919-493-7111^	wolves	Durham	NC	3/12/24	24 $ M N S

NOTE: ^ means the site is reachable using PC Pursuit.

348

This list is maintained by Phil Eschallier on lgnpl. Any additions, deletions, or corrections should be sent to one of the addresses below. The nixpub listings are kept as current as possible. However, you use this data at your own risk and cost -- all standard disclaimers apply!!!

Lists available from lgnpl via anonomous uucp.

+1 215 348 9727 [Telebit access]

login: nuucp NO PWD [no rmail permitted]

this list: /usr/spool/uucppublic/nixpub.short

long list: /usr/spool/uucppublic/nixpub

or from news groups pubnet.nixpub, comp.misc cr alt.bbs

E-MAIL . . . .

uucp: ..!uunet!lgnpl!{ phil ! nixpub }

domain: { phil ! nixpub }@LS.COM

COMPAQ, IBM, PC Pursuit, [SCO] XENIX, UNIX, etc. are trademarks of the respective companies.

■ INTERLINK/RELAYNET SYSTEMS

The following systems are Interlink regional network hubs. The Interlink is an ad hoc network made up of nodes running PCBoard BBS software. Like the FIDO network, distribution is hierarchical through these regional centers. At the end of 1989, there were 89 nodes on the Interlink network—not a large number by the standards of the Usenet or FIDO network, but respectable for a network in operation less than one year at that time. These 89 systems share over 100 conferences worldwide. The machines listed here are the regional network hubs in the United States.

System	Sysop	Data phone	Territory
Cheers	Bobbie Sumrada	(901) 373 5941	Southeast and south central
Compu-Data	Phil Gordemer	(609) 232 1245	Central East coast
Ed Hopper's BBS	Ed Hopper	(713) 782 5454	Central and southwest
Executive Net	Andy Keeves	(914) 667 4567	New York and New England
LANs	Philip Stults	(219) 884 9508	Central U.S.
Rose Media	Vic Kass	(416) 733 2285	Eastern Canada
Sleepy Hollow	Jim Fouch	(213) 859 9334	Western U.S.

The following systems are the main hub nodes of the RelayNet. Like the Interlink network, the RelayNet is an ad hoc federation of systems. In this case, the network uses an application layer translation system to port conferences between machines using different CMC software.

Hub ID	City	BBS name	BBS number	Baud	Node ID	Software	Sysop
Steering Committe of RelayNet:							
HUBMD	Bethesda MD	The Running Board	(301) 229-5623	19200HST	RUNNINGA	PCBoard	Bonnie Anthony
HUBNY1	Bronx NY	The Running Board	(212) 654-1349	38400HST	RUNNINGB	PCBoard	Howard Belasco
HUBIN	Indianapolis IN	IBM-NET Connection	(317) 882-5575	38400HST	BMNET	PCBoard	Rex Hankins
HUBNRI	Warwick RI	Eagles Nest	(401) 732-5292	38400HST	EAGLE	PCBoard	Mike Labbe
HUBSRI	Middletown RI	M.O.R.E.	(401) 849-1874	19200HST	MORE	PCBoard	J. Thomas Howell
HUBTN	Millington TN	The Party Line	(901) 873-2328	38400HST	PARTY	PCBoard	Mike Glenn
HUBVMC	Scarsdale NY	Activity BB Service	(914) 779-4273	38400HST		PCBoard	James Spinelli
Super Regionals:							
HUBCHAN	Cambridge MA	Channel 1	(617) 354-8873	38400HST	CHANNEL	PCBoard	Brian Miller
HUBKC	Kansas City MO	The Musical Chair	(816) 561-3006	38400HST	MUSICAL	PCBoard	Jeff Woods
HUBPETE	St. Petersburg FL	Computronics Comm Link	(813) 526-1265	38400HST	COMPTRON	PCBoard	Ken Hunt
HUBSD	Poway CA	DBoard	(619) 748-3644	38400HST	DBORED	PCBoard	William Parfitt
HUBSOMD	Hollywood MD	News/Info System	(301) 373-3530	19200HST	HNIS	PCBoard	Brandon Hayden
HUBZN	Middletown OH	Modem Zone	(513) 424-7529	38400HST	MODEMZNE	PCBoard	Don Cheeks
HUBCAVE	Oslo 3	ThunderBall Cave	(472) 567-018	19200HST	CAVE	PCBoard	Jon Orten
International Hubs:							
HUBCAT	1000 Lisboa	Cats BBS	(351) 152-4027	2400HST	IGUEL		Vitorino
HUBDIX	Holte Denmark	Online Support	(454) 541-0504	19200HST	DIX	PCBoard	Michael Willenbrack
YEBBSA	dah Saudi Arabia		(966) 266-0160	38400HST	YEBBS	PCBoard	Yarub Balkhair
HUBLINE	Amsterdam	Hotline BBS	(312) 089-1014	19200HST	HOTLINE	Spitfire	Piet Ebbes
HUBMETRO	Scarborough Canada	Metropolis OnLine Network	(416) 292-8757	19200HST	METRO	MajorBBS	Frank Sachse
HUBONT	Cambridge Canada	Cambridge Micro BBS	(519) 621-0561	19200HST	CAMBRIC	Spitfire	Armand Michaud
HUBSITE	Contrecoeur Canada	S.I.T.E.	(514) 587-5154	19200HST	SITE	PCBoard	Tony Dallaire

■ BULLETIN BOARD SYSTEMS

Here are a few of the many bulletin board systems sponsored by agencies of the federal government.

Software:	IBM-RBBS
Agency:	EXPORT-IMPORT BANK
Name/Speed/Word:	Exporters' BBS/300/1200/8N1
Data Lines:	(202) 566-4602, (202) 566-8180
Voice Lines:	(202) 566-4690
Access restrictions:	On-line registration
Sysops:	Bob Hughes, Joel Kahn
Features:	Files pertaining to import/export activities and banking.

Software:	unknown
Agency:	Environmental Protection Agency
Name/Speed/Word:	Pesticide Programs BBS/300/1200/2400/8N1
Data Lines:	(708) 557-3769
Voice Lines:	(708) 557-5484
Access restrictions:	On-line Registration

Software:	IBM-PCBoard
Agency:	USDA-NASS
Name/Speed/Word:	NASS BBS/1200/2400/9600/8N1
Data Lines:	(202) 472-1027
Voice Lines:	(202) 447-2339
Access restrictions:	On-line registration
Features:	IBM application files

Software:	IBM-RBBS
Agency:	Department of Commerce/National Bureau of Standards
Name/Speed/Word:	Data Management Information Exchange/300/1200/8N1
Data Lines:	(301) 948-2048
Voice Lines:	(301) 975-3269
Access restrictions:	On-line registration
Features:	Data and publications from NBS data management programs Lots of files; be careful, software is slow and unforgiving.

Software:	IBM-RBBS
Agency:	Department of Commerce/Office of Economic Affairs
Name/Speed/Word:	Economic News/300/1200/2400/8N1
Data Lines:	(202) 377-3870, (202) 377-0433
Voice Lines:	(202) 377-4450, (202) 377-1986
Access restrictions:	May browse; charges fees for regular access
Sysops:	Ken Rogers

Notes:	$25 registration buys two hours time; further time is charged at $.03/min. night and weekends and $.06 weekdays
Features:	ALL current economic reports, statistics, and forecasts of the Department of Commerce, Census Bureau, Department of Energy, Bureau of Labor Statistics, export opportunities, the National Trade Database, and more.

Software:	IBM-Fido
Agency:	Department of Commerce/National Oceanic and Atmospheric Administration
Name/Speed/Word:	Information Technology Exchange/300/1200/8N1
Data Lines:	(301) 770-0069
Voice Lines:	(301) 377-2949
Access restrictions:	On-line registration
Sysops:	Rich Kissel
Features:	NOAA and related data files; an Apple/Mac section has been added to the file area; most files are compressed

Software:	IBM-RBBS
Agency:	Department of Commerce/National Bureau of Standards
Name/Speed/Word:	Microcomputer Electronic Information Center 300/1200/2400/8N1
Data Lines:	(301) 948-5717 (301) 948-5718
Voice Lines:	(301) 975-3359
Access restrictions:	On-line registration
Sysops:	Ted Lanberg, Lisa Carnahan
Features:	Primarily devoted to computer security and anti-VIRUS efforts

Software:	IBM-RBBS
Agency:	Department of Commerce/Office of the Secretary
Name/Speed/Word:	Planning and Budget/1200/2400/8N1
Data Lines:	(202) 377-1423
Voice Lines:	(202) 377-2949
Access restrictions:	On-line registration
Sysops:	John O'Conor, Pat Spencer, Kathy Cooper
Features:	DoC Budget and Planning files (appropriations, etc.) and bulletins

Software:	IBM-RBBS
Agency:	Department of Defense/ADIAC
Name/Speed/Word:	Ada Information Database/300/1200/2400/8N1
Data Lines:	(202) 694-0215 (301) 459-3865
Voice Lines:	(703) 685-1477
Access restrictions:	On-line registration

Sysops: None listed
Features: DoD information, including reference manuals, on the DoD designated computer language for weapons systems software Ada

Software: IBM-PCBoard
Agency: Department of Education
Name/Speed/Word: Educational Research and Improvement/300/1200/2400/8N1
Data Lines: (202) 626-9853
Voice Lines: (202) 357-6524
Access restrictions: On-line registration
Sysops: Tom Litkowski
Features: Educational funding, enrollment, demographic, and other data; all data available in IBM ARC or ASCII Text formats

Software: IBM-RBBS
Agency: Department of Energy/Federal Energy Regulatory Commission
Name/Speed/Word: Commission Issuance Posting System/300,1200,2400/8N1
Data Lines: (202) 357-8997
Voice Lines: (202) 357-5570
Access restrictions: Public
Sysops: Sid Barinder
Features: Full text of FERC daily issuances, press releases; Commission agendas, reports, and filings

Software: IBM-RBBS
Agency: Department of Energy/USITC
Name/Speed/Word: ITC Energy/Chemical BBS/300/1200/2400/8N1
Data Lines: (202) 252-1948
Voice Lines: (202) 252-1354, (202) 252-1352
Access restrictions: On-line registration
Sysops: David Michaels, Sharon Greenfield
Features: Files and government reports dealing with synthetic chemicals/fuels

Software: Proprietary
Agency: Department of Interior/Geological Survey
Name/Speed/Word: Epicenter Determinations On-line
                   Information Service/300/7E2
Data Lines: (800) 358-2663, (303) 279-6374 in CO
Voice Lines: (303) 236-1500
Access restrictions: None listed
Sysops: Bruce Presgrave
Features: Earthquake occurrence information worldwide; login with "NEIS" then "QED"

Software:	IBM-Fido
Agency:	District of Columbia/Productivity Management Services
Name/Speed/Word:	No name given/300/1200/2400/8N1
Data Lines:	(202) 727-6668
Voice Lines:	(202) 727-6665
Access restrictions:	On-line registration
Sysops:	Danny Weiss
Features:	Files are mostly IBM, compressed, but some Apple and Text files available

Software:	Proprietary
Agency:	Federal Communications Commission
Name/Speed/Word:	Public Access Link/300/1200/8N1
Data Lines:	(301) 725-1072
Voice Lines:	None listed
Access restrictions:	No registration required
Features:	FCC fee and rules data; pending rules, hearings and applications

Software:	IBM-RBBS
Agency:	GSA/Information Resources Services Center
Name/Speed/Word:	no name given/300/1200/8N1
Data Lines:	(202) 535-7661
Voice Lines:	(202) 535-0825
Access restrictions:	Complete access available
Sysops:	Steve Tursky, Suzanne Taxin
Features:	Contains GSA material dealing with government contracts, suppliers, etc., as well as lists of who MAY NOT sell to the government.

Software:	IBM-PCBoard
Agency:	Library of Congress/Federal Library Committee
Name/Speed/Word:	AUTOMATED LIBRARY INFORMATION EXCHANGE 300/1200/2400/8N1
Data Lines:	(202) 287-9656
Voice Lines:	(202) 287-1374
Access restrictions:	On-line registration
Sysops:	Bruce Miller, Lee Power, Steve Palinscar, Bill Stockey
Features:	Library Science with emphasis on microcomputers; of most interest to other librarians

Software:	IBM-RBBS
Agency:	NASA/Information Technology Center
Name/Speed/Word:	no name given/300/1200/2400/8N1
Data Lines:	(202) 453-9008

Voice Lines: None listed
Access restrictions: On-line registration
Sysops: Carlos Ojeda, Maura Ennis
Features: NASA historical and statistical data; launch schedules; much of data in IBM ARC format; one file area dedicated to Apple/Mac files

Software: PBBS (proprietary)
Agency: NOAA/Space Environment Laboratory
Name/Speed/Word: Environment Service Center BBS
                      300/1200/2400/8N1
Data Lines: (303) 497-5000
Voice Lines: (303) 497-3284
Access restrictions: None listed
Sysop: Dick Grubb—software author
Features: Elaborate database on solar flair activity and sunspot cycles

Software: IBM-RBBS
Agency: National Science Foundation
Name/Speed/Word: Science Resources Studies/300/1200/2400/8N1
Data Lines: (202) 634-1764
Voice Lines: (202) 634-4636
Access restrictions: On-line registration
Sysops: Vanessa Richardson
Features: Research funding and grant information

Software: IBM-RBBS
Agency: National Science Teachers Association
Name/Speed/Word: Science Line/300/1200/2400/8N1
Data Lines: (202) 328-5853, (202) 328-4496
Voice Lines: (202) 328-5840, ext. 57
Access restrictions: On-line registration
Sysops: Alex Mondale
Features: Aimed at science educators; IBM and Apple files

Software: IBM-RBBS
Agency: VA Information Technology Center
Name/Speed/Word: VA Information Technology Center BBS/300/1200/2400/8N1
Data Lines: (202) 376-2184
Voice Lines: (202) 233-5571
Access restrictions: On-line registration
Sysops: Jay D. Anderson, Alan Toense
Features: Primary purpose is message base for vets to VA; file system aimed solely at IBM users

Software: IBM-PCBoard
Agency: Department of Agriculture
Name/Speed/Word: National Biological Impact Assessment Program 300/1200/8N1
Data Lines: (800) 624-2733, (703) 231-3858
Voice Lines: None given
Access restrictions: None
Sysops: Sanjay Dhawan, Don King
Features: Extensive database on agricultural genetics research and related
                     fields.

Software: IBM-TBBS
Agency: Federal Library and Information Network
Name/Speed/Word: Automated Library Information Exchange II 300/1200/8N1
Data Lines: (202) 707-9656
Voice Lines: None given
Sysops: Bruce Miller, Erik Delfino
Features: Telephone and address information on all Federal Libraries; li-
                     brary associations; information on library automation, online re-
                     search, CD-ROM, OCR, and more.

▪ THIRD-PARTY COMPUTER CONFERENCING SYSTEMS

Software: Notepad
 Vendor: Notepad Systems International
             575 Appleberry Dr.
             San Rafael, CA 94903
             (415) 492-8747
    Fax: (415) 499-3311

Software: Confer II
 Vendor: Advertel Communications Inc.
             2067 Ascot
             Ann Arbor, MI 48103
             (313) 665-2612

Software: Participate
 Vendor: Network Information (NWI) Inc.
             333 East River Dr.
             East Hartford, CT 06108
             (800) 624-5916
    Fax: (203) 282-0297

Software: proprietary CMC software
 Vendor: TRADENET Inc.
             2659 W. Guadelupe Rd.

Mesa, AZ 85202
(602) 968-7967

Software: Caucus
  Vendor: Metasystems Design (Metanet)
2000 N. 15th St. Suite 103
Arlington, VA 22201
(703) 243-6622

Software: Participate
  Vendor: Eventures Limited
2744 Washington St.
Allentown, PA 18104
(313) 763-8125

Software: Participate
  Vendor: Point Information Network Inc.
Box 151
Wyncote, PA 19095
(215) 635-4570

Software: Participate
  Vendor: Unison
700 W. Pete Rose Way
Cincinnati, OH 45203
(513) 723-1700
(800) 334-6122

Software: Picospan
  Vendor: The Well
27 Gate 5 Rd.
Sausalito, CA 94965
(415) 332-1716
(415) 332-6106—data; on-line sign up

■ THE MAJOR INFORMATION RETRIEVAL SYSTEMS

Products: Dialog, The Knowledge Index, and the Dialog Business Connection
  Vendor: Dialog Information Service Inc.
3460 Hillview Ave.
Palo Alto, CA 94304
(415) 858-3810
(800) 334-2564
Features: Many databases covering a wide range of subjects; probably the most comprehensive collection of databases in existence on one system; over 250 databases at time of writing

Products: BRS/Search, BRS/Brkthru, BRS/After Dark
Vendor: BRS Information Technologies (a subsidiary of Maxwell On-line)
1200 Route 7
Latham, NY 12110
(518) 783-7251
(800) 227-5277
Features: Very large single-point collection of Databases, like Dialog, but not quite so many, about 100; focused more on user-friendly interfaces, and a wide variety of service types

Product: Mead Data Central's NEXIS
Vendor: Mead Data Central
9393 Springboro Pike
Box 933
Dayton, OH 45401
(800) 227-4908
Features: Specializes in full-text databases, especially in the area of law, but many other full-text magazine databases, banking and brokerage reports, Associated Press, etc.

Product: ORBIT
Vendor: Orbit Search Service (a subsidiary of Maxwell On-line)
2500 Colorado Ave.
Santa Monica, CA 90406
(213) 453-6194
(800) 421-7229—outside California
(800) 352-6689—in California
Features: Highly focused on technical, scientific, industrial, and defense department databases, about 64 at the time of writing

Product: The Dow Jones News/Retrieval Service
Vendor: Dow Jones News/Retrieval Service
Box 300
Princeton, NJ 08540
(609) 452-2000
(800) 257-5114
Features: News and financial information, stock trading, and more market information than any other provider

Product: VU/TEXT
Vendor: VU/TEXT Information Services, Inc. (a subsidiary of Knight-Ridder)
1211 Chestnut St.
Philadelphia, PA 19107
(215) 665-3300
(800) 258-8080
Features: National, regional, and local newspapers, full text, are the focus of this system

Product: NewsNet
Vendor: NewsNet Inc.
945 Haverford Rd.
Bryn Mawr, PA 19010
(215) 527-8030—in Pennsylvania
(800) 345-1301
Features: Electronic trade and industry *newsletter* databases (about 300 of them); also AP Datastream Business News, UPI, Reuters International, PR newswires, and TRW credit reports

Product: Wilsonline
Vendor: H. W. Wilson Company
950 University Ave.
New York, NY
(212) 588-8400
(800) 622-4002—outside New York
(800) 538-3888—in New York
Features: Focus on library reference index; *Readers Guide to Periodical Literature, Book Review Digest,* index to legal periodicals: Art Index, etc.

■ PACKET SWITCH VENDORS

The following numbers and procedures may be used to get data on access points and other information from the four major providers of packet services in the United States.

Network: CompuServe Packet Network (CPN)
Vendor: CompuServe Information Service
Voice: (800) 635-6225
Data Access: (800) 848-4480
Procedure: At the "Host Name" prompt, type 'NETWRK'; the system will follow with a menu of services for searching the CPN database.

Network: Telenet
Vendor: US Sprint
Voice: (800) 546-2000
Data Access: (800) 546-2000
Procedure: At the "TERMINAL = " prompt, type 'D1' followed by a carriage return. At the following "@" prompt, type 'MAIL'; the system will respond by asking for a "USERNAME", type 'PHONES'; at the "PASSWORD" prompt, type 'PHONES' again. The system will follow with a menu of services for searching the database.

Network: PC-Pursuit
Vendor: US Sprint

Voice:	(800) 835-3638
Procedure:	Call for information

Network:	Starlink
Vendor:	Tymnet
Voice:	505-881-6988
Procedure:	Call for information

Network:	Tymnet
Vendor:	British Telecom
Voice:	(800) 635-6225
Data Access:	Your local Tymnet number
Procedure:	Type 'A' when the system asks for your "terminal identifier" or displays a stream of nonsense characters (this occurs at 1200 bps). At the "LOGIN:" prompt, type 'INFORMATION'; the system will respond with a menu of services for searching the database.

Network:	General Electric Packet Network
Vendor:	General Electric Information Services
Voice:	(800) 638-8369
Data Access:	Your local GEPN packet number
Procedure:	At any prompt, type 'PHONES'; the system will respond with a menu of services for searching the database.

BIBLIOGRAPHY

Arms, Caroline R. "A New Information Infrastructure." *Online,* 14 (5), 1990, pp. 15–22.

Arms, Caroline R. "Using the National Networks: Bitnet and the Internet." *Online,* 14 (5), 1990, pp. 24–29.

Bair, J. "Communications in the Office of the Future: Where the Real Payoff May Be." *Proceedings 4th International Conference on Computer Communications,* September 1978, pp. 733–39.

Basch, Reva. "The Seven Deadly Sins of Full-Text Searching." *Database,* August 1989, pp. 15–23.

Batterson, David. "2400-bps Modems are Revving up the Market." *PC Week,* May 22, 1989.

Batterson, David. "MNP Accelerates, Improves 2,400-bps Modems." *PC Week,* May 22, 1989.

Belitsos, Byron, and Misra, Jay. *Business Telecommunications.* Homewood: Irwin Press, 1987.

Bowen, Charles, and Peyton, David. *The Complete Electronic Bulletin Board Starter Kit.* New York: Bantam Books, 1988.

Bridges, L., Methvin, D., and Tracy, M. "Modems Call on Emerging Standards for 9600-bps Links." *PC Week,* September 11, 1989, pp. 65–71.

Brown, A. P. G. "Remote Database Access Using Remote Operations." International Open Systems 87. *Proceedings of the International Conference* Vol.1, 1987, pp. 377–89.

Buchinski, E. "Integration of Application-Level Protocols." *Computer Standards and Interfaces (Netherlands)* 5 (4), 1986, pp. 335–42.

Burg, F. M., and Put, P. "X.25: It's Come A Long Way." In Raviv, J. (ed.) *Computer Communication Technologies for the 90s.* B.V. (North-Holland) ICCC: Elsevier Science Publishers, 1988.

Carr, Jim. "Managing E-Mail." *LAN Magazine,* 5 (4), 1990, pp. 58–69.

Clippinger, John H., and Konsynski, Benn R. "Information Refineries." *Computerworld,* August, 1989, pp. 73–77.

Crowston, Kevin, Malone, Thomas, and Lin, Felix. "Cognitive Science and Organizational Design: A Case Study of Computer Conferencing." Human-Computer Interaction Vol. 3, 1987–88, pp. 59–85.

Delfino, Erik. "E-Mail Connections: It's Still A Jungle Out There . . . But It Is Getting Better." *Online,* 14 (5), 1990, pp. 31–35.

Delgado, Jaime, Medina, Manuel, Butscher, Berthold, and Tschichholz, Michael. "Use of SQL for Message Storage and Retrieval." In Speth, R.(ed.) *Message Handling Systems.* B.V. (North-Holland): Elsevier Science Publishers, 1988.

Dennenberg, R. "Standard Network Interconnection." Information Technology and Libraries (USA) 5 (4), 1986, pp. 314–23.

Duncan, Ray. "Sequential File Processing." *PC Magazine,* 8 (5), 1989.

Edwards, John. "How Bulletin-Board Software Compares with E-Mail Systems." *PC Week,* 3 (39), 1986, pp. 137–40.

Engelbart, Douglas, and Lehtman, Harvey. "Groupware: Working Together." *Byte Magazine,* 13 (13), 1988, pp. 245–52.

Engelbart, Douglas. "Authorship Provisions in Augment." *IEEE Digest of papers COMPCOM,* Spring, 1984, pp. 465–72.

Garman, N. "Common Command Language: Will It Really Happen?" *Online (USA)* 13 (4), 1989, pp. 49–50.

Grosch, A. N. "Computer-to-Computer Protocols." *Bulletin of the American Society of Information Scientists (USA)* 12 (5), 1986, pp. 8.

Glossbrenner, Alfred. *How to Look it Up Online.* New York: St. Martin's Press, 1987.

Glossbrenner, Alfred. *The Complete Handbook of Personal Computer Communications,* Third Edition. New York: St. Martin's Press, 1990.

Hammer, D. K. "Software Architecture of an X.400 Electronic Mail System." *Computer Communications* 11 (3), 1988.

Hammer, Michael, and Mangurian, Glenn E. "The Changing Value of Communications Technology." *Sloan Management Review,* Winter, 1987, pp. 65–71.

Hawkins, Donald T. "Information Delivery-Paper and E-mail." *Online* 14 (2), 1990, pp. 100–103.

Hildreth, C.R. "Communicating with Online Catalogs and Other Retrieval Systems: The Need for a Standard Command Language." *Libr. Hi Tech (USA)* 4 (1), Spring, 1986, pp. 7–11.

Hiltz, Starr Roxanne, and Turoff, Murray. "The Evolution of User Behavior in a Computerized Conferencing System." *Communications of the ACM,* 24 (11), November 1981.

Hiltz, Starr Roxanne, and Turoff, Murray. "Computer Support for Group Versus Individual Decisions." *IEEE Transactions on Communications* 30 (1), 1982.

Hiltz, Starr Roxanne, and Turoff, Murray. "Structuring Computer-Mediated Communication Systems to Avoid Information Overload." *Communications of the ACM* 28 (7), July, 1985.

Hughes, C., Cook, G., and McGrath, J. "A Survey of Computer Mediated Communications: Computer Conferencing Comes of Age." *Office Information Systems,* November 9, 1987, 20pp.

Johnson-Lenz, Peter and Trudy. "Computer Support for a Sustainable Culture." Draft paper submitted in 1989 to *In Context* magazine.

Johnson-Lenz, Peter and Trudy. "Groupware: The Process and Impacts of Design Choices." Addendum to *Computer-Mediated Communication Systems: Status and Evaluation,* by Kerr & Hiltz, San Diego: Academic Press, 1982.

Johansen, Robert. "Teleconferencing and the Future." *Computer Compacts,* 1 (4), 1983.

Johansen, Robert, and Bullen, Christine. "Thinking Ahead: What to Expect from Teleconferencing." *Harvard Business Review,* March/April, 1984, pp. 164–72.

Johansen, Robert, Hansell, Kathleen J., and Green, David. "Growth in Teleconferencing: Looking Beyond the Rhetoric of Readiness." *Telecommunications Policy,* December, 1981, pp. 289–95.

Kerr, Elain B., and Hiltz, Starr Roxanne. *Computer-Mediated Communication Systems: Status and Evaluation.* San Diego: Academic Press, 1982.

Kairi, Kalliopi, and Barnard, David. "Design and Implementation of an X.400 Standalone User Agent." *Computer Standards and Interfaces,* July, 1988, pp. 219–32.

Kiesler, Sara. "The Hidden Messages in Computer Networks." *Harvard Business Review,* January-February, 1986.

Kintzig, C., and Badine, S. A. "SMARTIX Network: Towards New Messaging Standards Applications." Presentation at Electronic Message Systems 87 Sponsored: Online Publications Pinner, Middlesex, UK: 1987.

Klemperer, K. "Common Command Language for Online Interactive Information Retrieval." *Libr. Hi Tech (USA),* 5 (4), Winter, 1987, pp. 7–12.

Kuehn, R.A. "Planning for Disaster Recovery (Telephone Systems)." *Business Communication Review (USA),* 18 (9), 1988, pp. 50–3.

Kuo, Feng-Yang "An Object-Oriented Approach to the Design of a Mail System for a Heterogeneous Environment." *Information and Management,* Nr. 15, 1988, pp. 173–82.

LaQuey, Tracy Lynn. *Users' Directory of Computer Networks,* University of Texas System Office of Telecommunications Services, 1989.

Learn, L. L., and Carpenter, G. L. "The OCLC Network: Its Architecture, Application, and Operation." *Hi Tech (USA)* 6 (3), 1988, pp. 43–60.

Malone, Thomas W., Grant, Kenneth R., Turbak, Franklyn A., Brobst, Stephen A., and Cohen, Michael D. "Intillegent Information-Sharing Systems." *Communications of the ACM,* 30 (5), 1987.

Malone, Thomas W., Yates, Joanne, and Benjamin, Robert I. "Electronic Markets and Electronic Hierarchies." *Communications of the ACM,* 30 (6), 1987, pp. 484–97.

Mamrak, S.A., Kaelbling, M.J., Nicholas, C.K., and Share, M. "A Software Architecture for Supporting the Exchange of Electronic Manuscripts." *Communications of the ACM,* 30 (5), 1987.

Martin, James. *Data Communication Technology.* New York: Prentice-Hall, 1988.

Matthews, Alan P. "Computer Graphics Technologies." *Microsystems,* July, 1984, pp. 42–11.

McCune, David. "An Introduction to NAPLPS." *Microsystems,* July, 1984, pp. 54–65.

McCune, David. "Graphics Subroutines in C for NAPLPS." *Microsystems,* August, 1984, pp. 87–93.

Meeks, B. N. "X.400 Grows Up." *Byte,* December, 1988.

Meeks, Brock N. "An Overview of Conferencing Systems." *Byte Magazine,* 10 (13), 1985, pp. 169–84.

Moritz, M. E. "If Disaster Strikes . . . (A Telephone Exchange)." *Telephony,* 200 (15), 1981, pp. 20–21.

Morrison, M. "The NISO Common Command Language: No More 'German to the Horses'." *Online (USA)* 13 (4), 1989, pp. 46–52.

Nye, J.M. "Overview of Communications Security and Vulnerabilities." *IEEE GLOBECOM '82. IEEE Global Telecommunications Conference,* Vol. 1, 1982, pp. 163–7.

Palme, Jacob. "Group Communication Functionality." Association Française de Normalization, Working Paper p.p. 27

Palme, Jacob. "Survey of Computer Based Message Systems." *Interact '84* conference papers, Amsterdam: North-Holland, 1984.

Palme, Jacob. "Extending Message Handling to Computer Conferencing." *Computer Communications Technologies for the 90s: Proceedings of the Ninth International Conference on Computer Communication.*

Palme, Jacob. "Group Communication is Message Systems The AMIGO Project." *Proceedings of the Eighth International Conference on Computer Communication,* September, 1986.

Pepper, Jon. "Data Compression and Error Correction Are Key to Increased Modem Throughput." *PC Week Connectivity.* 5 (30), 1988, pp. C/17-C/29.

Pitteloud, Joseph. "La Messageri Electronique X.400 se Consolide." Schluss aus Nr. 10, 1988.

Porter, D. D. "Information Retrieval for the NSFNET Community." *EDUCOM Bulletin (USA)* 23 (2–3), Summer-Fall, 1988, pp. 59–62.

Prosise, Jeff. "High-Speed Communications in DOS and OS/2." *PC Magazine,* September 26, 1989, pp. 307–319 and October 17, 1989, pp. 285–95.

Purser, Michael. "X.25 — The Fulcrum for Network Standardization." *Computer Communications,* 11 (5), 1988.

Quarterman, John S., and Hoskins, Josiah, C. "Notable Computer Networks." *Communications of the ACM,* 29 (10), 1986, pp. 932–71.

Quarterman, John S. *The Matrix: Computer Networks and Conferencing Systems Worldwide,* Bedford: Digital Press, 1989.

Rickard, Jack. "Electronic Information Services — Survival of the Specialized." *Boardwatch Magazine,* 3 (12), 1989.

Rickard, Jack. "Electronic Mail Call — Getting There Is Getting Easier." *Online,* 14 (5), 1990, pp. 37–40.

Salton, Gerard. "Another Look at Automatic Text-Retrieval Systems." *Communications of the ACM,* 29 (7), 1986.

Salton, Gerard, and Buckley, Chris. "Parallel Text Search Methods." *Communications of the ACM,* 31 (2), 1988.

Santo, Horst. "AMIGO: Advanced Messaging in Groups Interim Report." *Computer Networks and ISDN Systems,* Nr. 15, 1988, pp. 55–60.

Schneider, Stewart, and Bowen, Charles E. "Programming the Communications Module—The Heart of the BBS." *80 Micro,* July, 1984, pp. 152–58.

Schneider, Stewart, and Bowen, Charles E. "Controlling the Flow: The BBS File Structure." *80 Micro,* September, 1984, pp. 122–25.

Schneider Stewart, and Bowen, Charles E. "Storing and Retrieving Messages with Your BBS." *80 Micro,* October, 1984, pp. 156–59.

Schneider, Stewart, and Bowen, Charles E. "A Closer Look at Messages and Data-Base Files." *80 Micro,* November, 1984, pp. 152–55.

Schneider, Stewart, and Bowen, Charles E. "Using and Index for More Flexibility." *80 Micro,* December, 1984, pp. 136–39.

Schneider, Stewart, and Bowen, Charles E. "Getting the Message Across." *80 Micro,* January, 1985, pp. 132–34.

Smith, Ben. "High-Fashion UNIX on a PC." *Byte Magazine,* 14 (13), 1989, pp. 205–8.

Solanki, Dinesh. "Messaging X.400." *Proceedings of the Twelfth International Fiber Optic and Local Area Networks Exposition.* September, 1988.

Solomon, Richard J. "Broadband ISDN: With Computers, the Sum is Always Greater than the Parts." *International Networks,* 5 (2), 1987.

Squillante, Mark S., and Notkin, David. "Integrating Heterogenous Local Mail Systems." *IEEE Software,* IEEE Computer Society November, 1989.

Stanfill, Craig, and Kahle, Brewster. "Parallel Free-Text Search on the Connection Machine System." *Communications of the ACM,* 29 (12), 1986.

Taylor, Sandra Malloy. "Press Releases Online as a Source of Business Information." *Database,* 13 (2), 1990, pp. 53–56.

Turner, Steven E. "High-speed Modems for Computer Applications." *Telephony,* June 20, 1988.

Turoff, Murray. "The Anatomy of a Computer Application Innovation: Computer Mediated Communications (CMC)." *Technological Forecasting and Social Change,* Nr. 36, 1989, pp. 107–22.

Turoff, Murray, Hiltz, Starr Roxanne. "Exploring the Future of Human Communication via Computer." *Computer Compacts (Netherlands),* 1 (2), 1983, pp. 78–87.

Wilcox, R.O., Quinn, M.E., and Jensen, I.N. "The Telebase implementation of common command language." *Online Information 88. 12th International Online Information Meeting,* Oxford, UK: Learned Inf, vol. 2, 1988, pp. 507–15.

[No author given] "X.400: The Message is in the Medium." *Communications Engineering International,* September, 1987.

INDEX

A

Abstraction, 145, 156, 163
Access, 24, 27, 30, 31, 89–90, 149, 211
Accountability, 295
ACSNET, 104
Addressing, 93–96
Adequacy, 43, 75–77
ADMO, 244
Administration, 93–96, 115, 116
Advertel, *see* Confer
Agents, *see* User agents
AKCS, 288
Amiga, 53
AMIGO, 170
ANSI, *see* Standards
Apple, 9, 53
Applications, 34–41
ARC, *see* Compression
Arpanet, 163
ASCII, 147, 151

Asynchronous (store-and-forward) communications, 7, 29, 55–57, 101
Audit, 277, 295
Authoring, *see* Joint document authoring

B

Bandwidth, 99, 271–273
BIOS communications support, 74–75, 85
B-ISDN, *see* ISDN
BIX, 179–183
Boolean logic, 14, 122, 135
Branching structures, 137–144, 179–181, 183, 201–204
Broadcast, *see* Routing mechanisms
BRS, 14, 27, 48
BTLZ, *see* Compression
BYE, 20

C

CAS, 64
Caucus, 7, 78, 197–198, 233
CBBS, 19
CCITT, *see* Standards
CD-ROM, *see* Optical storage
Censoring, 212, 279
Centralized systems, 3, 11, 32, 67–88
Chairman, 199
Client-server architecture, 161–163, 167
Co-authoring, *see* Joint document authoring
Coconet, 147, 193–195
Comb structure, 124–126
COM, 158–159
Comment and conference orientation, 146, 181, 220
Communication structures, 124, 125, 143, 145, 210–213
Compression, 56–57, 59–60, 71, 273
CompuServe, 17, 30–32, 183–186
Confer, 6–7, 42, 124–137, 152, 259
Controllers, *see* Disk drives
Cost analysis, 225–232, 277, 281
CoSy, 8, 78, 180–183
CPN, *see* Packet switching
CPU, 46, 273
Crisis management, 9, 40, 224

D

DASnet, 287
Database management systems (DBMSs), 76, 240–248, 261
DECnet, 89, 231
Delphi, 188
Delphic voting, *see* Voting
Design, 5, 67, 88, 151, 265–270

Desqview, 200
Dialog information services, 14, 26, 241
Directories, 102–103, 107–109, 135, 173, 222
Disk drives, 1, 45
Distributed systems, 10–11, 89–93, 103–111, 160, 174–175, 195–197
Domain naming, *see* Routing mechanisms

E

EasyNet, 30
EDI, 38
Editing, 69–71, 120–122
Education, 32–34, 149
EIES, 117–124, 174
EIES2, 174–176
E-mail, 1–2, 29, 114–119, 136, 214, 215, 222–224, 274–275
EMISARI, 2–5, 30, 40, 117
Entertainment, 18, 30, 282, 283
Error detection, 19, 256, 257

F

Fax, 38, 275
Fiber optics, 61, 62
FIDO, 23, 93–95, 196–197, 284
File systems, 85, 86, 153–159, 162, 181, 257–264
Filters, 59, 118, 126, 133
FOSSIL, 74–75
Freeware, 18
Freeze-frame video, 27, 277

G

Games, *see* Entertainment

Gateways, 23, 27, 43, 65, 172, 288–291
GEnie, 186–188

I

IBM, 49, 78
Images, 147–149, 273, 277
Index management, 135, 156, 181
Information brokers, 13, 26-27, 67, 292
Interface, see User interface
Internet, 100, 103, 167, 172
ISDN, 61–62, 292–294
ISO, see Standards

J

Job role, see Roles
Joint document authoring, 43, 119, 136, 208

K

Keywords, 69, 118

L

LANs, 68, 89, 223, 292
LAPM, 57
Laptop computers, 42
Lemmpel-Ziv compression, see Compression

M

Magpie, 78, 201–203
Market coordination, 37
MCI, 23

Mead Data General, 16
Menus, see User interface
Metaphor, 3, 116–147
MetaSystems Design Group Inc., 43
MHS, 164
Microchannel bus, 49
Microwave, 65
MILNET, 104
MNP compression/error correction, see Compression; Error detection
Modem, 54–57
MOTIS, see Standards
MS-DOS, 52, 68, 77–88
MTA, 167–169
MTS, 137, 152, 259
Multimedia, 27, 277, 278
Multitasking operating systems, 53, 54, 79, 82–83, 93, 199–201
Multiuser systems, 53, 54, 79–88, 198–206
MVS, 53

N

NAPLPS, 147, 181, 236
Navigation, 11, 23, 69, 118, 119, 126, 142, 144, 181, 185
NewsNet, 16, 27
NISO, see Standards
Notepad, 8–9, 40, 227
NYNEX, see Gateways

O

Object-oriented programming, 174–176
Operating systems, 51–54
Optical storage, 48, 49
Orbit, 16, 27
OSI, 57–59, 161
OS/2, 85
Out-sourcing, 225–229

P

Packet switching, 62–64, 87, 231, 232
Participate, 8, 78, 137–143, 156–158
PC Pursuit, 87, 193
PDIS, 147, 237
People-link, 25, 188
PICK, 53, 85, 258
Picospan, 71, 137, 153, 155–156
PLANET, *see* Notepad
P-Link, *see* People-link
Point-to-point networks, 91, 93, 273
Political action, 31, 283, 284
Precision/recall, 14–16
PRESTEL, 147
Privacy, 279, 280
Problem resolution, *see* Crisis management
Prodigy, 148, 195–196
PSDNs, *see* Packet switching
Public switched telephone network, 78, 86–88

R

RAM, 46
Real-time communications, *see* Synchronous communications
RelayNet, 285
Remote login, 93, 100, 101
Roles, 114–115, 172, 211
Routing mechanisms, 11, 91, 96–97, 284

S

Satellite transmission, 66
SEA Inc., 60
Security, 69, 72, 173, 221
Shareware, 18, 150

Shells, *see* Multitasking operating systems
Single-user hosts, 26, 69
SMARTIX, 170–172
SmartNet, 285
SMTP, 163
Source path routing, *see* Routing mechanisms
SQL, 243–248
Standards, 38, 56, 63–65, 107, 108, 163, 173, 243, 271, 285
Starlink, 62
Status reporting, 256, 257
Storage systems, 47–49
Synchronous communications, 7, 29, 81–82, 101, 119–120, 136, 173, 221, 276

T

Tabulation, *see* Voting
Tailorability, 176–177, 183, 236, 274
TBBS, 78–79
TEAMate, 78, 203
Telenet, 62
Terminal software, 17–21, 150, 248–251
Threading, 140, 141, 157, 158
Topic drift, 137, 138
TSR, 73–74, 160
Tymnet, 62

U

UART, 50
UNIX, 83, 153, 190
Usenet, 11, 32, 45, 99, 191
User information, *see* Status reporting
User agents, 167–172
User interface, 71–72, 102–103, 113, 116–123, 142, 163, 190, 248–254, 278
UUNET, 197

V

VaxNotes, 90, 205–206
VMS, 84, 137
Voice mail, 29
Voting, 6–7, 9, 40, 43,124, 143

W

Well, 190–192

X

XBBS, 205
Xenix, 54
Xerox (Palo Alto Research Center), 9
X.400 standards, 107–109, 163–170,
    214, 244–248
Xmodem, 19